Thatcher's Britain

The politics And Social Upheaval Of The Thatcher Era

Richard Vinen

16

EasyRead Large

Copyright Page from the Original Book

TABLE OF CONTENTS

Richard Vinen teaches history at King's College London. His most recent books are *A History in Fragments: Europe in the Twentieth Century* and *The Unfree French: Life under the Occupation.* He reviews regularly for the *Independent* and the *Times Literary Supplement.*

Further Praise for Thatcher's Britain

'The really refreshing thing about Vinen's elegant and zippy book is that it eschews the narrow partisanship that has always disfigured so much writing about the Iron Lady and her times ... What this book injects into the Thatcher debate, in other words, is a welcome dose of sensible scholarly judgment'

Dominic Sandbrook, *Sunday Times*

'Vinen is very good on how the opinions of Thatcher and her ministers were in constant flux, and how on many issues there was no "Thatcherite" position. There is much to admire in this book'

TLS

'Vinen manages to be dispassionate on a subject where objectivity is hard to find'

Financial Times

'A marvellous book: well-written, lucid, balanced and devoid of the rather unpleasant bias present in so many tomes about Mrs Thatcher or Thatcherism ... Refreshingly honest'

Scotsman

'*Thatcher's Britain,* which is beautifully written with great wit and finesse, helps us to think straight about an era of visceral prejudice'

Literary Review

'A tight and sensible assessment of the era'

Observer

Also by Richard Vinen

A HISTORY IN FRAGMENTS
THE UNFREE FRENCH

For Emma

ACKNOWLEDGEMENTS

I am grateful to Andrew Wylie for selling this book and to Andrew Gordon for buying it. After Andrew Gordon moved on, Mike Jones and Rory Scarfe adopted my literary orphan and brought it up as though it was their own. Only authors know what a difference a good copy-editor makes and Bela Cunha is the best. She handled my manuscript with an impressive mix of rigour and good humour.

The first draft of this book was written in Houston, Texas. Houston is Thatcher's kind of town; she went there on her first visit to the United States in 1967 and returned to the meeting of the G7 a few months before she resigned as prime minister. Houston's appeal was not immediately apparent to me, and the fact that I grew to appreciate the city's charms owes much to the friendship of Sarah Fishman and Daniel Cohen. I am also grateful to Martin Wiener, whose influence is discussed in chapter 8, for arranging for me to enjoy the status of visiting scholar at Rice University. I also owe much to my students and colleagues at King's College, particularly Laura Clayton and Paul Readman.

All historians of modern Britain owe a debt to the Margaret Thatcher Foundation, which is making an extraordinary range of sources available on the web. I am particularly grateful to Chris Collins of the Foundation for his advice on a number of points.

Karl French read a draft of this book and made many helpful suggestions. Three professors also took time out from their own busy schedules to read my work and comment on it from their different perspectives. My father, Joe Vinen, represents that strand of the British establishment which shifted from the Labour Party to the SDP in 1981 and from *The Times* to the *Independent* in 1986. John Ramsden is a veteran streetfighter for Conservatism as well as being a distinguished historian of the party. Miles Taylor claims never to have voted; he belongs to that curious group of British historians who became post-Marxists without ever having been Marxists. All three of them were generous with their time and very perceptive in their comments.

My mother, Susan, and my sister, Katie, provided much practical and emotional support. Alison Henwood read my work, did her best to make me understand the workings of capitalism, and undertook more than her fair share of childcare whilst I was writing. I am, however, grateful to Alison for many things that are more important than any book and, most of all, for our children: Emma and Alexander.

INTRODUCTION

I remember where I was when it began. On the morning of 4 May 1979 I was in an 'O' level Latin class. Our teacher put a transistor radio on his desk and turned it on so that we could hear the speech that Margaret Thatcher read out from notes jotted on the back of a card as she entered 10 Downing Street:

> I would just like to remember some words of Saint Francis of Assisi which I think are just particularly apt at the moment. 'Where there is discord, may we bring harmony. Where there is error, may we bring truth. Where there is doubt, may we bring faith. And where there is despair, may we bring hope.'

My school was in Solihull, the second safest Conservative seat in the country,[1] and the whole place was pulsating with excitement at the Conservative election victory – all the same, I think that most of my classmates thought that the speech was pretty mad.

I remember with equal clarity where I was when it ended. I was walking down a back street near Euston station on 28 November 1990. I looked up and saw a sign that someone had placed against an office window. It said: 'She's gone.' Anyone seeing it that day would have known that Margaret Thatcher had resigned as prime minister.

It is not just self-indulgence that makes me begin this book with personal reminiscence. There was something about Margaret Thatcher's premiership that cut deeply into the personal lives of many British people. In 1985 psychiatrists produced an interesting piece of research that illustrated this. Generally, patients suffering from dementia forget things about the present whilst remembering things that are more permanent. For most of the post-war period, for example, many demented people knew that Queen Elizabeth II was the monarch but could not remember who was the prime minister. Under Thatcher things changed: 'Mrs Thatcher has given an item of knowledge to demented patients that they would otherwise have lacked: she reaches those parts of the brain other prime ministers could not reach.'[1]

References to Margaret Thatcher suffuse British culture. The head of drama commissioning at the BBC remarked in 2005: 'the Eighties and Nineties are the new Victorian drama. Contemporary writers are now looking to this era and Thatcher's influence is huge.'[2] Speeches delivered in her strange, unnaturally deep voice, the product of careful coaching by her advisers, are used, often incongruously juxtaposed with the music of Frankie Goes to Hollywood, as a soundtrack to television programmes about the 1980s. Her phrases – 'The Lady's not for turning' or 'There is no such thing as Society' – are quoted, though the first of these was coined by someone else and the second is usually quoted out of context. She features in films and plays. She has walk-on parts in novels such as Alan Hollinghurst's *The Line of Beauty* (2004).[2] There has even been a musical produced about her career.

This intense focus on Thatcher as a personality, or as a legend, has gone with a declining interest in what her government actually did. The most widely cited works on 'Thatcherism' – those by Gamble, Jacques, Jenkins (Peter), Jessop, Kavanagh, Riddell, Skidelsky and Young[3] – were written before Thatcher's resignation. Stuart Hall's influential article was published whilst Thatcher was still leader of the opposition.[4] Much was written by journalists, political scientists or left-wing activists, whose interest in Thatcherism was associated with a desire to devise strategies against it. Most of these people moved on to new interests when Thatcher fell. Even the emphasis on the extent to which Thatcherism's legacy has endured goes, curiously, with a tendency to downplay its importance – Margaret Thatcher is often now presented as though her main historical function was to serve as John the Baptist for Tony Blair.

There has also been a persistent tension in writing about the 1980s between an interest in Thatcher and an interest in Thatcherism. Academic writers, especially those of the Left, felt uncomfortable with the personalization of analysis – uncomfortable too, perhaps, with the ways in which attention to the character of Margaret Thatcher could slide into sexism.

In his article of January 1979, Stuart Hall used 'Thatcherism' six times and referred to 'Mrs Thatcher' only once. Discussion of the Thatcher government amongst the wider population always laid a heavier emphasis on Margaret Thatcher the woman. Striking miners were said 'universally' to use the Rider Haggardesque term 'she' for the prime minister.[5] Tory canvassers got so used to hearing the phrase 'that bloody woman' that functionaries in Central Office devised the acronym 'TBW' – until an unkind interviewer enlightened her, Mrs Thatcher herself thought that the letters stood for the name of a television station.[6] Most of all, there was a cloyingly fake intimacy in the way in which the name 'Maggie' entered general circulation. Demonstrators shouted 'Maggie, Maggie, Maggie, out, out, out.' Long-suffering audiences at Tory conferences were induced to sing the excruciating 'Hello Maggie' to the tune of 'Hello Dolly'. An excited Norwegian commentator celebrated his country's defeat of the England football team in 1981 by shouting into the microphone: 'Can you hear me Maggie Thatcher? Your boys took a hell of a beating tonight.'

The focus of my own book is on Thatcherism as a project rather than Thatcher as a person. My feeling is that John Campbell's biography of Margaret Thatcher has probably taken us as close to understanding the woman as we are ever likely to get – perhaps closer than she (a person with little taste for introspection) ever got herself.[7] Having said this, I think that the word 'Thatcherism' itself became the centre of a debate that sometimes obscured more than it revealed. Many scholars,[8] and at least one of Thatcher's own ministers,[9] assume that the term was invented by the sociologist Stuart Hall in January 1979. However, as time went on, many writers became uncomfortable with the word and, as was often the case with debates of the 1980s, the two sides of the political spectrum expressed themselves in remarkably similar ways. On the Right, T.E. Utley wrote that 'Thatcherism' was a 'monstrous invention'[10] that made the government seem more original than it really was. On the Left, Bob Jessop complained that his fellow Marxists had created a 'monstrous monolith' by presenting Thatcherism as a coherent phenomenon,[11] overemphasizing the importance of ideology and downplaying the role of division, conjuncture and disagreement.

In fact, the word 'Thatcherism' was quite widely used before January 1979 – Thatcher used it, in a flippant aside, in March 1975.[12] The mere fact that the term came into general use suggests a recognition that Margaret Thatcher was associated with something novel and distinctive. However, using the word 'Thatcherism' did not imply some platonic absolute of ideological purity that marked a complete break with everything that had gone before it. One should not assume that displays of pragmatism reveal Thatcherism to be somehow 'false' because it had failed to live up to abstract ideas that existed in the pamphlets of the

Institute of Economic Affairs or the mind of Alfred Sherman. Thatcherism was always about power, and it is the nature of power to adjust to circumstances.

The aims of my account are modest ones. I am aware that, as this book goes to press, I will for the first time be teaching students who were born after Margaret Thatcher resigned. I think there is a need for an account of this period that is designed for people who have no personal memories of it. I have tried to explain who the *dramatis personae* were, what they stood for, and to answer the simplest of questions: what happened next?

My account is more *événementiel* than most books on the Thatcher government. When Margaret Thatcher was still leader of the opposition, one of her advisers talked of the need to develop 'event-led communication'.[13] It seems to me that events such as the 1981 budget, the Falklands War or the miners' strike probably did more to communicate Thatcherism than the speeches of Sir Keith Joseph. I have stressed the difference between the Conservative Party in opposition from 1975 to 1979 and the party in government – as well as the differences between its various governments. Even my thematic chapters (notably that on Europe) are designed largely to show how thinking on particular issues evolved over time.

I have tried to strike a middle way between the very personalized biographical approaches that revolve around anecdotal details of 'Maggie' and the bloodlessly theoretical approaches that revolve around concepts such as 'relative autonomy of the state' or 'hegemony'. I have tried to give attention to the characters of people other than Thatcher and, in particular, to restore her ministers to the story. Thatcher's flamboyant style sometimes overshadowed that of her colleagues – one writer talked of 'a tyrant surrounded by pygmies'. A number of Thatcher's personal advisers or backbench supporters – Gardiner, Sherman and Mount – have also implied that the serious decisions were taken around Thatcher's kitchen table rather than in formal meetings of the cabinet. My own feeling is that Thatcherism makes more sense if it is examined in large measure through ministers. Studied in purely abstract terms, it is sometimes hard to pin down *what* Thatcherism was. It is, however, relatively easy to identify *who,* on the Conservative front bench, were Thatcherites. Few would, I think, deny this title to Howe, Lawson, Nott, Ridley and Tebbit. Ministers are crucial figures when it comes to seeing how the ideas dreamt up in think tanks were converted into policy.

There is one character in this story who was not a minister under Thatcher and never, indeed, a member of the Conservative Party during her leadership of it. I have given considerable attention to Enoch Powell. I should stress that the most important part of the chapter title 'Thatcherism before Thatcher?' is the question mark, and that my own answer to the question would be 'no'. Having said that, Powell does seem to me to be a uniquely important figure in the history of British Conservatism. He thought about many of the matters that concerned Thatcherites and he expressed his conclusions with a degree of clarity and force that they rarely achieved. He also thought about issues – 'Englishness', the end of Empire, Ulster – about which most Thatcherites were revealingly silent. Tory ministers regarded him with a mixture of admiration, exasperation and fear. If Thatcherism is to be understood in terms of intellectual history, Powell is vastly more important than any number of Austrian philosophers, American economists or earnest young men at the Adam Smith Institute. Powell is also important because he was a practising politician even if not, judged in conventional terms, a successful one. He understood the realities of power and, for this reason, was often the most eloquent commentator on the differences between Thatcherism and his own 'purer' vision of politics.

I think that I differ most sharply from other recent historians in terms of the historical context in which I seek to place Thatcher. David Cannadine, Peter Clarke and Ewen Green[14] – came to look at Thatcherism after having worked on earlier periods of British history. Not surprisingly, they were very exercised by the occasional references of Thatcherites to the nineteenth century or to 'Victorian values'; one of them even believed that he had invented this phrase.[15] I am sceptical about all this. I do not believe that Thatcherism seriously sought to make itself the heir to nineteenth-century liberalism, and I think that the occasional references by Thatcherite ministers to Gladstonianism probably had more to do with electoral strategy at a time when the Liberal/Social Democrat alliance was doing well in the polls than with serious thought about the nineteenth century.

I am also sceptical about interpretations that lay much emphasis on thinking in the immediate aftermath of the Second World War or on rejection of the 'post-war consensus'. In many ways, I see Thatcher as the defender of the post-war consensus (especially in the form in which it was expressed during the 1950s) against the 'progressive consensus' of the late 1960s and early 1970s (see chapter 1). Thatcher herself, and some of her ministers, made much of Friedrich Hayek's *The Road to Serfdom* (first published in 1945), which had sought to defend the free market against 'socialists of all parties'. It is not, however, clear that Thatcher herself read this book until quite late in her career.[16] I suspect that this work merely provided a convenient philosophical polish on things that Thatcherites wanted to do for reasons that had little to do with Hayek's thinking. When Norman Tebbit was interviewed in 1986, he referred to the writings of 'Fred what's his name'; only when an official from Central Office stepped in did it become clear that he was referring to Hayek.[17] Green presents Richard Law, the Conservative MP whose *Return from Utopia* (1951) defended free-market Conservatism against the encroaching state, as a kind of proto-Thatcherite,[18] but I doubt whether many people, other than historians who are concerned with Thatcherism's intellectual ancestry, have ever paid much attention to his book. It is unclear whether any minister in the Thatcher government had heard of Law at the time they held power.[19]

I see Thatcherism as rooted in a specific time – it emerged out of debates on national decline, trade union power and economic modernization during the 1970s and it ceased to be relevant when those issues became less pressing. If I was forced to give precise dates for a 'Thatcher era', then I would suggest 1968–88. The period stretched from Thatcher's 'What's wrong with Politics?' speech, which can be seen, though only in retrospect, as the first sign that Thatcher represented a distinctive political vision, until her Bruges speech of 1988, which can be seen as the first sign that Thatcherism was beginning to break up.

There are writers, of whom the most prominent is Simon Jenkins,[20] who see Thatcherism as having a life beyond Thatcher's resignation in 1990 and who, in particular, are interested in the way that Thatcher laid the foundations of New Labour. Obviously, Thatcher changed Britain in ways that mean that we all now live with her legacy. However, Thatcherism cannot be understood unless we recognize the remoteness of the recent past. Thatcher came to power less than thirty-five years after the end of the Second World War. Almost half the members of her first cabinet had fought in that war – three of them had been wounded;[3] four had been decorated for gallantry.[4] This compares to Margaret Thatcher's immediate successor as prime minister, who had grown up since the Second World War, or to his two successors, both men born after 1945. Tony Blair's first government in 1997 did not contain a single minister who had ever worn military uniform. Thatcher's world was dominated by the Cold War. For the whole of her premiership, there really were weapons of mass destruction pointed at London. This coloured not just her attitude to the Soviet Union but her attitude to Europe (especially West Germany), the United States, trade unions in Britain and Britain's status in the world. The political map changed almost beyond recognition as the Soviet Union reformed during the late 1980s; inability to adjust to these changes partly explains why Thatcherism became less successful during this period. The economy in the early 1980s was different from the economy of the early twenty-first century in ways that cannot be captured with mere statistics. As I lectured on Thatcherism in 2008, I looked at the rows of tiny, garishly coloured mobile phones that my students had laid out on the desks in front of them and I recalled how, when I myself was a student, the *Spectator* had run a series of articles devoted to the difficulty of getting the nationalized Post Office to install a new phone line in the magazine's offices.

This book is designed to be dispassionate. I was very much opposed to the Thatcher government when it was in power (or, at least, I often said I was – it is sobering to realize how hard I find it to recapture my own real feelings), and I have never been seriously tempted to vote Conservative. However, I have often felt exasperated by the partisan nature of writing on this subject and particularly by the sneering tone many authors adopt with regard to Margaret Thatcher herself.

Many French historians have managed to write interesting and sympathetic books about de Gaulle and his regime, even when they themselves had opposed him during his life. I feel that it is time British historians attempt to do the same for Margaret Thatcher. I have tried to avoid posing the Sellar and Yeatmanish question of whether or not Thatcher was a 'good thing'. However, it does seem to me that a little humility on this matter is in order from those of us who denounced Thatcher when she was in power. Many of us claimed repeatedly that the government's policies were so obviously wrongheaded that they were bound to bring some signal disaster. We should now have the grace to recognize that the signal disaster never arrived and that, at least in its own terms, the government was often – though not always – successful.

Perhaps I should finish the introduction by marking out the limits of this book. This is very largely about what Maurice Cowling, a historian sometimes seen as having been involved in the transformation of Conservative thought during the 1970s, labelled as 'high politics'. I have made three quite long excursions outside the high politics of the Tory party. One of these involves the Labour Party and the Social Democratic Party in the early 1980s, one of them involves the Falklands War and one of them involves the miners' strike of 1984–5. I think that all three were particularly important for the Thatcher government. I also think that analysts of Thatcherism have sometimes been too prone to treat all three as though they were acts of God. The electoral collapse of the Labour Party, British victory in the South Atlantic and the poor tactics of Arthur Scargill are invoked as evidence that Margaret Thatcher was 'lucky'. Thatcher clearly was lucky (no one would survive as prime minister for ten years unless they had some spectacular good fortune). But there was more to it than luck. Sometimes, the failure of Thatcher's enemies had deeper causes, often related to the social changes that had brought Thatcher to power in the first place; sometimes, it was due, to a greater extent than the government's critics have cared to concede, to skilful management by Thatcher and her colleagues.

Having said all this, I have not tried to write a social history of Britain in the 1980s. I have not, for example, attempted any serious research on whether British people during this decade were increasingly likely to define themselves in terms of consumption rather than work. I have discussed questions such as 'why did many British coal miners return to work before their union authorized them to do so during the strike of 1984–5?'; 'why did people buy their council houses?' or, for that matter, 'why did they vote Conservative?' on the basis of information that is already in the public domain.

Equally, this is not a history of the world from 1975 to 1990. Thatcher existed in an international context. Her positions on many issues, not just those directly relating to the Soviet Union, were born of the Cold War. Her political demise was in many ways associated with the fact that reform in the Soviet Union shot away the foundations of her political world. It would be possible to write a different kind of history that presented Thatcherism as one element in a global transition and which attempted to discern the extent to which changes in Britain were effects or causes of a change that brought down Soviet Communism and strengthened capitalism in most of the world. On the whole, my interests have been confined to looking at the extent to which British politics were influenced by events in the wider world. I have not attempted to say how far British policy influenced those wider events or, for that matter, to say very much about the extent to which Thatcherism might have been part of a wider pattern. Looking at the international context can be useful on one very simple level: it cuts Britain down to size. Thatcher led the British Conservative Party from 1975 to 1990. During these years, China saw all the extraordinary upheaval that lay between the death of Chairman Mao and the aftermath of the Tiananmen Square massacre. The year Thatcher became leader of the Conservative Party was also the year Vaclav Havel wrote his open letter to the president of Czechoslovakia – a brave and, as it seemed at the time, hopeless gesture of defiance against authoritarianism. In 1990 Havel, himself now president of the Czechoslovakia, dined in Downing Street. Between 1975 and 1990, Chile went from the worst years of state-sponsored murder to being, more or less, a democracy. All this reminds us that the Anglocentric obsession with Thatcherism as a 'revolution' needs to be judged against countries where politics really could be a matter of life and death.

Chapter 1

THATCHER BEFORE THATCHERISM, 1925–75

There is ... the sheer romance of it, which will remain alive for generations of readers in the wider world who may know little of late twentieth-century British politics and care even less. A woman from the provincial lower-middle class, without family connections, oratorical skills, intellectual standing or factional backing of any sort, established herself as leader of a great party which had represented hierarchy, social stratification and male dominance.

Alfred Sherman (adviser to Margaret Thatcher)[1]

I seem to have done very little in thirty years.
Margaret Thatcher, March 1956[2]

Margaret Thatcher did not share the fascination with her petit-bourgeois origins that was felt by so many of her admirers and enemies. The volume of her memoirs dealing with her time in Downing Street was published before that dealing with her life up to 1979. No doubt this was partly due to decisions taken by publishers and literary agents, but the order also reflects a feeling that Margaret Thatcher's early life made sense only when seen through the prism of her later career. Thatcher herself seems to have found the young Margaret Roberts to be an inscrutable figure. In her autobiography she thanks her 'memoirs team' for their skill in unearthing 'all the multifarious files where little bits of modern lives are written down and stored away[3] – as though her researchers had discovered a person previously unfamiliar to the adult Margaret Thatcher.

During her early years in parliament, Margaret Thatcher was usually seen as a typical Conservative lady. Her clothes, voice, pearls and general air of strained formality seemed to belong to the world of the garden party and the summer fête. An American diplomat who met her in 1973 described her as 'an almost archetypical, slightly to the Right-of-center Tory whose views are strongly influenced by her own middle-class background and experience'. It was clear that 'middle class' in this context meant 'upper-middle class' – the meeting had taken place over lunch at the Connaught Hotel.[4]

When she ran for the leadership of the Conservative Party in 1975, Thatcher's campaign team paraded her humble origins precisely because these origins seemed to run against the popularly held view of their candidate. One member of that campaign team – George Gardiner MP – subsequently published a biography of Margaret Thatcher.[5] It was one of the first full-length biographies; it was also, at least for a long time, the last book that was written by an author who had full access to Margaret Thatcher and to other members of her family.[6] Gardiner portrayed Margaret Roberts as the hard-working daughter of a Methodist grocer from the Lincolnshire town of Grantham. Grantham was almost turned into a brand name by Thatcher's associates. Thatcher's son was to name the enterprise at the centre of his business operations after his mother's birthplace.[7] But Margaret Thatcher rarely went back after she left home at the age of eighteen. Many of her ministers had, or at least affected to have, a visceral attachment to the area in which they had been born. Thatcher was never really happy anywhere except central London – for all her allegedly 'suburban' qualities, she regarded the retirement home that she and her husband briefly owned in Dulwich as being too remote.

Subsequent discussion of Thatcher was to make so much of the vices, or virtues, that she had allegedly acquired from her upbringing that it is sometimes hard to dig the real experience out from under the weight of subsequent mythology. Thatcher did not mention either her mother or her sister in her *Who's Who* entry. This provoked one Labour MP to build a psycho biography around Thatcher's alleged abnormality in this respect.[8] But Thatcher's memoirs contain a convincing account of her grief at her mother's death. Equally, most historians have underlined Thatcher's close relations with her father and the extent to which his example inspired her subsequent career. However, the precise details of Thatcher's relations with her father were rewritten in successive accounts. In one interview she expressed pleasure at the fact that her father had lived to see her on the government front bench.[9] In fact, as she recalls in her memoirs, he had died several months before she entered the cabinet.

Margaret Roberts was born in 1925. She was the second daughter of Beatrice, a seamstress who had run her own business before marriage, and Alfred, a tall good-looking man whose one indulgence seems to have been smoking, and who had been excluded from military service during the Great War on account of his poor eyesight. Alfred Roberts became manager of a grocery, and he saved enough money to buy his own shop in 1919. He was a devout Methodist and a well-known lay preacher. He was also a local politician. He had been a Liberal and was elected to Grantham Town Council as an Independent, though he seems to have been recognized as a functional Conservative by the time he became Mayor of Grantham in 1945. Certainly the Labour Party, which took control of Grantham Town Council in 1952, saw him as an opponent and ended his career as an alderman.

As John Campbell has shown, presenting the Roberts family as simply belonging to the 'provincial lower-middle class' ignores some important details. For one thing, Alfred Roberts was a good deal more prosperous by the 1930s than the average shopkeeper; he eventually bought two shops and employed several people. The gap between him and his neighbours was all the more marked because the Roberts family did not strictly speaking live in Grantham but in Little Gonerby, a working-class area built around a brewery. Alfred Roberts' political career also brought him into contact with other local notables – some of rather patrician background. The notion of Alfred Roberts as a sturdy exponent of free enterprise is also slightly misleading. His shop was a sub-post office and consequently, in a small way, an agency of the state.[10]

Margaret was a bright child and her father, who regretted his own lack of schooling, devoted great effort to her education. He sent her to the state elementary school in Huntingtower Road, which was said to be better than the school that was nearer to her house. In 1936 Margaret won a place at Kesteven and Grantham Girls' Grammar School. Grammar schools were to play an important part in Thatcherite mythology, but Thatcher did not belong to the post-war generation of grammar school children who enjoyed free places courtesy of the Butler Education Act (1944). She went to grammar school in an age when parents were still required to pay, though the fees were more modest than they would have been at a private school. KGGGS took some girls from quite humble backgrounds on scholarships, but Thatcher was privileged by the standards of the school, and of Grantham more generally. She was always well dressed and, perhaps the result of being a grocer's daughter at a time of rationing, better fed than most of her contemporaries.[11]

A girls' grammar school in the late 1930s was a good place to be educated. It was one of the few institutions in which young women could escape from male condescension. No one seems to have suggested that Margaret Roberts should study subjects 'appropriate for a girl' or to have objected to her decision to specialize in science. Economic depression had driven bright graduates who needed secure jobs into the teaching profession. Male casualties in the First World War had increased the number of spinsters who, like Muriel Sparks's Miss Jean Brodie, lived their lives through the girls whom they taught, and girls' schools, unlike those for boys, did not lose their youngest teachers to the armed forces during the Second World War.

In 1943 Margaret Roberts left home to read chemistry at Somerville College, Oxford. Oxford has educated twenty-five British prime ministers, including all the graduate prime ministers who took office in the second half of the twentieth century. Thatcher was not, however, the usual Oxford undergraduate. She was a woman in a male-dominated institution. She was a scientist in a university notable for its emphasis on the arts. Most of all, her university career began at a time when a large proportion of her male contemporaries were away fighting in the war. Her Oxford was one of blackouts and rationing rather than balls and punting.

Margaret Roberts was not a well-known Oxford figure. The only important political friend she made at Oxford was Edward Boyle, who was later to be her boss when she was a junior minister at the Department of Education in the 1960s and with whom she was to remain on good terms in spite of their differences. Julian Critchley, who came up to Oxford in the early 1950s, recalls: 'The talk ... was of great men who had just gone down, Robin Day, Peter Kirk, Jeremy Thorpe and Ken Tynan. Shirley Caitlin, later Williams, was talked of as Britain's first woman Prime Minister. No one mentioned Margaret Roberts.'[12]

Thatcher's relationship with Oxford was notoriously difficult.[13] The university refused to grant Margaret Thatcher an honorary degree (a distinction conferred on all previous Oxonian prime ministers). When she became prime minister, dons made much of her apparently mediocre academic record; her former tutor insisted that Margaret Roberts had been an unremarkable student. Thatcher's intellectual attainments generally were to be a subject of much discussion for the rest of her career. Her enemies derided her as a philistine of vulgar tastes who was interested only in knowledge that had some economic utility. There was much amusement when she told an interviewer that she was 'rereading Frederick Forsyth's *The Fourth Protocol'.*[14] Even her closest associates often implied that there was something deficient, or at least strange, in her intellect or education.'[15]

Yet occasionally we see glimpses of a very different kind of mind at work in Margaret Thatcher. She knew a great deal of poetry and had a special affection for Kipling, an unfashionable taste that she shared with George Orwell and Antonio Gramsci. She could be deeply affected by books such as Solzhenitsyn's *The Gulag Archipelago* or Harold Bloom's *The Closing of the American Mind.*[16] She disliked the poems of T.S. Eliot (the mere willingness to express dislike suggests that poetry mattered to her), but Anthony Powell overheard her talking about Helen Gardner's study of *The Four Quartets.*[17] Her interest in science was not purely utilitarian. She took pride in Britain's record of scientific achievement (particularly the number of Nobel prizes that its citizens had won) and, as secretary of state for science and education, she defended 'blue skies research'. Thatcher sometimes expressed disdain for 'intellectuals',[18] but she had a high, perhaps excessive, regard for 'first-class minds'.

Margaret Thatcher's last year at Oxford coincided with the return of the generation of men who had fought in the war. Almost the first political association she joined after graduating was called the '39 to 45' club. Throughout her career, Thatcher was to come up against men who had had 'a good war'. Especially when she was accused of having 'usurped' patriotism during the Falklands War of 1982, her opponents were to make much of her comparatively inactive role during the Second World War. David Ennals, a Labour

MP who opposed British intervention in the Falklands and who perhaps anticipated the fact that he was to be swept away in the Conservative landslide of 1983, pointedly reminded her that he had been 'storming up the beaches of Normandy' in the summer of 1944.

In the 1940s and 1950s the war pervaded politics in ways that made it all the more difficult for a woman who wanted to have a political career. Candidates campaigned in uniform and evoked their experiences of war at every opportunity.[19] Thatcher's first experience of elections came when she supported Squadron Leader Worth in Grantham in 1945. Her own attempts to become a candidate for a winnable Conservative seat brought her into competition with a succession of decorated heroes. At Beckenham her rivals included Major Ian Fraser MC. At Hemel Hempstead she lost out to Lieutenant Colonel Allason. At Finchley the two other names on the shortlist from which Thatcher finally emerged victorious were, respectively, a holder of the Military Cross and a former member of the Special Operations Executive.

How did Margaret Thatcher herself look back on the war and how did it shape her politics? Sharpeyed observers noted that Thatcher's references to the Second World War tended to concentrate on one year of the conflict: 1940.[20] Time and again, Margaret Thatcher was to refer to Dunkirk, the Battle of Britain and, most of all, our 'finest hour', a phrase that Churchill had used in a speech of 18 June 1940.[21] This focus on one year and, more particularly, on the months between May and September might be explained in all sorts of ways. It focused attention on a war that had been fought by a small group of men under the leadership of Winston Churchill and centred on the south of England. It avoided much reference to the large-scale industrial mobilization that came later in the war. It emphasized Britain 'alone'. In spite of her Atlanticist sympathies, Thatcher made little reference to the American role in the war. The Soviet Union was even more conspicuous by its absence – indeed the focus of her speeches on the early part of the war sometimes went with an emphasis on the fates of Finland[22] and Poland,[23] both countries that raised embarrassing questions about Soviet behaviour.

Thatcher's 'memory' of the Second World War was, like many aspects of her public personality, partly constructed by other people. Some of the 'Churchillian' references that so annoyed Thatcher's enemies had, in fact, been inserted into her speeches by advisers and ghostwriters.[24] The most systematic attempt to separate the 'good' war of Churchillian patriotism from the 'bad' war of increasing state power was made by Nigel Lawson.[25] Some of Thatcher's opponents also developed their own particular interpretation of the Second World War. They emphasized mass mobilization, working-class participation and plans for a new social order that were drawn up in 1943 and 1944. The phrase 'people's war', coined by the eccentric Communist soldier Tom Wintringham, was used frequently by the Left during the 1980s. Wintringham became an object of interest partly because his ideas could be used to attack the defence policy of the Thatcher government.[26]

The notion that Thatcher herself tried to rewrite the history of British participation in the Second World War to suit her political project is unfair. In public, she spoke respectfully of wartime projects for a new social order; indeed she was ostentatiously respectful towards the memory of the wartime leaders of the Labour Party, partly because she found it useful to contrast them with the supposedly lesser men who led the party later. She even occasionally spoke in terms that seemed very close to those who talked of a 'people's war'.[27]

It is true, however, that Thatcher focused most on the exploits of airmen and soldiers in 1940, rather than the more large-scale mobilization that came later. It is also true that this focus seems to have reflected the perception of the war that the young Margaret Roberts had at the time, as well as the more deliberately constructed view that Margaret Thatcher and her advisers found it useful to deploy in the 1980s. The two books on the war that struck Margaret Roberts most were the biography of Ronald Cartland, published by his sister Barbara, and the autobiography of Richard Hillary;[28] she was to say that the latter had affected her more than any other book she had ever read. Ronald Cartland was a soldier and anti-Munich Tory MP, who was killed in action during the retreat to Dunkirk.[29] Richard Hillary was a Spitfire pilot who was shot down and badly injured during the Battle of Britain.

Thatcher's perception of the war was different from that of most ruling-class Englishmen of her generation, the kind of men who were to dominate her first government in 1979. Such men had usually served in the war. Most of them had fought, not during the 'finest hour' of 1940, but during the bloody campaigns in southern Italy and Normandy. Thatcher's war was relatively simple: it pitted Britain against Germany, and right against wrong. Most serving soldiers saw something messier and less heroic. They belonged to a large and chaotic army made up mainly of conscripts. In personal terms, they remembered the war as one of squalor, confusion, fear, despair, separation and infidelity, as much as heroism. John Peyton, a Conservative MP who stood against Thatcher in the 1975 leadership contest and was later broken under the Thatcherite juggernaut, wrote:

> The Second World War was, for most of those over whom it cast its shadow, by far the greatest event of their lives. It reached down from its cosmic dimensions into their hearts, minds and bodies, and after its fearful passage, left them, as well as the world, changed.[30]

Peyton was captured, whilst hiding in a pigsty, near Dunkirk. He spent the next five years in a German prisoner-of-war camp. It was there that he learned that his fiancée had married another man and that his brother had been killed in the St Nazaire raid.

It is revealing to contrast Thatcher's view of the war with that of Peter Rawlinson, another of the politicians who was to be cast aside when Thatcher became prime minister. Rawlinson was wounded serving with the Irish Guards in North Africa. The shrapnel did not work its way out of his body until thirty years later, and the name of the young guardsman who had been blown apart whilst sitting next to him suddenly came back into his mind when he was writing his memoirs. Rawlinson's war was more ugly and morally ambiguous than Thatcher's. This was apparent in his personal memories of Thatcher's hero Richard Hillary: 'He wanted to join in a part of the gaiety of our youth, but as his had been burned away he would also sneer and scratch at us. We probably deserved it, but we had the grace to understand and to tolerate the savagery of the wounded man.'[31]

What was Margaret Roberts to do when she graduated? She rejected the obvious careers for a woman graduate of her class. She did not want to teach and she did not want to be a civil servant. Instead she went into industry and was hired as a research chemist by BX Plastics in Colchester. Here she was disappointed by the tedium of repeating simple tests. Moving to work at Allied Lyons a few years later took her to London, which was useful for her political career, and gave her slightly more scope for real research. It was still, however, not the kind of job that she wanted. For all her enthusiasm for business in principle, Thatcher was to make little of her own brief career in British industry; the CV that she prepared when she was a parliamentary candidate, and her *Who's Who* entry when she was elected to parliament, merely alluded to her having spent several years engaged in 'chemical research'.

Margaret Roberts also began the long haul that would eventually get her into parliament, a desire that she later claimed to have conceived quite suddenly in 1945 or 1946, as a result of a brief discussion of politics after a dance. It is hard to recapture now what an astonishing ambition this was. There were only twenty-four women MPs in the 1945 parliament. Being a Conservative woman Member of Parliament was particularly difficult. Of 618 Conservative candidates in the 1945 election, fourteen were women, and only one of these was elected. Most Conservative MPs were still public school men from upper-middle-class families. The Conservative Party was keen to recruit parliamentary candidates from a wider social base and constituency associations were no longer allowed to ask candidates to pay all of their election expenses. In spite of this, it was considered difficult to live on an MP's salary and consequently a political career was easiest for those who had a private income or who had a job, which being a research chemist was conspicuously not, that could be undertaken alongside parliamentary duties.

In 1949 Margaret Roberts was selected as a Conservative candidate for Dartford. As the local papers pointed out, she was the youngest woman Conservative candidate in the country. However, selection by the Dartford Conservative Association was hardly a political triumph. In spite of the fact that Dartford was a safe Labour seat, some party notables resented the selection of a woman. The Conservative MP for a neighbouring constituency wrote that he had been asked why 'a young girl of 23, Miss Margaret Robertson [sic], had been selected as Candidate for Dartford? Could not they have got some prominent business man?'[32]

The barriers that an unmarried woman with no money or contacts faced in getting a Conservative seat can be highlighted by looking at how easy some men found things. John Wells, an old Etonian who had had a 'good war', beat her to selection for a seat in Maidstone. His parliamentary career was notable mainly for his interest in inland waterways and horticulture. He came close to achieving political fame only during the brief period when he considered joining the Social Democratic Party and resigning his seat to allow Roy Jenkins to fight a by-election.[33] Paul Channon, later to be described as a 'lightweight' by Thatcher and to serve as an undistinguished minister in her government, had been chosen, whilst still an undergraduate at Christ Church, to fight a safe Tory seat once held by his father. James Prior, another of her future ministers, described how a casual acquaintance whom he met whilst driving his tractor back from the fields asked whether he would like to stand for the Tories in Lowestoft.[34]

Margaret Roberts's political prospects were transformed by Denis Thatcher – a man ten years her senior who had served in the Second World War. Denis Thatcher had very right-wing views on most matters – though he did not share his wife's support for the death penalty. His family seems, at least by the standards of the Home Counties middle class, to have been faintly bohemian, and he had contracted a brief wartime marriage.[35] In the 1980s Denis Thatcher was to tell a friend that he was a cavalier whilst his wife was a roundhead.[36] The couple met in 1950 and were married in December 1951. By all accounts the marriage was happy. It also transformed Margaret Roberts in material ways. She was now able to abandon chemistry and devote all her time to reading for the Bar, a more fitting occupation for a would-be Tory candidate. Denis was a wealthy man and on his way to being a millionaire by the time he sold the family business to Burmah Oil in the mid-1960s. Until she began to cash in on the fruits of her fame on the international lecture circuit in the 1990s, Margaret Thatcher's money came from her husband. In the 1980s she told the daughter of a friend: 'Marriages are made in heaven, but it is better if the money is made on earth.'[37]

In view of the frequency with which historians have evoked the influence of her father on Margaret

Thatcher, it is worth noting that she married a man who could hardly have been more different from Alderman Roberts. Her father had been, in a minor way, a public figure; her husband was careful to avoid any public statements at all once his wife embarked on her political career. Her father was a Methodist; her husband belonged to the Church of England, and, after marriage in a Wesleyan chapel, the couple began to practise a low-Church Anglicanism – Thatcher was not one of the three Tory MPs elected in 1959 who declared themselves to be Methodists. Her father had left school at thirteen to earn his own living; her husband had attended a minor public school (Mill Hill) and inherited the family business. Her father was a teetotaler who occasionally played bowls; her husband was a harddrinking ex-soldier who spent his weekends refereeing rugby matches.

Marriage and the Bar provided Margaret Thatcher with the basis on which to build a new political career. After having briefly withdrawn her name from the list of potential Conservative candidates, she began to look for a winnable parliamentary seat. Even with the advantages conferred by a rich husband, being selected for such a seat was not easy. Selection committees repeatedly asked her who would look after her young children. In a more subtle way, her social origins also counted against her. Anyone leafing through the *Who's Who* entries of candidates who were chosen ahead of Margaret Thatcher will notice some recurring patterns – 'the Carlton', 'country pursuits', 'Eton'.

It took Margaret Thatcher ten years of hard work to get into parliament,[38] but her persistence was rewarded in 1958, when she was selected as Conservative candidate for Finchley in North London. Her victory was narrow – she beat the last of her rivals by 46 votes to 43 – and, unusually, a 'handful' of members refused to observe the convention that the successful candidate should be given a unanimous vote of support at the end of the process.[39] The scale of Thatcher's achievement in getting selected for a safe Conservative seat can be illustrated by looking at her predecessor. Sir John Crowder, who had held the seat since 1935, was a Lloyd's underwriter who had been educated at Eton and Christ Church and served with the Household Cavalry during the Second World War. On being told that the shortlist for his succession contained both Thatcher and Peter Goldman, he said: 'We've got to choose between a bloody Jew and a bloody woman.'[40]

Thatcher held Finchley for the Conservatives, with a majority of 16,000, in 1959, and she was to do so again in every election, until she entered the House of Lords in 1992. It was a good springboard for an ambitious Conservative. Thatcher held her seat comfortably through three Labour victories in general elections so that her parliamentary career was never disturbed by the need to find a new seat – indeed she was one of only three Conservative MPs elected in 1959 who managed to hold exactly the same seats through the general elections and boundary changes of the next three decades.[5]

What was it like to be one of the twenty-five women MPs in the 1959 parliament? In her memoirs, Margaret Thatcher recalls the boisterous atmosphere of the House and the fact that women were effectively excluded from the smoking room, in which political deals were often hatched. However, she also insists that she felt unalloyed pleasure in her new role, that parliamentarians judged colleagues on their abilities, and that prejudice against women was less insidious than it had been in industry or at the Bar. Her parliamentary colleagues remember her arrival in parliament as being less comfortable. Peter Rawlinson first met Margaret Thatcher at a meeting of Conservative lawyers in the House of Commons. He recalled the occasion thus:

> She spoke even then ... with a vehemence rather too exaggerated for the subject and, I noticed, with an irritating emphasis on the wrong word, a habit she has never wholly lost. It was obvious that her 'contribution' had been designed merely to attract attention. She had of course attracted notice from every man in the room before she had ever opened her mouth. But that was not the kind of notice which she sought.[41]

Thatcher had recognized privately that some of the opposition to her candidature in Finchley had come from 'anti-woman' prejudice'.[42] Her attitude to the disadvantages under which women laboured was hard to read. Interviewed by the *Daily Express* in 1960, she said that she would send her daughter to university, rather than 'to finish abroad', and talked at length about the education and career appropriate for a woman. However, she also stressed the centrality of marriage for women and the importance of 'domestic arts'.[43] Some biographers argue that Thatcher's position on the rights of women changed as her career advanced – that, as time went on, she became less keen to ensure that other women had the advantages that she had enjoyed.[44] It is certainly true that Thatcher could be hypocritical. In later years she sometimes claimed that she had not worked when her children were young when she had, in fact, filled in the application to take her Bar exams when she was still in the maternity ward. It was not, however, just that Thatcher's position changed; rather that the whole nature of discussion around women's rights changed with the rise of feminism in the late 1960s and 1970s. Thatcher was emphatic that she was not a 'feminist',[45] and she often spoke of what she described as 'women's lib' with some disdain.[46] Addressing a group of children during a television programme in 1982, she said:

> I think most of us got to our own position in life without Women's Lib and we got here, not by saying 'you've got to have more women doing so and so' but saying 'look, we've got the

qualifications, why shouldn't we have just as much a chance as a man?' And you'll find that so many male bastions were conquered that way, whereas Women's Lib, I think, has been rather strident, concentrated on things which don't really matter and, dare I say it, being rather unfeminine. Don't you think that? What do the girls think, don't you think Women's Lib is sometimes like that?[47]

The truth was that Margaret Thatcher's sex, which had been a disadvantage when she was trying to get into parliament, was probably an advantage once she was in it, at least unless and until she tried to obtain one of the major offices of state. From 1959 until her entry into the cabinet in 1970, she benefited from the need for token women in certain kinds of position and from the attention that was given to someone relatively young and attractive.

For most of her time in parliament, Thatcher was a loyal party woman. She had promised the electors of Dartford in 1950 that she would vote according to her conscience and not the party line.[48] In fact, she voted against a Conservative three-line whip only once in her entire Commons' career, when she supported birching for young criminals. In any case, Thatcher's period as an ordinary backbench MP was comparatively short. She was appointed as parliamentary secretary to the Ministry of Pensions and National Insurance in October 1961 and she shadowed this department after the Conservative defeat in the general election of

1964. She worked through two further shadow posts: first at Housing and Land, from October 1965, and then as deputy to the shadow chancellor, Iain Macleod, from April 1966. She joined the shadow cabinet in October 1967 with responsibility for fuel and then took the transport brief in November 1968. In October 1969 she became shadow education minister. She was seen as effective and competent in the House of Commons. Education was a 'woman's job', but her post at Pensions and as deputy to Macleod had given her the opportunity to demonstrate a grasp of technical financial matters. The Labour MP Denis Healey had first been told of Thatcher by his colleague Charlie Pannell, who acted as her 'pair' and had a high opinion of her abilities. At first, Healey could not see anything special in the new MP, but, by the late 1960s, he had come to regard her with grudging admiration.[49]

What did Margaret Thatcher believe in during the 1960s? In the 1980s some historians talked about a post-war 'consensus' that revolved around the welfare state,[50] and the parallel lines on which the Conservative chancellor, R.A. Butler, and his Labour shadow, Hugh Gaitskell, had supposedly developed their economic policies. Interest in this phenomenon was sharpened by the frequency with which Thatcher herself denounced 'consensus'. Some of the fiercer Thatcherite ministers – Norman Tebbit[51] and Nicholas Ridley[52] – were particularly bitter in their attacks on Harold Macmillan. Thatcher's own relation with Macmillan was an interesting one. He was prime minister during her first four years in parliament, and gave her her first government office. In her memoirs, Thatcher talked of being 'uneasy with the general direction in which we seemed to be going' during the Macmillan government.[53] Macmillan's parliamentary private secretary listed Thatcher as one of four junior ministers who did not give the prime minister unqualified support.[54] If, however, Thatcher was dissatisfied with Macmillan, then she kept it quiet for a long time. Until at least 1979, she continued to praise Macmillan in extravagant terms. In one of the first interviews she gave as party leader, Thatcher suggested that Macmillan was a particularly important model for her.[55] She insisted that he was a visionary and the single twentieth-century politician that she admired the most – more, apparently, even than Churchill.[56]

Thatcherite dislike of Macmillan probably had as much to do with things that he said during the 1980s as with things that he had done during the 1960s. 'The Great Macmillan Speech' – with its evocation of Edwardian England, the tragedy of the First World War, the horrors of the Great Depression and the possibilities of new technology – had been a well-recognized and much parodied institution since the early 1970s. During the 1980s Macmillan injected it with new notes of sexism and snobbery (economic policy was evoked with references to nannies, family silver and the Brigade of Guards) to make his speech into an anti-Thatcher weapon. He ostentatiously supported her opponents in the cabinet and devoted his maiden speech in the House of Lords to attacking government economic policy. He republished *The Middle Way. Theories of a Mixed Economy* – a book he had first brought out in 1938 when under the influence of John Maynard Keynes.

There was, however, an irony in all this. Macmillan the elder statesman of the 1980s recalled himself as the young soldier of 1916 or the middle-aged parliamentary radical of 1938, but glossed over the small matter of his years as prime minister. He had, in fact, been a tough political operator, a vigorous defender of the free market and a bitter enemy of the Labour Party. It is true that Macmillan did not try to humble the unions or reduce state spending in the way that Margaret Thatcher's government was to do. But this was partly because he lived in different times – Thatcher wistfully remarked that Macmillan had presided over 'golden years', in which public spending had consumed only around 34 per cent of gross domestic product (it consumed around 42 per cent in 1984),[57] and in which inflation had seemed 'worrying' when it rose to 4.5 per cent.[58] It is interesting to ask how Macmillan would have behaved if he had still been an active politician when Britain began to face the problems of the 1970s. There is evidence that, in private, he anticipated some of the measures that Thatcher was to take (see chapter 7).

Thatcher's view of the post-war period was more subtle than that of some of her supporters. She usually used the word 'consensus' to describe a style of politics rather than to denounce particular politicians or policies. She was careful not to condemn the whole direction of British social policy since 1945; indeed, she sometimes confounded her opponents by citing with approval the documents that had influenced the immediate post-war period – the Beveridge Report of 1942 and the White Paper on Full Employment of 1944.[59] There was only one occasion on which she applied 'consensus' specifically to the three post-war decades of British history, and even then she was careful to note change across the period.[60]

Throughout the 1950s and 1960s some had campaigned against what they saw as the betrayal of free-market economics by all the major parties. Particularly important in this campaign was the Institute of Economic Affairs (IEA). The IEA was founded in 1955 by Antony Fisher, an entrepreneur who derived his fortune from battery chickens and his ideas from Friedrich Hayek.[61] Fisher recruited two economists – Arthur Seldon and Ralph Harris. The IEA was not a party political organization – the Liberal MP Oliver Smedley was closely involved in it and Seldon was, at least for most of the 1950s, a Liberal. The institute operated by publishing papers and organizing discussions, and it aimed to focus economic thinking on specific practical problems.

Some free-market Conservative MPs remained unsure about whether Thatcher was really 'one of us' on economic grounds until well into the 1970s.[62] Others regarded her as an ally, but one of uncertain value. When sounded out by Arthur Seldon about Margaret Thatcher in 1969, Geoffrey Howe wrote:

> I am not at all sure about Margaret. Many of her economic prejudices are certainly sound. But she is inclined to be rather too dogmatic for my liking on sensitive issues like education and might actually retard the cause by over-simplification. We should certainly be able to hope for something better from her – but I suspect that she will need to be exposed to the humanizing side of your character as much as to the pure welfare-market-monger. There is much scope for her to be influenced between triumph and disaster.[63]

The speech that Thatcher delivered to the Conservative Political Centre in October 1968 has attracted much interest from historians of Thatcherism because of its reference to controlling the money supply.[64] This was, however, a rather unusual expression of views on Thatcher's part; perhaps the only occasion in her life when she sought to tackle broad questions of political philosophy without having recourse to speechwriters. Parts of the speech seemed to allude to the critique of Heathite 'technocracy' that was being advanced at the time by Angus Maude and Enoch

Powell. However, this was hardly mainstream Thatcherism – she would never again hint that economic growth might not be a good thing. Nor did the speech have a great impact on perceptions of Thatcher's position: a *Times* interview in the following year was to conclude that 'she is no supporter of the Angus Maude wing of the Tory party'.[65]

The post-war political consensus was not just, perhaps not mainly, about economics. The single most important thing on which there was cross-party agreement during the 1950s was foreign policy.[66] In this area, Thatcher was an emphatic defender of consensus. She shared the belief that Britain should remain a great power. In pursuit of this status, she believed in a British nuclear bomb and in the maintenance of the Anglo-American 'special relationship' – she was later to claim that Macmillan's greatest achievement was his reconstruction of this relationship after Suez.[67] Thatcher also shared the belief widespread in the 1960s that the state had a duty to strengthen the family. She voted in favour of legislation to legalize homosexuality and abortion but she did so precisely because, like most other politicians of the time, she thought that this legislation would address 'anomalies' and 'special cases' rather than establish an alternative morality.

On social matters, as much as economic ones, the important point about the 'progressive consensus' was that it progressed. Sometimes, indeed, it might be argued that Thatcher was a defender of the 'post-war consensus' (i.e. that established in the late 1940s) against the 'progressive consensus' of the late 1960s. This was visible on two issues that Thatcher was most identified with. The first was crime and punishment. The *Sun* noted in 1970 that 'On issues ... traditionally close to the hearts of Tory women, she [Thatcher] is unhysterically, but firmly, in the law-and-order camp.' Thatcher favoured the restoration of the death penalty (though she wanted its use to be relatively sparing) and regretted that bringing back corporal punishment for young offenders was no longer realistic.[68] Thatcher was entirely consistent on support for the death penalty (her Liberal opponent in Finchley believed that it was her only strong conviction),[69] but her views, which would have seemed unexceptional for a Conservative parliamentary candidate in 1950, had begun to seem right-of-centre for a Conservative frontbencher in 1970.

The other matter that preoccupied Thatcher at the end of the 1960s was education, the subject on which she spoke for the opposition. She was contemptuous of radicalism on university campuses – though less exercised by this than her friend Sir Keith Joseph. More significant was the subject that began to dominate educational debate in the late 1960s: comprehensive schools. Since the Second World War, British schoolchildren had been divided, usually at the age of eleven, into the academically able, who went to grammar schools, and the majority, who went mainly to secondary modern schools. In the 1960s local authorities began to convert all schools into 'comprehensives'. Grammar schools were, in fact, very much a feature of the post-war consensus. It was, after all, success in exams that had given the men in Whitehall their notorious conviction that 'they knew best', and the 1944 Education Act, which gave birth to the post-war grammar school system, had been drawn up under the aegis of the arch consensualist R.A. Butler.

Thatcher defended grammar schools, though her position was, as was often the case, more nuanced than her later pronouncements, or those of her admirers, might suggest. She had expressed reservations about comprehensive schools ever since she had been a parliamentary candidate in Finchley, but she had also stressed that 'there was room for experiment ... It may be, she said, that comprehensive schools turned out to be wonderful.'[70] When she became shadow minister for education, the *Financial Times* believed that: 'On the vexed issue of comprehensive schools, Mrs Thatcher's position is moderate.'[71] Thatcher never suggested that changes that had already taken place should be reversed, or even that the transformation of schools into comprehensives could be stopped. Her aim seems mainly to have been to retain a few 'top tier grammar schools within a national system of mostly comprehensive education'.[72] A couple of years later she was to compare the relationship of direct grant schools (the grandest kind of grammar school) to state schools with the relationship between Paris fashion houses and Marks and Spencer (a remark that probably says something about her much vaunted admiration for M&S as well as her attitude to education).[73]

In 1970 the Conservatives won the election and Thatcher entered the cabinet for the first time, as secretary of state for education. The prime minister who made the appointment was Edward Heath. Like Thatcher, Heath had been born into a relatively humble background and educated at grammar school and Oxford. Service in the Second World War, which he finished with the rank of lieutenant colonel, gave him a belief in teamwork, efficiency and loyalty. It also gave him, as it gave his friend Denis Healey and his enemy Enoch Powell, a strange honorary membership of the English uppermiddle class – he drew his status from the pips on his shoulder rather than his background or wealth. After working as news editor of the *Church Times* and as a merchant banker (it says much about how his world differed from that of the Thatcherites of the 1980s that the first of these jobs was more highly paid and demanding than the second), Heath became a Tory MP in 1950 and made his mark as a successful whip, enforcing discipline on the other ranks after Suez. In 1965 Heath became leader of the party – the first one to be elected by Tory MPs rather than chosen by informal consultations amongst grandees. It was an astonishing achievement for a man of his origins – he succeeded a straight run of three Etonians.[74]

Thatcher voted for Heath in the leadership election, after Sir Keith Joseph told her 'Ted has a passion to get Britain right,' and she served loyally in his government. In spite of this, many came to talk as though Thatcherism was almost defined by opposition to the policies of her predecessor as Tory leader. Some of the tension between the two was personal, but some of it came also from the belief that Heath had, in fact, been elected to pursue radical free-market policies but had effected a 'U turn' and abandoned them. Thatcher's remark to the Conservative Party conference of 1980 – 'You turn if you want to. The Lady's not for turning' – was seen as an implicit rebuke to Heath.

Denunciation of Heath by free-market Conservatives revolved particularly around the conference for members of the shadow cabinet held at the Selsdon Park Hotel in 1970. The conference was designed to prepare the manifesto for the coming election and also, in the eyes of the Conservative apparatchiks, to ensure that frontbenchers actually understood the policies that the party had adopted in the previous few years.[75] The transcript of the meeting suggests that discussion amongst the shadow ministers was, in fact, rather disjointed and that the general thread of policy was often lost. The most revealing comments were those of Iain Macleod who tried to inject some sense of realism into the meeting: 'Absurd to go into details of administration now ... All we need is the decision en principe.' Macleod's words might almost have served as Heath's epitaph.[76]

Selsdon was, however, important to some people who did not attend the meeting. One of these was the Labour prime minister Harold Wilson, who coined the phrase 'Selsdon Man' to sum up 'the atavistic desire to reverse the course of twenty-five years of social revolution'. Selsdon, or perhaps Wilson's jibe about it, caught the imagination of some Tories. Nicholas Ridley, who felt slighted by the fact that Heath had removed him from a junior ministry in an economic department, founded the Selsdon Group in September 1973, ostensibly to defend the principles on which the Conservatives had been elected. Thatcher never joined it, and probably never really shared its view about what Selsdon had meant. A private briefing by the Conservative Research Department before she confronted a television interviewer in 1977 anticipated that there would be: 'Questions on the Selsdon Conference, what role Mrs Thatcher played and the final shape of the Selsdon policies. (Albeit that Selsdon itself is vastly exaggerated in Labour mythology.)'[77] However, when she became leader of the Conservative Party, Labour MPs asked whether her own economic policies would make her a 'Selsdon Woman' and, like many phrases that were originally intended as insults, this one was eventually adopted by Thatcher herself.

Heath undoubtedly did change course in certain respects during his four years in office. Having initially pledged to avoid intervention in industry, the government provided money for companies that were in difficulty and in 1972 institutionalized such support with the Industry Act. It was also in 1972 that the chancellor Anthony Barber sought to head off the prospect of rising unemployment with a budget that made borrowing cheaper. This provoked a boom in property prices, quickly followed by a train of bankruptcies and bank failures. It also provoked the resignation from the Central Policy Review Staff of Alan Walters, later to be Thatcher's personal economic adviser. Finally, in a bid to damp down inflation, partly caused by its own loose monetary policy, the government broke a manifesto commitment not to introduce controls over prices and incomes. After experimenting with voluntary agreements, it enforced a succession of statutory controls which seemed to illustrate all the absurdities of a managed economy. Geoffrey Howe, who became commissioner for prices and incomes, claimed that only some quick and discreet negotiations by his civil servants prevented the vicar of Trumpington from being prosecuted for raising the rates that he charged for brass rubbing in his church.[78]

Blaming Heath for changing course is, though, to miss the point. He was never a political fundamentalist. He thought of himself as a pragmatist and regarded adjustments to circumstances as natural. He saw the free market as a means to an end – that end being the modernization of Britain with a special view to making the economy fit for entry into the European Economic Community. Getting into Europe was, in fact, Heath's most cherished ambition and one that he achieved in 1973. In addition to this, the circumstances to which Heath had to adjust were uniquely difficult. Inflation came from the increased union militancy and consequent wage claims that had begun in the late 1960s. There was also a sharp increase in the oil price after the Arab–Israeli War of 1973. Heath's advisers had anticipated that prices might rise to six dollars a barrel or even to nine dollars, a possibility that they described as a 'crisis'. They actually rose to forty dollars.

A series of setbacks undermined the government. Iain Macleod, the chancellor of the exchequer, died unexpectedly in 1970. He had had the very qualities – charm, shrewdness, cynicism and an eye for electoral advantage – that Heath lacked, and it is possible that he might have been the one man capable of saving Heath from himself. Britain became locked in international disputes, the very triviality of which seemed to underline the decline of its power. Iceland declared that British ships would not be allowed to fish within 200 miles of its shores – thus forcing the Admiralty to admit that its aircraft carriers and nuclear submarines could not actually assure the freedom of the seas for British ships. The Ugandan dictator Idi Amin expelled people of Indian descent from his country. Ministers, including Margaret Thatcher, recognized that they were legally and morally obliged to take these refugees in. Doing so, however, damaged the government in the eyes of some Conservatives.

Heath also faced two more serious general problems. The first involved labour relations. The government had come to power with a pledge to introduce an Industrial Relations Act, which eventually came into force in early 1972. The aim of the act was to encourage unions to register with the state and to make agreements between unions and employers enforceable in special industrial courts. But it was introduced at a bad time, when labour militancy was rising, and suffered from a problem that ministers had not anticipated – unions simply refused to register under the legislation (the TUC expelled unions that did so) and effectively dared employers to take them to court. Far from bringing peace to industrial relations, the Heath government had to deal with a succession of disputes. In particular, the miners' strikes of 1972 and 1974 generated a visible sense of failure – the first caused power cuts and the second forced the government to introduce a three-day working week. The legislation allowing British governments to introduce a state of emergency has been on the statute book since 1920. It has only been used eleven times and five of these occurred between 1970 and 1974.

Above all, the Heath government faced problems in Northern Ireland. Ever since the 1920s much power in the province had been devolved to the Ulster parliament at Stormont. The province was dominated by the Unionist Party, which represented Protestant interests. In the late 1960s Catholics began to protest at the ways in which they were excluded from political power, and both sides took up arms to defend their interests. In 1969 there had been thirteen political murders in Ulster; in 1972, the *annus horribilis* for Heath in almost every way, there were 467 – the largest number of violent deaths in the province's history. The government tried to counter this threat with a succession of expedients – sending troops in to maintain order (and, initially, to protect the Catholic population), introducing internment without trial and conducting secret negotiations with leaders of the IRA – most of which made things worse.

Ulster was a particularly awkward issue for a Conservative leader because the Ulster Unionists had traditionally been allied to the Conservative Party on the mainland and because Ulster Unionist MPs at Westminister had taken the Conservative whip.[79] During the 'Troubles', this began to change. Unionism's leaders were now more plebeian and more radical. The Reverend Ian Paisley was the most flamboyant of the movement's new leaders. The tone of the new Unionism became more violent and its style – anti-European, self-consciously archaic, shot through with religious imagery – was far removed from Heathism.

In 1972 the British government suspended the Stormont parliament altogether and introduced direct rule in Ulster. The following year it organized negotiations amongst Ulster parties at that great centre of Heathite technocracy – the Sunningdale Civil Service College. At Sunningdale, the government imposed a 'power-sharing executive' that would have responsibility for some of the government of Northern Ireland. Far from being a solution, the Sunningdale agreement radicalized Ulster Unionism. Official and unofficial Unionists against Sunningdale fought the February 1974 election under a combined ticket which meant that only one of the twelve MPs returned by Ulster supported the agreement. This played a direct role in Heath's political demise.

After his general election defeat of February 1974, Heath was keenly interested in a parliamentary deal that might keep him in power. This meant talking to other political parties and particularly to the Liberals and the Ulster Unionists. Seven of the eleven Ulster Unionists who had been returned to Westminster still nominally took the Conservative whip in the House of Commons – though they had not in fact given much support to the government since March 1972. Heath hoped that they would continue to vote with his government on issues other than Ulster. The Unionists hoped that Heath would abandon Sunningdale in return for their support. In practice, however, Heath and his advisers found it hard to separate the Official Unionists from their more radical allies – it is difficult anyway to imagine how anyone could have built a political coalition that included the Liberal leader Jeremy Thorpe (pro-Sunningdale and about to be prosecuted for conspiracy to murder his male lover) and Ian Paisley (anti-Sunningdale and committed to 'save Ulster from sodomy').[80]

Problems in Northern Ireland sapped the energy of the government, and contributed to a general sense that its approach was not working. Ministers associated with law enforcement or the army were now obliged to spend their whole lives in the company of armed police officers. Politics on the mainland and in Northern Ireland intersected in awkward ways. The miners' strike of 1972 began just after British paratroopers had killed thirteen unarmed Catholic demonstrators on 'Bloody Sunday', and direct rule was announced just before the budget of March 1972. The mood of crisis that developed in Ulster spilled over into discussion of problems on the mainland. A report to the cabinet cited a Midlands MP who had warned that calling out troops in the coalfields would 'make a Londonderry out of every colliery'.[81]

Ministers and civil servants discussed industrial relations in apocalyptic tones – they were agitated by information from the security services about Communist infiltration of the National Union of Mineworkers – though the leader of the union, Joe Gormley, who led two successful strikes, was conspicuously non-Communist and may even have been an MI5 informant. In the aftermath of the 1972 miners' strike, a note to (or perhaps even by) the prime minister suggested: 'The use of violence to achieve social or political ends must increase as society becomes more complex, the vulnerable areas become more numerous, the methods of attack more sophisticated.' The letter added: 'The social revolution need not be destructive – although a growing number of people begin to think that it will have to be.'[82] Someone, presumably Heath, scribbled on this letter 'powerful: learn the lessons for...'

The Heath government was ill-equipped to deal with the crises of the early 1970s. Unforeseeable circumstances pose especially awkward problems for a government that presents itself, as Heath's did, as characterized by its capacity to plan the future. Heath was right to claim that his government came to power in 1970 with more detailed projects for action than any previous government. This was part of the problem, and he was probably more damaged by those projects for a new order in industrial relations which he tried to implement, than by those, for a more liberal economic order, which he abandoned. Heath's emphasis on rational discussion, modernization and planning made the chaos of the early 1970s seem all the more humiliating. In 1972 the machinery of government broke down in a very literal sense – during power cuts, senior civil servants sat in candle-lit offices, unable to get documents typed or photocopied.

Heath's corporatism – his desire to establish complicated mechanisms for negotiation between employers, unions and government – also made his problems worse. His government, in conspicuous contrast to Thatcher's, could not simply claim not to be responsible for strikes or negotiations. Heath had problems with both sides of industry. He made assiduous efforts to stay close to organized business – his secretary of state for industry, John Davies, had previously been head of the Confederation of British Industry. However, this did not produce a smooth managerialism. On the contrary, Heath was often shocked by the political incompetence of business leaders (including Davies), and the Conservative election campaign of February 1974 was damaged when the new head of the CBI (William Campbell Adamson) casually remarked that business did not really regard the government's policies on industrial relations with much favour.

Heath was bad at managing crisis. His fantasies about a 'technocratic' and 'apolitical' approach to government were really suited to France (the country that both fascinated and repelled Heath) rather than Britain. He placed great faith in civil servants, but men who were good at writing elegant reports proved strikingly bad at taking quick and unpleasant decisions. Far from being a detached purveyor of cool advice, William Armstrong (the cabinet secretary, who had won a place in Heath's heart by playing piano duets with him) became obsessed by the belief that Britain was on the verge of Communist revolution and eventually, after having had a nervous breakdown (which caused him to hide under his desk), had to be sent to the West Indies to recuperate.

The Conservatives needed someone who could rally support for their policies, but Heath was not the man for the job. In spite, or because, of his humble origins, he seemed patrician and his interests – classical music and yachting – did not suggest the common touch. He spoke badly when addressing a large audience and on television. The slogan of his 1966 manifesto had been 'action not words' and Heath's greatest weakness was, indeed, a failure to appreciate the importance of words. It is significant that his only memorable phrase – his description of Lonrho as the 'unacceptable face of capitalism' – came from his having mixed up 'face' and 'facet'. Despairingly his aides made a list of jargon that the prime minister should avoid: 'regressive, relativities, anomalies, unified tax system, productivity, threshold agreement, deflation, realignment'.[83]

The end of Heath's premiership came in February 1974. Against the advice of many colleagues, Heath called an election in an attempt to strengthen his hand in dealing with the miners' strike. He was unlucky in almost every respect during the election – even the weather was bad. In spite of it all, the Tories got more votes than Labour, but the Labour Party had 301 seats against the Conservatives' 297. After his attempts to stay in office with the support of smaller parties failed, Heath resigned on 4 March.[84]

Heath's failure was a precondition of Thatcher's success in a very direct way – it is hard to imagine that she would ever have become leader of the Conservative

Party if Heath had been elected for a second term. The Heath government came to provide some Thatcherites with a convenient epitome of everything that they opposed. Heath himself was an ideal enemy for Thatcher (almost as good as General Galtieri or Arthur Scargill). The venom of his attacks on her rallied her supporters whilst his own gloomy unclubability prevented him from rallying her opponents. Most of all, though, Heath laid the way for Thatcher in a more complicated fashion. He shared much of her diagnosis about what was wrong with Britain – economic decline, politicized trade unions. His failure seemed to discredit his own particular approach to those problems and this explains the fact that many of the Conservatives who had been close to Heath in the early 1970s were willing to support Margaret Thatcher's more dramatic radicalism ten years later. John Nott, a minister under both Heath and Thatcher, wrote: 'Perhaps Margaret Thatcher owes her election victory in 1979 to the appalling mess left behind in 1974 by a Tory Cabinet – of which she was a member.'[85] Arthur Scargill, a leader of the miners' union which broke Heath and was later to be broken by Thatcher, remarked in 1981:

> I think there are enormous differences between this Government and the Heath administration in terms of their application of Conservative policy. It's true that the working class movement learned a lot of lessons from 1970–74 but the ruling class learnt a lot of lessons as well.[86]

If Thatcher benefited from the Heath government in the long run, however, it was certainly not obvious in the early 1970s just how great those benefits would be for her personally. It was taken for granted that Thatcher was a competent minister but one whose sex would impose sharp limits on her career. Sir Gerald Nabarro, a right-wing Tory MP, wrote in 1973:

> Thatcher will probably go a good deal further without reaching the top. She is not prime ministerial material, but I suppose, conceivably, she might find her way into the Treasury ... if a brave enough Prime Minister could be found to appoint her Chancellor of the Exchequer.[87]

Chapter 2

THATCHERISM BEFORE THATCHER? ENOCH POWELL

I don't think he'd fit into Mrs Thatcher's Shadow Cabinet. He's just too powerful for the poor lady.

Mary Wills, working-class 'Powellite' from Ealing, interviewed mid 1970s[1]

[One of her] remarkable characteristics, which stamps her as a superb politician, is her ability to put up with things and go along with them, even though she doesn't agree with them, until the time comes when they can be dealt with. Now, not possessing that quality myself – having the loquacity which always impels me to say: 'I don't agree' – I admire this.

Enoch Powell on Margaret Thatcher, 1989[2]

In strict academic logic the Right Hon. Gentleman is right. In everything else he is wrong.

Margaret Thatcher to Enoch Powell, 1981[3]

Does Enoch Powell belong in a book about Thatcher at all? Thatcher was not one of the fifteen MPs who voted for Enoch Powell when he stood for the leadership of the Conservative Party in 1965. Powell would not have considered voting for Margaret Thatcher as leader of the Conservative Party – he said that the party would never stand for 'those hats and that accent'[4] – but, in any case, the question never arose because Powell had left the party by the time that Thatcher became its leader, and he never returned to it. Powell's support for Edward Heath in the 1970 election probably helped the Conservatives to win that election, and his advice to his supporters that they vote Labour in February 1974 probably contributed to Heath's defeat. In both these acts, he might have played an indirect and unintentional role in furthering Margaret Thatcher's career. However, Powell had little influence on the electoral politics of the British mainland after this, and he did not support Margaret Thatcher's party in the 1979 election: he described the result as 'grim'.

A historian of any aspect of post-war British history faces the dilemma of where to put Enoch Powell. His capacity for the striking expression of extraordinary opinions always commanded attention, but his eccentricity means that it is almost impossible to fit him comfortably into any wider movement. He spoke in terms that suggested a superhuman concern for rigour and logic (a journalist jibbed that he was 'lucid to the point of incomprehensibility'[5]), but these qualities were allied to a sense that politics should be informed by feelings that could not be rationally articulated.[6] He valued 'myth' and 'hallucination' and seemed at times to feel that there was something admirable about a rational man who based his life on things that a rational man would know to be untrue. One of the funniest passages in his writing concerns the 'simple faith' of Alec Douglas-Home. Without saying so in so many words, Powell hints that faith can be no great virtue in someone who is too stupid to see how implausible the tenets of Christianity are in the first place.[7]

Powell managed to combine an obsessive air of consistency with a capacity for the volte face. He changed his position dramatically on some of the issues that dominated his political career (Empire, Europe and race). He voted for three different political parties at various times but sometimes did so for reasons that were diametrically opposed to the stated policies of those parties. He was haunted by the death of a close friend during the war and sometimes expressed regret that he himself had not been given the chance to die in action: his whole career was suffused by fascination with the suicidal frontal attack.[8] Powell was always interested in matters of clinical insanity. As minister of health in the early 1960s, he worked hard to shut down Victorian mental hospitals ('the asylums which our forefathers built with such immense solidity to express the notions of their day')[9] and, in a characteristically eccentric moment, he persuaded the Queen's dressmaker to design new uniforms for the staff at Broadmoor. Anyone who studies his career must sometimes wonder whether Powell was not, to quote words that he used in his most notorious speech, 'literally mad'.

For all his eccentricity, however, it would be impossible to understand the political Right in late twentieth-century Britain without understanding something about Enoch Powell. Its whole style – from Roger Scruton's taste for hunting to Michael Portillo's affection for Wagner – owed much to Powell. He had a remarkable capacity for intimidating his fellow Tories. As prime minister, Harold Macmillan had the seating of the cabinet rearranged so that he could avoid Powell's stare, which, he claimed, made him feel like 'one of the more disreputable Popes being eyed by Savonarola'.[10] During the 1970 election, Heath's aides were tormented by anxiety about what Powell might say and one of them believed that the turning point of the whole campaign came on the day (15 June) that Heath said that he would take no more questions from journalists on the subject.[11] In the 1980s, when he was a backbench member of a small party with no hope of holding office again, Powell's long shadow could still darken the Conservative front bench. Ministers quoted his occasional expressions of approval with an almost childlike pleasure,[12] and they were frightened of his denunciation. One of them recalled: 'He was the only adversary in the House of Commons who ever seriously worried me ... Powell, by his appearance, voice and choice of words, radiated an authority which I had no immediate resources to match.'[13]

There were more specific links between Thatcher and Powell. Powell was seen as the purveyor of an ideology at a time when the Conservative Party still prided itself on being 'unideological': Iain Macleod first identified the phenomenon of 'Powellism' in 1965. Many of Thatcher's ministers – Geoffrey Howe, John Biffen, Nicholas Ridley, John Nott and Ian Gow – were, or had been, disciples of Powell. Some saw him as the political ancestor of Thatcher. Anthony Howard asked Powell in 1983 whether Thatcherism was 'Powellism by other means'.[14] Cecil Parkinson believed that Thatcher had succeeded Powell in a very direct way and that she had been invited to join the Economic Dining Club (an important free-market pressure group in the Conservative Party) to replace Powell when he left the party in 1974.[15] John Nott argued that the government in which he served from 1979 to 1982 was really 'Powellite' rather than Thatcherite.[16] Powell even provided Thatcherism with much of its language. When Keith Joseph talked of the 'ratchet effect' of socialism, or when Thatcher talked about subversion from 'enemies within',[17] they were, consciously or not, quoting Powell.

Most of all, however, Powell is worth studying alongside Thatcher precisely because of the *differences* between two outlooks that sometimes seemed superficially similar. Powell questioned every orthodoxy and took every argument up to, and sometimes beyond, its logical conclusion. Comparing him with Thatcher and her allies highlights the extent to which the success of her government was based on pragmatism and tactical flexibility. Thatcher is often seen as the enemy of the 'post-war consensus', but looking at Powell illustrates how many aspects of this consensus – Anglo-American alliance, a British nuclear bomb, the emphasis on great power status and on 'reversing decline' – she defended.

Even in purely personal terms, the contrast between Powell and Thatcher is revealing. Thatcher is interesting only because of her political career, and her life before she was elected to parliament was uneventful. Powell would have been an extraordinary and interesting man even if he had never entered politics.[18] He was born, the only child of two schoolteachers, in Birmingham in 1912. His brilliant career as a classical scholar took him through King Edward's Grammar School and Trinity College Cambridge to be professor of Greek at the University of Sydney, but he returned to England in 1939 to join up as a private in the Warwickshire Regiment. His military career was as meteoric as his academic one and Powell could have been a general if he had been willing to stay in the army for just another year or two. By the time he was thirty-four, the age at which Thatcher was first elected to parliament, he had already set two records – as the youngest professor in the British Empire and as the only man to hold every rank between that of private and brigadier in the British army during the Second World War. He was a published poet and could have been a professional clarinetist. As an essayist and reviewer, he could be as interesting on, say, the films of Jacques Tati or the travel writing of Wilfred Thesiger as he was on politics or history. Richard Ingrams was probably joking when he offered Powell the editorship of *Private Eye* (though with Ingrams, as with Powell, it is sometimes hard to tell) but, in fact, Powell was probably the only man in England who could have sustained the magazine's mix of paranoid denunciation and surreal humour.

Powell is now remembered mainly for a speech he made in April 1968 in Birmingham denouncing coloured immigration. Because of Powell's reference to the Tiber 'foaming with much blood', this became known as the 'rivers of blood' speech and it probably attracted more attention than any other statement in that whole tumultuous year. The British establishment was horrified by Powell's apparent racism, and Edward Heath sacked Powell from the Conservative shadow cabinet, thus ending his front-bench career. However, the mail that poured into Conservative Central Office was overwhelmingly favourable to Powell. He had struck a chord amongst part of the white working class – dockers and porters from Smithfield market marched in his support. For the next few years, polls showed that Powell was one of the most popular politicians in the country – sometimes more popular than the official leader of his party.

The 'rivers of blood' speech anticipated and influenced Thatcherism. Members of Thatcher's shadow cabinet repeatedly referred to the importance of 'immigration' as an electoral issue and Thatcher's remarks about the native population of Britain feeling 'rather swamped' were seen as an attempt to exploit public feeling on this issue (see chapter 4). Left-wing commentators sometimes saw Thatcher's 'authoritarian populism' as being an extension of Powell's.

However, the similarities between Thatcher and Powell can be overstated. For one thing, Thatcherites only ever saw immigration as one issue amongst many, while Powell, for a time at least, saw it as the most important issue in British politics. Some Thatcherites seem to have been interested in it because they saw it as a means of mobilizing electoral support for economic policies which might otherwise be unpopular, rather than because they saw it as a matter of central importance in itself. Thatcher's version of populism involved reference to the need for more severe repression of crime, particularly the restoration of the death penalty. Powell made little of crime and opposed the death penalty.

Furthermore, the key to Powell's populism was that it involved a form of politics that spilled out of the conventional party structures – it is significant that he admired Charles de Gaulle, who operated above parties and outside parliament. Though he always described himself as a Tory, Powell was not a conventional member of the Conservative Party. He had voted Labour in 1945, to 'punish' the Conservative Party for Munich, and his appeal after 1968 was largely to people who were not Conservatives. Powell himself voted Labour again in February 1974 (this time in an attempt to obtain British withdrawal from the European Economic Community). Later in the same year, he joined the Official Ulster Unionists and was elected to represent a constituency in Northern Ireland. And, though Powell adored the House of Commons and was a fanatical defender of the rights of parliament, he talked, with reference to both Europe and immigration, of matters that were so important that they could be decided only 'by the Nation itself'.

Thatcher, by contrast, never countenanced politics that spilt out of ordinary party structures. Her populism was a means to strengthen an existing party rather than to sweep it away. Her response to the 'rivers of blood' was to insist on the importance of the House of Commons: 'I hope Enoch will put his views before the parliamentary forum.'[19] More generally, Thatcher's relations with Powell after April 1968 were marked by the very quality that he most lacked: prudence. She knew how hostile the Conservative front bench was to Powell and understood the damage that could be done by association with him. She told an American diplomat in 1973 that 'John Biffen had once had a great future, but he was now ruined because he had made himself a disciple of Powell.'[20] But, if Thatcher was nervous of being associated with Powell, she was also nervous of being too clearly distanced from him. Association with Powell would damage an ambitious Conservative in the eyes of the party leadership; hostility to him could damage them in the eyes of the party's rank and file – David Hunt had difficulty in being selected to fight a safe Conservative seat after he attacked Enoch Powell at the party conference. Thatcher had a particularly awkward balance to strike: her own constituency association contained a number of Powellites,[21] but also a number of Jews. Powell was not anti-Semitic, but many Jews detected a whiff of late Weimar in his pronouncements and the reaction that they aroused. There was a studied ambiguity in Thatcher's public references to Powell.[22] Her speech to the Conservative Political Centre in 1968 contained an odd allusion to 'Enoch' as an exponent of planning – a reference that might be read as mocking or affectionate, or both.

Relations between Powell and Thatcher were made easier by the fact that Powell joined the Official Ulster Unionists shortly before Thatcher became leader of the Conservatives. In the article that first gave currency to the word 'Powellism', Iain Macleod wrote: 'I am a fellow traveller, but sometimes I leave Powell's train a few stations down the line, before it reaches, and sometimes crashes into, the terminal buffers.'[23] Powell's departure from the Conservative Party made it easier for his admirers in that party to be 'fellow travellers' without risking the crash into the buffers. Had he remained in the party, then Thatcher would have had to deal with some of his extraordinary outbursts. Sooner or later, the party would almost certainly have had to withdraw the whip from Powell. Had he joined a party that opposed the Conservatives, then equally Thatcher might have been expected to produce clear denunciations of Powell's views. As it was, however, Powell belonged to a party that no longer took the Conservative whip but also one that was not in direct competition with Conservative candidates (because the major parties of the mainland did not run candidates in Ulster). Thatcher could maintain a stance of benign neutrality towards Powell. When young Conservatives asked her to pledge that he would never be brought back to the Conservative front bench, Thatcher was able to reply that: 'Mr Powell is not even a member of the Party. He is an Ulster Unionist and we have no Conservative Party in Ulster. I really am not likely to have as a member of the Shadow Cabinet a person who is not even a member of the Party.'[24]

The emphasis on the post-1968 Powell as anti-immigrant populist is somewhat deceptive for anyone who wants to understand the links between Powellism and Thatcherism. Powell's support in the parliamentary Conservative Party was very different from his support in Dudley or Smithfield market. Indeed the Thatcherite Tory MPs who admired Powell most were often those who admired his attitudes to immigration least.[25] Geoffrey Howe was to become the staunchest opponent of racial inequality on the Conservative front bench: he had co-authored the Bow Group's pamphlet on 'Coloured People in Great Britain' in 1952.[26] In 1968 John Nott was one of just sixty-two MPs (seventeen of them Conservatives) who voted against the second reading of the Commonwealth Immigration Bill, which took British passports away from Kenyan Asians.

For men such as Howe and Nott, 'Powellism' meant primarily a certain attitude to economics. Powell had been one of three treasury ministers to resign from Macmillan's government in 1958 in protest at increased public spending. After 1963 he was a vociferous opponent of all forms of state intervention in the economy. He opposed nationalization, economic planning, high public spending, exchange controls and any government policy on prices or incomes. Increasingly, he argued that the sole economic duty of government lay in control of the money supply. His particular style of economic thinking fitted in with his propensity for absolutes and with a tendency to invest all possible matters of political importance into a single issue. A government that controlled the money supply and its own spending could thus be freed of concern for all other economic matters. Indeed, Powell argued that the operations of the free market would free government from the need to interfere in many matters that were not directly related to economics. It was, for example, unnecessary for the government to legislate against sexual discrimination by employers, who had an economic interest in hiring the best candidate: 'Everyone is entitled to conduct his own business to his own disadvantage; but those who do so are destined to be in a small and disappearing minority.'[27] Powell's admiration for capitalism did not necessarily imply admiration for capitalists. He had little time for the Heathite cult of the manager ('this new model army of gentlemen who know best') or for the Thatcherite cult of the entrepreneur. It was the market itself that Powell admired. He saw it as something natural and organic that contrasted with the artificial creations of the modern state, and he celebrated it in tones of romantic nationalism: 'The collective wisdom and collective will of the nation resides not in any little Whitehall clique but in the whole mass of the people – expressing [itself] through all the complex nervous systems of the market.'[28]

The journalist Samuel Brittan, an early exponent of monetarist economics and the half-brother of one of Thatcher's ministers, suggested in the late 1960s that Powell had 'read almost no economics' and that this fact accounted both for his ability to 'go to the heart of economic problems' and for the sometimes simplistic quality of his solutions.[29] There was an element of truth in this allegation. Most political defences of free-market economics were heavily encumbered with jargon, theory and algebra. What set Powell apart was simplicity. At a time when almost no one dared to defend the unfettered operation of the free market, Powell said that he often got down on his knees in church and thanked God for capitalism. On the fringes of the 1968 Conservative Party conference, he presented an alternative budget showing how income tax might be reduced to just over 20 per cent. He explained economics in terms of striking metaphors, often drawn from the cinema. He likened the experience of an incomes policy to that of being repeatedly made to watch a pornographic film: 'is it necessary to stay in our seats through another, and yet another performance?'[30] He described floating exchange rates in terms taken from *Those Magnificent Men in Their Flying Machines:* 'We'll go up tiddly pom; we'll go down tiddly pom.'

An emphasis on economics can, however, be as deceptive as an emphasis on race in understanding Powellism. Powell also spent much of his time thinking about Britain's place in the world. It was here that he stood most sharply apart from the 'post-war consensus' and here that Thatcher was most clearly part of that consensus. If the British governing classes agreed about just one thing in the years after 1945, that thing was that Britain ought to remain a 'great power'. It was thought indelicate of the American secretary of state to suggest that the loss of Empire might have called this role into question. Britain's power was seen to rest on the possession of the nuclear bomb, its 'special relationship' with the United

States and its capacity to maintain a military presence 'east of Suez'. Like most Conservatives, Thatcher supported all of these things – indeed the American alliance and British nuclear weapons were to be crucial features of her political position during the 1980s.

Powell was different. He had served in India during the war and it was India that brought him into politics. He saw a British political career as a route to becoming viceroy – though he conceived this ambition at a time when any private who had bothered to stay awake in his political education classes could have told him that British rule in India was finished. After a few years denying reality – according to one story he lectured Churchill on how many divisions he would need to reconquer the subcontinent – Powell accepted that India was gone. For him, this changed everything. Britain could no longer, and should no longer, be a world power. Powell turned against the stationing of British troops east of Suez. He also always disliked nuclear weapons and, by the 1980s, he had come to denounce Britain's status as a nuclear power. Much to the amusement of the cognoscenti of Conservative politics, he managed to cloud both these positions in Jesuitical ambiguity when he was Conservative spokesman on defence during the 1960s.

Most of all, attitudes to the Atlantic alliance illustrated the gulf between Powell and other Conservatives. From the moment that he first met American officials in North Africa in 1943 until his death in 1998, Powell had his own special relationship with America. It was one of pathological hatred. Indeed this was the most consistent theme in his politics – though his consistency was not particularly logical because a man who had first come to dislike America on account of its alleged efforts to dissolve the British Empire had no reason to maintain his hostility beyond the point at which he recognized that the Empire was finished. In any case, Powell's anti-Americanism went way beyond the bounds of logic. In 1945 he seems seriously to have believed that Britain would soon be obliged to fight the United States and to do so in alliance with the Soviet Union. He planned to go to Latin America 'for reconnaissance purposes' in the backyard of his country's enemy.[31] Powell never shared the Cold War fervour that made many Conservatives look to Washington (the American capital, for Powell, was a byword for the problems of racial mixing rather than for moral leadership). In 1978 Powell wrote that the 'portentous moralizing' of Solzhenitsyn, the exiled Russian writer whose denunciations of Soviet tyranny were much admired by Thatcher, was 'a bore and an irritation'.[32] During the 1980s, hostility to America was reflected in his complaints about the subordination of British foreign policy to that of America and, more strikingly, in his assertion that the Americans were conspiring, for their own strategic reasons, to evict the British from Ireland.

Powell's insistence that Britain was no longer a great power intertwined with his thinking about other things in ways that also underlined how different Powellism was from Thatcherism. The first of these was economic decline. Almost the whole of the British establishment began to be obsessed by Britain's economic decline relative to other countries – particularly those of continental western Europe – from the late 1950s. The obsession reached its peak in the 1970s. The promise to 'reverse decline' was an important part of both Heath's and Thatcher's political project. In both cases, such a reversal was seen as important partly because it would allow Britain to play its 'natural' role as a world power. Powell was the most articulate critic of British 'declinism'. He believed that it was based on a deceptive historical comparison (with Britain at the apogee of her relative prosperity in the Victorian era) and a deceptive geographical comparison, with continental western Europe. 'Why? [he asked] compare Britain with France and Germany rather than America or Canada' (whose performance in the 1970s was less impressive) or, for that matter, with 'China or Peru'. He was sceptical about the value of the graphs and tables that permeated so many documents on Britain's state in the 1970s – 'To be happy it is not necessary to beat the statistical record all comers.'[33] As a true free marketeer, he disliked the idea that it was for the state to establish what level of production was desirable and, unlike many who thought themselves free marketeers, Powell recognized that the most important human desires might not be economic ones: 'But this question of growth brings us near to whatever real meaning can be attached to the idea of a "strong" economy. Ultimately, that idea is subjective – it has to do with what people feel and what people want. The only rational meaning of a "strong" economy is one where people put their efforts and resources to the use which gives them what they consider the greatest satisfaction.'[34]

Powell's view of Britain's role in the world was also tied to his view of what 'Englishness' should mean at home. Most British politicians saw decolonization in coolly rational terms. Emotion was usually injected only by nationalists in Asia and Africa or by sentimental right-wingers who sought to defend the Empire. Powell managed to portray decolonization as a romantic adventure for the British themselves: 'our generation is one which comes home again from years of distant wandering. We discover affinities with earlier generations of English, generations before the "expansion of England", who felt no country but this to be their own.'[35] Powell wanted the end of Empire to mark a clear break with Britain's recent past. He despised the constitutional fudges that allowed the Empire to be transmuted into the Commonwealth – he claimed that the most important speech of his political life involved denouncing the insertion of an 's' after the word 'realm' in the 1953 Royal Titles Bill. Powell became an English equivalent of the French royalist thinker Charles Maurras – trying to defend the *ancien régime* of Church, aristocracy and monarchy, after his own countrymen had forgotten what these things meant. Powell never tried to hide his own origins. He always spoke with a Midlands accent and revelled in his plebeian tastes – his wife made him promise that he would never ask her to cook tripe. However, he regarded the rituals and ranks of the English ruling class with the same scrupulous respect that he had, as a young officer in India, displayed towards the Hindu caste system. When Alec Douglas-Home renounced his peerage in order to become leader of the Conservative Party, many intelligent Conservatives were shocked because they saw Home's appointment as undemocratic or simply because they believed that he was not a good candidate for the job. Only Powell thought that renouncing a peerage was wrong because being the fourteenth earl was itself an important position with inalienable rights and responsibilities.

The struggle against modernization brought Powell up against the whole current of the post-war Conservative Party – a party that was obsessed with forms of modernization that Powell saw as destroying the real genius of England. Powell's most bitter antagonist in this respect was Edward Heath, but Margaret Thatcher was a kind of modernizer too and some of her dealings with Powell in the 1980s revealed how little she understood of his Toryism. Thatcher could not, in particular, understand why Powell, who had no male heir, refused to accept a life peerage after he lost his seat in the Commons in the general election of 1987.

Powell's preoccupation with a certain variety of Englishness accounts for a view of politics that laid a heavy emphasis on sovereignty, and this ties in with the two issues that separated him from the Conservative Party: Ulster and Europe. Powell believed strongly in the Union of England and Ulster – his belief in the integration of Ulster into British political structures was, in some ways, a more absolutist position than the support for Home Rule espoused by more traditional Unionists. Powell's views on this matter were also more absolutist than those of Thatcher – who combined vague professions of belief in Unionism with a half-hearted search for constitutional expedients that might solve the province's problems. Ulster was to be the single issue on which Thatcher and Powell were to clash most strongly (see chapter 9). After Thatcher signed the Anglo-Irish agreement of 1985, Powell told her the penalty for treachery was to fall into public contempt.

On Europe, Powell was initially favourable to Britain's entry into the Common Market – partly because he saw it as a means of promoting free trade and partly because he relished something that seemed to undermine Britain's pretensions to being a world power. In 1969 Powell changed his mind. The resignation of de Gaulle, whom he admired, seems to have precipitated this change. Almost any other politician would have regarded the exit of a notably anti-British statesman from the European scene as making things easier. Perhaps Powell had hoped that de Gaulle would turn the Common Market into a looser and less political federation or perhaps he found de

Gaulle's Anglophobia easier to bear than the condescension that younger French politicians displayed to Britain. Whatever the reason, from then on Powell insisted that Britain's entry into the EEC would involve an unforgivable renunciation of the rights of the British parliament. Eventually Europe was to bring Powell and Thatcher back together. Powell welcomed what he saw as the *souverainisme* of Thatcher's 1988 Bruges speech. This reconciliation on Thatcher's political deathbed should not, however, disguise the fact that the Conservative Party was – for most of the period after 1969 and most of the period during which Thatcher led it – the most pro-European of the major British political parties.

Some of Powell's admirers liked to imply that Thatcherism was really Powellism in power. Thatcher and Powell would probably both have recognized that this was a contradiction in terms. If Thatcherism meant anything, it meant power. Thatcher held office, in the government or her party, for most of the time that she was a member of parliament. She only once voted against a three-line whip and she imposed firm discipline on her own party when she was leader. She never resigned from any position and was emotionally broken when she was finally forced out of office.

Powell, by contrast, was one of nature's refuseniks. He voted against the government 115 times between 1970 and 1974, more than any other Conservative MP. He refused office twice, resigned once and forced his party leader into sacking him once. Nicholas Ridley, one of his greatest admirers, conceded in December 1968: 'he is probably an awkward colleague in any administration because if he is not resigning, he is probably threatening to resign'.[36] He was in the cabinet only for a couple of years and, though he enjoyed administration, he seemed to think that ministerial office had a corrupting effect on its holders. His attitude to office-holding is illustrated by his extraordinary position in the Official Ulster Unionists. Joining the party ensured that he would never again hold ministerial office at Westminster; insisting on full integration into the political structures of the mainland ensured that he would never hold office in a devolved Ulster government at Stormont.

In 1959, shortly after he had resigned from the government but at a time when the Tories seemed safely ensconced in power for years to come, Powell wrote an essay in the *Political Quarterly* on 'opposition'. He argued that an opposition 'must have a categorical imperative: "Do this, and this alone, if you would be saved." There must be a great simple, central theme, branching into all fields and subjects of debates.'[37] By this definition, Powell was a great oppositionist. He could always find some single great theme to which all other issues should be subordinated. Thatcher, by contrast, could never afford such political fundamentalism. She wanted power and knew that government meant the continuous juggling and balancing of different issues. In 1988 Thatcher commented that Enoch Powell 'commanded influence without power' and drew an interesting comparison between him and David Owen (another MP from outside the Conservative Party who was sometimes admired by Thatcherites): 'when you have been in Government you know that it is not a question of right or wrong – it is often a question of shades of grey'.[38]

Powell came to recognize that Thatcher's capacity to wait, compromise and tolerate ambiguity were useful qualities, and ones that he conspicuously lacked. Nevertheless he could never entirely tame the urge for political self-destruction that lay at the heart of his own character. On 16 November 1990, when her hostility to Europe had isolated her in her own party and when she faced a challenge for the leadership from Michael Heseltine, Powell wrote a letter to Norman Tebbit, the effective manager of Thatcher's leadership campaign, in which he offered to do anything that he could to defend Thatcher against her opponents in her own party.[39] Worldly Conservatives must have realized that Powell's support was a sure sign that Thatcher was finished.

Chapter 3

BECOMING LEADER

It wasn't an election. It was an assumption.

Norman St John-Stevas on Thatcher becoming leader
of the Conservative Party (1975)[1]

After 1975 it suited some Conservatives to describe the Thatcher leadership as the product of an almost supernatural process. The party made much of loyalty to the leaders and, for this reason, never liked to discuss the means by which they were chosen or deposed. There was also a slightly forced gallantry in the way that senior Tories talked about Margaret Thatcher. No one wanted to admit that a respectable woman had been involved in anything so sordid as an internal party conflict. All the same, Thatcher did come to power through an election and one that left many of her colleagues feeling uncomfortable. Norman St John-Stevas had been a loyal supporter of Edward Heath who also had good personal relations with Margaret Thatcher. In the 1975 contest for the leadership of the Conservative Party, he had voted for Heath in the first round but then voted for Thatcher in the second round after Heath's withdrawal. For all his talk of 'assumptions' St John-Stevas illustrated the complicated mixture of personal and political calculations that lay behind the decisions of so many people (including many who did not like Thatcher or who did not believe that she could win) to cast their votes for the successful candidate in the second round.

In 1973 Thatcher's star had seemed to be in decline. Even the tiny minority of well-informed people who had once thought that she might one day lead a government had begun to think that they had probably been wrong. The American ambassador wrote in May 1973: 'Once touted as a potential first woman Prime Minister; it is most doubtful that she could, or does, realistically expect to lead her party.'[2] A group of sympathetic journalists at the *Spectator* magazine thought that she looked tired and that she seemed not to have the stomach for a future fight. The defeat of the government in the February 1974 election did not offer her any obvious opportunity. She had, after all, been a member of a government that was now seen to have failed.

In the middle of 1974 Heath undertook a U-turn in electoral tactics to match the U-turn in policy that he had undertaken in government. He sought to adopt a more emollient tone and began to suggest that the country might benefit from a 'national government'. He promised that, if elected, he would appoint to his cabinet people who were not members of the Conservative Party. This change of policy alienated both sides of his party. Those who favoured a government of national unity suspected that it would, in fact, be most feasible if Heath stepped aside as a potential prime minister; they were taken aback by his refusal to countenance such a possibility. On the other hand, those in the party who most resented the 'betrayal' of the pledges that it had made in the 1970 election were hardly likely to welcome the possibility of a government that was based on consensus between the parties. It is significant that Thatcher and Keith Joseph were the only prominent Tories who avoided reference to a government of national unity during the general election campaign of October 1974.[3] However, Thatcher had still made no open move against Heath; she still held a post in his shadow cabinet and she still campaigned for the party that he led.

Heath's second, and slightly more decisive, defeat in the general election of October 1974 put his own position as party leader in jeopardy. The party had no mechanism by which a serving leader might be challenged. Ten years earlier, a leader who had endured two successive election defeats would probably have been discreetly eased out by party elders, who would almost certainly have chosen William Whitelaw as the natural successor. As it was, Heath established a committee to look into means by which an election for party leader might be conducted. It was agreed that a challenger who collected a certain number of signatures from their parliamentary colleagues could force an election and that this election would take place in two rounds, unless one of the candidates obtained the support of an absolute majority of members of the Conservative Party in the House of Commons in the first round.

Who, however, was to oppose Heath? Senior ministers who had served in his government were reluctant to seem disloyal – Whitelaw, in particular, refused to stand against his leader. Sir Keith Joseph was the obvious standard bearer of the free-market Right. Since the election of February 1974, he had articulated a vision of Conservatism that emphasized the importance of reviving free enterprise and reducing the power of the state. Initially he had conducted his arguments inside the Tory leadership. He had persuaded Heath to let him establish a Centre for Policy Studies to examine the causes of British decline, which, in practice, soon came to mean proselytizing for a new kind of economic policy. In meetings of the shadow cabinet in the summer of 1974, Joseph urged an approach to inflation that would lay greater emphasis on free enterprise and controlling the money supply. Finally, Joseph broke cover in speeches at Upminster (22 June 1974), Leith (8 August) and Preston (5 September). In them he attacked the power of trade unions and excessive levels of public spending. He urged more emphasis on fighting inflation and less on lowering unemployment. The first two speeches – whilst arguing that the whole post-war period had been excessively 'socialist' – focused on attacking the Labour Party. The speech at Preston laid a more explicit emphasis on the specific faults of the Heath government, in which Joseph had so recently served. It contained a particularly striking and wide-ranging passage of self-criticism:

> To us [i.e. the members of the Heath cabinet], as to all post-war governments, sound money may have seemed out-of-date; we were dominated by the fear of unemployment. It was this which made us turn back against our own better judgement and try to spend our way out of unemployment, while relying on incomes policy to damp down the inflationary effects. It is perhaps easy to understand; our post-war boom began under the shadow of the 1930s. We were haunted by the fear of long-term mass unemployment, the grim hopeless dole queues and the towns which died. So we talked ourselves into believing that these gaunt, tight-lipped men in caps and mufflers were round the corner, and tailored our policy to match these imaginary conditions.[4]

Joseph, the son of a wealthy Jewish building magnate, had been born in 1918. After Harrow, he studied law at Oxford and served in the Royal Artillery during the war, in which he was wounded. Returning to Oxford, he was elected to a fellowship of All Souls where, a portent of things to come, he embarked on an ambitious research project, seeking to distinguish between tolerance and indifference, that was never finished.[5] He had some things in common with Enoch

Powell and was sometimes described as a 'Powellite'. However, the two men were very different. Powell's comment on Joseph said much about both of them: 'He was always a butterfly, not only in the sense that he had a mind which loved flitting from flower to flower, and sipping honey where honey could be sipped, but he was a butterfly, not a hawk.'[6] In his own eyes, of course, Powell was a hawk: solitary, high-flying, clear-sighted and utterly ruthless when it came to the kill.

Joseph, by contrast, was a sensitive and humble man, who changed his mind repeatedly. Unlike many Tories, Joseph took the writings of economists and social scientists seriously. He had first become interested in the free-market ideas expounded by the Institute of Economic Affairs in 1964 and embraced such ideas with increasing enthusiasm over the next six years. However, after 1970 Joseph went along with Heath's economic policy and proved to be one of his most enthusiastic spending ministers, a fact that Joseph himself stressed with masochistic pride. More significantly, he often seemed to back away from his own conclusions when people argued with him or simply when, as a minister, he was faced with the human consequences of implementing his own logic.

Joseph was not, in fact, a free-market fundamentalist in the manner of Powell. He believed in the 'enterprise' part of 'free enterprise' where Powell believed mainly in the 'free' part. Joseph thought that it might actually be necessary for the state to stimulate such enterprise and particularly that it might be necessary to direct British education along more practical lines, an idea that Powell loathed.

Where Powell saw himself as a prophet in the desert who drew his ideas from solitary reflection, Joseph surrounded himself with advisers. Particularly important among these was Alfred Sherman. Like Joseph, Sherman was a Jew in his mid fifties, and, like Joseph, he was an intellectual of sorts. In almost every other respect the two men were different. Sherman was an autodidact from the East End. He was short, physically unprepossessing and enormously energetic. In many ways, he was a mirror image of the 'polytechnic trots' who were beginning to exercise influence in the Labour Party. He had hung around the fringes of educational institutions (studying chemistry at Chelsea Polytechnic and later taking a course at the London School of Economics); he had fought for the Republicans in the Spanish Civil War and later served with field intelligence in the British army during the Second World War. For most of his life, he scraped a living through schoolteaching, journalism and political lobbying. The only political office he held was that of councillor for Kensington and Chelsea. In politics he moved from youthful Stalinism towards a mixture of free-market economics and defence of 'traditional' moral values.

Sherman had an extraordinary capacity for making enemies. When he died, a right-wing journalist wrote:

> Mean-spirited, spiteful, envious and resentful, he never had a good word to say about anyone else's intellect and overvalued his own. He had moved to the political Right from the millenarian Marxist Left, without abandoning its sectarian habits of mind. He thought that a firing-squad was too good for anyone who disagreed with him ... [he] was also prey to temper tantrums that would have disgraced an overtired three-year-old.[7]

Sherman was brilliant at devising hurtful phrases – he once said that giving ministers policies was like giving an impotent man a condom. He embraced unpopular causes. He invited Jean-Marie le Pen, the leader of the French Front National, to a fringe meeting of the Conservative Party conference. He spent much of the later part of his career defending Serbian war criminals – his interest in the Serbian cause was probably increased by the fact that his former patron, Margaret Thatcher, was pro-Bosnian.

Relations between Sherman and Joseph sometimes resembled the relations of inverted domination across social classes depicted in Pinter plays. Sherman, the nominal servant, bullied his master mercilessly. His influence increased after Joseph began an autocritique about his own participation in the Heath government – famously, Sherman refused to shake Joseph's hand when the two men met after Joseph's 'betrayal of his principles' in office. Joseph went along with Sherman's criticism of the Heath government, though Joseph hated the personal animosities that such criticism provoked – eventually he scuttled from one office to another (bent under the weight of a briefcase filled with books) as he tried to escape from arguments with his own colleagues.[8]

The Labour Party could not have hoped for a better leader of the opposition than Sir Keith Joseph. He was neurotic and prone to crack under pressure. He had a hopelessly academic approach to policymaking: a Conservative journalist wrote that he was 'inclined when in doubt to call for more paper as looser men will call for more wine'.[9] His political conversion of the mid-1970s related to his own life in ways that might have interested a psychologist. He began to embrace 'family values' at the moment when his own marriage was breaking up, and he talked about the need for strong management at a time when his family company had fallen into difficulty. He had an almost unique gift for picking the wrong cause at the wrong time. Having been a life-long opponent of the death penalty, he seemed to change his mind in response to the Birmingham pub bombings of 1974: the six men convicted of these offences, who would have hanged if the death penalty had been in force, turned out to be innocent. Most of all, he suffered from a catastrophic political weakness – a propensity to see the strength of his opponents' arguments. The result of all this was that he often cut an absurd figure. With characteristic brutality, Sherman described him as the 'antithesis of a leader'.[10] Denis Healey said that he was a mixture of 'Hamlet, Rasputin and Tommy Cooper'.[11] Joseph's cabinet colleagues were only too well aware of his weaknesses. Hailsham recorded the opinion of much of the establishment: 'a silly man and always wrong';[12] 'dotty and lacks moral fibre for office';[13] 'Keith is an albatross: lost 1974 by larger than nec. May bring us down. Clever-silly. Attracts barmies.'[14]

As it turned out, Joseph destroyed his own chances of leading his party before the hard men of the Labour front bench got a chance to put the boot in. On 19 October 1974, he made a speech at Edgbaston in Birmingham. It was designed partly to emphasize that his political vision was not confined to economic matters and thus, perhaps, to illustrate his suitability for the leadership of the Conservative Party.[15]

The speech was a characteristic Joseph performance: impassioned, based on an eclectic range of sources and ranging over a wide variety of subjects, in the course of forty minutes, Joseph cited Rousseau, Orwell, Gladstone and Freud. It was partly inspired by Alfred Sherman's reading of the works of the Italian priest and Christian Democrat politician Luigi Sturzo[16] – anyone other than Sherman, or Joseph, would have asked themselves whether the leader of a party that lasted for three years before being swept away in the fascist revolution was a good model for a practical politician. The speech also owed much to Joseph's own concern about social deprivation, and it drew on information that he had gleaned from the Child Poverty

Action Group (a body that was close to the Labour Left). Joseph rode one of his favourite hobby horses (left-wing infiltration of the universities), attacked aspects of the 'permissive society' and paid tribute to Mary Whitehouse (a Christian housewife who had attracted much derision with her campaign against depictions of sex on television). All of this would probably have been fairly uncontroversial. However, towards the end of the speech, Joseph called attention to the dangers 'for the national stock' that he saw in the large numbers of children being born to mothers from the lowest social and educational categories, and suggested that these groups should be encouraged to practise birth control. This was an argument with something to offend everyone. The Left was shocked by its eugenicism; the Right was shocked by the vision of comprehensive schools handing out contraceptives to retarded teenagers.

Joseph was horrified by the reception of his speech and reacted in the worst possible way. He sought to explain himself in a long letter to *The Times.* At the same time he seemed to apologize and to accept that: 'I may have damaged – things in which I rather deeply believed.'[17] These were not the tones of a potential prime minister. Eventually, Joseph decided that he could not be a candidate for leadership of the party. On 21 November, he told Margaret Thatcher of his decision. According to her own account she then said, quite spontaneously: 'if you're not going to stand,

I will, because someone who represents our viewpoint *has* to stand.'[18]

How good did Thatcher's chances of beating Heath in the leadership election seem? She had certain advantages. One of these had been given to her by Heath himself. After the election defeat of February 1974, he had moved her from Education to shadow the Department of the Environment. Here she defended a Tory proposal to abolish the rates and to encourage home ownership through an implausibly complicated mechanism by which special tax concessions to building societies would prevent anyone from paying interest of more than 9.5 per cent on their mortgage. Both these proposals would have increased the financial problems of central government, and the second of them would have been seen as absurd by anyone who understood anything of free-market economics. Privately, Thatcher had doubts about both proposals. That she was willing to defend them in public illustrated her willingness to go along with things that she did not believe in for the sake of political expediency. It may also have made her a stronger figure in the Conservative Party. Her new role meant that she assumed a greater prominence in the general election of October 1974 than she had done in any previous election (even the one that had been held just six months previously). For a time it also made her seem to be associated with the most moderate wing of the Conservative Party's debate on economic policy. Paul Johnson wrote in the *New*

Statesman that Conservative policy 'oscillates wildly between the lavish spending promises of Mrs Thatcher and the austere Powellism of Keith Joseph'.[19]

After the second of his election defeats, Heath moved Thatcher again to assist the shadow chancellor, Robert Carr. This provided Thatcher with a good platform for a leadership bid. It gave the sense that she had the kind of wide policy experience (particularly with regard to economics) that might be useful for a prime minister, and it allowed her to display her ability to master detail and to concentrate (she continued her work on this brief even when running for leader of the party). Most of all, Thatcher emerged as a performer in the House of Commons. When she attacked wealth tax, the chancellor, Denis Healey, dubbed her the 'Passionaria of privilege'. She replied: 'Some Chancellors are macroeconomic; some are microeconomic. This one is just cheap ... If he can be Chancellor, anyone can be Chancellor.' The riposte does not seem very impressive when seen in cold print, but it (or perhaps just the fact that a Conservative was willing to stand up to Labour's resident front-bench bully) apparently excited the parliamentary Conservative Party.

Thatcher also benefited from the absence of competition in the first round of the leadership election. William Whitelaw might have won the vote if he had stood in the first round. He was well connected, experienced and popular – though his virtues were probably more visible to those who had served with him in government than to backbench MPs. However, Whitelaw refused to stand against Heath. The only other candidate in the first round of the leadership election was Sir Hugh Fraser. Fraser's background – he was a Scottish aristocrat who had been born in 1918 and served with distinction in the Second World War – was reminiscent of Whitelaw's. Unlike Whitelaw, though, Fraser had no senior ministerial experience, no reputation for 'sound' judgement and no happy family life (his wife was shortly to leave him for Harold Pinter). Fraser might almost have been picked to illustrate the weaknesses of old-style Tories.

Thatcher's support did not come from the front rank of British politics. It seems that almost no one from the shadow cabinet voted for her in the first round of the leadership election. Julian Critchley labelled Thatcher's victory a 'peasants' revolt' of backbenchers. The reality was slightly more complicated. Thatcher's most important supporters were backbench MPs, but they were not just ordinary backbenchers. A few, such as Norman Tebbit, had only recently entered parliament and would, under Thatcher, make considerable reputations. More important than these were men who exercised particular influence but whose careers had been thwarted in ways that left them bitter towards Edward Heath.

The first backbencher whose influence mattered was Edward du Cann. Du Cann had grown up in difficult circumstances (his father abandoned him and his mother) and risen through grammar school and the City. He had been on the Tory front benches briefly during the 1960s but got on badly with Heath. He resented Heath's much-quoted remark that the company Lonrho, of which du Cann was chairman, represented the 'unacceptable face of capitalism'. Du Cann did not hold ministerial office in the 1970s, but he did chair the 1922 Committee of backbench Tory MPs.

As chairman of the 1922 Committee, du Cann, and the 'Milk Street mafia' who met at his City offices, played an important role in precipitating the challenge to Heath and in swinging support behind Thatcher. Du Cann himself was talked of as a potential leader for a time. He said in November 1974 that he would not stand. His decision sprang partly from the reluctance of his wife and partly from the worry that his business activities might become the subject of unwelcome scrutiny – partly too, perhaps, from the fact that being leader of Her Majesty's Opposition is a badly paid job by the standards of the City. Du Cann summoned Margaret and Denis Thatcher to his grand Lord North Street house to tell them of his decision, and to offer her his support for her own candidacy; he likened the Thatchers' manner to that of a couple who had come to be interviewed for a job as 'housekeeper and handyman'. Du Cann's memoirs give the impression that he had not entirely abandoned prime ministerial ambitions and it may be that his support for Thatcher owed something to the assumption that she would not be elected (or not last if she were elected) and would therefore help clear the way for an eventual candidacy of his own.[20]

George Gardiner was similar to du Cann in some respects. He too had grown up as the impoverished child of a single mother and risen up through grammar school. In spite of having taken a first in politics, philosophy and economics at Balliol, he was very self-consciously not a member of the establishment (a word that obsessed him). He had served in the ranks in the Pioneer Corps during national service. He worked as a journalist on provincial newspapers and eventually wrote for the *Daily Express* (no one could have been further away from the style of *The Times* or even the *Daily Telegraph).* He espoused a succession of unfashionable right-wing causes (capital punishment, support for white rule in South Africa). He claimed (perhaps a little too insistently) that he was proud to be a backbencher and had never wanted ministerial office. He vaunted his own lack of scruple – boasting about how he had rigged an election to the Oxford University Conservative Association and, later in life, revelling in the fact that John Major had called him a 'bastard'. Gardiner loathed Heath and was willing to deploy all his dark arts in support of Margaret Thatcher.

Airey Neave – an Etonian barrister – came from a more conventional background for Conservative politicians. He was widely known as the first English officer to have escaped from Colditz Castle. It seemed likely, however, in 1974 that this would remain his sole claim to fame. He had held only minor ministerial office. He believed that Heath, as Conservative chief whip, had told him that his poor health made it impossible for him to hope for further preferment and he seems to have nurtured a bitter dislike of Heath ever since this episode.

In 1974 Neave was willing to back almost any candidate who stood a chance of ejecting Heath from the leadership. Initially, he was part of a group of MPs (organized by Nigel Fisher) who supported du Cann. Fisher was on the Left of the party; he was one of those who believed that the Conservatives should enter a government of national unity, but that such a government would be made easier if Heath himself ceased to be leader, and he had discreetly been seeking to ease Heath out of the leadership ever since the February general election.[21] When du Cann withdrew, Fisher felt that he could not organize Thatcher's campaign; he planned to vote for her against Heath, but reserved the right to support someone else in the second round of the election. Fisher turned the leadership of his group over to Neave, who was a reassuringly unThatcherite figure – his political views and background fitted into the mainstream of the Conservative Party. Neave was also a skilled plotter, one who spent much of his adult life in the shadow lands where Conservative politics meet the secret services. His most successful strategy was to hint to his fellow Conservative MPs that support for the Thatcher candidacy was weak, and that voting for her was therefore a means of damaging Heath and bringing out more serious candidates in the second round of the leadership contest.

Thatcher's candidacy was greatly helped by the behaviour of the opposing camp. Indeed, it is revealing that no one really knew who ran Heath's campaign: the main suspects – Kenneth Baker, Tim Kitson and Peter Walker – all denied that they had been campaign manager.[22] In any case, Heath was an impossibly awkward candidate. His innate sulkiness had been exacerbated by the humiliations of defeat in two general elections and Thatcher's challenge for the leadership. Heath's belated attempts at seduction were so clumsy and blatantly insincere that they probably lost him votes. On 4 February 1975 Margaret Thatcher got 130 votes on the first round of the leadership election, Heath got 119 and Hugh Fraser got 16.

Even to her supporters, Thatcher's success against Heath probably came as a surprise. At this stage, other candidates threw their hats into the ring. Geoffrey Howe represented the free-market wing of Conservativism and might have damaged Thatcher by taking votes that would otherwise have gone to her, but he had a soporific style – his friend Denis Healey famously likened him to a dead sheep – and seemed faintly embarrassed by his own candidacy. William Whitelaw was the single most popular candidate, and the one anointed by Heath, but Heath's support had probably become a liability by this stage and

Whitelaw's failure to stand in the first round had come to seem like weakness by the time of the second. John Peyton, an intelligent and interesting person but one whose carefully cultivated reputation as the rudest man in politics was hardly calculated to win his colleagues over, stood, as did Jim Prior. Some believed that Thatcher's campaign team had deliberately encouraged additional candidacies in the second round in order to split the potential anti-Thatcher vote. Margaret Thatcher won 146 votes in the second round – Whitelaw got 79, Prior and Howe both got 19 and John Peyton got 11.

Thatcher's election as leader of the Conservative Party was a triumph. The very improbability of a woman from her background winning such a position helped to create an aura around her that was to last for many years. But there was no certainty that Thatcher would succeed, or even survive, in her new position. Private interviews conducted with Tory MPs many years later suggested that the profile of the average backbencher who voted for Thatcher in the leadership election anticipated certain traits that would later become associated with Thatcherism. Her supporters tended to have constituencies in the south of England rather than the north or Scotland, and they were less likely than the supporters of her opponents to have been educated at the grandest of public schools, especially Eton.[23] However, this hardly constituted a social base for a new kind of politics. In fact, Thatcher's election had little to do with ideology. She had played down many of her beliefs during the campaign. Though she was seen as being on the Right of the party, Thatcher was not clearly identified with economic radicalism – indeed, as has been suggested, her public positions on rates and the subsidization of mortgages in 1974 had made her seem rather loose on matters of public spending. A few MPs, such as Ian Gow, appear to have seen rebellion against Heath in terms of a new emphasis on controlling the money supply, but these men were against Heath rather than for Thatcher. The candidate most associated with economic radicalism in the second round of the leadership election was Geoffrey Howe. Indeed, in some ways, Howe was the Thatcherite candidate in 1975. His campaign was managed by Gow, who was to become Thatcher's famously loyal parliamentary private secretary during the early 1980s, and was supported by Norman Fowler, who had previously urged Keith Joseph to stand. The election often revolved around trivial questions of personal style. Thatcher's opponents in the first round had made much of an interview in which she had allegedly incited old-age pensioners to hoard tinned salmon as a hedge against inflation; Whitelaw's campaign in the second round had been damaged by comic photographs of him pretending to wash dishes at home.

Thatcher had been almost no one's first choice for the leadership, probably not even her own. Many had voted for her either because they disliked Heath or because they regarded him as an electoral liability. Thatcher had come to seem the candidate who stood the best chance of rallying the party after Heath but support for her was very qualified and provisional. Few Conservative MPs would have shed any tears if she had been quietly ousted after a year or two to make way for some more established party figure.

Chapter 4

OPPOSITION, 1975–9

Well, what are we going to do after she gets in if she gets in?

Lord Carrington to Lord Hailsham, March 1977[1]

In the mid-1970s, leaders of both parties recognized that old remedies were not working. The oil crisis, the new radicalism of the trade union leaders and Britain's entry into the EEC all shook British politics. Some Conservatives talked in almost apocalyptic terms and saw their own plight as part of a wider international crisis caused by the advance of Communism. The first letter that Margaret Thatcher ever received from Ronald Reagan was sent on what Reagan himself described as a 'dark day' – it was 30 April 1975, the day that Saigon fell to the Vietcong.

Some thought that the British economy was on the verge of collapse. The Americans were particularly contemptuous (perhaps because the plight of the British provided a partial distraction from the problems they themselves were facing). Henry Kissinger told Gerald Ford: 'Britain is a tragedy – it has sunk to begging, borrowing, stealing, until North Sea Oil comes in.'[2] Edmund Dell, chief secretary to the treasury in the Callaghan government, wrote later that 'everyone I know' regarded the autumn of 1976, when the Labour government had to ask the International Monetary Fund for money to prop up sterling, as the 'worst period of their lives'.[3]

However, judging what political consequences might spring from financial crisis was complicated by the fact that there was a gap between feelings amongst the elite and those amongst the mass of the population. The arcane financial negotiations or gloomy prognostications of long-term industrial decline that so obsessed economists and politicians meant little to most British people. For them, the mid-1970s was a time when wages were higher than ever before and when inflation had eaten much of their debt. Opinion polls suggest that quite large numbers of British people look back on the hot summer of 1976 as the *happiest* time of their life. The Queen's Silver Jubilee in 1977 seemed to reflect a nation that was conservative (with a small c), consensual and at ease with itself. A group of Tory MPs, some of whom were to be closely associated with the most radical policies of the Thatcher government in the 1980s, wrote privately that the Jubilee showed the extent of 'national unity' and the desire for 'continuity'.[4]

There was, in any case, little reason to suppose that economic and political upheaval would lead to the election of a Conservative government led by Margaret Thatcher. For much of their time in opposition, the Conservatives were divided, confused and scared.

Internal party documents sometimes evoked radical projects only to dismiss them as unrealistic or dangerous. Much discussion amongst shadow ministers revolved around how they should react to what their political opponents were doing, rather than how they should shift the political debate on to their own ground.

The sense of crisis in the British political elite was greatest from the beginning of 1974, when the National Union of Mineworkers seemed to be running the country, until the autumn of 1976, when the International Monetary Fund seemed to be running the country. However, people anticipated all sorts of different potential outcomes of this crisis. Thatcher recognized in September 1975 that the assumptions of post-war British economic policy were being rethought, not just in the Conservative Party, but across the whole political spectrum.[5] Peter Jay, son-in-law of James Callaghan and soon to be appointed British ambassador in Washington, wrote a series of articles in *The Times* in which he suggested that economic crisis might destroy British democracy – a prospect that was taken seriously by a number of economists and political scientists. The paper's more flippant columnists identified a whole genre of such writing, which they christened 'Doomwatch'.[6] Auberon Waugh wrote in the *New Statesman:* 'the party system is finished and the country is crying out, in its timid and furtive way, for a Gaullist constitution administered from the Centre-Left ... [by] Denis Healey.'[7] Waugh may have been mocking his readers, but members of Thatcher's shadow cabinet did have a sneaking admiration for Healey,[8] and did discuss the prospect that they might be drawn into a government of national unity, led by a Labour moderate.

In 1975 Thatcher's personal position was insecure. As secretary of state for education, she had withdrawn free school milk and this had prompted the *Sun* to ask its readers whether she was 'the most unpopular woman in Britain'.[9] For almost her whole time as leader of the opposition, Thatcher's personal poll ratings were below those of the Labour leader. Rank-and-file Conservatives were famous for their loyalty to the party leader, but, at first, this loyalty counted against Thatcher because she was seen as a usurper who had deposed Heath. Thatcher's own entourage feared that she might get a rough ride when she attended her first party conference as leader in the autumn of 1975.[10] Most particularly, they feared that she might be disliked by the middle-aged suburban ladies (people supposedly much like Thatcher herself) who made up an important part of the Conservative Party's membership.

It was probably not until after the 1983 general election, if then, that Thatcher was able to impose obedience on her senior colleagues. Her position was particularly weak before the 1979 general election. A significant group of members of her shadow cabinet were older than her;[6] almost all of them had more ministerial experience. Senior Conservatives were knitted into a network of regiments, smart Oxbridge colleges and public schools from which Thatcher was excluded. Most of them lunched or dined regularly at clubs that would not have let a woman across the threshold.

A prime minister has powers of patronage; loyalty can be bought with office. A leader of the opposition, especially a Conservative opposition, is in a more awkward position. A place on the opposition front bench may be less attractive and less lucrative than the other jobs available to prominent Tories: Lord Carrington spent much of the late 1970s flying around the world on behalf of Rio Tinto Zinc. The more patrician shadow ministers were not always assiduous in their attendance: at the shadow cabinet meeting of 11 April 1975, six – Carrington, Thorneycroft, Peyton, Prior, Jenkin and Edwards – were absent.

Finally, Thatcher faced a problem on the other side of the House of Commons. She had been elected leader when the prime minister was Harold Wilson – a man widely despised in Conservative circles, and outside them for that matter, for his shiftiness and interest in short-term political manoeuvres. Thatcher had certain advantages in confronting such a man – though it was generally believed that he got the better of her in their exchanges in the House of Commons.

In the spring of 1976 Wilson resigned unexpectedly and was replaced by James Callaghan. Callaghan was a more difficult opponent for the Conservatives than

Wilson. He seemed, as a member of Thatcher's shadow cabinet recalled, 'good, comfortable and conservative'.[11] He came from a Portsmouth naval family (his father had once served on the Royal Yacht), and he had fought the 1945 election in his naval officer's uniform. He had risen up through the union movement without going to university. He was self-consciously not 'clever' (unlike Wilson) and not an intellectual (unlike Healey). He was much given to homely references to music hall songs or to his farm in Sussex. Callaghan had been parliamentary adviser to the Police Federation in the 1950s and 1960s. As home secretary, he had introduced legislation that excluded many black and Asian holders of UK passports from entry into Britain. He had condemned 'permissive morality' and called for a return to traditional values in education.[12] Thatcher recognized in private that Callaghan was 'the Baldwin of modern politics';[13] she was probably the only person on the Conservative front bench who did not consider this to be a compliment.

Callaghan presented particular problems for Margaret Thatcher personally. He was sixty-four (four years older than Wilson) but his age seemed an advantage – where Wilson had looked tired, Callaghan looked wise. Callaghan was the first prime minister in British history to have held all three of the most important ministerial positions (chancellor, foreign secretary and home secretary), and he made much of Thatcher's comparative lack of experience. He responded to

Thatcher's attacks in the House of Commons with a studied condescension that made her appear shrill. When she complained about his 'avuncular flannel', Callaghan responded that he had difficulty in imagining her as his niece.

Thatcher's shadow cabinet was primarily made up of people who had served in the Heath government and included all of the men who had stood against her in the second round of the leadership election. The shadow chancellor was Geoffrey Howe, a barrister, educated at Winchester and Trinity Hall Cambridge. He had played an important part in devising new approaches to trade union law and was also associated with Powellite economic views. In retrospect, he looks like one of the most important of Margaret Thatcher's associates. He was shadow chancellor throughout her period as leader of the opposition, chancellor during the first difficult years in government, when he showed a notable doggedness in sticking to unpopular policies, and held senior positions until shortly before Thatcher's own fall. Thatcher's opinion of Howe was, however, not high. She thought him excessively cautious and, perhaps most importantly, there was something about his style that did not suit her. He spoke in a soft voice. For all his clarity of purpose, he valued collegiality (a favourite word of his), was on good terms with his Labour opposite number and regarded his son's involvement in left-wing demonstrations with rueful pride.

Whitelaw was made deputy leader of the Conservative Party. He epitomized everything that Margaret Thatcher was not. He came from a wealthy family with well-established Conservative traditions – his grandfather and great-grandfather had both been Tory MPs. His father, a Scottish squire, had died of wounds received during the First World War. After Winchester and Trinity College Cambridge, Whitelaw had served as an officer in the Scots Guards during the Second World War. He managed to convey the impression that his political career was governed by notions of public service and that he was untainted by any hint of personal ambition; though men entirely without personal ambition do not often become cabinet ministers.

Most surprisingly, Thatcher brought Reginald Maudling back to the Conservative front bench as foreign secretary. Maudling was relatively old and had resigned as home secretary in 1972, when it became clear that one of his business associates was to be prosecuted for corruption. He was an arch pragmatist. Though he resigned from government before Heath's U-turn of 1972, he probably believed in the later policies that Heath then pursued more than any of the ministers who implemented them. Maudling seemed to stand for everything that Thatcher might be expected to react against, and he was notably rude to, and about, Thatcher personally. His appointment may have reflected Thatcher's weak position and consequent need to maintain good relations with parts of the party that did not share her views. It may just have reflected her poor judgement of people. Maudling was a big, extrovert, easygoing man. He had all the qualities that Howe (or Joseph for that matter) lacked. Thatcher seems to have been genuinely impressed by him, and particularly by his much-vaunted 'first-class mind'. Indeed, Thatcher once asked Maudling what he would do if he were chancellor,[14] a remark that must have been interpreted as a snub to the shadow chancellor, whose opinions on any matter outside his immediate area of concern were usually dismissed.

Conservative Party institutions were reformed when Thatcher became leader, but it is hard to argue that these reforms marked a move towards the radical rethinking of policy. Some insiders complained about lack of clarity in any direction at all. Michael Wolff, who had been director of Conservative Party Organization under Edward Heath, was sacked. The chairmanship of the Conservative Research Department (CRD) was transferred from Ian Gilmour to the anti-Heathite Angus Maude. However, Chris Patten was kept as director of the CRD. Patten had been born in 1944 into a lower-middle-class Catholic family and had been educated at Balliol. He had spent almost all his adult life as a functionary of the party or the state. He had begun working for the CRD in 1966, been seconded to the Cabinet Office from 1970 to 1972 and worked as an assistant to Lord Carrington during his tenure as chairman of the party. An unideological figure who had been close to Heath,

Patten represented everything that Thatcherites most despised, and some of them came to think of him in terms of visceral disgust.[15] At the time, however, he was a less controversial figure. *The Times* noted that he 'retained the confidence of a variety of Conservatives who do not have confidence in each other'.[16] Thatcher seems to have shared this confidence in him. She kept him in his post until he himself was elected to parliament in 1979.[17] Patten had one great virtue: he had a good feel for electoral politics – it was he who, as chairman of the party, was to be the architect of John Major's unexpected victory in the general election of 1992. Patten asked the one question that Thatcher's less worldly advisers often neglected: 'Will people vote for this?'

Often Thatcherism in the 1970s seemed to come primarily from outside the shadow cabinet, and sometimes it came from outside the Conservative Party. Part of the impetus came from a group of energetic backbenchers. George Gardiner and Norman Tebbit were particularly important in attacking the Labour Party in parliament. In economic terms, the most important member of the group was Nigel Lawson. Lawson came from a wealthy Jewish family. He had been educated at Westminster and Christ Church, where he had been a favoured pupil of Roy Harrod, the keeper of the Keynesian shrine. He had escaped the institutionalized humiliations with which the English upper classes usually teach boys to hide their cleverness; he even managed to spend his national service in command of his own torpedo boat whilst his contemporaries sweated on the parade ground at Catterick. He began working life as a journalist on the *Financial Times* – where young men are encouraged, in the anonymity of the Lex column or the leader articles, to point out where ministers and captains of industry are getting things wrong. After his election as an MP in 1974, he bombarded front-bench colleagues with notes explaining what their economic policy ought to be.

John Hoskyns was probably Thatcher's most significant adviser from outside parliament. Hoskyns had been an army officer before going into business and making a modest fortune in computer software. A Wykehamist who owed his introduction into the inner counsels of the Conservative Party partly to the fact that he had served in the Rifle Brigade with the son of R.A. Butler, Hoskyns was hardly of plebeian origin. But he was, like many of Thatcher's early associates, intensely conscious of his own status as an outsider – after meeting Lord Plowden, the 'mandarins' mandarin', he wrote in his diary: 'It was clear that I was one of the few people he had ever talked to who was not in *Who's Who.*'[18] A patriot who had become obsessed with reversing British decline, Hoskyns was much given to military metaphors and apocalyptic talk of 'saving' the nation – his father had been killed during the desperate fighting to cover the British retreat at Dunkirk in 1940. Hoskyns was a believer in systems and all-encompassing theories and spent a year drawing a huge diagram to illustrate how all aspects of British decline were linked up. He became Thatcher's adviser in 1975, went to work for her full-time in 1977 and continued to advise her during her first two years in office.

Ideas were also developed outside the formal Conservative Party apparatus. Thatcher and her entourage had meetings with monetarist economists – notably Alan Walters, Patrick Minford and Gordon Pepper. Study groups and committees proliferated in and around the party during the late 1970s. It is hard to tell how many of the radical ideas that were thrown around in such bodies were taken seriously by mainstream Conservative politicians, including Thatcher. Chris Patten argued that pluralism and tolerance would prove productive: 'Let a thousand flowers bloom.' John Hoskyns, who would probably have put weed killer on anything planted by Patten, argued that wide-ranging and open debate would provide Tories with 'a sort of intellectual limbering up' that was a conscious alternative to the party 'sailing into office with a cast-iron "plan", which turns out to be inappropriate (as in 1970)'.[19]

Whole new movements were established on the political Right during the 1970s. The National Association for Freedom (NAFF) was founded by the twin brothers Norris and Ross McWhirter (the latter was murdered by the IRA in 1975). Its nominal leader was Viscount de L'Isle, a war hero and former governor general of Australia who had once been a

Conservative MP, and the movement's council took in a disparate collection of famous names – including Douglas Bader, the fighter ace, and Winston Churchill, grandson of the great man. Thatcher later claimed that she gave the NAFF 'as much support as I could',[20] and a few of the movement's leaders – such as Nicholas Ridley and Rhodes Boyson – were to become ministers under Thatcher, though it was never formally affiliated to the Conservative Party. The association was particularly concerned to assert the rights of individuals against those of trade unions. It supported legal action by people who had been dismissed for refusing to join trade unions in workplaces governed by the closed shop.

In retrospect, some of those close to Thatcher seem to be fairly eccentric. John Gouriet, Robert Moss and Brian Crozier were members of the NAFF. Gouriet described the trio as Thatcher's 'liege men'. All talked darkly of the threat posed by internal as well as external subversion. Moss, who was partly responsible for Thatcher's 'Iron Lady' speech of January 1976, wrote spy stories. Crozier sometimes seemed to be living such a story[21] – he introduced Thatcher to a network of shadowy agencies, in which right-wing politics, business interests and Western intelligence services overlapped. Thatcher, Carrington (who was sceptical of the whole business), Whitelaw and Joseph sat for a time on a secret 'Shield' committee to study 'security questions' and Crozier hoped to establish a Counter Subversion Executive. None of these activities seem to have had much influence on government policy after Thatcher's election.[22]

The most passionate advocate of a new Conservatism on the front bench was Keith Joseph. He remained as head of the Centre for Policy Studies and Thatcher gave him a roving brief to rethink party policy – she had considered making him shadow chancellor, but been dissuaded from this by Whitelaw. The tone of Joseph's policy proposals was one of agonized uncertainty. He made much of the potential problems raised by every action that he proposed. Chris Patten wearily suggested that 'There must be some advantage in him [Joseph] shifting his argument from the more painful consequences of a different approach to wealth creation, to the reasons for such a new approach and the benefits that would flow from it.'[23] Joseph often backed away from the implications of his own proposals. In one strategy document, he wrote: 'We shall perhaps help if we can really nerve ourselves to remove supplementary benefits for dependents of strikers.'[24] In the subsequent shadow cabinet discussion of his own proposals, however, it seemed that Joseph had failed to nerve himself for this particular challenge: 'Sir Keith referred to the question of strikers' benefits. He wondered whether the Party wished to add yet another to the several controversies which its programme might inevitably involve.'[25]

In common with almost all prominent Tories, Joseph did not believe a new economic policy would be enough to win an election and turn the country around. He made much of matters such as violence on television, immigration and the break-up of the family. He suggested that the death penalty might be an important issue – though it was hard to imagine that this could be made a matter of party policy and though many of the most important Conservative front-bench spokesmen (including Joseph) had usually voted against its reintroduction.

Joseph's attempt to mark a break with the recent past of his own party ran into opposition from his colleagues. The shadow cabinet that met to discuss a paper he had prepared in April 1975 was particularly outspoken: 'I do not agree with one little bit' (Maudling); 'too much misery in Keith's paper' (Raison); 'hairshirts have gone too far' (Atkins). Many members of the shadow cabinet did not believe that the Heath government had been an unqualified failure. They thought that there was a general and irreversible drift to the Left in British politics, and they also pointed out that countries in continental Europe seemed to have successful economies in spite of having pursued some of the policies that Joseph denounced. According to one account, the meeting to discuss Joseph's paper finished with talk of subsidizing 'jobs that would otherwise be lost' and Heseltine's statement: 'This is being done increasingly in the capitalist world.'[26]

Some in the shadow cabinet argued that the real faultline in British politics lay in the Labour Party, rather than between the two parties, and that it was the duty of Conservatives to support Labour moderates against left-wing infiltrators.[27] Thatcher was never tempted by the idea of an alliance with the Right wing of the Labour Party, which would almost certainly have meant the end of her own career as leader. However, some shadow ministers clearly still hankered after a government of national unity – the idea that had been promoted by Heath in 1974. Keith Joseph countered this notion with the argument that a major faultline of British politics cut across the Conservative Party on issues 'like crime and punishment and immigration'.[28] He recognized that there was a division in the Conservative Party between those whose primary interest lay in getting back into office as soon as possible and those who accepted a long *cure d'opposition* as necessary in order for the party to renew its ideological purity. Joseph foresaw the risk that the Labour Party might be forced to call an early election, before the Conservative Party was ready for office, or that the Labour Party might institute a siege economy and call the Conservative Party into a national government designed to manage the crisis – thus encouraging Conservatives to embrace the controls and heavy state intervention that some of them had flirted with under Heath.

Constitutional reform was widely discussed amongst Conservatives during this period. In a much quoted television lecture of 1976, Lord Hailsham drew attention to the dangers of what he called 'elective dictatorship'. Far from looking for ways to ensure that a future Thatcher government might have the means to effect radical change, many Conservatives were looking for ways to introduce more checks and balances into the British system. Even men who featured prominently in the demonology of the Left – such as the founder of the Special Air Service[29] or the chairman of Rio Tinto Zinc[30] – seem primarily to have seen politics during the mid-1970s as a defensive operation. They talked of the need for a written constitution or for the institution of proportional representation.

Monetarism – a belief in controlling the money supply as a means of controlling inflation – was seen as the most important element in the economic policy of the first Thatcher government. Things seemed less clear in opposition. The very intellectual success of monetarism in the mid-1970s meant that it transcended conventional political divisions. The three most prominent journalists to be associated with the doctrine were Peter Jay (a Labour supporter), Samuel Brittan (the half-brother of Leon Brittan and a friend of many Conservatives, but a man whose politics revolved around nostalgia for a truly liberal Liberal Party) and William Rees-Mogg (a Tory). Conservatives faced particular problems in 1976. On the one hand, this looked like a moment of opportunity, because the Labour Party's popularity was damaged by economic problems. On the other hand, Callaghan implemented rather monetarist policies, partly under pressure from the IMF.

Monetarism raised awkward questions for Conservatives. It ran against Tory pragmatism as well as against the party's policy in the recent past. In May 1976 Reginald Maudling submitted a paper to the shadow cabinet in which he underlined the benefits of pay control and dismissed the role of controlling the money supply in combating inflation.[31] Defence of monetarism in the shadow cabinet was surprisingly muted. Keith Joseph's most quoted reference to the new economic doctrine during the 1970s came in a speech – 'Monetarism is not enough' – that was, characteristically, designed to draw attention to the limits of the very theories that he was expounding.[32] Geoffrey Howe was in favour of monetarist policies but aware that they were hard to sell to voters. He simply argued that the party should emphasize 'proper management of the money supply (without much attempt to popularize this unintelligible proposition – except by arguing the case against big public spending, and big borrowing by the government and internationally)'.[33]

Divisions over economic policy were in any case not clear-cut in the shadow cabinet. In a memorandum to President Ford, Henry Kissinger described the internal politics of the Conservative Party thus:

> Themselves divided on inflation policy between the advocates of statutory wage controls and 'strict monetarists', the Tories clearly are waiting to see if Labor can make a voluntary incomes policy stick with the unions – where the

Conservatives failed with a statutory policy ... Mrs Thatcher has tried to occupy a middle ground, resulting in a lack of clear public understanding of what exactly Tory policy is on this vital issue.[34]

The notion of Thatcher occupying the 'middle ground' may in retrospect seem odd, but it would not seem strange to one whose only knowledge of her came from reading her remarks when she was leader of the opposition. Thatcher's economic ideas were shrouded in ambiguity, which may have reflected both an uncertainty in her own mind and a desire to avoid taking unpopular positions. Unlike some of her colleagues, she did not rule out wage control in all circumstances.[35] Though she had alluded to the money supply as a cause of inflation as far back as 1968, she rarely came across as a monetarist in the economic statements that she made as leader of the opposition.

The conflict between monetarism and wage control intersected with views on trade unions and economic management more generally. Advocates of wage control were not 'soft' on other matters. On the contrary, their views were often tied to fierce anti-unionism. In his paper attacking monetarism, Maudling wrote:

All economic problems are basically political problems, and politics are about power. The sole and overwhelming reason why an incomes policy is needed is to deal with the monopoly power which the unions now possess and, even more important, are now fully conscious that they do possess. So long as they continue to wield power to destroy individual businesses or indeed, complete industries, and the threat of bringing the entire economy to a halt, any talk of a return to 'free collective bargaining' or the ... 'free market' is meaningless. The simple fact is that for years now the unions have increasingly demanded, with effective menaces, excessive wage increases which have inevitably led to excessive cost and price increases. That is what has happened. That, and the other side of the union coin, their total unwillingness to co-operate in raising productivity, constitute the 'English disease' which has become the despair of our friends and the bane of sterling.[36]

Monetarism, on the other hand, did not imply a general hostility to 'corporatism'. There was no reason why control of the money supply should not coexist with control (perhaps even statutory control) of wages. Indeed, the European country seen to have practised monetarism most successfully, and which provided a model of economic success for many Conservatives in the 1970s, was West Germany – a country in which both employers and workers were organized into powerful unions and in which the government certainly did take a view about desirable levels of wage settlement. Nigel Lawson, an admirer of German monetary discipline, suggested to Thatcher that the Tories might outflank Labour and the unions by proposing to legislate for the establishment of German-style work's councils.[37]

Geoffrey Howe was keenly aware of the complexities at work here. He was a monetarist and, as it turned out, tougher than most of his colleagues when it came to applying control of the money supply when in office. However, Howe was subtle and cautious in his approach to wage negotiations and trade unions. He did not believe, à la Powell, that the government should just let employers pay their workers anything they liked and then sit back whilst everyone took the consequences. He insisted that he was for a policy for incomes if not an incomes policy.[38] More generally, Howe favoured a recognition that society was composed of organized interests as well as free-floating individuals. This was partly a reflection of his professional background. It would have been a bit rich for a QC at the English Bar to preach the virtues of an unrestricted free market to other people. Furthermore, he had specialized in labour law and drawn his clients from the Welsh valleys – so, unlike some of his colleagues in the shadow cabinet, he actually knew a few trade unionists.[39] Howe drafted a report in 1977 in which he talked of the need for 'concerted action', the pooling of economic advice from many quarters and discussion with the 'major interest groups'. His emphasis was on education and the flow of information rather than binding arrangements, and he wanted to work 'on a basis compatible with existing British institutions'.[40]

In spite of Howe's cautious tone, or perhaps because of it, this was one area of economic policy on which Margaret Thatcher took a clear stand: she hated it, and her denunciation of it seems to have blended into her general propensity to bully her shadow chancellor. She scrawled her objections across his report and, when he replied in characteristically and annoyingly emollient terms, she wrote that she was 'frightened to death' of the proposals.[41] When Howe drafted a speech on trade unions in which he talked of the 'corporate world of an industrial society', Thatcher wrote: 'Should not use this word – it is too close to "corporatism".'[42]

In their attitude to trade unions, as in so much else, the notable thing about the Conservatives was how cautious they were. Many of them were bitter about the way in which the Heath government had been brought down by the miners (for this reason, hostility to unions was not confined to those most identified with Thatcher). However, the downfall of Heath also made Conservatives tread warily in this area. In the autumn of 1977 John Hoskyns and Norman Strauss (another businessman who had become interested in politics) prepared a report entitled 'Stepping Stones', which was to play an important role in the mythology of Thatcherism. Hoskyns and Thatcher both wrote dramatic accounts of a report that was so radical in its insistence that the union issue should be put at the centre of Conservative policy that the chairman of the party tried to have all copies destroyed.[43]

The actual text of the Stepping Stones report seems rather less dramatic. Much of it consisted of a breathlessly urgent statement of the obvious – there was always a touch of the management consultant about Hoskyns. Reactions to the report amongst senior Tories were interesting. There was no simple Right/Left divide in the shadow cabinet. Whitelaw seemed the most enthusiastic supporter of the report; John Davies was its most severe critic. John Biffen – alway sceptical about plans, even planning to abolish plans – was against. Most of all, by this stage, Conservative leaders were preoccupied by the electoral advantage that might be extracted from a trade union policy. For this reason, they were particularly keen to avoid publicizing their internal discussions and to avoid anything that might give the impression of 'splits' in the party. Patten sought, much to the annoyance of the report's authors, to assimilate Stepping Stones into the general thrust of Conservative policy and particularly electoral strategy. Jim Prior, seen by Thatcher, at least in retrospect, as the major obstruction to Tory radicalism on the trade unions, remained shadow minister for employment. Patten argued that new initiatives on the matter were rendered unnecessary by the fact that opinion 'is already moving our way'.

Trade union policy was an area on which Thatcher's advisers and speechwriters seemed to be pitted against the members of her shadow cabinet – Norman Fowler talked of a division between 'Pymites' (i.e. those loyal to Francis Pym, the shadow agriculture minister and a believer in moderation) and 'Shermanites'.[44] Advisers did much to set the tone for Thatcher's pronouncements, but it seemed safe to assume that front-bench spokesmen would define the policy. John Nott wondered whether grandees such as Carrington and Whitelaw had even condescended to register the existence of Sherman and Hoskyns.[45] In 1977 Robert Moss attacked Prior's attitude to the closed shop: 'He appears to be confused about everything except the need to appease the unions by giving them a licence to conscript labour.' Whatever her private opinions, Thatcher allowed it to be thought that she backed Prior.[46] During the 1979 election, Thorneycroft, the chairman of the party, insisted that Thatcher remove an aggressive passage on trade unions from a speech that had been written for her by the journalist Paul Johnson. Thatcher was cross, or at least had become cross by the time that she described the incident in her memoirs, but she tore up the offending pages.[47]

Conservative attitudes to trade unions during the 1970s had much to do with the Tories' attitudes to continental Europe. The Federal Republic of Germany was held up by many Conservatives as a model that Britain would do well to imitate. The phrase 'social market' was taken from the Germans and picked up by the Right of the Conservative Party.[48] Discussion in shadow cabinet was often about how German political models might be rendered into British idioms, and sometimes this meant literally addressing questions of translation. Geoffrey Howe regretted that there was no English word for *'Konzertierte Aktion'*[49] and Reginald Maudling felt that the English language needed an equivalent of 'Erhard's single favourite word "conjuncturpolitik".'[50] Thatcher never liked foreign words (in her more austere moments she even disapproved of 'bourgeois') and, as has been explained, she was suspicious of Conservative interest in 'concerted action'. However, even she recognized that circumstances for cooperation between unions, management and the state were better in Germany, where the extreme Left was weaker, unions were less prone to strike, and labour productivity was higher. Whatever she may have said later, Thatcher's statements in the 1970s reflected a belief that Britain needed to be more like West Germany.

Throughout the late 1970s the Conservatives who were to be most associated with Thatcher's policy during the 1980s were remarkable for their lack of confidence in the possibility of radical change. Economics was the issue that lay at the centre of their thinking, and the issue on which their policies, once in government, were to break most sharply with the past. However, one of the most consistent themes to be found in internal party documents was that the Conservative Party would not win an election on economic policy, certainly not on a Thatcherite one.

Scepticism about this was found across the party (from Joseph on its radical wing to Patten on its centrist one); it was expressed by both Howe and Lawson – the two men who were to dominate economic policy-making from 1979 to 1989.

The comparative weakness of Thatcherism in the Conservative Party was reflected in two documents from 1978. The first was apparently drawn up in secret by a small committee chaired by Lord Carrington. It concerned the prospect of confrontation between a future Thatcher government and the trade unions. After talking to senior civil servants, Carrington's committee concluded that 'no government can win these days in the way that Mr Baldwin's Cabinet triumphed during the General Strike of 1926, by maintaining essential supplies and services', and that a Labour government would find it easier than a Tory government to take on the unions.[51]

Perhaps it was not surprising that a committee chaired by Carrington and advised by senior civil servants should produce such a pessimistic view of the chances of breaking with the recent past. More striking was a document on 'themes' drawn up by Angus Maude and others in early 1978. The MPs who drafted the document were mainly backbenchers who had entered parliament fairly recently. Some of them were to be seen later as important figures in the Thatcherite revolution – two of them, Lawson and Tebbit, were to be very important indeed. One might have expected such a group to embrace radical ideas. In fact, their report seems in retrospect astonishingly averse to change or risk.

> We believe people are fed up with change, and with new systems that don't work. There is a deep nostalgia, in part for what is thought of as a comfortable past, but chiefly for a settled, civilized life. Continuity is vital, and that is in tune with a Conservative approach ... we must be very careful how we handle 'Time for a Change' as a theme ... Most people (we hope) want what we are seeking – a major change of trend and style of government – but not a great radical upheaval, based on promises of a Brave New World.[52]

The report suggested that patriotism would play well, if delivered with a 'rather special Disraelian panache', as would the independent nuclear deterrent – 'it is humiliating for Britons to rely solely on Yanks, Frogs and Krauts for their survival'. However, the more novel aspects of Conservative policy that had come to the fore since the deposition of Heath were treated in almost dismissive fashion: 'We are not keen on "Freedom" as a great philosophical theme. "Stop messing us about" is much nearer home ... "Capitalism" is not a good word, and we do not think even "Free Enterprise" rings many bells.'

Given that Thatcher and her allies were so conscious of the weakness of their ideas in their own country and their own party, why did Thatcher survive as leader of the party at all, and why did she win the general election of 1979? A great deal of the answer to both questions is luck. Thatcher was lucky in her enemies inside the Conservative Party. When advised by Carrington to praise his successor in public, Heath said: 'Why on earth? I do not think she is any good. I am much better and ought still to be there.'[53] This lack of grace made him less effective as an opponent, and probably eroded the support that he had initially enjoyed amongst rank-and-file party members. At first Reginald Maudling looked like the most dangerous opponent of Thatcher and her ideas in the shadow cabinet. Maudling, however, was a vain, idle man who was prone to have his first drink of the day at ten o'clock in the morning. His interventions against Thatcher were too tactless to rally his colleagues. He was also mired in corruption allegations that surrounded his association with property developers. In 1976 Thatcher was able to sack him from her front bench without having to endure anything more than an exchange of rude words.

Thatcher was also lucky in the behaviour of her opponents on the other side of the House of the Commons. Many commentators argued that the 1979 election was lost by the Labour Party rather than won by the Conservatives. By most measures, the Labour ministers had been successful. They had survived the financial crisis of 1976, they had brought down inflation and contained public spending. In many ways, they (and particularly the chancellor, Denis Healey) had done the very things that Keith Joseph had blamed the Heath government for failing to do. Part of the problem for Labour leaders, however, was the fact that they were competent managers of a crisis rather than inspired purveyors of a new doctrine. Once the Labour Party had lost its belief in Keynesian economics, which it seemed to have done by the autumn of 1976, then it was split between Tony Benn, who espoused more radical government intervention in the economy, and Denis Healey, who seemed to be motivated by an alternating desire to please the International Monetary Fund, with financial stringency, or the British electorate, with generosity.

In his budget of 1978, Healey swung towards generosity, apparently motivated by the belief that an election was imminent. As it turned out, Callaghan did not call an election in the autumn of 1978. The reasons for his delay are a matter of debate and may not have been entirely clear in his own mind; he may just have wanted to cling on to power for a few more months. However, Callaghan had also seen private polls that suggested that the Labour position in the country was not as strong as generally assumed in the autumn of 1978. Equally, he seems to have believed that the medium-term prospects for the economy were relatively good. He had only a small majority in the House of Commons, but he thought that the Liberals and the Nationalist parties from Scotland and Wales would have their own reasons for not wishing to force an election on him. Most of all, he calculated that the enthusiasm of the trade unions for a Labour victory would prevent them from causing too much trouble.[54]

The last of these calculations turned out to be wrong. Two key trade unionists – Hugh Scanlon of the engineers and Jack Jones of the Transport and General Workers Union (TGWU) – had been good at restraining their own supporters, the former helped in this by his own reputation as a left-winger. However, both men retired. Scanlon's replacement was a more 'moderate' figure, Terry Duffy, who consequently lacked authority over his own troops. The new leader of the TGWU, Mostyn Evans, seems simply not to have understood the wider political context in which wage negotiations took place.

Changes in the trade unions mattered to Labour even more than usual in the late 1970s. The party's economic policy revolved around a 'social contract' between government, employers and trade unions, which sought to impose a voluntary limit on pay rises. These arrangements were due to expire in July 1978, but the TUC and the government now came into conflict. The former wanted a return to free collective bargaining; the latter wanted to limit annual pay rises to 5 per cent. The government did not impose its will by law but it did try to enforce limits in the public sector and it did threaten private companies that paid more than 5 per cent that they would be penalized by the loss of government contracts.

In the winter of 1978–9 there was a series of strikes. The first of these was at the Ford Motor works, but more serious for the government's image were those by a variety of municipal employees. The total number of days lost in strikes was relatively small – smaller than it was to be five years later when the Conservative government faced down the miners. However, the strikes were politically damaging for three reasons. First, they were mainly by workers whose activity, or inactivity, had a direct impact on the public. Cancellation of hospital appointments or the sight of uncollected rubbish piled in the streets made an impression that the interruption of industrial production would not have done. Secondly, a hostile press was able to make much of individual incidents that seemed to display particularly cavalier attitudes to the public – the refusal of a few Liverpool gravediggers to bury corpses in February 1979 probably came to loom larger in the mind of the average reader of the *Daily Mail* than, say, the General Strike of 1926. Finally, a large part of Labour's appeal, and especially Callaghan's appeal, had lain in the belief that they would maintain smooth relations with the unions. By the spring of 1979 intimacy with the trade unions had come to seem a weakness rather than a strength. Callaghan was damaged by a small incident that received wide coverage. On 10 January 1979 he returned from an economic conference in Guadeloupe and told an impromptu press conference at Heathrow that most of the world would be surprised by the notion that Britain was in chaos. The *Sun* newspaper gleefully printed the headline 'CRISIS WHAT CRISIS?' alongside a picture of Callaghan's suntanned face.

Even after the strikes, however, Labour's defeat was not inevitable. Most opinion polls showed the Conservative Party ahead during the spring of 1979, but the lead was not a big one. Thatcher's sex introduced an element of unpredictability into the election. Some Tories believed that voters would not countenance a woman prime minister; others believed that a female leader would give them unique appeal to working-class women – particularly, perhaps, to that growing group of women who worked themselves and who were married to Labour-voting men.

As it turned out Margaret Thatcher won the election with a majority of forty-three seats. The electoral swing to Conservatism was sharper in the south of England than in the north. In other respects, the Conservative vote defied expectations. Thatcher's critics and friends alike had laid a heavy emphasis on her appeal to the middle classes – yet the swing to the Conservatives in 1979 came primarily from the working class, and especially the skilled working class. Middle-class voters (or, at least, university graduates) were actually less prone to vote Conservative in 1979 than they had been in the previous election. The heavy emphasis on Margaret Thatcher's appeal to women, and the fears about her possible lack of appeal to men, sat oddly with the fact that the swing to the Conservative Party was higher amongst men than amongst women. Finally, and in conspicuous contrast to the previous election, the swing to the Conservatives was highest amongst young voters (especially, it seems, amongst those aged twenty-five to thirty-four).[55]

The election victory did not simply mark the return of an ordinary Conservative government brought by the ebb and flow of electoral tides. The key to its novelty was Thatcher herself. Opinion polls showed that she was not popular with the electorate, and Conservative strategists had been worried by this. In 1976 Keith Joseph had argued that the leader should adopt a 'national' tone and that she should display 'her warmth and humanity' whilst men like him should do the dirty business of attacking the government.[56] In 1979 it looked as if this strategy had failed. Interviewing her in September 1978, Brian Walden brought out a paradox in Thatcher's public image. On the one hand, she was reluctant to identify herself with specific controversial policies. Yet, on the other hand, her tone was – in some almost indefinable way – new: 'Instead of the reassurance we've come to expect from Conservative leaders, Mrs Thatcher's [speeches] conveyed a sense of imminent danger.'[57] Voters thought that Thatcher was particularly 'divisive'.

None of this means that Thatcher was a liability to her party in 1979. The electoral advantage that a party derives from its leader does not depend on popularity with the whole electorate. Thatcher was regarded with disdain by many traditional Conservatives and with active dislike by many committed Labour supporters. Neither of these groups mattered – because they were both made up of people who were unlikely to change their vote. Thatcher does, however, seem to have appealed to a small but important group of voters – those who had not previously voted Conservative but were willing to consider doing so.

Thatcher's appeal did not depend on identification with particular policies – such identification, particularly in economic matters, was weak. It did depend, in a more complicated way, on the sense that she was identified with certain values, with a kind of moral mood music. This moral mood music was in part the product of a deliberate strategy. Internal party documents often talked about the benefits that the party might derive from an emphasis on non-economic issues. However, the sense of Thatcher's personal identification with particular values was not the result of a deliberate strategy by her entourage. Sometimes it seems to have come about partly by accident; sometimes it was Thatcher's enemies who helped to build her image by the very vehemence of their attacks. A banal speech entitled 'Britain Awake' delivered at Kensington Town Hall on 19 January 1976 caused the Red Army newspaper to label Margaret Thatcher 'The Iron Lady' – a soubriquet that was to be enormously useful to her. Similarly, Thatcher's brief remarks about white Britons feeling 'swamped' by immigrant cultures (delivered during a television interview on January 1978) had not been planned by her advisers – some of them were, in fact, rather shocked by the remarks.[58] None the less, they did exactly what some Conservatives had urged in private for the previous four years – communicated a sense that a Conservative government would be tough on immigration.

The very uproar that greeted some of Thatcher's remarks probably served her party's electoral purposes. It contributed to the sense that she had a dramatically new approach, without forcing her to specify how such an approach might translate into policy. In fact, there was often a disjuncture between image and policy in 1979. Thatcher was seen as tough on defence (though the perceived gap between the parties was smaller than it was to become in 1983), but Conservatives had promised to do nothing more than maintain Labour's rate of increase in spending (privately some of the economic spokesmen jibbed at even that). The Conservatives were seen as tough on immigration though in practice their policies differed little from those of the Callaghan government.[59] They were seen as tough on trade unions though they had in fact refused to go along with the NAFF's campaign to ban the closed shop. They were seen as tough on capital punishment though Thatcher ruled out all the measures (a referendum, deselection of anti-hanging MPs by Tory constituency associations, the application of a whip in a House of Commons vote) that might have made the restoration of the death penalty possible.

If the election of 1979 was a triumph for Thatcher, it was conspicuously not a victory for Thatcherism, as it was to be defined in the following decade. Very few expected the ruthless monetarism of the first Thatcher government or the energetic sale of state assets that marked the second. Well-informed people would have laughed aloud it they had been told that, within a decade, trade union power would be sharply reduced. On the day after the election victory, Thatcher's adviser John Hoskyns wrote in his diary: 'I somehow could not get excited about the victory celebrations because I knew that the chances of the new government achieving anything where so many had failed were small. We might as well get some sleep and conserve our energies.'[60]

Chapter 5

PRIMITIVE POLITICS, 1979–83

Now that the (hundred day?) honeymoon is over, and at least until the fruits of our policies show up (which will not be for some time yet), they will attack us for whatever we do; for 'primitive monetarism' if we continue on our present course and for weakness, U-turns and general Heath/Barber recidivism if we do not. There is no way in which we can avoid being attacked, whatever we do: we must be guided by the reflection that it is better to be attacked for the right policies than for the wrong ones and concentrate on getting our own message across, for which purpose incidentally, 'primitive' language is essential: nothing else will be understood.

Nigel Lawson to Geoffrey Howe, August 1979[1]

On 5 May 1980 members of the Special Air Service stormed the Iranian embassy in London, in which a number of hostages were being held by armed Iranian dissidents. They blew holes in the wall, abseiled down from the roof and killed all but one of the dissidents.

In some ways, this was a turning point in world history. Ever since the 1960s, Western politicians had been haunted by the notion that, to paraphrase Baldwin, 'The guerrilla will always get through.' In 1970 fear of terrorist reprisals had forced the Heath government to release the Palestinian hijacker Leila Khalid and, shortly before the storming of the Iranian embassy by the SAS, American special forces had botched an attempt to rescue American hostages in Tehran – a failure that almost certainly sealed the fate of President Jimmy Carter and ensured the election of Thatcher's friend Ronald Reagan. Thatcher's government seemed to have acted with a determination and ruthlessness that had not been seen in major Western democracies since 1945. There had always been links between the SAS and the Conservative Party. MPs such as Carol Mather, Stephen Hastings, Fitzroy Maclean (it was Maclean's stepson who led the assault on the Iranian embassy), and Thatcher's own patron, Airey Neave, had served with the regiment. The SAS seemed to epitomize a new mood in British life. The cabinet secretary recalled that Thatcher was the 'nearest thing to Queen Elizabeth at Tilbury' after the operation. As luck would have it, a dinner brought permanent secretaries and the prime minister together on the day after the storming of the embassy: the 'Sir Humphreys' were uncomfortably aware that their own caution was now unfavourably compared with the dynamism of the army.[2] The SAS's subsequent exploits in the Falklands and in Ulster launched a whole new genre of books about 'special forces',[3] and established the regiment's reputation as a Thatcherite praetorian guard. One soldier recalled that the prime minister 'practically had her own bunk at Hereford [the SAS headquarters]'. The founder of the Special Air Service, David Stirling, had once been regarded with embarrassment by senior Conservatives.[4] Thatcher brought him in from the cold – he was knighted in 1990.

The storming of the Iranian embassy mattered so much partly because it was almost the only success that the Thatcher government could claim during its first three years in office. For many, it was the unoccupied burnt-out shell of the Iranian embassy – in which the dope smoke of squatters mingled with the lingering smell of cordite – that symbolized the early Thatcher years more strikingly than any military triumph. Even Thatcher's friends were often at a loss to find anything good to say about her government. Unemployment increased sharply, as did, at first, inflation. A leading industrialist was quoted as saying that the 'removal of Mrs Thatcher' would be the best thing that could happen to the economy.[5] Young men in several cities rioted during the summer of 1981, and some observers seem seriously to have believed that the whole fabric of British society would collapse. In July 1981 Sir Nicholas Henderson, appointed by Thatcher as British ambassador to Washington and a keen supporter of the Conservative government, wrote in his diary:

The news at home is unredeemably bad; economic decline, rising unemployment, hunger-strike deaths and violence in Ulster, riots in many towns in England. I find that the hopes I entertained exactly two years ago that we might be going to turn over a new leaf under Maggie have been dashed. Our plight is worse than two years ago because we appear to have tried something new and it has failed.[6]

Henderson would have been even more distressed if he had seen the report from the newly installed American ambassador in London, which was summarized for the president: 'Thatcher has lost her grip on the political rudder ... With no British leader seeming to have a clear idea of where or how to go, some political turbulence is likely, with adverse effects on the country's reliability as a US ally.'[7]

The great and the good of British public life, including some cabinet ministers, wanted the government to reverse its economic policies. However, the most troubling comments on the government's record came in the form of 'support' by John Kenneth Galbraith, a professor at Harvard and probably the best-known economist in the world at the time. He insisted that Britain was a good place to test new economic thinking because the British rarely translated economic despair into physical violence. He told Geoffrey Howe:

I would not wish at all to discourage the Chancellor from continuing with his monetarist experiment. I would indeed deplore it if he stopped because [Milton] Friedman would then be able to say that the policy would have worked if only he had given it another six months.[8]

Thatcher was lucky to survive this period. Conservative performance in opinion polls was consistently bad and Thatcher's personal rating was lower than that of her party. She was fortunate that her cabinet colleagues did not rebel against her – though their reluctance to move directly against her may have sprung from a belief that the force of circumstances would do their work for them. The very difficulty of the first few years in office became an important part of the Thatcher myth. Lawson had called for 'primitive language' that would differentiate the government from all the complexities and compromises of the Heath period. It was often Thatcher's enemies who provided this language. The violent attacks on Thatcherite economic policy conveyed a sense of high drama and often concealed the extent to which the government had, in reality, compromised. Thatcher's parliamentary private secretary divided the cabinet into 'heroes', who supported Thatcher, and 'reptiles'. Her supporters came to relish their own 'heroism' in having pursued unpopular policies in the face of apparently impossible odds. Thatcher and her closest associates were much given to analogies that drew on the Second World War, and their recollections of this period are peppered with references to Dunkirk, El Alamein, Stalingrad and the Battle of Britain.

Overwhelmingly, Thatcherism, from 1979 until 1982, was discussed in terms of economics. Foreign policy, crime and immigration had all been important to the formation of Thatcher's image before 1979, but it was hard to take the radicalism of opposition into government on these issues – partly because Thatcher's appeal had often depended on tone rather than on particular policies that were different from those of her opponents. The economy would in any case have forced itself on the attention of any British government during this period. The 1979 election was held at a time when the economy seemed to be in good shape. Inflation, which had been over 20 per cent per year, had been pulled down to 8 per cent. In 1978 the British government had been released from the controls over public spending that the International Monetary Fund had imposed in return for loans in 1976.

The apparent prosperity of the British economy did not last long and merely masked the problems that the new government inherited. Denis Healey, the Labour chancellor, had looked forward to 'sod off day' when he would no longer have the representatives of the IMF looking over his shoulder.[9] He exploited the freedom he gained on this day to increase public spending in 1978. Public finances were less healthy in 1979 than they had been a year earlier. To this was added the effect of public-spending commitments made before the election. The Labour government had appointed a commission, under Professor Hugh Clegg, to look into public-sector pay increases. During the election campaign the Conservatives had felt obliged (against the advice of the shadow Treasury team) to promise that they would honour the Clegg Commission's recommendations. This alone meant an increase in public spending. The Labour government had also promised Britain's NATO allies that they would increase defence spending in real terms by 3 per cent per year for several years and the Conservatives honoured this commitment[10] – it would have been hard to avoid increases in defence spending at a time when international tension had risen sharply. In any case, the Conservatives had spending commitments of their own; they had promised to increase pay for soldiers and policemen.

Even the government's good fortune seemed to come with dark linings inside the silver clouds. High oil prices had undermined the Heath government and done much to precipitate the general economic crisis of the 1970s. However, in the 1960s oil had been discovered in the North Sea. Exploiting it was difficult but, as technology improved and the oil price increased, it became obvious that Britain would eventually become an oil exporter. Some politicians came to look on North Sea oil as the magic potion that would solve every British problem. It would support the pound, provide fresh investment for industry and, so Machiavellian Tories hoped, undermine the power of the National Union of Mineworkers. The Labour minister Edmund Dell wrote that politics in the

1970s had been like a 'game of musical chairs' in which both parties prayed that they would be in office when the oil started to flow.[11] In 1980 Thatcher won this particular game because large-scale British extraction of oil began at almost the same moment that the world oil price, driven up by the Iranian revolution of 1979, reached a new height. In the long term, North Sea oil obviously did help the government – if only by giving it new resources to tax. However, sterling's new status as a petrocurrency – along with the government's emphasis on controlling the money supply and, eventually, the fact that the dollar was weakened by deficit spending under Reagan – meant that the pound rose sharply against other currencies. The managers of industries that depended on exports raged against the effects of oil on the exchange rate. Britain's leading motor manufacturer told the CBI conference that he wished the government would 'leave the bloody stuff in the ground'.

In its bid to balance the books, the new government was driven to some strange expedients. In November 1979 it brought forward by two months the date on which companies exploiting North Sea oil were required to pay £750 million of petroleum revenue tax. In the spring of 1981 Nigel Lawson, the financial secretary to the treasury, met the chairman of the Committee of London Clearing Banks, and suggested that the banks might like to take over a proportion of the government's fixed-rate credit export scheme, i.e. effectively, to subsidize the government. When the chairman refused, the government imposed a 'once and for all' levy of 2.5 per cent of all non-interest-bearing deposits the banks held, thus raising £400 million.[12] Both measures were justified on the grounds that 'peculiar circumstances' (respectively high oil prices and high interest rates) were giving the companies concerned 'windfall profits'. The various measures against windfall profits, extraordinary ones for a government that was ostensibly committed to defend free enterprise, provoked only one, rather halfhearted, resignation by a parliamentary private secretary.[13]

Public spending increased during the first few years of the Thatcher government, driven up partly by the commitments on public sector pay and defence described above, and partly by side-effects of the government's own policies. The need to make nationalized industries more efficient often meant, in the short term, granting them more money for investment. Equally, the sharp rise in unemployment during the early 1980s meant that the social security budget increased. Some of the changes that the first Thatcher government made related to accountancy rather than the actual level of spending. Ever since the 1960s, government departments had calculated their future spending in terms of 'volume' or 'funny money', as it came to be known. Thus, for example, the Ministry of Defence's budget would effectively commit the government to spend 'whatever a destroyer happens to cost in five years' time'.

Automatic adjustment to inflation meant that civil servants and contractors had little incentive to cut costs. The government now began to move towards the calculation of future spending in terms of cash to be spent.

One of the government's most difficult tasks was a negative one: it resisted pressure, some of it from Conservative MPs, to impose tariffs or import controls. In the short term, the only market that could easily be 'freed' was that in the national currency itself. On 23 October 1979 the government announced the abolition of exchange controls. If controls had been kept, then the City of London would never have assumed the international role that it did during the 1980s. Economic policy in the 1960s and 1970s had been overshadowed by persistent neurosis about a 'sterling crisis'. The fact that Britain was now an exporter of oil made such a crisis less likely: indeed, a fall in the value of the pound was widely considered to be desirable. All the same, abolishing exchange controls was a risk that, literally, kept the chancellor of the exchequer awake at night. Enthusiasts for the free market were quite often to claim that this was the single most important measure imposed by the first, or perhaps any, Thatcher government.

The word that mattered most for economic debate in the early 1980s was 'monetarism'. Monetarism suggests that there is close relation between inflation and the money supply. The fashion for monetarism owed something to the American Milton Friedman, who had won the Nobel prize for economics in 1976. The links between Friedman and British Conservatives were in fact fairly limited,[14] and many British ministers were not unqualified admirers of his thinking or, indeed, of American monetarism more generally.[15] Friedman did, however, exercise a certain influence over the 'primitive language' of British economic debate. His influence derived mainly from presenting a television programme, *Free to Choose,* in 1980, which may have been broadcast by the BBC in an attempt to make amends for the prominence that they had previously given to Galbraith's more dirigiste approach,[16] and which probably contributed to a public perception that monetarism was just another term for free-market economics.

Monetarism did not necessarily go with any other aspect of right-wing economic policy. It was not always associated with a desire to cut public spending or increase the role of the free market. It could be used as a justification for not having any other sort of economic policy. Enoch Powell had embraced it precisely because he thought that it freed the government from all manner of other economic tinkering. Perhaps the 'purest', and certainly the most Powellite, monetarist in Thatcher's cabinet was John Biffen. However, Biffen could be sceptical about other aspects of Thatcherite economics. After leaving the government, he summed up his position thus: 'I am a monetarist, but I am not a great supply-side

Conservative, so I accept higher levels of taxation and public spending than many of my colleagues.'[17]

The word 'monetarism' was bandied around in a fairly cavalier manner. John Hoskyns wrote: 'informed opinion in the country at that stage still seemed to think that "monetarism" was some brutal, possibly slightly mad, celebration of man's basest acquisitive instincts, rather than an important and highly technical body of theory and knowledge, in which the US Federal Reserve and the German Bundesbank had considerable and successful experience, and we had virtually none'.[18] Disarmingly, Hoskyns admitted that his own understanding of monetarist theory was imperfect. After meeting Gordon Pepper, an economist and high priest of one of monetarism's sects, he wrote in his diary: 'Pepper talks so fast and so technically it's really hard to follow.'[19] John Sparrow, a banker who had advised Thatcher since 1977 and whom she was to appoint as head of the Central Policy Review Staff in 1982, said: 'I have never described myself as a monetarist, largely because I have never understood what monetarism as one subject is.'[20] A stockbroker said: 'It is monetarism as a fashion rather than as an economic theory which has gripped the City. We are businessmen and solicitors, not economists, and "controlling the money supply" has the same intuitive appeal today that "priming the pump" had in the heyday of Keynesianism, twenty years ago.'[21] Enoch Powell complained that monetarism had simply become another word for 'government economic policy'.[22] Sometimes it was used as a term of abuse. Denis Healey, who had in fact practised fairly monetarist policies for part of his own term as chancellor of the exchequer, talked of the Thatcherites as being 'sado monetarists' or 'punk monetarists'.

Monetarists were divided about the means by which their insights might be implemented. Gordon Pepper, who had once advised Thatcher, denounced most in the Thatcher government as mere 'political' monetarists who had not fully embraced the creed. Thatcher talked of some of her colleagues as 'fair-weather' monetarists. Lawson wrote that the civil service contained 'non-believing monetarists' who were willing to implement monetarist theories with a degree of rigour that a believer would not have countenanced. Particularly prominent amongst 'non-believing monetarists' was Sir Douglas Wass of the Treasury.[23] Wass had expressed his own scepticism about monetarism during the 1970s and, as shadow chancellor, Howe had developed some of his own ideas in a lecture that was itself designed partly to reply to some of Wass's public statements.[24] In government, however, Howe found that Wass (perhaps hoping to see the government skewered on its own economic logic) was a loyal executor of policy.

Monetarism was not new. Thatcher had talked about controlling the money supply since 1968 and Joseph had described himself as a monetarist (though stressing that he was not just that) in the 1970s. The more urbane Conservatives, aware of how their party distrusted abstraction, were careful to stress that their own monetarism did not depend on arcane theory – particularly theory that had been expounded in foreign accents. Howe wrote: 'It is a great pity that its [monetarism's] practical, common sense importance has been so confused by arid, theoretical dispute. Certainly the words should never have become a term of political abuse.'[25] Nigel Lawson regarded David Hume as the true founder of monetary theory, and said:

> In essence, monetarism is simply a new name for an old maxim, formerly known as the quantity theory of money. So far from being the controversial brainchild of an eccentric American professor, it was – in one form or another – the common belief and shared assumption of politicians and administrators of all political parties throughout the industrialized world for the century and more that preceded the Second World War.

> It consists of two basic propositions. The first is that changes in the quantity of money determine, at the end of the day, changes in the general price level; the second is that government is able to determine the quantity of money. In practical terms, this was translated into the twin axioms of the pre-Keynesian consensus: that the primary economic duty of government was to maintain the value of the currency, and that this was to be

achieved by not increasing its supply – a constraint which operated quasi-automatically for a country on the gold standard, as Britain was for most of the pre-Keynesian period.[26]

The problem for men such as Howe and Lawson was that common sense is difficult to translate into concrete policy and that the monetary system of Britain in the 1980s was more complicated than it had been at the time when Hume was writing. Nigel Lawson, as financial secretary to the treasury, made much of the Medium Term Financial Strategy, by which the government announced targets for the money supply. In practice, though, government targets for the money supply were rarely met. Simply measuring the money supply was difficult. M0 sought to measure the amount of cash in the economy, M1 (the measure that the Heath government had used) took in some bank accounts, M3 (the most important of the measures used under Thatcher) was a broader category that took in all bank accounts but excluded money held by building societies. All these measures were artificial to some degree; all of them hinged on distinctions that would be subverted by the very changes that the Thatcher government promoted. Who, in 1990, would have based monetary policy on a distinction between banks and building societies?[27] Often government policy in one area created new problems in another. The abolition of exchange rate controls, for example, made the 'Corset', an instrument that had been used to control lending by banks, useless.

Interest rates were the main instrument of British monetary policy. The aim of high interest rates was to deter borrowing and hence to reduce the total amount of money in circulation (purists insisted that interest rates reduced *demand* for, rather than supply of, money). However, the effect of interest rates (for those who believed in them as an instrument of monetary policy at all) was hard to determine. Nigel Lawson recognized that sometimes high nominal interest rates were undermined by high inflation. Sometimes high interest rates might actually cause the money supply, or at least that bit of the money supply which the government measured, to increase: 'The increase in short-term interest rates was itself making bank deposits, a major component of M3, particularly attractive to hold.'[28]

The debates in the Thatcher cabinet were as much between different kinds of monetarist as between monetarists and their opponents. Many around Thatcher disliked high interest rates. John Hoskyns and Alan Walters, Thatcher's economic adviser, were worried that they had created an over-valued currency, which was damaging British industry. They found support from the Swiss economist Jurg Niehans, who argued that it was indeed interest rates, rather than the price of oil, that had pushed the pound so high. Thatcher herself was uncomfortable with high interest rates because of the political damage that they might do by making life expensive for home owners. In opposition, Conservatives had been much exercised by the question of how home owners with mortgages might be protected from the impact of high interest rates[29] – but, apart from the scheme that Margaret Thatcher had briefly defended in 1974 to control mortgage rates, they had not come up with anything. Gordon Pepper argued that a more direct control of the money supply – through 'Monetary Base Control' – would allow interest rates to be lower.[30] Treasury ministers, however, argued that British financial structures were different from those of America and Switzerland where Monetary Base Control had seemed to work. The government found no alternative to high interest rates – though the Treasury eventually backed away from an exclusive emphasis on controlling M3 and came to pay more attention to the value of sterling.

Opposition to government policies reached its peak around the time of the budget in March 1981. The budget aimed to lower the Public Sector Borrowing Requirement (PSBR), partly because Thatcher hoped that this would allow her chancellor to lower interest rates, and thus to relieve the pressure on industry. Having failed to cut public spending, the only way in which the chancellor could hope to cut the PSBR was by raising taxes. Raising taxes in a recession ran against the whole current of post-war economic thinking and there was real astonishment when the budget did this.[7] There is still debate about the political origins of the 1981 budget – in particular about whether or not its general thrust was the result of Howe's own initiative or whether it was imposed on him by Thatcher and Walters.[31] There is also debate about the economic significance of the budget. Ian Gilmour sees it as 'an elaborate camouflage for monetarist failure' because an interest in monetary targets was replaced by an interest in the PSBR.[32] Patrick Minford sees the budget as marking a shift within monetarism as the government moved from a pessimistic 'Friedmanite' approach, which assumed that only real economic pain would lower inflationary expectations, to a monetarism of 'rational expectations', which assumed that inflation would come down if the government was perceived as determined to cut its own spending.[33]

The budget provoked much muttering on the Conservative back benches – as well as a call for the chancellor's resignation from the Tory Sir Peter Tapsell. It also produced the single most dramatic denunciation of government economic policy. Two professors of economics – Robert Neild and Francis Hahn – drew up a letter stating:

> A) There is no basis in economic theory or supporting evidence for the Government's belief that by deflating demand they will bring inflation permanently under control and thereby induce an automatic recovery in output and employment;

B) Present policies will deepen the depression, erode the industrial base of our economy and threaten its social and political stability;

C) There are alternative policies; and

D) The time has come to reject monetarist policies and consider urgently which alternative offers the best hope of sustained recovery.

The letter was then signed by 364 economists, a group that was drawn together quickly via networks of personal contacts during the Easter holiday. Signatories included most of those who had served as chief economic adviser to the Treasury since 1945. They were drawn from the grandest of universities – fifty-four of them from Cambridge. The letter did not set out alternative policies to those of the government; its signatories would not have agreed about what those policies should be. Some were Keynesians who believed in counter-cyclical finance, some advocated import controls and tariffs. Stephen Nickell later admitted that he had not agreed with everything in the letter but felt government monetary policy was too tight and that the letter was 'the only game in town'.[34]

Wynne Godley was the most articulate and widely reported of the government's economic critics. He was professor of applied economics at the University of Cambridge and had served as a government adviser after having worked at the Treasury as a young man. The son of an Irish aristocrat, he had once been a professional oboist and had married the daughter of the sculptor Jacob Epstein. His denunciations of government policy – delivered with a pained manner and in an impeccably uppermiddle-class accent – were sometimes illustrated with references to his brother flying Swordfishes during the Second World War. His patrician manner and cultural refinement impressed even – his enemies would have said *especially* – those who understood nothing of economics.

Godley spoke about the consequences of government economic policy in particularly pessimistic terms. He and Francis Cripps argued that the budget was 'severely disinflationary [and] will cause a hyper slump such as Britain has never seen before'.[35] Godley said that he foresaw 'apocalypse' if government policy was not changed.

The British economy did not collapse. In fact, it began to recover soon after the 1981 budget. This contributed to a Thatcherite mythology of the 1981 budget. It was portrayed as 'the turning point in post-war British economic management': a moment when a small, determined group defied conventional wisdom, held fast against apparently impossible odds and consequently began to reverse decades of economic decline.[36]

The government's critics disputed all of this. They argued that ministers claiming credit for upturns in the economic cycle was as irrational as ministers claiming responsibility for 'a sunny day'.[37] Some of them believed that the economic recovery was 'below trend' and would actually have been more pronounced if the government had pursued different policies. Others attributed recovery to the fact that the government had discreetly abandoned some of its more rigorous policies, and that its monetary policy became increasingly loose as time went on. The storm over the March 1981 budget helped to conceal another important economic turning point, which came during a cabinet meeting on 23 July 1981, when even some of Thatcher's most loyal ministers resisted public spending cuts. All these subtleties were, however, difficult to convey and particularly difficult after such a large number of prominent academics had put their names to such a brief and bald prediction of imminent disaster.

The government and its supporters in the City became increasingly contemptuous of criticism by economists. Those ministers who had read economics at university during the years of Keynesian orthodoxy, such as Nigel Lawson or John Nott (who had studied under the aegis of Robert Neild), felt particular glee at the discomfiture of the professors. One stockbroker derided 'Uncle Wynne Godley and all':

> I can't quite put my finger on it, but somehow they don't seem to have brought off whatever it was that they were trying to achieve. Rather like the Charge of the Light Brigade, they meant well

but have ended up as slightly humorous subjects. They formed up in their cloistered courts, mounted on a motley collection of nags, clutching a variety of largely obsolete weapons, blunderbusses, spears and lances, and then weren't quite sure where they were going.[38]

In some ways, attention to the precise details of government economic policy in the 1980s – to the various definitions of the money supply, the various means of controlling it, the various alternative indicators and targets – can be deceptive. As Lawson's reference to the need for 'primitive language' suggested, the government's most important task was often just to communicate an air of resolution and clarity. There was a touch of the tribal war dance in its early economic policies. The aim was to illustrate the government's determination as dramatically as possible. In this sense, government economic policy was remarkably successful. At the end of 1982 most people did not understand the details of government economic policy, and many of those people who did were not very impressed. However, the British people had a general sense of a new kind of economic policy – one that made the government responsible for lowering inflation and absolved it of responsibility for unemployment and, most importantly, one that would be pursued ruthlessly beyond the point at which earlier governments had backed down.

How did debates on economic policy affect the members of the government themselves? Broadly, Thatcher took her opposition front bench into office with her. John Peyton was the only member of her last shadow cabinet who did not serve in her first government. However, the cabinet still contained a number of people who were sceptical about the government's most radical plans. Journalists divided the cabinet into 'wets' (those who were sceptical about radical policies) and 'dries' (those who were most committed to them). The 'wet'/'dry' division was often talked about in relation to other divisions. The 'wets' were seen as nostalgic for an old-style 'One Nation' Conservatism (though the One Nation group in the party had actually contained many Thatcherites) and for the 'post-war consensus' that had allegedly once existed.

Ministers themselves used the terms 'wet' and 'dry'. Lord Thorneycroft, who had been appointed as chairman of the party partly because Thatcher assumed that his brief association with Enoch Powell in the late 1950s would have made him 'dry', told journalists that he was afflicted with 'rising damp'. Lord Hailsham claimed that he sat in cabinet 'oozing'. The divisions were never, however, clear-cut or simple. Belief in a particular kind of policy did not necessarily go with loyalty to Margaret Thatcher. Whitelaw and Carrington were both on the whole loyal to Thatcher as an individual though they were both 'old-style' Tories rather than ideological radicals. Whitelaw's version of loyalty sometimes involved dissuading Thatcher from giving too much prominence to dries – such as Joseph or Ridley – whom he saw as lacking political sense. Carrington seems to have honoured a tacit deal with Thatcher whereby he was allowed a relatively free hand in the conduct of foreign policy in return for not interfering in domestic policy. Howe and Lawson were 'dry' on economic policy, but not, as it turned out, unconditional in their loyalty to Thatcher.

'Wet' implies ineffectuality and the 'wet'/'dry' division was also often associated with a social division between traditional Conservative grandees and self-made men from humbler backgrounds. By this definition, Sir Ian Gilmour was a typical 'wet'. He was the grandson of an earl and the son of a wealthy stockbroker. He had been educated at Eton and Balliol. He criticized the government's economic policy in a series of 'coded' speeches when he was a minister, and then did so more openly after his dismissal in 1981, but his former colleagues pointed out that he had not protested very often, or very effectively, in cabinet discussion. Other 'wets' fit the bill less neatly. Peter Walker, secretary of state for agriculture in Thatcher's first government, had left grammar school at the age of sixteen and begun his political career as one of the last protégés of the imperialist Leo Amery, which meant that he was, before being converted by Edward Heath, hostile to British membership of the EEC. Walker made his fortune in the City. Slater Walker, in which he was a partner, was famous for squeezing value out of assets – so much that the 'dry' Nigel Lawson had pointed out in the 1970s that most people feared having their companies taken over by it more than they feared nationalization.[39] Walker was also an effective minister, more so than Thatcherite ministers such as Keith Joseph.

In the short term Jim Prior was the most important of the 'wets' because, as secretary of state for employment, he occupied an economic ministry. He played up to his image as a red-faced country squire, but he too was a more complicated figure than he looked at first glance. He had been born into the prosperous middle classes – his father was a country solicitor – and he had been to Charterhouse and Cambridge with the novelist Simon Raven (he is said to have been the model for Peter Morrison in Raven's *Alms for Oblivion* sequence of novels). Prior entered agriculture via a first-class degree in estate management rather than an inherited family farm. His emollient manner disguised a ruthless streak – he maintained amicable relations with trade union leaders, but it was on his advice that the government first acquired the services of Ian MacGregor, the man who was to preside over the breaking of the National Union of Mineworkers.[40]

Michael Heseltine fitted into no category at all. He was a self-made businessman, though one whose 'humble origins' were very relative – only those who looked down from the heights of Eton, Christ Church and the Grenadiers could imagine that Shrewsbury, Pembroke and the Welsh Guards constituted a plebeian background. He was a ferociously unconsensual politician, and in the 1970s he had almost started a brawl in the House of Commons by waving the Mace at the government benches. His personal relations with Thatcher were bad, he favoured certain kinds of economic intervention (sometimes, admittedly, a kind that amounted to little more than exhortation) and he paraded his concern for the unemployed of Liverpool. On the other hand, Heseltine's emphasis on complicated managerial systems was often better at delivering public spending cuts than the more obviously freemarket approaches of his colleagues.

Ministers who disliked the economic policy of the first Thatcher government tried, in retrospect, to explain why they had not opposed it more effectively. Gilmour suggests that individual ministers were too absorbed in their departmental briefs to have time for broad economic discussion – an interpretation that does not work well for Gilmour, whose duties, as lord privy seal and as deputy to Carrington at the Foreign Office, cannot have been terribly onerous. More plausibly, Thatcher succeeded in securing acquiescence for her economic policy by placing the majority of economic ministries in the hands of people who were broadly sympathetic to her aims, by controlling cabinet agendas and by ensuring that key decisions were taken outside meetings of the full cabinet.

Ministers who disliked Thatcher's economic policies ended up grumbling amongst themselves, leaking to the press and hoping for some reversal in Thatcher's fortunes, but they never coordinated any public protest against her. Thatcher was able to pick them off one by one. Gilmour, the one whom she feared least, was sacked in 1981 along with Christopher Soames, Churchill's son-in-law, who, as Thatcher noted, could not have been crosser if he had been sacked by his own housemaid.[41] Prior was manoeuvred out of Employment and sent to Northern Ireland in 1981. Walker, the man who might have done most damage on the back benches, was kept in the cabinet almost to the end of the Thatcher government.

Most importantly, there was no simple Left/Right spectrum on which the Thatcher cabinet can be placed. Even on economics, no position was clearly marked out. In particular, enthusiasm for combating the unions was not confined to those who were 'dry' on monetary policy. Since the 1940s Thatcher had been saying that the trade unions were too powerful. However, it was often nonmonetarists who, believing that controlling pay was the key to controlling inflation, were most exercised by union power. Though dissatisfaction with the unions had played an important part in the Conservative election victory of 1979, the party did not come to power with many manifesto commitments on the subject. Once in power, the Conservatives were divided about other new laws. Some in the cabinet believed that James Prior was too soft in his approach to the unions and too reluctant to bring in new laws, but reluctance to legislate was not just a sign of pro-union sympathies or lack of determination. Union legislation was complicated, hard to enforce and sometimes associated with the corporatism of the Heath government. Prior himself believed that less formal means would be more effective in taming union power. There was no single Thatcherite view on the subject. Geoffrey Howe was in favour of legislation – partly because as a lawyer he believed in the usefulness of law, and partly because he thought that giving unions a more clearly defined legal status might make them more responsible. John Nott, by contrast, was sceptical of bringing too much law into an area that ought to be governed by the operation of the free market.

In practice, the laws that the government introduced were limited. The Employment Acts of 1980 and 1982 required ballots to be held over closed shops, provided government funds for trade union ballots, and diminished the legal immunities that unions enjoyed, especially with regard to secondary picketing. The laws were comparatively modest. Unions were not yet required to hold ballots before strikes and there was no attempt to ban the closed shop (rather than to provide compensation for those who might be dismissed as a result of it). Legislation was primarily aimed to allow parties who felt themselves to be aggrieved to sue trade unions – rather than to grant the government itself new powers. Thatcher's own position was complicated. When George Gardiner led a backbench rebellion of fifty or so Conservative MPs who voted for more severe legislation on trade unions, he was given to understand that Thatcher was privately sympathetic to their proposals, as were some of her fiercer ministers.[42] However, as was often the case, Thatcher's understanding of the need to maintain a radical image seems to have gone alongside an understanding of the dangers that might go with too many radical policies – her later governments were to introduce more measures to control the unions (in 1984 and 1988), but these added relatively limited scope to the laws that had first been drawn up by Prior in the early 1980s. Only in 1990 did the government finally make it illegal to refuse employment to non-union members, and thus end the closed shop.[43]

Alongside these measures were general circumstances that shifted the balance of power against the unions. Some ministers believed that rising unemployment was an important part of these circumstances – ensuring that workers who kept their jobs were more nervous of doing anything that might jeopardize them. At first glance, a statistical overview does not lend much support to this theory: the number of strikes rose during the high unemployment of the early 1980s.[44] Probably, in truth, the links between unemployment and labour relations were complicated. To take the most obvious example, the miners' strike of 1984–5 coincided with a period of high unemployment. This did not deter the miners themselves – because they were striking to keep pits open and defend jobs, it probably encouraged them. On the other hand, fear of unemployment may well have deterred workers in other industries (notably steel) from helping the miners.

The most important focus for Conservative thinking about the trade unions was in the nationalized industries, where highly unionized workforces came up against employers who depended on the state to underwrite their wage bill. The Thatcher government was at first remarkably uncertain in its approach to public-sector strikes. The biggest strike of the period was that at British Steel in 1980 – it lasted thirteen weeks, involved 155,000 workers and cost 8 million working days. Some believed that the government had forced the management of British Steel into making a low pay offer. The reality seems to have been more complicated. The strike exposed divisions between the management of the company and the government (Thatcher had already decided, in private, to sack its chairman, Sir Charles Villiers),[45] as well as within the management and within the government. The secretary of state for employment rebuked the chairman of British Steel for having made too low an offer and was in turn rebuked by the prime minister. At least one of Thatcher's advisers believed that the whole strike had been brought about because the management of the company had made an unrealistically low offer and that it had almost had catastrophic consequences: 'If the steel strike had ended in humiliation for the Government, it is quite possible that Thatcher would not now be a household name.'[46] Thatcher was to insist that the steel strike had ended in victory for the government, if not for the management of the company. However, her government was careful to persuade other nationalized industries to avoid strikes – in particular, it provided money for a generous pay settlement to the National Union of Mineworkers in 1981 (see chapter 7).

Not all employers wanted weak trade unions. Large companies often felt that they were most threatened by unofficial strikes, and strikes of any kind were in fact least common in firms where all workers were grouped into a single union. Michael Edwardes, managing director of British Leyland – the single company in Britain that was most notoriously afflicted by strikes – insisted that he wanted 'stronger and fewer unions', so that they would be more reliable interlocutors.[47] In opposition, some Conservative frontbenchers had talked of the need to involve both sides of industry in discussion. In spite of her horror of 'corporatism', Thatcher herself had once insisted that she wanted to transform unions rather than to destroy them. She had seemed to follow the internal politics of the TUC with interest and, for example, to relish 'Hughie Scanlon's' attacks on Clive Jenkins.[48] She had, as late as 1978, invited Conservatives to join their unions. During Thatcher's first years in government, all this was forgotten. Tories regarded bodies that brought them into contact with trade unionists – notably the National Economic and Development Council – with disdain and rarely thought much about trade unions, except when they were forced to do so by strikes.

What of organized business? During the 1970s the Conservative Party had sometimes seemed like the political wing of the Confederation of British Industry (CBI) and, indeed, the former head of the CBI, John Davies, sat on the Conservative front bench for much of this period. Relations took a turn for the worse during the early years of Thatcher's leadership. Donald MacDougall, the economic adviser to the CBI, had previously been one of the Treasury officials behind Heath's loose monetary policies and not surprisingly he suggested that most industrialists were committed to the very economic policies that Thatcherism seemed against.[49] Donations to the Conservative Party had increased when business was scared after the 1974 elections.[50] However, they seem to have dropped off later in the decade – perhaps because the Labour government seemed less threatening or perhaps just because business leaders, used to back-slapping bonhomie, did not take to Margaret Thatcher.[51]

In the early 1980s manufacturing was battered by the recession. Its representatives called for lower interest rates and a lower pound. The chairman of ICI told Thatcher that he was considering moving its operations abroad. Terence Beckett, the head of the CBI, promised his members that he would give the government a 'bare knuckle fight' over their policies. Some of the more radical Thatcherites despised the CBI almost as much as they despised the TUC; they associated it with corporatism and disliked the representation it accorded to the heads of the nationalized industries. When John Hoskyns was approached with the suggestion that he might run the CBI, Alfred Sherman told him that the whole thing should be shut down.[52]

The gulf between industry and the Thatcher government was never as wide as a few well-reported spats made it seem. ICI did not move and Beckett was said, after pressure from his members, to have apologized to Thatcher.[53] Companies continued to make political donations to the Conservative Party and few of them seem to have been tempted to change this, even when the creation of the Social Democratic Party offered them a pro-capitalist alternative – indeed, Tory MPs were deterred from joining the new party by the fear that they might lose lucrative business contacts.[54] Regardless of the effects that government policies on interest rates may have had on their companies, senior executives benefited from cuts in the top rate of income tax – in at least one case, a senior executive gained enough money from this in just two years to pay for the donation that his company had given to the Conservatives during the 1979 election campaign.

Some Conservative politicians had always known that their policies would mean unemployment. Nigel Lawson was one of the few candidates in the October 1974 election who had dared to tell his own constituents the 'harsh truth' that he regarded unemployment as a price worth paying in order to beat inflation.[55] During a private meeting with economists in July 1975, Geoffrey Howe had remarked that the effects of unemployment had to be made 'harsher ... for those elements of the labour force that were insufficiently mobile' – though he also recognized that these consequences had to be made 'less harsh ... so that frictional or disinflationary unemployment should be made less unpalatable and likely to cause social strain'.[56] Not even the most radical thinkers, however, anticipated the levels that unemployment actually reached in the 1980s. Keith Joseph had argued in the 1970s that post-war governments had been excessively influenced by the need to avoid a return to the mass unemployment of the 1930s, but he based his arguments on the assumption that the level of post-war unemployment was naturally low. When he talked about the acceptability of increased unemployment, the numbers that he had in mind amounted to hundreds of thousands – not millions.[57] A CBI economist had warned him in the 1970s that monetarist policies might mean over a million unemployed, but Joseph had dismissed this as 'rubbish'.[58]

By late January 1982 unemployment stood, for the first time since the 1930s, at over 3 million. High unemployment under Thatcher proved to be unusually long lasting – its level did not drop much until 1986. This was partly because unemployment is usually a 'lagging indicator', which only declines sometime after a general improvement in the economy. More significantly, it was because economic recovery, when it came, involved less labour-intensive industries and drew 'new' people, such as married women, into work rather than creating jobs for the unemployed.

Unemployment haunted British culture in the early 1980s. Regularly the presenter of the nine o'clock news read out a list of factories closed and jobs lost in each region of the United Kingdom. Ken Livingstone, the left-wing Labour leader of the Greater London Council, arranged for the number of unemployed people to be printed on a banner and hung across County Hall, opposite the Houses of Parliament. Alan Bleasdale's *The Boys from the Blackstuff,* a television series about unemployed Liverpudlians, popularized the phrase 'gissa job'. Reference to unemployment statistics produced some of the most contrived lines in the history of English pop music. The Angelic Upstarts entitled one of their albums *Three Million Voices;* the Birmingham band UB 40 were named after the form used to claim unemployment benefit.

Why did the Thatcher government survive such high levels of unemployment? One answer focuses on the state of the political opposition. In 1979 the Labour Party was bitterly divided. Callaghan, widely blamed for the party's election defeat, was bound to go. The potential leader that the Tories feared most was Denis

Healey. Healey was a tough operator. He had been beach master during the allied landings in southern Italy and was on good terms with the military – a fact that some senior officers made ostentatiously clear when they were faced with cuts in defence spending during the early 1980s. Twice in his career he was offered the secretary generalship of NATO. However, Healey had been exhausted by his time in government. His abrupt manner had made him powerful enemies in his own party and he was so concerned to try to obtain the support of the Left of the party that he was cavalier towards his natural supporters on the Right. In 1980 he lost the second round of the leadership contest to Michael Foot.

Foot was old (he had been born in 1913), famously indifferent to his appearance and unworldly. He was prone to talk about his pet interests – the novels of Disraeli, the poetry of Byron and the evils of British foreign policy in the 1930s – at times when his audience might have expected him to address matters of more immediate concern.[59] He was the last Labour leader to be chosen by MPs, but it was not clear that they really wanted him. A few right-wingers had already decided to leave the party and voted for Foot in order to saddle Labour with an unelectable leader; some left-wingers voted for him on the assumption that he would soon step down in favour of Tony Benn.[60] Foot was, as many rightwing Tories recognized in private, an impressive orator, a patriot and a man of principle, but no one thought that he would make a good prime minister. During a television broadcast in 1982, a child asked Thatcher to list three things that she admired about Foot. After having said that he had a journalist's ability to meet a deadline, Thatcher seemed genuinely unable to think of any other admirable quality in the leader of Her Majesty's Opposition.[61]

Foot quickly found himself in an absurd position. He had spent his whole career on the Left of his party. He supported unilateral nuclear disarmament and British withdrawal from the European Community. However, his leadership was destabilized by a new kind of left-winger that had risen up in constituency parties during the 1970s. The activists campaigned to make the decisions of party conference carry more weight and to shift the election of the party leader from Labour MPs to an electoral college that represented trade unionists and party members. They also campaigned to ensure that Labour MPs should be forced to face reselection by their constituency associations. Only eight Labour MPs were deselected, and some of them were being punished for sloth rather than right-wing political opinions, but the fear of losing their parliamentary seat struck terror into the hearts of men who often saw their parliamentary salary as a reward for decades of work in trade unions or the party.

The most important figure for the Left of the Labour Party was Tony Benn. Benn was the son of a Labour minister and, when his older brother was killed in the war, he became heir to a peerage. He managed to renounce his place in the House of Lords, changed his name from Anthony Wedgwood Benn to Tony Benn and progressively reduced his entry in *Who's Who* until it disappeared altogether. Having been a modernizing technocrat in the 1960s, he became increasingly interested in workers' control of industry during the 1970s. He became more left-wing and ostensibly plebeian as his contemporaries became grander and more conservative. Wilson quipped that Benn 'immatured with age'.

Benn provided Labour left-wingers with a figure around whom they could unite. He was not a Marxist – his claim that Marxism was 'one of the world's great religions' was just the kind of thing that no Marxist would have said – but his very lack of concern for the theoretical niceties that often obsessed Marxists made it easier for him to draw together a broad coalition of fashionable left-wing causes – feminism, anti-racism, Irish nationalism and support for nuclear disarmament. By 1978 half of Labour Party members were said to favour Benn as leader of the party. Bennism was also convenient for the Tories. His 'extremism' and combination of privilege and working-class affectation made him an easy target.

Having not competed for the leadership of the Labour Party, Benn then competed against Healey for the deputy leadership, a post that served no purpose except to generate acrimony. Healey won narrowly, though Benn got a large majority of votes from constituency activists. The party became so absorbed in its internal quarrels that its leaders sometimes seemed to have little time to address the electorate. Its campaign in the 1983 election was notoriously inept – partly, it seems, because prominent members of the party had lost all hope that they could win. The Labour manifesto, pulled together at the last moment, was a long, rambling document that was full of promises to all sorts of interest groups. It appeared to pledge the party to the unpopular policy of unilateral nuclear disarmament – though Callaghan openly attacked such a policy and Healey deployed Jesuitical subtlety to try to talk his way around it. The manifesto became known as the 'longest suicide note in history', a phrase usually attributed to Gerald Kaufman but which seems to have been coined by Peter Shore, a man who would, at almost any point other than 1983, have been regarded as being on the Left of the Labour Party.[62] The Tories were so confident that the manifesto would damage Labour that Conservative Party officials bought and distributed 1000 copies.[63]

For all its problems, the Labour Party was ahead of the Conservatives in the polls for a large part of Thatcher's first government. Furthermore, it seemed for a time that Labour's problems might generate an even bigger problem for the Tories. In January 1981 the 'gang of four' former Labour ministers – Roy Jenkins, Shirley Williams, David Owen and Bill Rodgers – issued the 'Limehouse Declaration' calling for a 'realignment' of British politics. Two months later they formed the Social Democratic Party (SDP), which was to work in alliance with the Liberals.

At first the SDP/Liberal alliance was extraordinarily successful. It almost won a by-election in Warrington (a 'safe' Labour seat), and it won by-elections in Crosby and Hillhead (Tory seats). Psephologists had played an important part in the foundation of the new party and, for a time, it seemed that the party attracted support on a scale that almost defied conventional measurement. There was a brief heady moment when polls showed that up to 50 per cent of the electorate would support it. The Tories were particularly vulnerable to the SDP at the height of its success and one projection suggested that the Conservatives might hold just one seat, not Finchley, in a general election.

But the alliance failed to live up to the hopes entertained by its most enthusiastic supporters and in particular it did less damage to the Conservative Party than might have been expected. The SDP had famous leaders and numerous potential supporters, but it lacked that intermediate class of local activists that sustained other parties. Labour MPs who joined the SDP tended to be metropolitan. They were less likely than their colleagues who stayed in the party to have experience in local government, or even to live in their constituency. The SDP had awkward relations with trade unions – the electoral college, which had given considerable power to the unions, was the ostensible reason that the 'gang of four' gave for their breach with Labour. Most SDP MPs and a majority of the party's members supported the Thatcher government's 'anti-union' laws. Ian Gilmour, who was personally and politically close to Roy Jenkins, predicted that the SDP would fail because it was not rooted in 'interests'. The SDP's leaders were good at getting Conservative voters, but hesitant about trying to recruit Conservative MPs. They liked to think of themselves as left-wing and, in any case, they had fewer contacts with the Tories. Only one Conservative, Christopher Brocklebank-Fowler, joined the new party.

The SDP suffered from other problems that became more apparent as time went on. Roy Jenkins, a biographer of Asquith, had good relations with the Liberal leader, David Steel. However, most Liberals in the 1980s were not at all like Asquith. Large numbers of them were interested in causes such as nuclear disarmament, which the leaders of the SDP disliked, or gay liberation, to which they were politely indifferent. 'Grassroots' was a favourite Liberal phrase. Liberals were good at municipal politics and suspicious of the extent to which the SDP was a party of London-based national figures. At local level, Liberal activists were often like Michael Meadowcroft, from Leeds, who sometimes seemed to feel that his politics – like his enthusiasm for trad jazz and real ale – might be spoilt if it ceased to be a pursuit of a minority.

The division of Liberals against the SDP went with a split within the SDP that divided Roy Jenkins from David Owen. The latter, having come up against Liberals in the rough-and-tumble of West Country politics, had mixed feelings about alliance with them.[64] In addition to this, Owen was less enthusiastic than Jenkins about Europe. There was also personal tension between the two men – Bill Rodgers maliciously compared Owen's reactions to Jenkins's successful re-entry into British politics to that of a rebellious adolescent boy who finds that his girlfriend is attracted to his father.[65] Owen and some of his supporters were eventually to split with the other founders of the SDP, over a proposed merger with the Liberal Party, in 1988.

Thatcher was lucky in her dealings with the opposition parties – lucky that she was not forced to call an election at the moment when the SDP was at its peak and lucky in that she finally went to the country at a time when both elements of the opposition were in a bad state and when the Falklands War had strengthened the Tories. Not all of it, however, was luck. There was, for one thing, a structural element in the crisis of the Left. The large, and relatively homogenous, working class that had voted for the Labour Party in the early 1960s simply did not exist any more. The SDP and the hard Left of the Labour Party both drew support from a part of the middle class. The trade unions played an odd role in the Labour Party – it was the Left that voted to give them power in the electoral college and voters often associated union leaders with 'extremists', though some trade union leaders were fighting a rearguard action against left-wing influence in the party.[66]

The political manoeuvres of the early 1980s often showed that Thatcher and her supporters had precisely the quality that their opponents reproached them for lacking: pragmatism. This was particularly visible in the way that the Conservative Party dealt with potential defectors to the SDP. At a time when the Labour Party was riven with paranoia about traitors and threats of deselection, the Tory leaders were subtle. Peter Walker, the leading Cabinet 'wet', was entrusted with persuading disaffected MPs not to leave the party. A number of MPs who had been tempted to defect were later given office in Thatcher governments, though one assumes that their discussions with the SDP were known to Tory whips.

Tory survival also revealed something about the British electorate's real attitude to unemployment. Some observers thought society as a whole would break down in the face of very high unemployment. In the early 1980s there was a succession of riots – in Toxteth (Liverpool), Brixton (south London), Handsworth (Birmingham) and St Paul's (Bristol) – and some (including at least one cabinet minister) assumed that these reflected the failure of the government's economic policy. However, riots seem to have been rooted in responses to aggressive policing and in racial conflict rather than unemployment – though it was true that unemployment was one of the many things that black people resented (over half of people drawing supplementary benefit in Handsworth were from ethnic minorities).[67] Many areas of high unemployment – Yorkshire, Scotland, Newcastle – did not see riots. Attempts to mobilize the unemployed generally failed. The 'People's March for Jobs' of 1981 and 1983 were organized by trade union activists rather than by the unemployed themselves.

In some ways, however, the ubiquity of references to unemployment in British popular culture of the 1980s was deceptive. Everyone knew about it, everyone knew that they ought to care and most people probably did care, but they cared about it in an abstract fashion. A pious concern for the unemployed was expressed in even the most unexpected quarters – one researcher found that almost half the merchant bankers he interviewed said that the government was 'not doing enough' for the unemployed.[68] Regarding unemployment as an 'important issue', however, did not necessarily mean that it was one that had much effect on people's own lives. Voters consistently told researchers that unemployment was a 'more important problem' than inflation. Eventually, pollsters learned to ask a different question: 'Which threatens you and your family most?' Now 49 per cent of people said rising prices whilst only 43 per cent said unemployment.[69]

Unemployment divided the British working class. It was higher in Wales, Scotland, Northern Ireland and the north of England than it was in the south east. It hit certain groups – young men without qualifications, old men who had worked in declining industries, black people – harder than it hit the general population. Those with jobs were consistently optimistic about their chances of keeping them and their economic prospects generally; those without jobs were pessimistic about their chances of regaining the standard of living that they had once enjoyed.[70] Practical expressions of solidarity between the employed and unemployed were rare. Unions had difficulty in persuading their members to donate money to support centres for the unemployed – many of these were reduced to the humiliation of having to take money from the Manpower Services Commission, established by the Thatcher government.[71]

Unemployment benefit in the 1980s was distributed according to clear rules that were applied across the whole country – there was little scope for the local disputes over dole payments that had sometimes aroused the unemployed during the 1930s. Benefit payments were sufficiently low to cut many unemployed people off from the company of those who remained in work, which itself reduced the possibility of working-class solidarity, but they were not so low that they induced the desperation that might have come from the prospect of starvation. Many unemployed people did not vote and a significant minority of those who did voted Conservative. To the chagrin of left-wing sociologists who interviewed them, large numbers of unemployed people accepted government explanations for unemployment[72] – a good example of the successful diffusion of Lawson's 'primitive language'.

Chapter 6

UNEXPECTED VICTORY: THE FALKLANDS

[T]he Falkland Islands. Never heard of them, right? Me neither – at least not until last evening ... 1,800 British-origin sheepherders, pursuing a peaceful life on some wind-blown specks in the South Atlantic, now targeted by Argentine amphibious assault units – who, in turn, may soon be attacked by the largest naval armada ever to steam out of British ports since Suez? Yes indeed, the whole thing certainly does sound like Gilbert and Sullivan as told to Anthony Trollope by Alistair Cooke.

Diary entry by American diplomat James Rentschler for early April 1982[1]

It was the very best sort of war: fought at a distance against a second-class enemy and with no fear of retaliation on the homeland. And our servicemen were all regulars. It was a bit like the Boer war but without the Boers.

Julian Critchley (Conservative MP)[2]

There are 780 Falklands Islands of which only two are inhabited. In 1982 they had a population of about 1,800 people, just over half of whom lived in the capital, Port Stanley, on East Falkland, and 600,000 sheep. The islands are 8000 miles from Britain and 400 miles from Argentina, which has claimed sovereignty over them since the nineteenth century.

The Falkland Islands (or Malvinas) mattered deeply to Argentina. Schoolchildren learned about them in their textbooks. There was an annual Malvinas Day and Argentine sovereignty over the islands was asserted in the country's constitution. Every Argentine politician for generations had talked about the need to 'restore' Argentine rule over the islands.

Until Argentine forces invaded them in the spring of 1982, the Falkland Islands meant almost nothing to the British. John Nott, the secretary of state for defence, had to refer to the globe in his office to remind himself where they were. Many British people vaguely assumed that they must be somewhere beyond Shetland, and British sailors were sometimes mystified to learn that the task force sent to liberate the islands would sail south rather than north.

The Falklands had no strategic or economic value – a fact pointed out in an essay by Dr Johnson that had first been published in 1771, and which was unearthed by journalists who, in 1982, were desperate for any information about the islands. Sheep farming was the main means by which Falkland Islanders made their living. Most did not, in fact, own their own land, which belonged in large part to the Falkland Islands Company. Contact with Britain depended on annual visits by an Antarctic exploration ship, *Endurance.* The Falklands were a British dependency, administered by a governor and garrisoned by a force of a hundred or so Royal Marines, some of whom helped to diminish the population by sweeping local girls off their feet and taking them back to the delights of married quarters in Portsmouth or Arbroath. Not all Falkland Islanders had full British citizenship, and legislation the government planned to introduce would have further reduced their rights in this regard. In any case, the British community in Argentina was considerably larger than the population of the Falklands.[8]

For some years the British government had made discreet, though not very urgent, efforts to extricate itself from the Falklands. Simply giving them to Argentina, however, was complicated by the bitter hostility of the islanders. Nicholas Ridley, a junior minister at the Foreign Office, had conducted negotiations with Argentine officials whilst trying to reassure the islanders that their interests would not be neglected. There was an element of farce in the negotiations: Ridley met his Argentine counterpart whilst pretending to paint watercolours at the Hotel du Lac in Lausanne, and he once minuted that it would be helpful to his cause with the islanders if the Argentinians could be as rude as possible to him during his passage through Buenos Aires. Ridley's tactless candour probably caused more problems than his slightly inept efforts to cover his diplomatic tracks. He told the Argentinians that Britain did not care about the Falklands. He also told the islanders that, if the Argentinians invaded, the British would 'kick them out'. Both these statements were true, but the Argentinians eventually interpreted the claim 'not to care' about the Falklands as meaning that they would face no serious opposition if they invaded; the islanders interpreted the promise to 'kick them out' as meaning that they had infinite licence to obstruct negotiations with Argentina.[3]

The Falklands were not at the front of the minds of British ministers in 1982. Defence policy revolved around the threat of conquest or annihilation posed by the Soviet Union, a threat that seemed to have increased since the late 1970s. The government also had to worry about Northern Ireland and about the Middle East (the Israelis invaded Lebanon in June 1982). Even the small proportion of British intelligence analysts which was concerned with affairs in Latin America worried more about the threat that Guatemala posed to Belize than the threat that Argentina posed to the Falklands.[4]

Matters were made more complicated by politics in Argentina. The country had been under military rule since 1976 and General Leopoldo Galtieri, who had become leader of the junta in December 1981, was trapped by a variety of competing pressures. The government had turned away from the corporatism of the Peronist years, cut public spending and tried to revive the private sector. When these policies seemed not to work, the finance minister had attempted to revive the economy with a 'shock approach' of austerity and cuts in public spending. In purely economic terms, the junta's Argentina had much in common with Thatcher's Britain, a fact that Cecil Parkinson, a junior minister with responsibility for trade, noted during an official visit.[5] Unlike its British counterpart, however, the Argentine government could not afford to sit back and hope that its economic policies would eventually produce results. Economic discontent blended into opposition aroused by the severe repression (ostensibly directed against 'Marxist insurgents') during the late 1970s, when the army had murdered thousands of people. Even the Americans were pressing Argentina to improve its human rights record, and some military leaders seem to have recognized that they needed to prepare for a return to civilian government. However, the army was determined that any liberalization of the political system should not involve awkward questions about the fate of those who had 'disappeared'. Galtieri wanted to extend his tenure as head of the army, which was due to end in November 1982,[6] and to do so he needed to maintain good relations with other powerful military leaders – particularly Jorge Anaya, Argentina's senior admiral. Retaking the Falklands seemed an obvious way in which to win over public opinion and buy the support of the navy.

An intelligent man might have waited to see whether the Falklands could be acquired through negotiation or whether the British defence cuts of 1981 (of which more below) might reduce Britain's capacity to defend the islands. But Galtieri was not an intelligent man, and thirty years of peace-time soldiering and heavy drinking had not sharpened his intellect. In any case, he needed a quick success abroad in order to secure his government at home. On 19 March 1982 an Argentine scrap-metal merchant with a contract to dismantle a disused whaling station landed and planted an Argentine flag on South Georgia, an island 600 miles away from the Falklands that was inhabited only by a few members of an Arctic research station.[7]

On 2 April Argentinians landed on East Falkland itself. They did not mean to start a war and they went to some lengths to avoid causing casualties – though the British garrison inflicted quite heavy casualties on the attackers. The Argentinians shipped the entire garrison back to Britain via Montevideo on the very day that they were captured – hardly something that they would have done had they anticipated that those same soldiers would help retake Port Stanley ten weeks later.

The Argentine assumption that there would be no war over the Falklands was initially shared by many in Britain. The islands were a long way away, and they stood in the middle of a particularly rough part of the Atlantic Ocean. Argentina would find it relatively easy to resupply her garrison and, crucially, to provide air support for her troops. Douglas Hurd, a junior minister at the Foreign Office, probably knew more about the Falklands than any other British politician – his father had been a director of the Falkland Islands Company. Hurd assumed that 'The chances of a successful outcome, through either diplomacy or war, seemed hopeless.'[8] Even after British ships had been sent to the Falklands, military journalists were still laying bets that the fleet would be turned around within a week and that the matter would be settled by negotiation.

The debates in the House of Commons, and the more private discussions amongst Conservative MPs, which took place in the aftermath of the Argentine invasion were so ferocious precisely because it appeared that the Falkland Islands were all but lost. The likely casualties of these debates seemed to be Lord Carrington, the foreign secretary, who was seen to have devoted too little attention to the Falklands and who did indeed resign, John Nott and perhaps even Margaret Thatcher herself. In the Conservative Party indignation at the loss of the Falklands was greatest amongst those MPs (Winston Churchill, Julian Amery and Alan Clark) who felt nostalgic for an era of British military greatness. There was also much foaming at the mouth on the Labour benches. The Labour leader, Michael Foot, had been a fierce opponent of appeasement during the 1930s, and he now summoned up all his rhetorical fervour to indict the government for giving in to a 'fascist dictator'.

Why did the British fight over the Falklands? One possible answer to this question has the British armed forces rescuing politicians from the consequences of their own folly. On 30 March Admiral Sir Henry Leach, the First Sea Lord and thus the most senior officer in the Royal Navy, came to the House of Commons in full dress uniform. He asked to speak to the prime minister and was eventually shown into her office, where he found her in conversation with John Nott. When the prime minister asked him what could be done, Leach insisted that it would be possible to assemble a fleet that would include the aircraft carriers *Invincible* and *Hermes,* and which could be sent on its way to the Falklands within a few days. Veering off purely military questions (as senior officers were to do frequently in the next few months), he added 'if we do not [recapture the Falklands], if we muck around, if we pussyfoot, if we don't move very fast and are not entirely successful in a very few months' time we shall be living in a different country whose word will count for little'.[9]

The contrast between heroic determination on the part of the admiral and 'pussyfooting' on the part of politicians was made all the more striking by the fact that John Nott had just imposed a round of defence 'cuts' (actually reductions in the rate of increase of spending) that had fallen particularly hard on the navy. Nott, a cabinet 'dry', was motivated partly by the general need to cut public expenditure – the defence budget had been more protected than any other aspect of government spending during the previous three years. He was also influenced by thinking about strategic priorities. The share of British defence spending devoted to the navy had increased ever since 1950, but the value of ships (especially surface ships) was unclear. Some projections of war with the Soviet Union anticipated that fighting would last only for a week before nuclear weapons were used, in which case transatlantic convoys were unlikely to play a large role. Anyway, surface ships were vulnerable to attack from the air or from submarines – a fact that was to be made painfully clear to both the British and Argentine navies during the Falklands War. Britain was about to upgrade its submarine-based Trident nuclear weapons system and the spending for this came from the naval budget, thus reducing money available for surface ships.[10] Finally, in a bid to satisfy Treasury demands for further public-spending cuts, Nott had agreed to sell the aircraft carrier *Invincible;* he seems to have done so partly in the hope that his cabinet colleagues would baulk at such a tangible loss and the sale had still not been completed.[11] The cuts earned Nott the undying enmity of the senior naval officers, who lobbied against him with an enthusiasm that bordered on mutiny. The navy's resentment of Nott's policies was most openly displayed in May 1981 when officers (including the First Sea Lord) were ostentatious in their support for Keith Speed, the navy minister who had been sacked for opposing the cuts.[12]

Retaking the Falkland Islands posed a series of particularly awkward military problems. Simply getting the fleet to the South Atlantic was difficult. Some operations would have been tricky even without the presence of an enemy. Troops had to be moved from one ship to another in order to ensure that excessive numbers were not concentrated on a single vulnerable ship just before the landing. Several helicopters crashed in the course of the campaign; in one of these accidents, twenty-one members of the Special Air Service were killed.

The fleet was vulnerable to missiles, which hit three British ships. The landing on East Falkland took place without the level of air cover that strategists regarded as adequate. To avoid direct encounter with Argentine forces, the landing took place on the western side of East Falkland – away from the main centre of population, and the main concentration of Argentine forces, in Port Stanley. The site of the landing, however, created problems of its own. The original plan to helicopter troops across the island had to be abandoned because so many helicopters had been lost when one of the transport ships was hit by a missile. The result was that heavily laden soldiers had to walk across difficult ground in cold weather before facing their enemy.

Coordination between the different components of the task force was difficult. The operation was primarily a naval one until troops were established on East Falkland, and the senior officer in the South Atlantic was Rear Admiral Sandy Woodward, the commander of the task force. However, lines of command could be blurred. Commodore Michael Clapp (the naval officer responsible for amphibious operations) and Brigadier Julian Thompson (the senior marine with the fleet) were outranked by Woodward but technically answerable to the task force headquarters back in England. General Jeremy Moore commanded troops in the Falklands, but he remained in England until the landing had taken place and, due to a fault in radio systems, was unable to communicate with his subordinates for a crucial period whilst he was on a ship travelling from Ascension Island to the Falklands.

Personal and institutional friction affected the task force. The navy, army and air force all regarded each other with suspicion. The Royal Marines were technically part of the navy but functioned more like part of the army. Fierce rivalry separated them from the Parachute Regiment. When journalists sought to explore how far their reports from the task force would be censored, one of them asked whether they would be allowed to file a story about a fight between a para and a marine in which one of them was killed.[13] When his cautious superior seemed likely to overrule an attack, a lieutenant colonel in the Parachute Regiment said: 'I have waited twenty years for this moment and now some fucking marine goes and cancels it.'

In spite of all this, the British had some advantages. The British navy was used to conducting operations in distant waters and the Royal Marines Commandos were trained for cold weather and amphibious warfare (the Argentinians were notoriously unprepared for the former). British commanders had good information about the Falkland Islands and, in particular, they could draw on the expertise of Major Ewen Southby-Tailyour, a latter-day Erskine Childers who had whiled away time whilst he was stationed in the Falklands preparing a map of the shoreline for the use of his fellow yachtsmen.[14]

Britain was also fortunate in her allies. The administration in the United States was divided in its attitude to the conflict. Some officials with links to Latin America were keen not to break with Argentina, as was Jeane Kirkpatrick, the ferociously anti-Communist American ambassador to the United Nations.[15] Ronald Reagan was initially reluctant to come out in support of either side, and Alexander Haig, the secretary of state, was sent to negotiate in London and Buenos Aires to see whether he could broker a compromise. His efforts failed. However, even as negotiations continued, other sections of the administration provided the British with copies of intelligence reports. Caspar Weinberger, the secretary for defence, was particularly helpful. Most importantly, the Americans granted the British access to the base in Ascension Island, a place that was technically British territory, but which had been leased to the United States.

Britain's staunchest ally was France. The French president, François Mitterrand, wanted the Western alliance to be strong in the face of the Soviet Union and he had no desire to see a member of that alliance humiliated. Furthermore, as a member of a resistance organization, he had been infiltrated into France in February 1944 on board a British torpedo boat (commanded by Jane Birkin's father). He had special reasons to feel grateful to Britain in general, and the Royal Navy in particular. In the face of strong opposition from his foreign minister, but with the support of his prime minister and defence minister, Mitterrand threw France's weight behind Britain's cause. The French had supplied Exocet missiles to the Argentinians. Mitterrand was warned that further sales of French armaments would be damaged if potential buyers thought that the French had helped the British counter Exocets, but he overruled the objections. Further sales to Argentina were blocked and the paperwork for some missile sales to Peru was carefully lost, in case the Peruvians passed their missiles to Argentina.[16] French pilots went to Scotland so that their British comrades could hone their skills in practice dogfights against Mirage and Super-Etendard jets, with which the Argentinians were equipped.[17]

France pressed other European countries to support sanctions against Argentina. It also had an important influence in the United Nations – persuading francophone countries in Africa to support, or at least not to oppose, the British position. To most people's surprise, the Soviet Union did not use its veto in the Security Council to prevent a motion condemning Argentine action – a motion that the British were able to use as a justification for their action.

Most of all, however, the British were lucky with their enemy. Galtieri responded so little to attempts to broker a peace that American diplomats concluded that he was drunk. He reinforced the garrison in the Falklands to a counterproductive extent – ensuring that the soldiers ran low on food – but kept back some of his best troops to guard against a possible Chilean attack on the mainland.

After the event, two groups of people made much of how close-run the Falklands War had been. On the one hand, left-wingers who believed that Thatcher had derived an 'unfair' political advantage were keen to stress how 'lucky' she had been.[18] On the other hand, soldiers and, particularly, sailors argued that British defence spending had been reduced to a dangerous extent and that the war would probably have had a different result if Argentina had invaded after the Nott Defence Review had been fully implemented.

At the time, those involved in planning the expedition had different views about its chances of success. Shortly before the landings, the commander of the task force told journalists that he regarded the odds in favour of British victory as twenty to one. Privately he seems to have been less sanguine. He wrote:

> Lose *Invincible* and the operation is severely jeopardized. Lose *Hermes* [the other aircraft carrier and Woodward's flagship] and the operation is over. One unlucky torpedo, bomb or missile hit, or even a simple but major accident on board, could do it.[19]

Later Woodward was disconcerted to find that the overall commanders of the operation back in the UK believed that it would have been feasible after the loss of an aircraft carrier and, once troops were safely ashore, that it could probably have worked without either of them.[20]

In fact, questions about victory or defeat were never really just matters of military calculation. Britain had the second largest navy in NATO. It was absurd to imagine that it was incapable of taking the Falklands; the question was always what price, in terms of money and casualties, the government was willing to pay to achieve this aim. James Prior said that he had no faith that the British people would have continued to support the war if their forces endured serious casualties – though members of the cabinet had apparently been warned that they should expect casualties of 'up to three thousand'.[21] Cecil Parkinson admitted that there was uncertainly about Thatcher's own emotional reaction to casualties. Until the sinking of the *Sheffield* destroyer, some were convinced that she would be unable to countenance sending men to their deaths.[22]

It was often those with most military experience, and/or knowledge of military history, who felt most nervous about retaking the Falklands. Recollections of the Normandy landings haunted discussion of the operation. Several members of the cabinet had been junior officers during the Second World War and still remembered trying to fight their way off the beaches in June 1944. Lord Hailsham recalled that he had been taught that such operations should never be undertaken without air superiority.[23] Many officers had studied D-Day at Staff College.[24] Max Hastings, the most prominent of the journalists to accompany the task force, was actually writing a book about the Normandy landings as he sailed south on board the *Canberra*.

The humiliation of another maritime expedition, that undertaken to Suez in 1956, was also in the minds of those who decided to invade the Falklands. This was a powerful memory in the Conservative Party and in the armed forces – a number of naval officers who went to the Falklands had previously served in the Suez expedition. John Nott wrote: 'Whitelaw, Lewin [chief of the general staff] and I, in the early stages, thought "Suez, Suez, Suez".'[25]

Both Normandy and Suez were misleading analogies. The former had been undertaken against an unusually numerous, determined and well-dug-in enemy. The Falklands expedition might more usefully have been compared with the easier allied landings in North Africa, Sicily, Salerno and Provence, or even with the commando raids on Dieppe and St Nazaire. As for the Suez expedition, its failure was political rather than military and the political context of the Falklands was quite different since the Americans, who had done so much to undermine Suez, always recognized that the Argentinians were the aggressors in 1982.

Misleading though they may have been in purely military terms, references to Suez and the Second World War contributed to a sense that the Falklands had a special kind of historical significance. The Second World War was a totem of Britain's lost greatness and Suez was a symbol of its more recent decline. Thatcher seemed to have recaptured the first and reversed the second. She certainly thought of the Falklands in terms derived from the Second World War – though, characteristically, her interests centred on Britain the lone hero of 1940 rather than Britain as an element in the coalition of 1944.

The Falklands War fitted into a certain image of Britain. It was a 'clean' war, in which both sides sought to avoid civilian casualties and respected the rights of prisoners – indeed scrupulous respect for the rules of war meant that the British refused to interrogate captured Argentine officers about the very dirty war that they had conducted against civilians in their own country.[26] British soldiers could afford public scrutiny of their actions in the Falklands in a way that they could not have afforded scrutiny of their actions in Ulster. The war was fought by a small professional force, one of the many respects in which it differed from the Normandy landing. Units of the British armed forces that had particular cultural resonance were deployed. The navy, especially the surface fleet, was associated with all the myths of Nelson and Drake – names that popped up with predictable frequency in 1982. The Falklands struck all sorts of chords amongst those who cared for the Royal Navy. Sandy Woodward belonged to the last generation of British naval officers who had begun their careers as thirteen-year-old cadets at Dartmouth. Admiral Sir Henry Leach bore an especially resonant name. His father, Captain John Leach, had commanded the *Prince of Wales* and gone down with his ship in 1941. Amongst the land forces, regiments that were seen as particularly professional and/or particularly smart were sent to the Falklands. Guardsmen were taken straight from ceremonial duty at Buckingham Palace to the South Atlantic and even a detachment of the Household Cavalry was added to the British force, perhaps on the grounds that officers who had spent most of their adult lives playing polo would have a unique insight into the Argentine mind.

Though few British people had known much about the Falklands before 1982, the rainy, green countryside of the islands – without large towns, a significant immigrant population or any apparent crime – looked British, or, rather, they looked as many conservatively minded Britons liked to imagine their own country to be. The governor of the Falklands insisted that the landscape over which he ruled was 'Herriot country'.[27] Visiting the Falklands, the Conservative MP Alan Clark was moved by the sight of 'jolly fair-haired children [from a nursery school], to be collected by their mums. A completely English scene'[28] (after failing to get into Eton, Clark's own son had been sent to school in Switzerland). Clark believed that the war had been fought 'in obedience to a blood tie' and he cited members of the Parachute Regiment who told him that they felt happier defending 'our people' than 'mucking around in the Third World'.[29]

What long-term effects did the war have? In terms of the British armed forces, the answer is relatively little. Two years after the Argentine surrender, a senior officer from the armoured corps told Hugh McManners, a student at the staff college who had served as a commando in the Falklands, that the war had been a 'sideshow'.[30] British defence policy continued to revolve around tanks, nuclear weapons and preparations to fight the Red Army. The military careers of men who had distinguished themselves in the South Atlantic did not always flourish. McManners left the army to devote his life to journalism and rock music. Southby-Tailyour also resigned and returned to yachts and writing. Even Rear Admiral Woodward never became First Sea Lord, perhaps because his success in the Falklands had removed any inclination that he might ever have had to disguise his view that he was cleverer than his comrades-in-arms.

The war was also a sideshow for most politicians. MPs who fancied themselves as experts on matters military had a good few weeks making portentous speeches and scoring points off ministers. Having had a 'good' war, however, was no guarantee of future success. Being mistaken for a privy councillor on an RAF flight to Port Stanley in the summer of 1982 was in many ways the high point of Alan Clark's career. The speeches of David Owen attracted much attention during the war, but the long-term effect of his prominence was probably to isolate him further from his colleagues in the Social Democratic Party. During the parliamentary debate that followed the Argentine invasion, Michael Foot had probably seemed the politician most likely to gain from events. Always keen to make trouble for Thatcher, the Tory backbencher Edward du Cann had said that Foot 'speaks for us all'. A year later, after the general election of 1983, Foot looked like the most significant political casualty of the war.

The Falklands was not a Thatcherite war – or, at least, it was not much associated with qualities that had most often been imputed to Thatcher's government in the first three years of its existence. The Falkland Islands themselves did not incarnate the thrusting enterprise that supporters of the government usually praised; a visiting Labour minister in the 1970s had said that the economic prospects of the islands were much like those of the 'Welsh mining valleys'.[31]

The only cabinet minister to speak against the military expedition was John Biffen, a monetarist. Outside the cabinet, Jock Bruce-Gardyne (an arch-monetarist MP and junior minister at the Treasury) was embarrassed by the leak of a letter that he had written to a financial journalist, in which he mocked the whole Falklands adventure.[32] Nicholas Ridley, another 'dry', had been the key figure in negotiations to dispose of the Falklands and was said to have regarded the operation to retake the islands as 'mad'.[33] Fighting the Falklands War meant throwing concern with public spending out of the window. On the advice of Harold Macmillan, Thatcher did not even invite the chancellor of the exchequer to sit in her war cabinet.

Alan Walters, Thatcher's economic adviser, had a genuinely free-market solution to the crisis. He suggested that a plebiscite should be held and that the Argentinians should be given the chance to offer the islanders a fixed sum of money per head in return for accepting Argentine sovereignty. Walters suggested that the first offer would be £50,000 and that, assuming an initial rebuff, 'Granted the acquisitive obsession of the Argentines, their second bid would be likely to be raised to heights which the Falklanders could hardly refuse.' Walters drafted his plan as the task force sailed south but wisely he did not show it to any senior minister until Christmas 1983.[34]

If it was not a 'Thatcherite war', was the Falklands 'Thatcher's war'? She had no military experience and, though she had been considered 'sound' on defence, she had never taken any interest in the details of military matters. Her vision of British 'greatness' up until 1982 was one that involved British participation in the Western alliance against Communism, not lone British action in pursuit of a purely British aim.

In some ways, the very incongruity of Thatcher's position was her strength. She was the perfect war leader – uncompromising about the end and pretty much indifferent about the means. Thatcher did not share the *Boys' Own* obsession with particular weapons, units and tactics that still gripped many Conservative MPs. Her attitude was summed up in her brisk response to an adviser who worried about finding enough ships to transport British troops – 'The world,' said Thatcher, 'is full of ships.'[35]

During the early stages of the war Alan Clark predicted that Thatcher would be a 'hero' in an 'unassailable' position if she won – and that this was, indeed, the reason why some in her own government hoped that she would lose. Julian Critchley believed that the Falklands marked a new 'imperial' phase in Thatcher's government. Historians generally have suggested that Thatcher was 'rebranded' in the aftermath of the Falklands. The precise form that the rebranding took, however, is open to doubt. One writer suggests that she became 'late imperial' and 'little Englander' – though these are very different things.[36] The Falklands is hard to fit into any more general transformation of Thatcherism. It preceded, and to some extent created, the electoral victory of 1983, which, in turn, produced a period of economic liberalization – though, as has been stressed, the Falklands War itself had nothing to do with free-market economics. It preceded, though less directly, a period in which Thatcherism came increasingly to mean opposition to European integration and looking with favour on the alliance with the United States, but in the immediate aftermath of the war Thatcher was grateful for the help of 'our European friends', by which she meant, especially, the French.

The most obvious political result of victory in the Falklands was the transformation of Thatcher's position in the Conservative Party. Up until this point, she had been an oddity: she was a woman, she came from outside the traditional ruling class and she had held no great office of state before becoming prime minister. There was always the risk that she would be deposed if her party came to see her as an electoral liability and the greatest threat to her probably came not from those who most opposed her policies but from those patrician grandees (Whitelaw and Carrington) who might, in a crisis, decide to put their loyalty to their party, and their own careers, ahead of loyalty to their leader.

On the day that Port Stanley fell, all this changed. Enoch Powell was one of the most self-consciously masculine and military members of parliament. He was also still regarded by many Conservatives as the expression of the conscience of their party. During the early stages of the war, he had reminded Thatcher of her soubriquet 'Iron Lady' and added: 'In the next week or two this House, the nation and the Right Hon. Lady herself will learn of what metal she is made.' After victory in the Falklands, Powell said:

> Is the Right Honourable Lady aware that the report has now been received from the public analyst on a certain substance recently subjected to analysis and that I have obtained a copy of the report? It shows that the substance under test consisted of ferrous matter of the highest quality, and is of exceptional tensile strength, is highly resistant to wear and tear, and may be used with advantage for all national purposes.

Powell's laboured joke delighted Thatcherites. Ian Gow, Thatcher's parliamentary private secretary, had the extract from Hansard framed so that she could hang it on her wall.

The woman with no experience of defence or foreign policy was now a warrior queen. The dinner to celebrate British victory was attended by seventy men (many of them in uniform and weighed down with medals) and one woman. Carrington's career was over; Whitelaw would never be able to challenge Thatcher. In many ways, the Falklands saw the passing from the political stage of the whole generation whose outlook had been moulded by military experience of the Second World War. Nott asked for Cecil Parkinson to be included in the war cabinet precisely because he wanted someone to counterbalance Whitelaw and

Pym, both of whom had been junior officers in 1945.[37]

The effect of the Falklands War in the country at large was more difficult to assess. Thatcher talked of the nation having found itself in the South Atlantic. She associated the spirit of the Falklands with a denunciation of trade union militancy (the return of the task force coincided with a rail strike) and with a call for economic revival. Her political opponents were bitter about the exploitation of military victory for internal ends and made much of the ways in which the Falklands allegedly benefited the Tories in the 1983 election.

In fact, less than a third of Conservative candidates referred directly to the Falklands during the 1983 campaign, though many of them made more general remarks about the restoration of British prestige,[38] and few voters admitted that the Falklands had exercised any influence over them. The point about the electoral significance of the Falklands, however, was precisely that it mattered only when mixed with other ingredients. One of these was defence. The election was fought at a time when tension between the Soviet Union and the West was high and when the Labour Party supported unilateral nuclear disarmament.

Did the Falklands create a new kind of populist patriotism? The *Sun,* a keen supporter of Margaret Thatcher since 1979, presented itself as 'the paper that supports our boys', and Tory MPs attacked the BBC as the representative of an elite that had lost touch with the true national spirit. In fact, the new spirit was more complicated than it looked at first glance. The editor of the *Sun* was involved in battles that pitched him against the other tabloid newspapers (the *Star* had introduced bingo for readers in the spring of 1981, thus launching a new circulation war) as well as against some of the *Sun's* own journalists and printers, who resented their paper's political stand. Surveys showed that most *Sun* readers were Labour voters and that almost a third of them thought that the *Sun* was a Labour newspaper. The paper's most notorious headline 'GOTCHA!' – printed after a British submarine sunk an Argentine cruiser – was withdrawn in later editions to be replaced by 'DID 1,200 ARGIES DIE?' Many people took a more nuanced view of events than the pronouncements of their representatives suggested. When the chairman of the BBC, George Howard, appeared in front of a committee of MPs, Tories shouted him down, but 57 per cent of Conservative voters thought that attacks on the BBC were unfair.[39]

Curiously, the most important 'Falklands factor' may have worked on the Left. The Communist historian Eric Hobsbawm wrote shortly after the end of the war that it had mobilized a 'public sentiment which could actually be felt' and that 'anyone of the Left who was not aware of this grass roots feeling ... ought seriously to reconsider his or her capacity to assess politics'.[40]

One of the most striking features of the Left's behaviour after 1982, and especially of the Labour Party election campaign in 1983, was precisely the sense of lost confidence on the part of its leaders in their ability to judge the public mood.

Chapter 7

VICTORY FORETOLD: THE MINERS

She planned it very, very clever – you've got to admire her ... It all fit in, in that ten year from '74 to '84 ... she was determined that, at *any* cost ... she wasn't going to be humiliated and defeated the same way Ted Heath was ... it was all geared up for her to *smash* the National Union of Mineworkers – and by God, it worked. It's hard to say it, but it worked.

Miner, who had been on strike in 1984 and 1985, from Bilsthorpe Colliery, Nottingham[1]

On 5 March 1985 British miners, or at least those who remained loyal to their union, returned to work, a year after they had gone on strike. The executive of the National Union of Mineworkers had agreed to support the return in order to avoid the humiliation that would have been inflicted on the union if miners had simply drifted back to work as and when they could hold out no longer. The miners marched to their pits behind the banners of their union lodges, often accompanied by brass bands. Some trade unionists claimed that the strike had been a success because it had slowed the programme of pit closures put forward by the National Coal Board or simply because the miners had kept their dignity.

No one was fooled. The miners had been crushed. They had gone on strike to prevent pit closures. After a year of grinding poverty, they had got nothing. The National Union of Mineworkers had lost members and money: legal action had rendered it technically bankrupt. The miners were divided. About half of them were working by the time the union finally gave up the fight. After the strike, some men, most of whom had opposed the strike, left the NUM to form the Union of Democratic Miners. The membership of the NUM, which had stood at almost a quarter of a million during the strike, had dropped to fewer than 100,000 by the end of 1987.[2] A small group of miners regarded any return to work as a 'betrayal'. When Arthur Scargill, the president of the NUM, led men from his own Yorkshire pit back to work, they were turned away by pickets from the Kent coalfield, which was still on strike.

The very fact that parts of the Left had invested such symbolic importance in the miners meant that their defeat was all the more resonant. Ever since Margaret Thatcher's election as leader of the Conservative Party, her supporters had feared that union resistance might destroy her economic policies. This fear was laid to rest in March 1985. Norman Tebbit wrote that Thatcher had broken 'not just a strike, but a spell'.[3]

Everyone had always known that conflict between the NUM and a Thatcher government was likely. When Brian Walden interviewed Margaret Thatcher in September 1977, he described, in detail and with a series of cartoon illustrations, strikes by the NUM under a future Conservative government.[4] Some believed that the Tories had returned to office in 1979 with a fully worked-out plan to defeat the NUM. They pointed, in particular, to the report on nationalized industries drawn up by Nicholas Ridley in 1977,[5] which contained a 'confidential annex' on 'countering the political threat' to the government's plans to render the nationalized industries more efficient and financially accountable. The annex anticipated a large public-sector strike. It identified coal as the industry in which this was most likely to happen and laid out tactics by which such a strike might be countered. It anticipated cutting off supplementary benefit to strikers, deploying 'a large mobile squad of police' and encouraging hauliers to hire non-union drivers who might be willing to cross picket lines.

The Ridley report, or at least that part of it which had been leaked, acquired vast importance in the eyes of those who supported the miners' strike of 1984–5.[6] However, it was not much discussed in the inner circles of the Conservative leadership during the years immediately before the miners' strike.[7] The selective leaking of the report, and then the even more selective way in which that leak was discussed and recalled, was deceptive. The report was primarily about questions of management and finance in nationalized industries, rather than about labour relations. Furthermore, the Ridley report was one of a series on nationalized industries, and the ideas expressed in these reports were radical hopes discussed in opposition – no one was sure which parts of them, if any, would be implemented. In any case, Ridley (like other Conservatives) was cautious about confrontation with the unions. He regarded some strikes as unbeatable and thought that in many nationalized industries: 'Since they [the unions] have the nation by the jugular vein, the only feasible option is to pay up.' Indeed, Ridley's most significant recommendation was that the government should set aside money to pay large wage claims. He divided unions into three categories: those (electricity or sewerage) that had the power to bring the country to an immediate halt; those that could inflict serious damage only with a more long-term strike; and those (such as the Post Office or education) to which the government was not particularly vulnerable. Ridley put coal in the second of these categories and anticipated that the government would be able to resist a strike in this sector for 'about six weeks'.[8]

The real significance of the Ridley report was not so much that it provided a novel and specific programme for action, but rather that Ridley, with his characteristic bluntness, set out in writing what many Conservatives were thinking. There was no peculiarly Thatcherite approach to the miners. This was an issue on which there was a consensus across the party. On the one hand, everyone – including, and perhaps especially, those who had been most loyal to Heath – resented the humiliation of 1974. On the other hand, everyone – including those, such as Keith Joseph or John Biffen, who were seen as most radical – recognized that beating the miners would be difficult. The most pessimistic shadow ministers thought that it might be impossible.[9]

The extent to which all Conservatives shared an approach to the miners is illustrated by Harold Macmillan. He is often presented as the arch appeaser of the miners. His remark that the National Union of Mineworkers was, along with the Vatican and the Brigade of Guards, one of the 'great powers' that no British prime minister could afford to annoy was quoted ad nauseam.[9][10] When the government yielded to the miners in February 1981 (see below), John Hoskyns, one of Thatcher's advisers, wrote that the prime minister herself had accepted the 'Macmillan doctrine'.[11]

Private conversations suggested that the Macmillan doctrine was closer to the Thatcherite orthodoxy than its author's public declarations suggested. In January 1974 Alan Clark talked to Macmillan and recorded the exchange thus: 'the miners had to be bought off until North Sea Oil came on stream; that it should not be too difficult to outmanoeuvre Len Murray [general secretary of the TUC]; that McGahey [Communist leader of the Scottish miners] wasn't popular in the

TUC; that the real agitator was *(Scrimgeour* was it? – the words came thick and fast and I was transfixed)'.[12] The name that Clark heard as 'Scrimgeour' was presumably Scargill. In short, Macmillan advocated a tactical retreat until a future government might be strong enough to take on the miners, and in the long run he anticipated a confrontation that would involve Scargill as the most important figure on the trade union side.

Once in power, however, the Thatcher government was in no hurry to take on the miners. Towards the end of 1980, the annual pay negotiations between the miners and the National Coal Board were complicated by two things. First, NCB managers wanted to close those pits that were never likely to make a profit. Secondly, the term of office of Joe Gormley as leader of the NUM was coming to an end. Gormley was a staunch monarchist who wrote newspaper articles on horse racing and who accepted a seat in the House of Lords. His politics were rooted in a view of working-class interests that would have horrified young left-wingers of the early 1980s – he wrote that he wanted a society in which everyone 'would have a Jaguar out front to take him to work and a Mini at the side to take his wife to the shops'.[13]

For all his moderation, Gormley was good at getting wage rises for his members. He had won battles with the Conservative government in 1972 and 1974, and he took on the Thatcher government in early 1981 over wages and pit closures. Ministers discussed their chances of holding out if there was a strike. They knew that stocks of coal were high, but they found that this was not enough. Too much of the coal was stored at the pitheads rather than in the electricity generating stations. There was no guarantee that the coal could be transported if railwaymen supported a miners' strike. The particular kind of coke used for starting up power stations was also in short supply. In February the government backed down. It agreed to make more money available to fund higher wages and a halt to pit closures.

In April 1981 Gormley retired as leader of the NUM. His successor was Arthur Scargill. Scargill was relatively young (born in 1938), earnest and vain. He seemed remote from the beery bonhomie of British trade unionism – or, for that matter, from the brusque melancholy of Mick McGahey, whose own chances of leading the NUM had been undermined by the manoeuvres of Joe Gormley. Amongst those who worked most closely with him, Scargill's strange 'mixture of ruthlessness and sensitivity' aroused an exasperated affection.[14] In the wider Labour movement, though, his arrogance annoyed even those – such as Eric Heffer – on the hard Left.[15] Tabloid newspapers and Tory politicians implied that Scargill could not really represent his working-class members. Miners seem to have felt differently. Scargill got almost three quarters of the vote in a large turnout. There were few trade union leaders who had a clearer electoral mandate than him.

Was Scargill a revolutionary? He had been a Communist in his youth and he talked about the tactics of revolution when he was interviewed by the *New Left Review.*[16] Some Conservative ministers made much of his Marxism.[17] However, Scargill had broken with the Communist Party in 1962. The NUM took money from Soviet miners and from the trade unions of Soviet-controlled Afghanistan during the strike of 1984–5, but there is no evidence that it did much in return. Furthermore, the Soviet Union conspicuously failed to do the one thing that might have helped the NUM during its strike – prevent the export of Polish coal to Britain.

Scargill's most marked characteristic was his parochialism. His roots were in Yorkshire, where he had spent his whole life. He felt uneasy when he was obliged to leave his home ground, and he sometimes claimed that he had rejected a place at grammar school because he did not want to go to school in a different town. On being elected president of the NUM, he moved the headquarters of the union from London to Sheffield. Far from looking ahead to some future revolution, Scargill often seemed to be looking back to his own youth. He was obsessed by a single incident in 1972, when he and a group of flying pickets had succeeded in forcing the closure of a coke depot in Saltley in Birmingham. He was to claim in 1981 that this was: 'The greatest victory of the working class, certainly in my lifetime.'[18]

If Scargill was looking to the past, the government was looking to the future. It regarded the settlement of February 1981 with the miners as a tactical withdrawal rather than a defeat, and from then on it began to prepare for a future conflict with the miners. Discussions about beating a future miners' strike (which had involved politicians, civil servants and outside advisers from the very moment that Thatcher arrived in Downing Street) acquired a new urgency.[19] David Howell, who, as secretary of state for energy, had presided over the settlement with the miners and who was described by Gormley as 'wet behind the ears',[20] was replaced by Nigel Lawson. Lawson built up stocks of coal at power stations and increased the use of oil in electricity generation. He also made special arrangements, so secret that they were hidden from his own cabinet colleagues, to transport vital chemicals into power stations by helicopter. Against protests from his own constituents, he insisted that a new 'super pit' was opened in the Vale of Belvoir, thus helping to make the Nottinghamshire coalfield more productive and Nottinghamshire miners more secure than their colleagues elsewhere.[21]

In June 1983 Lawson was made chancellor and was replaced as secretary of state for energy by Peter Walker. Thatcher says that she wanted Walker to preside over a future miners' strike because he had shown himself a 'tough negotiator' in dealings with the EEC – an odd claim since the government ostentatiously refused to play any direct part in negotiations during the miners' strike – and because he was a 'good communicator', who might be expected to influence public opinion.[22] Perhaps Thatcher's private thinking was more complicated. Walker's willingness to oppose her economic policies in cabinet must have impressed on her the fact that he was a man who did not scare easily. Besides, it made sense to associate a cabinet 'wet' with the government's strategy: it meant that a rebellion within the cabinet was less likely and that someone relatively dispensable could be sacked if things went wrong.

Other appointments also seemed to pave the way for a strike. Nicholas Ridley, who had written the much-discussed plan of 1977, was appointed secretary of state for transport in 1983, and thus made responsible for getting coal from pits to power stations. The Central Electricity Generating Board was obviously going to be important in any future coal strike. Nigel Lawson had no confidence in its head, Glyn England. This was partly because England had been appointed by Tony Benn in 1977 and was a supporter of the Labour Party (he was soon to join the Social Democratic Party). More importantly, perhaps, it was because England resented being obliged to waste money on maintaining large stocks of coal.

England was replaced by Sir Walter Marshall. Marshall was a physicist, who had run the Atomic Energy Authority. In the government's eyes, he was made attractive by the fact that he had quarrelled with Benn over the benefits of nuclear energy. His style also commended itself. He was an extraordinary man from a humble background who had taken a Ph.D. at Birmingham University at the age of twenty-two. His almost incomprehensible accent and manner set him apart from the establishment men who usually ran nationalized industries. He relished dramatic gestures and was unafraid of confrontation. His character was illustrated by the fact that he once arranged for a train to be crashed at full speed: ostensibly this spectacular and expensive experiment was designed to show that the containers in which nuclear waste was transported were hard to break. Marshall's greatest failing, as Lawson admitted, was an almost complete lack of interest in, or knowledge of, finance. His appointment showed how ordinary business considerations were subordinated to the need to defeat a coming coal strike.[23]

The most awkward appointment of all was that of the chairman of the National Coal Board. Edward Heath had appointed Derek Ezra to the post in 1971. He was a member of the Liberal Party and the epitome of post-war corporatism, and had worked in the mining industry ever since leaving the army in 1945. He was close to Joe Gormley – the two men sometimes went away for weekend retreats together – and the NCB was known in Whitehall as the 'Derek and Joe show'. Ezra stood for everything the Thatcher government disliked. Ministers blamed him for the defeat of the

Tory government in 1974, and they suspected that he had not been sorry to see the government back down in February 1981. It was clear that Ezra would not be reappointed when his contract expired at the end of 1982.[24] In the short term, Ezra's deputy Norman Siddall got the job, but Siddall, for medical reasons, was unwilling to stay on beyond the autumn of 1983. Lawson believed that the chairmanship of the NCB was the 'most political' position in British industry and would have liked to appoint a politician to it. He considered Roy Mason, a Labour MP who had attracted much admiration amongst Conservatives for his vigorous policies when Northern Ireland secretary and who had, perhaps more importantly, crossed swords with Scargill when the Left had tried to deselect Mason as Labour candidate for Barnsley.[25]

In the end, the candidate chosen was Ian MacGregor, who had been born and raised in Scotland but had enjoyed a successful business career in the United States. He had kept in touch with business in Britain – serving as deputy chairman of British Leyland and then becoming chairman of British Steel. In spite of his experiences in British business, however, his overall attitude remained rooted in the American climate of free enterprise, in which unions could be crushed or circumvented – he once casually mentioned to a Tory minister that a strike in Wyoming, 'so far as he knew', was still going on.[26]

Like Scargill, MacGregor had a great capacity for self-dramatization and, sometimes, for self-deceit. He repeatedly referred to his confrontation with the miners in terms of 'war', 'storm troopers', 'Rommel' and the 'Gestapo'.[27] Characteristic of him was his attempt to suggest in his autobiography that Peter Walker had lost his nerve and tried to impose a compromise settlement on the NCB during the closing weeks of the strike – a claim that seems to have been the exact reverse of the truth. MacGregor exasperated almost all who worked with him – he was nearly as unpopular with industrialists as Scargill was with trade unionists.[28] Senior managers at the NCB were driven to despair.

MacGregor's term of office began in September 1983. The appointment was seen by the NUM as a provocation. Scargill was increasingly vocal in his public claims that the Coal Board had a 'hit list' of pits which were due to close. However, the NUM constitution required a 55 per cent majority in any ballot to authorize a national strike. Scargill held strike ballots three times on pay and/or pit closures in 1982 and 1983. Every time, he failed to secure the majority he needed – on the first occasion, the case for a strike was undermined by an article Joe Gormley had written in the *Daily Express* urging the miners not to strike. From Christmas 1983, however, leaders of both the NUM and NCB seem to have known that a strike was on the way.[29]

In early 1984 MacGregor agreed with the government that the Coal Board must reduce its deficit. This meant closing pits. MacGregor talked to his area directors – characteristically he referred to them as 'field commanders'.[30] The toughest of them – in Scotland, South Wales and the North East – resisted a sudden new pit closure in their area, which might disturb their relations with the unions and their own carefully laid plans. George Hayes in South Yorkshire was less assured and more willing to go along with orders he was given in London. On 1 March 1984 Hayes told a meeting of union representatives that the Cortonwood pit was to close. The announcement came as a surprise. Strictly speaking, Hayes had not followed the agreed formal procedures for the announcement of pit closures. There were still reserves of coal left at the pit and, indeed, miners had been transferred to it within the previous few weeks. Miners across South Yorkshire walked out in protest over the closure of Cortonwood, and they were followed by miners in Scotland.

At a meeting between the NCB and the unions on 6 March, MacGregor outlined the need for further cuts in spending, and Scargill deduced from this that the board intended to close about twenty pits. The national executive of the NUM now invoked rule 41 of their constitution, which allowed individual areas within the NUM's federal structure to call their men out on strike. Scargill rejected calls for a national ballot and, instead, convened a national delegate conference. This conference duly decided to support the strike – though it also changed the union's constitution so that the threshold for authorizing strike action, if a ballot were to be held, was lowered from 55 per cent to 50 per cent.

Members of the government had been waiting for the strike for years, but they had not anticipated that it would begin under terms that were so favourable to them. Spring was the worst time for the miners to go on strike – because they would have to hold out for at least six months before they could hope for the fuel demands of winter to begin to bite. Furthermore, government plans had anticipated a complete halt in coal production. As it turned out a significant minority of miners worked throughout the strike. The NUM was a federation of regional bodies and, though there was no national ballot, a number of regions did hold ballots at local level, and most of these decided against the strike.[31] In a few areas almost all miners kept working throughout the strike. In Leicestershire there were just thirty strikers; in south Derbyshire there were seventeen.[32] Particularly important were the Nottingham miners. Some of them struck but most worked through the strike. They had political traditions that separated them from miners elsewhere in the country, and their jobs seemed safer than those of their colleagues elsewhere. They voted against a strike in a local ballot and subsequently for the most part stayed at work.

The absence of a national ballot weakened the position of the NUM executive. It made it difficult for leaders of the Labour Party and other unions to defend the strike. It made it easier for Nottinghamshire miners and their allies to argue that the strike was illicit.[33] Ministers were, in fact, far from sure that a national ballot would not favour a strike. However, the NUM executive was trapped by its own rhetoric. Once Scargill and his allies had talked of not letting miners 'be voted out of jobs', it was hard for them to hold a ballot without appearing to have given in; the fact that so much Conservative legislation revolved around encouraging ballots exacerbated this position.

The government insisted that the coal strike was a matter between the NCB and the NUM. This policy of 'non-intervention', however, turned out to mean an extraordinary amount of activity. A cabinet sub-committee was established encompassing Whitelaw (responsible for 'civil emergencies'), Walker, Brittan (the home secretary), Lawson, Tebbit (then minister at the Department of Trade and Industry but also, as former secretary of state for employment, responsible for much of the legislation that might be used against unions), King (secretary of state for employment) and Ridley.

The government's first task was to prevent the use of the very union legislation that it had just enacted. MacGregor wanted to sue the NUM under laws designed to prevent secondary picketing.[34] Walker believed that doing so would bring the striking miners sympathy from other workers, not least their own colleagues in Nottinghamshire.[35] He won the argument and the NCB suspended its action – subsequently other chairmen of nationalized industries were also discreetly discouraged from using laws against secondary picketing.[36] Thatcher and Tebbit were both later to claim rather ungraciously that the strike might have been 'won' earlier if 'Thatcher's laws' had been used.

The alternative to using civil law against secondary picketing was to use criminal law against individual pickets. Trying to stop men from working with violence, or the threat of violence, was an offence. In the strikes of 1972 and 1974 this had not been a particularly important issue: the NUM itself tried to avoid physical violence and the police had been less concerned to protect the right to cross picket lines; at Saltley in 1972 the police had lent Scargill their public address system so that he could tell his men that they had won. In 1984, though, striking miners faced the fact that large numbers of workers, including some of their own colleagues, intended to go to work, and that the authorities were determined to protect their right to do so. Some picket lines became violent – though the miners themselves often distinguished between pushing against the police lines, which they regarded as legitimate, and throwing bricks, which they resorted to only when they believed that the police had broken some unspoken compact by mounting baton charges.

For all their preparations, ministers were not confident that the strike would fail. There was no real agreement about how long coal stocks would last. Tebbit believed that they would run out by January 1985; the Central Electricity Generating Board thought that it could hold out until at least November of that year. Walker deliberately avoided making promises that there would be no power cuts until he was sure that the promises could be kept.

When Walker's assurance that the lights would stay on finally came, in January 1985, its effect on the morale of the strikers was powerful precisely because Scargill had repeatedly claimed that power cuts were imminent. The tactics of the miners came to seem desperate and undignified – miners' support groups urged their members to switch on electrical appliances at six every evening, in the hope of causing a power surge that would shut down the national grid. Scargill's personal involvement distorted the miners' tactics in other ways too. In particular, he diverted pickets to the Orgreave coke plant. He seems to have done this partly because he was hoping to relive the triumph that he had enjoyed at Saltley in 1972, and partly because he had been jostled by police on the picket line at Orgreave. At one point, there were 10,000 pickets, about 7 per cent of all striking miners, at Orgreave, a place that did not, in fact, have great strategic significance.[37]

The NUM organized the strike under increasingly difficult conditions. The NCB did not use recent trade union legislation against the NUM, but other companies that had been damaged by the secondary picketing of the miners eventually did go to court, as did miners who objected to the strike. The first sued under laws designed to prevent secondary picketing and the latter argued that the union's constitution required a ballot before launching a strike. The NUM was declared in contempt of court, and, when it failed to pay a fine, its assets were sequestered.

Other trade unions might have helped the NUM. Railwaymen, steelworkers, dockers and electricians could have impeded the movement of coal, or its use in factories and power stations. The National Association of Colliery Overseers and Deputies, which was responsible for the supervision of pit safety, might have shut down all coal mining in Britain. Twice – once when dockers walked out in July and once when pit deputies seemed on the verge of striking in September – it seemed that a sympathetic strike by other workers might stop the production or movement of coal. The fact that the strike never spread to involve workers who were not members of the NUM was partly the result of skilful concessions by the government. The NCB's attempt to force pit deputies to cross NUM picket lines was abandoned when it seemed that this might provoke all deputies into striking. Railwaymen were given a deliberately generous pay settlement to keep them happy during the miners' strike.

The miners and their would-be allies also fell victim to wider changes in industry. The National Dock Labour Scheme imposed rigid restrictions on the ways that ships could be loaded or unloaded, but important ports – Dover and Felixstowe – were outside this scheme. Besides, increasing amounts of freight were transported in containers that were relatively easy to load and unload. Much freight was also moved by lorry, and lorry drivers – men who worked on their own and in some cases owned their own trucks – did not fit neatly into a traditional working-class culture. Lorry drivers were important in breaking a succession of strikes during the 1980s and their willingness to transport coal in 1984 and 1985 was crucial. The two unions representing electricians were recognized by the government as the one group who almost certainly had the power to bring the country to a halt, but electricians often gained from the very technological change that damaged workers in old-fashioned heavy industry. The electricians' unions were on the Right of the labour movement and had been the object of much solicitous attention from the government.

Steelworkers ought to have been natural allies of the miners. Bill Sirs, leader of the Iron and Steel Trades Confederation, knew that miners, railwayworkers and steelmen (the Triple Alliance) were all members of the 'old' working class, increasingly marginalized in a union movement that was becoming dominated by white-collar workers.[38] However, the steelworkers had lived through their own bruising strike of 1980.

Now they wanted to protect their industry and in particular to prevent the closure of one or more of the large steel plants at Scunthorpe (in Lincolnshire), Ravenscraig (in Scotland) or Llanwern (in Wales). A blast furnace is damaged if it is allowed to go cold. The steelmen were sometimes able to arrange special deals with the NUM that would allow enough coal in to keep the furnaces operating, but such deals became increasingly difficult as time went on and, as ever, Scargill proved particularly awkward. When the NUM sought to extend the strike by preventing the movement of iron ore by rail, a move that would have cost jobs in the steel industry, Bill Sirs said that he was not willing to allow his industry to be sacrificed on the 'altar of the coal strike'.

For someone who was believed to be a revolutionary, Scargill was remarkably bad at maintaining relations with workers outside his own industry. The NUM did not ask the TUC for help until September 1984. The alliance of coal, steel and rail unions had hinged partly around personal friendship between Joe Gormley, Bill Sirs and Sid Weighell (of the National Union of Railwaymen). Weighell's replacement by Jimmy Knapp and Gormley's replacement by Scargill made things more difficult. Scargill sometimes seemed to go out of his way to antagonize his fellow trade unionists. He had said before the strike that his men would 'throw lorries in the ditch' if transport workers tried to get past picket lines. During the strike itself, Scargill wrote to Bill Sirs: 'The fact that you have acquiesced in the use of scab labour is something that will be on your conscience for the rest of your life. You are a disgrace to the very concept of the Triple Alliance and all that it was supposed to do.'

The attitude of other unions to the miners' strike was not just a function of crude economic self-interest. Workers in other industries felt sympathy for the miners, but they were disturbed by the NUM's refusal to hold a strike ballot and also by violence on picket lines – especially after a taxi driver, David Wilkey, was killed by a concrete block that pickets dropped on his car as he drove a miner to work in Wales.

The National Association of Local Government Officers (NALGO) illustrates the complexities of the union movement at the time of the miners' strike. Early in the strike, the union expressed support for the miners and gave £10,000 of its own funds to the NUM. However, five NALGO branches withheld subscriptions in protest at the donation, and, in August 1984, 200 branches challenged their union's financial support for the miners. They were not numerous enough to force a ballot on the matter, but the union's leaders were sufficiently impressed by the opposition to stage a discreet retreat: they gave no further money to the miners.[39]

Sometimes it seemed that the violence associated with the miners' strike might spill into the trade union movement itself. When Norman Willis, the leader of the TUC, condemned 'violence from either side' at a rally of miners in Wales, someone lowered a noose so that it hung menacingly above his head. When John Lyons, of the electricians' union, attended the TUC conference in the autumn of 1984, he took a bodyguard in case he was attacked by miners or their supporters.[40] Even miners who supported the strike sometimes came to blows with each other. Mick McGahey, the deputy leader of the NUM, was loyal to Scargill – even though McGahey's own comrades in the Communist Party had their doubts about the strategy of the strike. In March 1984, however, McGahey was beaten up, apparently by men who regarded his willingness to countenance a return to work as a 'betrayal'.

Once it had become obvious that the miners would not bring the country to a halt, how was the strike to end? Much was made of the need for negotiation and for 'face-saving formulae'. Ministers, however, did not want to save Arthur Scargill's face. They feared that the NUM would make almost any deal appear to be a victory for the miners, and they were concerned that any settlement should involve the acceptance of the 'right to manage' in the coal industry – many ministers privately believed that the NUM itself had effectively run many pits before the strike. Restoring 'the right to manage', however, raised questions about whose power was being restored. The truth was that ministers despised NCB managers – regarding them as too close to their own workers, too keen on subsidy and craven in the face of the NUM.

From the government's point of view, the strike was about circumventing the power of management as much as crushing that of the union. The appointment of MacGregor was calculated to disrupt management traditions at the NCB; he was almost obsessively hostile to Hobart House (the NCB's headquarters in London). The government did not entirely trust MacGregor himself, though. Throughout the strike, ministers pressured him to adjust his tactics – particularly when it came to public relations – and, according to Walker, the cabinet even discussed dismissing MacGregor during the strike.[41] Towards the end of the strike, Peter Walker heard that MacGregor was talking to the leaders of the TUC about terms on which the strike might be ended. Walker was keen that no agreement should be reached that might be presented as even a partial victory for the NUM. He wrote to MacGregor in strong terms.[42]

The ideal solution for the government was simply that miners should return to work with no agreement. Throughout the strike, some miners kept working, and the numbers increased as workers lost faith in their leadership or in the chance of gaining anything. Statistics about working miners became an important part of the propaganda war that was conducted between the two sides. NCB officials, scornful of the government's claims, sent out spoof Christmas cards at the end of 1984 that alluded to the game of 'New Faces' that was being played as colliery managers sought to identify miners who had returned to work.

Thatcher claimed that February 1985 was the crucial month in which, for the first time, there were more working miners than strikers. The NCB's private figures suggest that the majority of miners were back at work on 1 March 1985 – just days before the NUM finally called the strike off.[43]

Who represented the working miners? A Nottinghamshire miner, Chris Butcher, known as 'silver birch', met journalists from time to time. David Hart, an old Etonian, apparently close to MacGregor though not to Peter Walker, who had made and lost a fortune in property development and who lived in a suite at Claridge's, attempted to coordinate actions amongst working miners.[44] The official leaders of the NUM in Nottinghamshire – Ray Chadburn and Henry Richardson – supported the strike, though they also asked for a ballot. During the strike, Nottingham miners began to eject pro-strike officials and replace them with men who were working. Roy Lynk was the most important of the new leaders and, after the strike ended, he became general secretary of the newly formed Union of Democratic Miners.

There was never – for all the rhetoric – a clear-cut division between 'scabs' and strikers. Nottinghamshire miners observed the go-slow (that had begun in 1983) throughout the strike. Some of them stopped work in March 1984 and returned to work only when their own area balloted against a strike; others insisted that they would have gone on strike if a national ballot had favoured one, and even that they personally would have voted for a strike in such a ballot. Equally, quite large numbers of men went on strike but then returned to work before March 1985. In some areas that had observed the strike, the return to work acquired a momentum of its own. Early on, men had feared ostracism if they crossed picket lines. However, the weight of social pressure began to shift as more men returned. Those who were back at work spread rumours of reprisals that might be taken against men who stayed out. The belief that anyone who was away from work for twelve months would have to undergo a medical examination before they could go underground again was especially influential – many middle-aged men, who had spent years breathing coal dust, knew that they did not stand much chance of being passed fit.[45]

The actions of men who worked in areas where the strike was solid are hard to explain. Their enemies accused them of selfishness, but many men's pursuit of 'material advantage' earned them years of ostracism and fear. Some left their mines or the industry when the striking miners returned. One striker suggested that men who risked such penalties must be mentally retarded.[46] Some men broke the strike in ways that seem deliberately perverse. In Staffordshire pits most strikers had returned to work by November 1984. A pro-NUM account of the strike suggested that those who had always been lukewarm in their support for the strike generally went to work in the buses provided by the Coal Board. However, men who had once been 'hardline' chose to walk in, thus exposing themselves to abuse from pickets: 'a symbol of guilt that amounted to self-inflicted punishment'.[47] At Cortonwood, where the strike had begun, four men returned to work just twenty-four hours before the official strike ended.[48] It is hardly likely that men who had stayed out for a whole year could not face one more day without pay. Did they want to display their contempt for the union when they finally realized that all the suffering of the past twelve months had been for nothing? Did they want to prove, perhaps only to themselves, that it was not fear of the picket line that had kept them out?

The strike was riven with hypocrisy on all sides. Coal Board managers wanted to see Scargill defeated, but they often also hoped that the government would provide further subsidies to keep pits open. Ministers pretended that the strike was a matter for management when they were, in fact, giving orders to the chairman of the NCB. Trade union leaders pretended that they wanted the miners to win, though privately many of them loathed Scargill and believed that he was damaging the labour movement. One senior civil servant claimed: 'I remember being told by one union leader that, if we did not destroy Scargill, he would never forgive us.'[49] Eric Hammond, of the electricians, was the only trade union leader to condemn the NUM executive during the strike itself – at the Labour Party conference of 1984 he said that the miners were 'lions led by donkeys' – but other trade unionists, notably Gavin Laird of the engineers and David Basnett of the General and Municipal Workers Union, were widely known to be hostile.[50] Leaders of the Labour Party such as Roy Hattersley, and even Tony Benn, supported the miners in public long after they had conceded in private that the strike was bound to fail.[51]

The return to work involved all sorts of uncomfortable deceptions. Pickets had talked a language of solidarity and uncompromising determination. They had said that they would never work with 'scabs', and that they would hold out for the rights of their comrades who had been dismissed for offences committed during the strike, but sacked men were not reinstated and no one in the enclosed and dangerous conditions of a pit could afford to refuse all dealings with men who had broken the strike. Anyway, the division between striker and 'scab' cut across communities and families in awkward ways. One woman in South Yorkshire was particularly vehement in her denunciation of men who had broken the strike. Her male relatives sometimes left the room when she talked about the matter – they could not bring themselves to tell her that her own son had gone back to the pit in February.[52]

The position of strikers was sometimes oddest of all. They and their supporters insisted that they were striking to 'protect their children's jobs', but how many people really wanted their sons to become miners? How many men, for that matter, wanted to be miners themselves? Interviews conducted with miners and their families by sympathetic historians and journalists suggest that on a personal level strikers were often motivated by the desire to escape the pits. Men who had worked in the industry since they left school, and who were used to going underground every morning, were suddenly able to travel and to spend all day in the open air – for all the well reported violence, picket lines were safer places than coal mines. One Yorkshire miner recalled: 'It were the best twelve months of me life. I hadn't seen a complete summer since I were fifteen. I right enjoyed it. I walked miles.'[53] Many men left the industry at the end of the strike. Some of them were militants driven out by management harassment, or working miners who were bullied by former strikers; some, though, seem simply not to have wanted to go back to the coalface.

Doubt about whether or not mining was a desirable job was illustrated by the family of Iris Preston. Her two sons were miners and she campaigned vigorously during the strike to defend their jobs. Both her sons went on strike, but one of them, Tarrance, refused to undertake picket duty. After the strike, Tarrance asked his mine manager if he could be paid redundancy money. When the manager said no, because the pit was not going to be closed, Tarrance resigned. He said that he could not bear working with 'scabs'. His mother, though, recognized that Tarrance had been unenthusiastic about his job even before the strike and that, after it, he was simply frightened by the prospect of underground work. However, she, the mother, preferred not to think about the reasons for this fear because her other son was still working underground.[54]

There was also something oddly double-edged about the way in which the British public responded to the miners' strike. Every opinion poll showed that the public was dissatisfied with the power exercised by trade unions and that this dissatisfaction had helped to bring the Conservatives to power in 1979. The Conservatives had always been open about their desire to curb union power, and their more specific plans to deal with the NUM had been widely discussed since the late 1970s. Beating the miners was not a radical Thatcherite policy that broke with mainstream Conservatism. Conservatives disagreed about timing and tactics but almost all of them agreed about the need to defeat the NUM, and the defeat was eventually achieved under the leadership of the most important cabinet 'wet'. Indeed support for government on this issue, and on unions generally, went much wider than the Conservative Party. Members of the Social Democrat Party, allegedly the defender of the 'post-war consensus', were often particularly enthusiastic about containing trade union power. In the summer of 1984 David Owen, a leader of the SDP and a man who had in 1972 put up striking miners in his London house, urged Thatcher not to back down to the NUM.

Why then, as Thatcher's ministers sometimes asked themselves,[55] did the Conservative Party not get more credit for the outcome of the coal strike? Its poll ratings were poor in the spring of 1985 and it suffered heavy losses in local government elections soon afterwards. The strike left a nasty taste. This was partly because of the winner. It would have been hard to find a more unattractive face of international capitalism than Ian MacGregor. The nasty taste was also associated with the nature of the losers in the strike. Trade unionists and strikers were often portrayed in contemptuous terms. Descriptions of workers at the British Leyland plant at Longbridge in Birmingham or of printers in Fleet Street made much of their laziness, 'Spanish practices', and (in the case of printers) high pay. The miners were different. No one thought that they were lazy or dishonest. Coal mines were harsh and dangerous places: thirty miners were killed at work in the year before the strike. A number of politicians knew all too well what it was like to work in a mine: Neil Kinnock and Roy Jenkins were both the sons of miners. Keith Joseph had spent a week working in a mine near Rotherham during a university vacation in the 1930s; with his characteristic honesty, he admitted that he would not have cared to spend a second week there.

The very hopelessness of the strike increased the regard in which miners were held. They were not striking for higher pay or shorter hours. Towards the end of the strike, it was not clear that they were fighting for any material benefit at all. Dennis Skinner, a left-wing Labour MP and ex-miner, said that the strike was: 'The most honourable strike this century [because it] was not about money but about people fighting for their jobs, communities and the futures of their children.'[56] Many Conservatives who did not want the miners to win were, nevertheless, fascinated by their courage. The historian Raphael Samuel, writing shortly before the miners accepted defeat, advanced an interesting theory as to why this was so. Samuel was sympathetic to the strikers, but he also recognized that they were in a curious way conservative, and even that they incarnated some of the 'Victorian values' that were sometimes associated with Margaret Thatcher. The miners represented solidarity and tradition. The very efficiency with which the government dealt with the strike – the careful preparation, the deployment of well-equipped policemen, the centralization of power – all seemed 'unEnglish'. One miner complained that the roadblocks which he had to get through were 'Soviet style'; a miner of Polish origin likened the government's action to that which was taken against the Solidarity trade union in Gdansk.[57]

People who regarded themselves as 'traditional Tories' and as defenders of an 'organic' and settled society were particularly prone to self-deception when they recalled the strike. In truth, such people had often been particularly exercised by trade union power and were keen to see the miners beaten, but they began to feel uncomfortable about their victory after the event. In 2005 the journalist Peregrine Worsthorne wrote: 'the physical methods ... adopted by the Thatcher revolution to put down the Scargill miners were ... alien, owing more to France's brutal revolutionary tradition of treating all protests as incipient insurrections – a tradition loyally upheld by the CRS [riot police] to this day – than to Britain's preference for beer and sandwiches in Downing Street'.[58] No one reading this passage would guess that Worsthorne had poured abuse on the miners during the strike itself, or that he had said in private that the chairman of the NCB deserved to be fêted 'as Wellington after Waterloo'.[59]

The truth, perhaps, was that the British people wanted the miners to be beaten, but they did not want to be associated with the means by which this victory was achieved. In a strange way, Thatcher's very success in the miners' strike laid the way for her eventual failure. Concern about the power of the trade unions had been one of the most important reasons for Thatcher's electoral popularity. When the most terrifying of the British trade unions had been broken, the usefulness of her style of politics had ended. Expressing admiration or concern for the miners became a discreet way in which Conservatives could distance themselves from the government. Harold Macmillan, the man who had recognized, back in 1972, that the miners would one day have to be beaten, delivered his maiden speech in the House of Lords in

November 1984: 'It breaks my heart to see what is happening to our country – this terrible strike with the best men in the world, who beat the Kaiser and who beat Hitler too, who never gave in. Pointless, endless. We cannot afford that.' In January 1985 an obscure upper-class Tory MP made a speech in which, whilst deploring the miners' aims, he stressed that the strikers had something to 'teach us about solidarity'.[60] The MP was Anthony Meyer, who was five years later to become the first person to challenge Thatcher for the leadership of the Conservative Party.

Chapter 8

SERIOUS MONEY, 1983–8

Sexy greedy *is* the late 80s.

Caryl Churchill, *Serious Money* (1987)

The 1983 election ought to have been Margaret Thatcher's great moment of triumph. She had been the emblematic figure of the Conservative Party during the election, and that election produced a sharp increase in the party's majority, from 43 to 144. The Labour Party was even more inward-looking after the election than it had been before. The party's new leaders, Neil Kinnock and Roy Hattersley, were good at dealing with internal dissent in their own party but famously ineffective in their attacks on the government. Senior Tories regarded them with a contempt that they had never shown to Foot or Healey, and senior Labour politicians doubted whether Kinnock could ever win a general election.

Thatcher was now strong enough to insist that her own supporters dominate the cabinet. Not all of her appointments worked. She abandoned plans to make Cecil Parkinson foreign secretary when she discovered that his mistress was pregnant; he was forced to resign from the government altogether a few months later when the scandal broke. As for Leon Brittan, he just looked wrong for the part of home secretary and had to be moved in 1985. Two more durable appointments were Nicholas Ridley and Norman Tebbit. Ridley, who came into the cabinet in 1983, was the younger son of a viscount. His father had insisted that he study engineering at university in order to be able to make his own living. However, Ridley was, in some ways, a rather unworldly man who had wanted to be an architect (he was the grandson of Edwin Lutyens), and who spent his spare time painting watercolours. Thatcher said that he 'could have been a figure from Wilde or Coward'.[1] Ridley, a chain smoker who did nothing to disguise his upper-class drawl, made no concessions to populism; in March 1990 he said: 'Every time I hear people squeal, I know that we are right.' Norman Tebbit was a very different kind of man. He had been in the cabinet since 1981 but he now became more prominent and in 1985 was made chairman of the party. He was a grammar-school boy from Edmonton who had become a pilot during his national service – fighting his way out of a burning Meteor jet at an age when some of his future cabinet colleagues were still at university. He was a more careful politician than Ridley (John Mortimer described him as 'an illusionist without illusions') and one who never caused offence unintentionally. What united Ridley and Tebbit was contempt for the pre-1974 political order and fierce personal loyalty to Margaret Thatcher.

The most momentous of Thatcher's ministerial promotions after the 1983 election was that of Nigel Lawson. He became chancellor, a position that he held until his resignation in 1989. No cabinet minister, other than the prime minister, stayed in a single post for longer than Lawson, and in many ways Lawson was second only to Thatcher in the influence that he exercised over British politics during the period. Elected to the House of Commons for the first time in 1974, and not appointed to the cabinet until 1981, he had risen fast. Other men who enjoyed such meteoric careers – Brittan or John Moore – were marked by the perception that they were Thatcher's creatures. Lawson, by contrast, was known as one of the few ministers who regularly stood up to the prime minister. He was the only senior minister who had never been talked about as a possible leader of the party – his disdain for certain kinds of public relations and his impatience with those whom he regarded as his intellectual inferiors made it inconceivable that he would ever build an independent following. Curiously, these qualities were strengths rather than weaknesses. Thatcher never regarded him as a possible rival, but she could also never dismiss him as a political runner-up. Though he sometimes reflected on the charms of being foreign secretary, Lawson himself had effectively achieved the highest of his ambitions when he entered Number 11 Downing Street. This gave him an aura of success and self-confidence, as well as the knowledge that a return to the back benches would not mean cutting off his career before its peak.

For Tebbit and Ridley, Thatcherism was intertwined with personal loyalty to the prime minister. Lawson was different. He was, more than any other member of the cabinet, prone to reflections on political philosophy and he was keen to put the government's actions into the broad sweep of history. Ross McKibbin suggested that Lawson was not a Thatcherite at all.[2] The truth was more complicated. Lawson emphatically was a Thatcherite, as Thatcher recognized.[3] But, for him, loyalty to Thatcherism meant loyalty to a set of ideas (ideas that he regarded himself as particularly qualified to expound) rather than loyalty to a person. For Lawson, Thatcherism was not 'whatever Margaret Thatcher herself at any time did or said'.[4]

In spite of her new parliamentary majority and Thatcherite hegemony in the cabinet, Thatcher recalled the aftermath of the 1983 election in curiously melancholy terms. Early Thatcherism had often seemed ascetic. There was a sense that economic virtues – thrift, independence, responsibility – were to be encouraged as much because they were virtues as because they were economic. After 1983 the economic benefits of Thatcherism seemed more dramatic and more widely experienced. Privatization, the sale of council houses, rising property prices and deregulation in the City of London sometimes seemed to offer people the very thing that the first Thatcher government had defined as being impossible – money for nothing.

The new economic mood of Thatcher's second term was felt first in the City of London. In the early 1980s jobbers (who bought and sold stock and made their profits from the differences between the prices of these two operations) were required to be separate from brokers (who acquired stock on behalf of their clients and charged a fixed commission). Gilts were sold, on behalf of the government, by a single broker and then sold on by a small group of other recognized dealers. Only individuals, rather than corporations, were allowed to be members of the Stock Exchange and, in practice, this excluded foreigners. Until 1973 women were not allowed to be members of the Stock Exchange. In 1971 Graham Greenwell, a partner in a broking firm that employed a number of people who would become advisers to Margaret Thatcher, objected to 'modernization' of the City in these terms: 'In essence, both the Stock Exchange and the Baltic [Exchange] are private men's clubs and not business institutions ... The Stock Exchange is not an institution which exists to perform a public service.'[5]

The City was dominated by small institutions that had been established for a long time. Nepotism and back-scratching flourished. Lord Carrington remembered how his Eton housemaster had advised him that stockbroking (along with farming and the army) was a suitable profession 'for a really stupid boy'.[6] S.G. Warburg, a merchant bank founded by a German-Jewish émigré in 1946, was the only firm that stood outside the culture of the City. It pioneered

Eurobonds and also, in the battle for control of British Aluminium in 1958–9, suggested that shareholders might have the right to sell their shares to the highest bidder regardless of the wishes of the company's management. S.G. Warburg, however, was the exception that proved the rule. Respectable bankers regarded it as pushy and vulgar.

The Stock Exchange was, in fact, facing the prospect of prosecution by the Office of Fair Trading for restrictive practices when the Conservatives came to power in 1979. Ministers in the first Thatcher government were not inclined to stop this prosecution. Many of them believed that British financial institutions gave insufficient support for industry. This belief often featured in the theories of industrial decline that influenced the Conservative Party so much in the late 1970s (see below), and it had been strengthened by the way in which banks had apparently sought profits in property rather than industrial investment during the 'Barber boom' of 1972–3. Thatcher had no particular affection for the City – she said that her father had seen the Stock Exchange as a form of gambling.[7] Disdain for the City was especially marked amongst those ministers who had actually worked in it. This was true of John Nott, secretary of state for trade from 1979 to 1981, who had chosen to begin his business career with S.G. Warburg in 1959 precisely because of Warburg's reputation for being an outsider in the City club.[8] It was also true of Cecil Parkinson,[9] who headed the Department of

Trade and Industry during the few months between the 1983 election and his public disgrace. However, Parkinson decided on a change of tactic. In July 1983 he called off the OFT in return for a promise that the Stock Exchange would reform itself.

The reforms were to be implemented on a single day (the 'Big Bang') on 27 October 1986. Brokers and jobbers were no longer to be separate, fixed commission was to be abolished, corporate membership of the Stock Exchange was to be permitted and the trade in gilts was to be opened to anyone who could obtain a licence. The Big Bang did not seem likely to bring unqualified benefits for those who worked in the City. Just before the deregulation of the City, one of the biggest of the UK merchant banks, Morgan Grenfell, had a stock market capitalization of £664 million; this compared to £5 billion for the American Citicorp and almost £20 billion for the largest Japanese investment bank.[10] Many thought that British institutions would be elbowed aside in a more aggressive market, and that a brief flurry of investment, as new opportunities opened up, would be followed by redundancies and bankruptcies. As one American banker put it: 'Sure as dammit, 50 per cent of the Eurobond and gilt traders are going to be driving taxis in five years' time, and the best business to be in will be a secondhand Porsche dealership.'[11]

As it turned out, few traders ever drove taxis. The prospect of reform meant that banks and brokers became bigger. Firms merged in order to create companies that would be able to work in several different areas. Foreign banks bought their way into the City. All of this brought new prosperity. Brokers and jobbers were bought out at generous premiums. Barclay's Bank bought the broker De Zoete and Bevan and the jobber Wedd Durlacher Mordaunt in 1986. It was said to have paid close to £150 million for the two; three years earlier the estimated capitalization of *all* brokers on the London exchange put together had been between £150 and £200 million.[12] The desire to acquire expertise pushed up salaries. The average income of directors in Morgan Grenfell had been £40,000 in 1979; by 1986 it was £225,000. At the stock broker Cazenove, profits during the same period (to be divided amongst a pool of partners that had barely increased at all) multiplied by seven.[13]

The City of London was also transformed by a new attitude to mergers and acquisitions. In 1985 Burton brought Debenhams for £579 million – the largest takeover in stock market history; by the end of 1989 there had been twenty acquisitions for more than £500 million. Hanson Trust, which bought the Imperial Group for £2,564 million in 1986 and Consolidated Gold Fields for £3,275 million in 1989, specialized in such operations. Particularly important to the City after the Big Bang in the late 1980s were 'hostile takeovers', that is to say takeovers, such as the one of British Aluminium that had so shocked City opinion in 1958–9, that were opposed by the existing management of the target companies. The mid-1980s saw a wave of such takeovers. Newspapers ran vituperative advertisements in which the managers of firms that were locked in battle abused each other in an attempt to win shareholders over to their side. Share prices were pushed higher and corporate finance departments became ever more aggressive in their pursuit of victory. The language of the takeover began to penetrate the whole world view of prominent Conservatives. Norman Tebbit suggested that the Church of England was like a poorly managed company that would benefit from the attentions of Charles Hanson.

One takeover bid which, though relatively small in business terms, had particular political significance was the attempt by the American company Sikorsky to take over Westland helicopters in 1985–6. The Sikorsky bid was supported by the Westland management but, against Thatcher's wishes, Michael Heseltine, the defence secretary, conjured up an alternative bid by a consortium of European companies. Westland divided the cabinet, caused the resignation of two ministers and almost brought Thatcher herself down (see chapter 11). It also revealed how interwoven the worlds of Conservative politics and corporate finance had become. Hanson Trust and News International, both companies whose owners were close to Thatcher, rode to the support of the Sikorsky bid; GEC, an established British industrial company, was the key component in the European consortium. This was not, however, a simple matter of political positions 'expressing' economic interests. In purely economic terms, the Westland company was not very important (until the artificial pressure of a contested takeover pushed its share price up, the company was valued at around £30 million) and many of the companies that became involved in its affairs did not really have any business interest in helicopters. The truth seems to have been that business and political interests were entangled in complicated ways, and that politics drove business as much as the other way round. Two figures in the takeover battle (John Nott, at Lazard, which advised Westland, and James Prior at GEC) had been ministers in Thatcher's early cabinets. Gordon Reece, who advised Westland, was an important figure in Thatcher's inner court. Indeed, the most significant lesson of Westland was that the state influenced the economy even after a supposedly free-market revolution. Westland was, after all, a defence company that would always do most of its business with governments – the only debate was whether the governments in question should be European or American. Furthermore, all the companies involved understood the importance of political patronage. The chief executive of GEC had worried, even before the Westland affair, that his takeover of Plessey might be blocked,[14] whilst the government's decision not to refer Hanson Trust's takeover of Imperial to the Monopolies and Mergers Commission was widely seen as a reward for Hanson's intervention during the Westland affair.

The wealth associated with the new City came to obsess cultural commentators. In March 1986 Nicholas Coleridge, himself the son of the chairman of the Lloyd's of London insurance exchange, identified the 'New Club of Rich Young Men':

> It is difficult to estimate the number of young investment bankers, stockbrokers and commodity brokers earning £100,000 a year. Perhaps there are only a couple of thousand, but they are so mobile and noisy that they give the impression of being far more numerous. Most are aged between 26 and 35, and two years ago they were being paid £25,000, in some cases even less, until the opening of the City markets precipitated an epidemic of headhunting and concomitant salaries.[15]

Caryl Churchill's play *Serious Money,* which was first performed at the Royal Court Theatre in March 1987, was set amongst the traders of the London International Financial Futures Exchange. It was intended as an attack on Thatcher's Britain. However, the cast (mainly earning the minimum Equity wage of £130 per week) developed a horrified fascination with traders who earned £40–£50,000 per year by the time they were twenty-three. Traders themselves seemed to relish the image of them that Churchill portrayed: on two occasions banks booked every seat in the theatre for works outings.[16] The whole style of the City – flickering screens, arcane jargon and implausibly large sums of money – seemed glamorous. Some writers felt that the City was supremely 'postmodern'; though Cecil Parkinson, the principal architect of the Big Bang, claimed, rather improbably, to have been a disciple of F.R. Leavis.[17]

Merchant banks gave money to the Conservative Party, and an increasing number of men who had begun their careers in banks or as brokers became advisers to ministers and, eventually, ministers themselves. John Richardson, a corporate financier at Cazenove, was an early admirer of Margaret Thatcher, and his subsequent recruitment by N.M. Rothschild may have owed something to the bank's celebrated talent for maintaining political contacts. Some saw a strand of Thatcherism as an instrument of London finance: 'City interests received political and ideological expression through Sir Keith Joseph's conversion to monetarism and anti-statism and through the role of leading City commentators and financial journalists as the organic intellectuals of a new economic strategy.'[18]

In spite of these links, there were always tensions between the Thatcher government and the City. The fact that a successful banker could expect to be paid several times the salary of a cabinet minister did nothing to smooth relations. Thatcher was said to disapprove of the cavalier attitude to the law that some banks took – the exclusion of Morgan Grenfell from almost all privatization business was believed to be a punishment for the improper actions of some of its executives during the battle to take over Distillers in 1986.

The success of the City also raised questions about the whole nature of Thatcherism. The members of Thatcher's first government had been haunted by the idea of Britain's relative economic decline. Geoffrey Howe's first budget speech compared the statistics relating to British productivity with those of France and West Germany. Three interpretations of British decline had a particular influence on the Thatcherites. The first of these was the report on the state of British engineering prepared by a committee under the chairmanship of Sir Monty Finniston. The report had been commissioned by the Labour government in 1977, but it was finished in 1979 and, in large measure, implemented under Thatcher. Finniston's committee blamed Britain's poor economic performance partly on the low prestige of British engineers and partly on the poor quality of British technical education, particularly relative to that in France and Germany.

The second interpretation was contained in the dispatch that Sir Nicholas Henderson, about to retire as ambassador to Paris, composed in March 1979 on 'British Decline: its causes and consequences'. Henderson too made much of the need to improve the status of engineers. More generally he talked about the need for technological modernization, for fewer strikes and less shop-floor resistance to management. He also argued that Britain was too rooted in a comfortable pastoral vision of itself and too resistant to industrial values. He bemoaned the propensity of intelligent young people to go into the civil service or the City rather than into industry. The dispatch was leaked, as Henderson almost certainly intended that it should be, and published in the *Economist.* It provided Thatcher's supporters with useful ammunition against the Labour government during the election campaign.[19] Thatcher referred to the dispatch with approval soon after she took office,[20] and, indeed, cited it again in one of the last speeches that she made as prime minister.[21] She brought Henderson back from retirement to become British ambassador in Washington.

And thirdly, Martin Wiener, an American historian, published *English Culture and the Decline of the Industrial Spirit, 1850–1980,* in 1981.[22] Some of the arguments of this book ran parallel to those of Henderson – one of Thatcher's advisers wrongly believed that Henderson had 'quoted Wiener' in his dispatch[23] – and also to the arguments that were advanced, a few years later, by the English historian Correlli Barnett.[24] Wiener argued that British industrial decline was rooted in aristocratic values and a celebration of rural Arcadia that had been passed to the middle classes via British public schools and ancient universities. Wiener contrasted the British middle classes unfavourably with those of other nations, especially Germany and America, and argued that they had become excessively inclined to seek their fortunes in the 'gentlemanly capitalism' of merchant banking rather than in manufacture. Shirley Robin Letwin (a Tory intellectual who was herself hostile to the assault on gentlemanly values and liberal education) lamented that her friend Sir Keith Joseph had made the 'Barnett/Wiener thesis' into a 'Thatcherite theme song'.[25]

There was something odd about the enthusiasm with which some Conservatives embraced the various theses about Britain's 'anti-industrial culture' in the early 1980s. They had *étatiste* implications. Their proponents often thought that redemption might come through nationalized industry – Finniston had run British Steel. Henderson was fascinated by the *grands corps* of elite civil servants who exercised such power over the French economy. The very notion of 'relative decline' suggested that the state ought to determine the 'right' economic performance for a country. Enoch Powell, a true free-marketeer, regarded economic decline as a meaningless concept. He also expounded the Arcadian vision of Englishness that men like Wiener regarded as responsible for industrial decline; Wiener's book is shot through with disapproval of Powell. The oddest feature of Wiener and Henderson, when seen through the prism of the later Thatcher government, is that both men seemed closer to Heathite technocracy than to Thatcherite free enterprise.[26] Heath had, indeed, been staying at the Paris embassy in the month before Henderson sent his dispatch, and it seems likely that he had some influence over the views that Henderson expressed.[27]

Far from suggesting that the state was causing problems for society, proponents of the 'antiindustrial culture thesis' suggested that society itself had problems that might be cured by state intervention. John Hoskyns, an admirer of Henderson's dispatch, wanted 'ten years of vulgarly probusiness and pro-industry policies'.[28] He supported special grants for engineering students and, in January 1981, he wanted the government to bail the computer company ICL out of its financial difficulties, partly on the grounds that it was in a 'growth' industry.

The deregulation of the City had important implications for theories of national decline. First, and most simply, it was less obvious that Britain had declined. Reversal of fortunes was especially obvious amongst the upper-middle classes. In 1979 Nicholas Henderson had envied the privileges of the French *grands corps;* by the mid-1980s, members of the French elite drooled at the thought of the money earned by 'les golden boys' in the City. In 1985 Jacques Attali – the man who best epitomized the French educational and administrative elite – published an admiring biography of the London banker Siegmund Warburg.[29]

The new direction of the British economy went with new thinking about Europe. John Redwood and Peter Lilley, important figures on the anti-European wing of the Conservative Party, had made their fortunes in the City.[30] Conservative enthusiasm for European integration during the late 1970s and early 1980s had gone, in part, with a belief that British capitalism had lessons to learn from France and West Germany. This belief was less influential as the City of London became more successful. Increasingly, it seemed that Europe might learn lessons from Britain; in certain respects, particularly with regard to privatization, it did. Judged as financial centres, Paris and Frankfurt looked provincial, and the important competitors for London were now New York and Tokyo.

The success of the City also had implications for the kind of economy that might be possible in Britain. Talk about decline in the 1970s and early 1980s had often gone with a belief that Britain's fortunes were tied to the success of manufacturing. British merchant banks were blamed for being too interested in short-term returns and too prone to invest abroad. The City was seen as a feature of Britain's archaic economy. In the mid-1980s all this began to change. Conservative talk about the possibility of an economy based on service rather than industry, which had looked like rather desperate special pleading in the early 1980s, suddenly began to seem plausible.

Notions about decline had also gone with a wider sense about the whole of British society. Theorists of decline had made much of the survival of 'pre-industrial' values in Britain – values that they associated with the ruralism of the upper classes and with the outdated ethos of the public schools. An odd feature of such theories was that the very people who propounded them so often seemed to epitomize the qualities that they denounced. This was true, to an almost absurd extent, of Sir Nicholas Henderson. Henderson had spent his formative years in the Vanbrugh gardens that surround Stowe School. His life in France revolved around hunting parties and tastings of vintage claret. Even his perception of national decline was rooted in a Foreign Office view of the world: one that saw prosperity as primarily useful because it supported the exercise of national power or prestige.[31] He had an almost *ancien régime* sense of status – after dining with the rector of the Sorbonne, he fussed about whether Oxford dons were still being waited on by flunkeys in white gloves. He epitomized the archaic aspects of the British diplomatic service: he had run a ruthless campaign of press leaks to undermine the team sent by a cabinet think tank in the mid-1970s to enquire into why, for example, the British embassy in Paris needed eleven official cars when the French embassy in London made do with one.[32]

Ministers in the first Thatcher government were also notable for their lack of contact with the industrial virtues that they extolled. The only minister who had much direct experience of industrial technology was the prime minister and, perhaps because of this, she was always rather hostile to attempts to make the British education system more 'practical'.[33] Indeed, so removed from the world of industry were most ministers that discussion of 'anti-industrial culture' often became a means by which they attacked each other. Wiener's book almost provided the occasion for a libel action between two former cabinet colleagues. On Christmas Day 1984 Rupert Edwards gave his father, Nicholas Edwards, the secretary of state for Wales, a copy of Wiener's book. Inspired by his reading, Nicholas Edwards made a speech in which he denounced British companies for their lack of entrepreneurship. He cited GEC, then noted for its refusal to plough its large cash reserves back into the business, as an example. Jim Prior, chairman of GEC and, until recently, a cabinet minister, complained and threatened to sue. Edwards apologized.[34] Rupert Edwards, whose present caused such trouble, had been schooled in the gritty realities of industrial life at Radley and Trinity College Cambridge. After graduation he (like the sons of many of Thatcher's ministers) went to work in the City.

The striking feature of the new prosperity that came from the City was that it strengthened, and was strengthened by, the very culture that the 'declinists' had denounced. There was much talk about the role of 'barrow boys' and cockney dealers. Grimes, the dealer in *Serious Money,* has 'one CSE in metalwork'. In reality, however, it was members of the established upper-middle class who were the big winners from the prosperity of the City. Kate Mortimer was a more typical figure than Grimes. She became the first ever female director of a UK merchant bank in 1984. In social terms, however, she was hardly a parvenu. Her father had been bishop of Exeter and she had built up a network of powerful friends (including a future Tory minister) whilst working in the Central Policy Review Staff during the premiership of Edward Heath. Most bankers had been educated in the very institutions that Wiener and Barnett blamed for Britain's 'anti-entrepreneurial' culture. Oliver Letwin was a banker and adviser to Margaret Thatcher, as well as being the son of Shirley Letwin, who had expressed such hostility to the 'Wiener/Barnett thesis'. Oliver Letwin illustrated the full range of his 'liberal education' by publishing *Ethics, Emotion and the Unity of the Self* in 1987, the year before he published *Privatizing the World.* The young men who left Oxford and Cambridge and went into the City in the mid-1980s had sometimes acquired a fascination with wealth by watching the television series based on that supreme celebration of aristocratic values, *Brideshead Revisited,* in 1981. Many of these people poured their new money back into old commodities: country houses, well-stocked wine cellars and expensive public-school educations for their own children.

The new confidence of the aristocracy and upper-middle class in the 1980s was summed up in the phrase 'Sloane Ranger'. Sloane Rangers were young women from good families who were characterized by their gentility, conservatism and interest in country pursuits. Peter York and Ann Barr, the journalists who popularized the term, described how the 'Magic Money ... brass without muck' of the City funded this new group. The epitome of the Sloane Ranger was Lady Diana Spencer, who married the Prince of Wales halfway through the first Thatcher government. The curious relationship between the old world of the hunt ball and the new world of the post-Big Bang City was illustrated by the widely reported rumour that, in the late 1980s, the Princess of Wales was having an affair with a man who worked in the corporate finance department of the bank that had once stood for everything that was most vulgar in the financial world: S.G. Warburg.

Most British people had probably never heard of S.G. Warburg. For them, the economic effects of the 1980s were felt as a result of less spectacular changes. One of these was privatization. The Conservatives had never liked nationalized industries, but had not on the whole tried to translate this dislike into action. Before 1970 they made only one attempt to reverse a nationalization (that of the steel industry). Thatcher said, shortly before her election to parliament in 1959: 'The government could not de-nationalise things as easily as they had been nationalised.'[35]

A group of Conservatives dreamt of more radical denationalization. Nicholas Ridley had produced an internal party report on the matter in the late 1960s.[36] The Heath government had sold off a few insignificant companies – the Thomas Cook travel agency and a network of pubs in the North West – that had come into the possession of the state, more or less by accident, at various times. However, more significantly, it had nationalized Rolls-Royce when the company seemed on the verge of bankruptcy – a move that was defended by Margaret Thatcher.

Ridley had chaired a second internal party committee to investigate 'problems in the nationalized industries' that began work in 1976 and reported in 1977. Denationalization had many advantages for the Conservatives. It would cut state spending (since most nationalized industries enjoyed large subsidies), and the sale of state assets might even bring money to the government. Denationalization would also weaken the unions, which were strong in nationalized industries, and might create a more flexible free-market economy. It would even change the formal structure of British industrial leadership – since the heads of nationalized industries were represented in the Confederation of British Industry.

In spite of all this, the Conservatives were hesitant in their approach to nationalized industries. Keith Joseph summed up matters with his usual mixture of radicalism and uncertainty:

> Presumably we do not think that denationalization is practicable. Who would buy under Labour threats? Can we go half-way – BP? We must study. Anyway, I assume – but I may be wrong – that we are agreed to manage them [nationalized industries] at arm's length, phasing out subsidies, and seeking to cut overmanning as

hard as we can. I am very conscious of a reservoir of disenchanted experience among our colleagues, and hope that suggestions will be made for fruitful thought and study.[37]

Ridley's report of 1977 on the nationalized industries became notorious for the way in which one of its annexes seemed to anticipate a confrontation between a future government and the miners (see chapter 7). However, the proposals in the main part of the report, and the discussions that preceded it, were modest. Even in internal party discussions, Tories did not suggest that all nationalized industries suffered from the same kinds of problem or were amenable to the same kinds of reform. Nationalized industries considered to control 'natural monopolies' were on the whole regarded as unsuitable for sale. Ten years before the first British Gas shares were traded on the Stock Exchange, a radical group of Conservatives in a private party document concluded that 'the denationalization of the gas industry would be neither practicable nor beneficial'.[38] The denationalization of the British National Oil Corporation (achieved just two years after the Conservatives came to power) was regarded as a 'long-term ideal'.[39]

The idea that it would be possible to sell large numbers of state-owned enterprises was seen as almost quixotic. Managers of nationalized companies were reluctant to discuss the idea – partly because they feared the confusion that would be caused if they moved in and out of the private sector.[40] When Norman Fowler, shadow minister for transport, presented some modest proposals about privatization to his colleagues, he was worried that they might be seen as too radical – he later concluded that they got through only because the shadow cabinet was not terribly interested in transport.[41] In 1976 the CBI insisted that they wanted the existing balance of private and public sector companies left as it was.[42] For much of the 1970s, Conservatives, including Thatcher and Joseph, seemed more concerned to defend the existing 'mixed economy' against further nationalization than to sell off companies that belonged to the state.[43] Enoch Powell presented denationalization as one of the means by which he would reduce taxation in the alternative budget that he presented on the fringes of the Conservative Party conference in 1968, but this was after his front-bench career had ended and Powell later recognized that his proposals had been 'political satire'. The most enthusiastic proponent of denationalization before 1979 was not an MP or a businessman but Michael Ivens, a poet whose distaste for state power had, in his youth, taken him close to anarchism and who, in the 1970s, ran the free-market pressure group Aims of Industry.[44]

The 1979 manifesto barely mentioned denationalization. The truth was that 'privatization' (a word that began to be widely used in 1981 and which Thatcher always disliked) was easier to talk about than to implement.

It was not terribly clear who, in law, owned a nationalized corporation and ownership had to be transferred to special companies before it could be sold to anyone.[45] It was hard to value companies that had no existing share on the stock market, no profits and, in some cases, nothing that anyone in the private sector would have recognized as a set of accounts. The Tory discussion papers of the 1970s had recognized that any value that might be ascribed to nationalized industries, for the purposes of forcing them to make a certain return on capital, was pretty much 'arbitrary'. Should such companies simply be given away to the public or to their employees? This possibility was discussed – though, in truth, some parts of nationalized industries had such liabilities that they might be worth less than nothing. Should shares be offered by tender – that is to say, should buyers be invited to bid for them? Should shares be offered at a price that had been fixed after consultation with bankers and, if so, how was the government to ensure that the bankers, who had an interest in undervaluing shares that they also underwrote, did not take advantage of the ambiguity surrounding valuation?

The government embarked on early privatizations with trepidation. When Cable and Wireless was sold to the public in 1981, the value of the shares offered (around £240 million) was the largest that had ever been sold in a company that had no previous stock market valuation. There was no way of telling how the market would react to such an offer. Some privatizations seemed to confirm the government's worst fears. Amersham International was a spin-off from the nationalized nuclear industry – its assets were largely composed of patents on unproven technologies. The government offered its shares at a fixed price that was, as it turned out, much below what the market was willing to pay. The lucky buyers made quick profits. A year later, the sale of Britoil produced the opposite kind of problem. This time the sale was conducted by tender. However, when the bids were in, a few casual remarks by a Saudi Arabian minister knocked 20 per cent off the price of oil. No one wanted Britoil shares and the underwriters were left with heavy losses.

Companies could be privatized only if they had the right kind of managers. Getting such people was easier said than done. Occasionally, a successful industrialist could be tempted into running a nationalized industry that seemed on the verge of privatization – this was how Sir John King was brought to British Airways. However, before privatization had begun, it was hard to persuade anyone to endure the travails of public sector management in the hope that they might still be there on the day of stock market flotation. Matters were not made easier by Margaret Thatcher who insisted that managers of nationalized industries were performing a 'public service' and should not therefore expect to be paid the kind of money that they might attract in private companies.[46] Some strong-willed chairmen were more concerned to hold their industrial empires together than to increase market choice or profitability. Denis Rooke bullied the government into selling the gas industry as a unified whole; Walter Marshall resigned as chairman of the Central Electricity Generating Board rather than preside over the break-up of his beloved conglomeration.

Most of all, though Conservatives were rarely very open about this, privatization raised questions about party politics. In general terms, it was obviously in Conservative interests that large numbers of people should own shares of any sort and, more particularly, that they should own shares in companies that might be renationalized if Labour were to regain power. However, the very threat of a Labour government also made privatization difficult. Until the summer of 1982 it seemed likely that the Tories would lose the next election, and highly possible that the Labour Party would form the next government. Labour was committed to renationalizing privatized companies in a manner that would deprive shareholders of all profits; Tony Benn talked of nationalization without any compensation at all. This made it hard to sell shares in state-owned companies; every privatization prospectus was required to spell out Labour Party policy.

After the Conservative election victory of 1983, things changed. The chance that a Labour government might reverse privatization policy now seemed remote. Privatization was pursued with new ambition and energy. Until 1983 annual receipts from privatization never exceeded half a billion pounds. After 1983 they were never less than one billion pounds, and they peaked in 1988–9 at £7.1 billion. The change was seen in the privatization of British Telecom in 1984. Previous privatizations had involved relatively small companies, ones that had often been nationalized recently and ones that did not do business directly with the general public. British Telecom was a national company that did business with almost every householder in Britain. It was also the holder of what had seemed to be a natural monopoly. Its privatization was facilitated partly by technological change, which seemed to undermine its monopoly and also to offer new possibilities for profitability as a private company. BT shares were sold at a fixed price and with special provisions to ensure that ownership of the shares should be as widely distributed as possible. The share sale was publicized with a vast mailshot and telephone answering service – at one point, over 36,000 enquiries per day were being fielded.[47]

The sale was, in terms of the government's ambitions, a success. British Telecom was followed by other big sell-offs – British Gas in 1986, British Airways and the British Airports Authority in 1987, the electricity generating companies in 1990. By the time Thatcher left Downing Street, forty companies, employing a total of 600,000 people, had been sold off. Privatization was also a notable success for the City of London: banks were engaged to advise all the relevant parties in each privatization and to underwrite the shares that were issued. The grander banks tended to be sniffy about the comparatively small fees that were offered for underwriting privatizations,[48] and very indignant on the rare occasions when some unexpected movement in the share price forced them to do something in return for those fees.[49] However, privatization work in the UK reinforced the general sense that London-based banks were the frontier warriors of corporate finance, and provided them with the route to more lucrative work overseas as other countries began to sell-off state assets. N.M. Rothschild established a special department (employing Oliver Letwin and John Redwood) to 'sell' privatization abroad.

In some ways, the focus on the very visible transformation that was brought about by the sale of shares obscured the wider problems that Conservatives had identified with state control of industry. Privatization, in itself, did not necessarily bring greater efficiency or more competition. The airline industry illustrated the contradictions in the Thatcherite approach. In the 1970s Freddie Laker's Skytrain had offered cheap transatlantic fares in competition with British Airways. Thatcherites, such as John Nott and Cecil Parkinson, had seen Laker as a kindred spirit.[50] Thatcher herself praised him and supported his legal actions against the British government to ensure his right to operate. However, during the 1980s Laker brought an anti-trust suit against British Airways in the American courts – a case that made privatization difficult and eventually forced the government to delay it. Then Thatcher became the enemy of Laker. She appealed directly to the US president in a bid to quash the anti-trust suit and protect British Airways.[51] There were other ways in which British Airways seemed to benefit from government's willingness to smother competition. A sharp-eyed merchant banker noticed that the privately owned airline British Caledonian seemed to find it difficult to get routes or landing rights when their state-owned rival was being prepared for privatization.[52]

Privatized companies were not always models of the free market. Several of them preserved monopolistic positions. Their prices were often subject to control and the government sometimes retained a 'golden share', which allowed it to veto certain operations, particularly the sale of 'strategic' companies to foreign buyers. So far as could be told, productivity in most companies increased more dramatically in the period preceding privatization than in that immediately after it.[53] A supporter of privatization would no doubt have argued that increases in productivity were brought about by the prospect of privatization; an opponent would argue that state-owned companies were being fattened for sale through sleights of the accountant's hand that disadvantaged taxpayers or customers.

The proportion of the British public that held shares increased from 7 per cent to 29 per cent during the 1980s. However, this change was not as dramatic as it sounded. The proportion of shares held by individuals rather than institutions in 1990 was still lower than it had been in 1950. Furthermore, shares in privatized companies did not really change people's attitude to shareholding in general, or to the management of companies. Most people bought shares in privatized companies because the shares were easy to buy, and because they were known to command an instant premium. Few buyers went on to buy other shares or followed the fortunes of the companies that they 'owned' with any great attention. Indeed, Edward du Cann, the chairman of the 1922 Committee and an intermittent nuisance to the Thatcher government, had probably done more through his promotion of unit trusts during the 1960s to promote share ownership than Nigel Lawson or Cecil Parkinson.

Did privatization have a wider impact on British society? In 1986 government ministers began to talk about 'popular capitalism' (Thatcher had vetoed Lawson's original formulation of 'people's capitalism' because it sounded too 'East European'). Popular capitalism was never, in fact, that popular. This was partly because, for the reasons described above, the distribution of shares was not as spectacular as it looked. It was also because take-up was not spread across all social classes or even all regions. The typical customer who enquired about buying shares in British Telecom was 'male, middle-class and over 45'.[54]

The government did gain from privatization. In the simplest terms, it made money from selling state assets. The culture of industry changed. Privatized industry, especially when privatization was accompanied by the break-up of companies, created a less benign climate for the exercise of union power. The government found it easier to distance itself from pay negotiations once companies had been sold off. A whole section of the establishment, with which Thatcherites had had such fraught relations, was swept away when management of nationalized industries ceased to exist. There were political gains too. Nationalization/privatization is an area in which political parties find it hard to change the status quo. Just as the Conservative Party had hesitated to put denationalization forward as a policy during the 1970s, or even during the first Thatcher government, so the Labour Party realized after 1983 that renationalization would be a complicated and messy operation – one that would alienate some voters, cost a lot of money and make merchant bankers (probably the same ones who had gained from privatization) even richer. Gradually, Labour's threats about renationalization were abandoned. In 1989 Enoch Powell remarked that 'the transfer of ownership and control of industries and services to a wide public gave the Conservative government precisely the sense of irreversibility that is daunting to political opponents'.[55]

Privatization brought relatively small profits to individual buyers, and benefits tended to be enjoyed by people who were already wealthy. The sale of one sort of state asset, however, was different. This was housing. In 1979 about a third of all housing in Britain was owned by local councils – making the British state the largest landlord in western Europe. Many council houses had been built quickly during slum clearance campaigns in the 1960s. Rapid building had all sorts of unfortunate consequences. When Tottenham's Broadwater Farm estate, which was to be the scene of a violent riot in 1985, was built, the council architect realized, after the building contracts had been signed, that important features such as drainage had been omitted. About 2000 large estates – each of which contained between 500 and 2000 properties – were regarded as particularly difficult places in which to live. These estates tended to be composed of flats in high-rise buildings that had been built in line with the modernist fashions of the 1960s. Raised walkways and underground car parks – ideas that looked good on the drawing board – encouraged crime and vandalism. Difficult estates soon got into a vicious circle because only people with no choice would agree to live there and/or because councils deliberately allocated them to 'problem' families.[56]

The Conservative Party was particularly keen to sell council houses. Partly this was a matter of crude politics. They knew that council tenants were likely to vote Labour and that home owners were more likely to vote Tory. Proponents of the free-market also pointed to the 'rigidities' in the labour market that were created by council houses – because tenants were reluctant to abandon their safe and subsidized housing and move to areas where work might be more available. This argument was used with increasing frequency during the 1980s as unemployment rose in the north of Britain. Patrick Minford, a Thatcherite economic cheerleader with a taste for boldly implausible claims of statistical exactitude, argued that the rigidities of the housing market pushed the rate of unemployment 2 per cent above its natural level.[57]

Some Tory strategists considered simply giving council houses away to their tenants. This idea was abandoned, partly because it would have outraged middle-class home owners who were still paying mortgages. Instead, in 1980 the government introduced the 'right to buy' council houses. The right was granted to all tenants who had occupied a property for three years or more (this was lowered to two years in 1984). Prices were fixed at a fraction of the market rate that diminished according to the length of time that the property had been occupied – eventually some tenants were able to buy their houses for just 30 per cent of the market value. The implementation of the scheme was one of many things that brought the government into conflict with Labour-controlled councils. Legislation forced councils to allow sales and also prevented them spending their share of receipts from sales, at a time when the government was keen to cut all public spending.

Over a million council houses were sold in the 1980s. Subsidy of housing was the one area of government spending that dropped sharply during the 1980s. The receipts from council house sales amounted to £17,580 million in the ten years after 1979 and, until 1984, sale of council houses raised more money than the rest of the privatization programme put together.[58] The government also made political capital out of the policy. Those who bought their houses at reduced prices were understandably grateful.[59] More importantly, perhaps, home ownership was popular with the population as a whole, and the sale of council houses forced Labour councils into a position where they looked as though they were against home ownership in general.

The wider social and political effects for which some had hoped from the sale of council houses were harder to discern. About a sixth of all council properties were bought by their tenants. This did not, however, transform a feckless underclass into a breed of sturdy householders. On the whole, houses rather than flats attracted buyers, and many sales took place in relatively desirable locations in southern England. Buyers were mainly middle-aged, married couples from the skilled working class. Council policies for the allocation of housing had tended to favour people who were defined as 'respectable' when distributing the most desirable properties for rent, and the sale of council houses gave an added advantage to this already privileged section of the working class.

Council house sales on problem estates in areas of high unemployment were low – they amounted to between 1 and 5 per cent of properties.[60] Council estates looked more like social ghettos than ever before. The least desirable estates were the ones in which people were least likely to buy. Tenants in such places did not have the money to buy, even when granted substantial discounts, or to pay the high service charges and rates that went with difficult estates. A building society survey of council tenants in 1983 found that many of them did want to own their own homes, but that only about a fifth of them wanted to buy the properties in which they currently lived.[61]

The economic benefits that some had hoped to see from the sale of council houses were elusive. Sales would hardly contribute to labour mobility if the only people who bought were those who already had jobs in relatively prosperous areas. Furthermore, property ownership created its own 'rigidities', which were particularly marked for former council houses because tenants were prevented from realizing the full profit from their acquisition if they sold within a short period of buying. Indeed the most mobile population in Britain was composed of tenants on difficult council estates – where turnover sometimes reached 40 per cent per year.

Most Tories argued that the sale of council houses was justified on grounds that transcended economic or political calculations. They believed that the ownership of property made people into better citizens with a 'stake in society'. Thatcher was a particularly strong exponent of the virtues of home ownership[62] – though she and Denis had not bought their first house until the late 1950s. There was, however, a tension in Conservative attitudes to home ownership during the 1970s and 1980s. Housing was an area in which the free market conspicuously did not function. Council housing was subsidized by the state; private landlords were prevented from charging a market rent for their property by legal controls; owner occupiers benefited from subsidy in the form of tax relief on their mortgages. The Thatcher government increased the operation of the free market for rental accommodations – by cutting subsidies to council houses and by relaxing rent controls. It did not, however, intend to expose home owners to the unrestricted free market. Thatcher herself had once been the front-bench advocate of the Conservative Party's extraordinary proposal, during the general election campaign of October 1974, that the government should prevent repayments on all mortgages from rising above a certain level.

Thatcher never felt comfortable with the notion of direct government subsidy to mortgage payers. She was, however, an enthusiastic proponent of subsidizing home ownership via the tax relief that was granted on mortgage repayments. Lawson disagreed with her. His belief in property-ownership was less fervent than hers – he had sold his London house on moving into Number 11 Downing Street in 1983. He wanted to make the revenue system simpler and more efficient.

He was also keener on a genuine free market in accommodation that would mean the revival of privately owned housing for rent.

Lawson and Thatcher reached an unwieldy compromise by which the amount on which tax relief could be granted was increased – though not as fast as the price of houses increased during the late 1980s. The total tax relief granted to mortgage holders increased from £1,639 million to £5,500 million between 1979 and 1989; subsidy to local authority housing dropped from £1,258 million to £520 million during the same period.[63] House price inflation – driven by a general sense of middleclass prosperity as well as by tax advantages – became a defining feature of the late 1980s. Attempts to revive the privately owned rental sector produced few results, largely because its economic logic was overridden by a British (or at least English) obsession with home ownership. Inflation of house prices was particularly marked in London and parts of the south east. There were times when the average London house 'earned' more than its owner.

The housing market was also transformed by the blurring of the division between building societies and banks (many of the former were 'demutualized' and then reborn as banks), and by the removal of the formal or informal restrictions that had previously existed on the granting of personal credit. In the ten years to November 1988 non-housing loans given by UK banks increased from £4 billion to £28 billion; during the same period, housing loans increased from

£6 billion to £63 billion.[64] Borrowing on this scale sat oddly with a government that talked about the need to live within one's means.

During the booming 1980s the City was always haunted by the fear of a bust. There were many who could still remember the disastrous year of 1974 when shares had plunged. There was also, perhaps, a strain of apocalyptic puritanism in English middle-class culture. The very articles that gave currency to the notions of new prosperity in the City almost invariably finished with some allusion to the prospect of future crisis. A character in Caryl Churchill's *Serious Money* muses on how 'it' will all end: 'Will it be Aids, nuclear war or a crash?'

As it turned out, the end (or at least a kind of end) came with a storm. On Friday 16 October 1987 an extraordinarly high wind, said to be the most severe since 1703, hit southern England. Ancient trees were uprooted, roads were blocked, the plate glass on the new buildings that housed London banks shattered and the whole City was brought to a halt by power cuts. The following Monday world stock markets crashed – a crash that seems to have been exacerbated by automated computer trading systems that sold stock in an attempt to prevent loss. The value of shares quoted in London fell by more than a quarter in a single day – the most dramatic fall in history. Briefly it seemed that the whole transformation of the City during the previous few years might just have been a dream.

Things were not as bad as they had looked on 19 October 1987. Equity prices mainly recovered within a year. In the long run total employment in the City did not drop. The crash did, however, have an important effect on government policy. Nigel Lawson cut interest rates, partly to boost confidence in the UK and partly because he wanted to avoid the pound rising against the currencies of other countries that were cutting rates. The government was, in fact, faced with an odd situation since sterling was rising against other currencies at a time when Britain's balance of payments deficit was also rising. The political divisions over currency and interest rates were now very different from the ones that had existed in the early 1980s (see chapter 5). Thatcher, who had once been so concerned to lower interest rates, was now worried about the possibility of inflation and willing to see sterling reach its 'natural' level. Lawson wanted to keep sterling and interest rates low. The argument was to help bring Thatcher down (see chapter 11).

At the time, Lawson's budget of March 1988 seemed to be a triumph. It looked as though he had headed off the dangers of recession that had loomed just six months earlier. In addition to this, his budget had two striking features. First, he announced that he would be repaying public sector debt (the last chancellor to do this had been Roy Jenkins in 1968), and he added that 'henceforth a zero PSBR will be the norm'. Secondly, Lawson cut income tax. The basic rate was reduced from 27 pence in the pound to 25 and the top rate was reduced from 60 pence to 40. The second of these cuts was relatively unimportant in terms of government revenue, but significant in terms of public perception; for the first time since the Second World War, rich people in Britain could expect to keep most of the money that they earned. Someone earning the average male income in 1988 (£245 per week) would, after Lawson's budget, pay a slightly higher proportion of their income in taxes, rates and national insurance contributions than someone in the same situation would have done ten years previously. Someone earning five times the average male income would be paying about 15 per cent less of their income in tax.[65]

In the long term, Lawson's budget came to be seen in a less favourable light. In some respects it seemed like a negative version of Geoffrey Howe's budget of 1981. Whereas Howe's budget earned retrospective admiration for having dared to increase taxes during a recession, Lawson earned retrospective condemnation for having cut taxes at a time when the economy was 'overheating'. Lawson himself claimed that his budget was misunderstood – that people failed to appreciate how well public spending had been contained or how small tax cuts were as a proportion of GDP. Even he, however, recognized that the tone of the budget contributed to a sense of expansiveness in the economy.

Perhaps, in fact, the single most important measure in the budget was one that appeared at first comparatively trivial. Mortgage tax relief was to be limited to covering £30,000 per property rather than £30,000 per borrower. The main effect of this was to prevent unmarried couples (who were taxed separately) from obtaining tax relief on £60,000 of mortgage. Implementation of the decision, however, was deferred for four months (apparently for administrative reasons). The effect of this deferral was to further heat the property market as people hurried to complete purchase during the last few months when they would be entitled to double tax relief.

The aftermath of the 1988 budget was curious. Everyone had expected that the crash would primarily affect shares; as it turned out, it affected the one thing that the British middle classes had come to regard as safe: houses. From October 1988, for the first time since the 1940s, UK property prices dropped. They continued to do so until the early 1990s. This was, so far as most people were concerned, the most visible sign of a wider economic downturn. It was a downturn that was to strain the relations between Lawson and Thatcher, with important political consequences for them both.

Chapter 9

DIVIDED KINGDOM?

If we are to act in the name of patriotism, as our party has traditionally been respected for doing, we must define the patria.

Keith Joseph, 1975[1]

Mr President, before I begin, there is just one thing I would like to make clear. The rose I am wearing is the rose of England.

Margaret Thatcher to Conservative Party conference, 1986[2]

For most of the period since the partition of Ireland in 1920, the United Kingdom had been an uncontentious administrative formality that aroused few strong feelings. In the decade after 1968, though, questions of devolution inside the British Isles became increasingly pressing. This was most obvious in Northern Ireland, where the violence of the Provisional IRA, and their loyalist opponents, came to overshadow all other political developments in the 1970s. Events on the mainland were less dramatic. Nationalist parties gained some purchase in both Scotland and Wales during the 1970s. The Labour government responded to this by putting forward plans for a limited 'devolution' of powers to local parliaments. Thatcher's shadow cabinet was trapped by a commitment to Scottish devolution given by Edward Heath in 1968. For this reason, the Conservative Party claimed to support devolution, but opposed the particular form that was proposed. In practice, devolution divided both parties. Alick Buchanan-Smith, the Tory spokesman on Scotland, resigned in protest at the party's failure to support devolution more vigorously, as did his deputy, Malcolm Rifkind. Meanwhile George Gardiner, who had been an important figure in Thatcher's leadership campaign, organized opposition to devolution. In the end, referenda in Wales and Scotland in March 1979 did not produce the majority that had been required under the legislation for such measures to be introduced. In the 1970s two governments fell partly because of nationalist movements inside the United Kingdom. Heath might have been able to cobble together a parliamentary majority in 1974 if he had still been able to depend, as previous Tory leaders had, on Ulster Unionist support (see chapter 1). Callaghan was finally forced into calling an election in 1979 partly because the Scottish Nationalists, angry at his failure to deliver devolution, withdrew their support, and partly because a member of the Social Democratic Party, a representative of Catholic nationalists in Northern Ireland, angry at the government's failure to reform the Ulster electoral system, abstained in the key vote.

When Margaret Thatcher came to power in 1979, the constitutional questions of the 1970s seemed to have been settled, or at least to have reached the kind of stasis that is produced when no one believes that any further settlement is practicable in the near future. Scotland and Wales were not to have devolved government. Northern Ireland was to remain in a peculiar constitutional limbo – it was ruled from London, though its parliamentary representation at Westminster was smaller than an equivalent population on the mainland would have enjoyed and though the legislation underwriting its position had to be renewed every year. Furthermore, because of anti-terrorist laws, its inhabitants did not enjoy all the rights that they would have done on the mainland. In terms of party politics, a stasis had also been achieved. Until 1974 the Official Ulster Unionists had taken the Conservative Party whip. This was no longer the case when Thatcher became the leader of the party, though the Conservatives, like all the major mainland parties, refrained from contesting elections in Ulster.[10]

The Conservative Party did field candidates in Scotland and Wales, but its electoral success in these areas was more limited than that which it enjoyed in England. In part, this was due to a long-term decline that predated Thatcher. Wales was an area of heavy industry (coal and steel) and nonconformist religious traditions. Even the presence of Lloyd George's son on the Conservative benches after 1945 did not make the Welsh susceptible to the charms of Toryism. The

Conservative electoral performance in Wales was not, in fact, disastrous during the Thatcher years – they gained seats in the 1983 election, though their gains were more limited than those they made in Britain as a whole, and for several years they managed to find a secretary of state for Wales, Nicholas Edwards, who sat for a constituency in Pembrokeshire and who could make semi-plausible claims to be Welsh. However, Conservative support in Wales dropped quite sharply in the late 1980s and the Tories began to look like a foreign army of occupation – the head of the Welsh Development Agency had formerly been chairman of the Monaco branch of Conservatives Abroad.[3] There was an increasingly strong sense of cultural divide between Wales and the Thatcher government. Every single Labour leader that Thatcher faced between the resignation of Harold Wilson in 1976 and her own resignation in 1990 (i.e. Callaghan, Foot and Kinnock) sat for a Welsh constituency.

The proportion of people in Wales who defined themselves as 'Welsh', rather than 'British', had dropped to a low point of 57 per cent after the failure of devolution in 1979. Two years into the Thatcher government, this proportion had risen to 69 per cent.[4] Thatcherites seemed sometimes to take it for granted that Wales would epitomize everything that made them uneasy. Sir Keith Joseph once told an audience in Cardiff that the Welsh language had no word for 'entrepreneur'; he was disconcerted when a member of the audience asked him what the English word might be.

The problems of Scotland were more painful for the Conservatives. There had once been a strong Scottish Conservative Party and important figures in the party – Willie Whitelaw and Alec Douglas-Home – thought of themselves as Scottish. Thatcher had been greeted rapturously during a brief visit to Scotland shortly after she became leader of the party and she seems to have assumed that the country of Adam Smith would be 'naturally' Thatcherite – indeed, that the Scots 'invented Thatcherism'.[5] This assumption, perhaps cultivated by the small group of free-market radicals at St Andrews University, was wrong. The Conservative Party lost votes in Scotland throughout the 1980s, as Labour, the Nationalists and the Liberal/SDP Alliance gained them. In March 1982 Roy Jenkins, who had been born in Wales and who sounded like a caricature of an upper-middle-class Englishman, won the Glasgow Hillhead constituency from the Tories in a by-election. By 1983, there were only eleven Conservative MPs from Scotland.

Almost every statistic showed that Thatcherism made less progress in Scotland and Wales than in England – or, more precisely, than in the south of England. Ministers with responsibility for Wales boasted of a 'Welsh economic miracle' during the late 1980s, sometimes implying that this miracle was the result of rather unThatcherite policies that they had pursued in the principality. It is true that unemployment dropped sharply in Wales during the second half of the decade, that foreign companies were persuaded to bring inward investment, and that industries associated with the provision of services or high technology rose as the old industries of steel and mining declined. This was not, however, a miracle that would have survived much scrutiny by a statistician: the Welsh economic recovery of the late 1980s looked dramatic precisely because Welsh industry had taken such a bad hammering during the recession of the early 1980s. Furthermore, an increase in employment did not bring a dramatic increase in household income. Many of the new jobs were comparatively unskilled and lowly paid. Often men who had held down well-paid jobs in heavy industry were replaced by women who held more precarious positions on assembly lines. Even the best jobs were less lucrative than those being created in London and the South East. Employment in banking and financial services increased from 50,000 to 75,000, but these were mostly clerical jobs in 'back offices'.[6]

The Scots were particularly resistant to attempts to strengthen the private sector. The proportion of people employed by the public sector was higher in Scotland than in England, as was that of people who belonged to trade unions. Scots were less likely to own shares than English people and, in particular, were less likely to buy shares in the companies that were privatized during the mid-1980s. Scots were more likely to live in council houses and, again, were less likely to buy such houses under the Conservative legislation of the 1980s.

The imposition of Thatcherite economic policies outside England was made more difficult by the fact that the ministers for Wales, Scotland and Northern Ireland often saw it as being their job to maintain public subsidies for the areas under their aegis. Debates on the steel industry, for example, did not simply pit Treasury ministers against those with more interventionist instincts; they also pitted the secretary of state for Scotland, who was determined to defend the steel works at Ravenscraig, against his counterpart for Wales, who tried, with less success, to defend the works at Port Talbot. The tendency of regional ministries to become centres of opposition to certain Thatcherite policies was exacerbated by Thatcher's own use of these offices as a political Siberia to which her most determined cabinet opponents could be exiled: Peter Walker was allowed to run a semi-autonomous economic policy in Wales from 1987 to 1990, as an alternative to keeping him in an economically sensitive ministry with influence over England.

All the problems presented by Wales and Scotland during the 1980s were dwarfed by those of Northern Ireland. In 1920 Ulster had been granted home rule. A parliament met at Stormont. The majority of the province's population were Protestant and electoral manipulation ensured that Protestants monopolized political power. Quite important parts of the British post-war settlement simply never applied to Ulster. The welfare state was more limited, and, not surprisingly, worked in ways that tended to advantage Protestants over Catholics. The education system was divided, to a much greater extent than on any part of the mainland, along religious lines. Birching for young offenders, the abolition of which on the mainland had so offended Margaret Thatcher, remained in force in Northern Ireland until the 1980s.

During the first two decades after the Second World War, conservatively minded English people sometimes regarded Ulster as a tranquil land, one which was refreshingly free of the 'troubles' caused by left-wing activism, trade union power and immigration on the mainland. Brian Faulkner, the Ulster prime minister, remarked in 1963: 'I doubt whether there is any other country which has shown such universal political stability as Ulster.'[7] By 1968 all this had changed. The Civil Rights movement began the long period of violence that the Northern Irish came to refer to as 'the Troubles'.

More than 850 people were killed by terrorists in Northern Ireland during the 1980s. Violence was particularly acute early in the decade. In 1980 and 1981 Republican prisoners went on hunger strike in an attempt to regain the special status as political prisoners that they had enjoyed until 1976. The government made no concessions and ten hunger strikers eventually starved themselves to death; each death provoked riots. Bobby Sands, the most prominent of the strikers and the one who died first, was elected to parliament during the last months of his life.

In spite of all this, Northern Ireland in the 1980s never produced the sense of general crisis of the British state that it had produced during the early 1970s. Politicians on the mainland were less fearful that disorder in Ulster might become associated with disorder on the mainland. The rate of killing was lower than it had been for most of the 1970s and this reflected a new strategy by the IRA, which now recognized that it was in for a long war. The government too dug in for a struggle with no immediate end in sight. The legal and constitutional initiatives of the 1970s were replaced by policies of 'Ulsterization', which meant, so far as possible, replacing the British army with the Royal Ulster Constabulary, and 'criminalization', which meant prosecuting terrorists for particular offences rather than interning whole categories of people.

There was no particularly Thatcherite view on Northern Ireland. The Conservative Party had fought the 1979 election with a vague proposal to introduce 'regional councils' in Ulster. This proposal seems to have been designed to assuage Unionist desire for home rule without re-establishing the Stormont parliament. Two people who were close to Thatcher – Airey Neave and Ian Gow – had a strong interest in Northern Ireland; both were assassinated by Irish republicans. But these men were political fixers rather than policy makers.

In any case, Neave was dead by the time that Thatcher formed her first government and Gow resigned from the government in protest at its Ulster policy. There were Conservative MPs who cared about the union of Britain and Ulster but these were isolated figures – such as Ivor Stanbrook[8] or Sir John Biggs-Davison – who often took a range of slightly eccentric positions that prevented them from forming a coherent group. The behaviour of Ulster Unionists themselves seemed increasingly at odds with the economic dynamism of Britain in the 1980s – Ferdinand Mount, once head of Margaret Thatcher's policy unit, wrote in 1986: 'the Unionists appear so irredeemably *foreign,* far more alien, say, than Mr Lenny Henry or Mr Clive Lloyd.'[9] Mount's remarks would have offended Unionists even more if they had realized that he had authorized the section on Ulster in the draft Conservative manifesto for 1983.[10] After the Anglo-Irish agreement of 1985, of which more below, Unionists finally broke their last formal links with the British Conservative Party. They also sought to organize their forces on the British mainland, with little success. The affairs of Ulster barely impinged on the electorate of the mainland. James Black contested the 1986 Fulham by-election on a 'Democratic Rights for Northern Ireland' ticket. He got 98 votes – placing him just behind John Creighton's Connoisseur Wine Party (127 votes) and Screaming Lord Sutch's Monster Raving Loony Party (134 votes).

Thatcher's own attitude (or perhaps, more precisely, her lack of a clear attitude) to Ulster can be highlighted, as is often the case, by comparing her position with that of Enoch Powell. Powell, to Thatcher's surprise,[11] supported 'integration' – that is to say he wanted Northern Ireland to be ruled by the Westminster parliament under the same terms as the rest of the United Kingdom. He also opposed any measure that seemed to dilute the sovereignty of the British government or to suggest that the Irish Republic might have any voice in Ulster affairs. Powell's focus on what he saw as vital matters of sovereignty went with near indifference to the day-to-day question of terrorism.

Thatcher, on the other hand, was obsessed with terrorism. Some of her closest associates were killed or injured by republican terrorists and she herself came close to being killed when IRA volunteers planted a bomb next to her hotel room during the Conservative Party conference at Brighton in 1984. The passage in her memoirs that deals with Northern Ireland is in large measure a recital of killings and bomb attacks. Often Thatcher seemed to see Northern Ireland as one front in a world-wide battle between democracy and terrorism[12] rather than as a specific place that raised particular constitutional issues for the British government.

In terms of policy, Thatcher claimed to be a unionist rather than an integrationist. In theory, she wanted to restore devolved government; in practice, she never made any move that brought such restoration closer. Throughout her government, Northern Ireland continued to exist in constitutional limbo with its status, as well as the anti-terrorist legislation that had most effect on people from Northern Ireland, being renewed every year. Far from seeking clarity about the status of Northern Ireland, Thatcher often seemed intent on generating the greatest possible degree of ambiguity. This was particularly obvious in talks with the Republic of Ireland about the status of Ulster, talks that ultimately produced the Anglo-Irish agreement of 1985. The Anglo-Irish agreement was designed to give the Republic some say in the affairs of Ulster. The defining quality of the agreement was lack of definition. It gave the government of the Republic of Ireland a consultative role in the affairs of Ulster, without specifying what that might mean. Even the negotiation of the agreement generated peculiar doubts – at one point Margaret Thatcher insisted that discussions of this matter should circumvent ordinary political and diplomatic channels entirely, and that they should be conducted orally by the cabinet secretary, thus leaving no written record. This vagueness provoked the violent hostility of Unionists, who often convinced themselves that the anodyne phrases of the agreement must carry some secret meaning that would be apparent to the Vatican or the CIA.

Thatcher's relations with the secretaries of state for Northern Ireland revealed much about the oddity of her own position over Ulster. Many of them were driven to distraction by her unwillingness to grasp the detailed problems of the province. She repeatedly suggested some border adjustment that would put all Catholics into the Republic and bring all Protestants into the six counties; she had repeatedly to be reminded that most Northern Irish Catholics lived nowhere near the border.[13] She was much given to historical analogies; she once compared Ulster Catholics to Germans in the Sudetenland, hardly a point calculated to reassure either side. It says much about Thatcher's general attitude that her favourite Northern Ireland secretary was not Douglas Hurd or Jim Prior (both subtle men) but Tom King. Thatcher recognized that King had no great grasp of detail but felt that his 'manly good sense' was what Ulster needed.[14]

If Thatcherite economics failed in Scotland and Wales, they were not even attempted in Ulster. In 1977 Geoffrey Howe wrote a despairing report in which he commented on the extent to which Ulster Unionism had become effectively allied with the Labour government on the mainland: 'Ulster shows so many signs of becoming (like the North East) a "natural" for state-subsidized Socialism.'[15] In practice nothing was done to assuage Howe's fears after the Conservative election victory of 1979. One British journalist wrote of the 'Independent Keynesian Republic of Northern Ireland, where monetarism remains unknown'.[16] Jim Prior, secretary of state for

Northern Ireland from 1981 to 1983, had been, along with Peter Walker, one of the most determined defenders of pre-Thatcherite economic policy to remain in the government. Most of the Conservatives who filled the various posts at the Northern Irish Office were smooth, often rather patrician, men who seemed equally distant from both the culture of Ulster Unionism and that of those who were directing economic policy in London. Rhodes Boyson, who was responsible for industry in Northern Ireland when Douglas Hurd was secretary of state, was probably the only one of them who would have described himself as a Thatcherite, and even he conducted an interventionist policy when he got to Belfast.

Economic intervention in Ulster was mainly rooted in pragmatism rather than ideology. Unemployment in the province was higher than on the mainland and it was twice as high among Catholics as among Protestants. Economic failure and terrorist violence fed each other and the government recognized that subsidizing jobs might have political benefits even if it did economic damage. It was estimated that 90 per cent of all industrial jobs in the province were supported by some kind of government subsidy.[17]

The state was more visible in Northern Ireland than it was on the mainland – not least because of the agencies associated with security. About 40 per cent of all jobs in the province were in the public sector.[18] Such jobs could be sustained only by moving money across the Irish Sea. Subsidies from the mainland to Ulster rose from £100 million in 1972 to £1.6 billion in 1988–9 (£1.9 billion if money from the European Community and money spent on the army were taken into account). One curious result of all this was that average household income in Northern Ireland, racked by unemployment and state dependency, overtook that in Wales, which had 'adjusted' so well to the new realities of freemarket economics.

Huge areas of Thatcherite politics meant nothing in Northern Ireland. Crushing the power of local authorities was unnecessary because direct rule had already stripped those authorities of much of their power, partly to prevent them from favouring Protestants. Council housing in Northern Ireland was under the control of a central Housing Executive. On a less formal level, paramilitary groups took a keen interest in the housing of 'their people', and it is unlikely that the sale of council houses on, say, the Garvaghy Road would have been brisk even if the government had tried to implement such a policy. The level of government subsidy to housing in Northern Ireland dropped by only 27 per cent, during a period when it fell by 79 per cent on the mainland.[19]

If direct rule weakened local authorities, it strengthened another agency that was sometimes seen as being inimical to Thatcherism: the civil service. Decisions that might have been taken by elected politicians anywhere else were taken by administrators in Northern Ireland. 'Apoliticism', which Thatcher's ministers often regarded with suspicion on the mainland, seemed eminently desirable in Ulster. The whole sprawling Ulster state produced complexities that only specialists could hope to understand, and this increased the power of both the Northern Irish civil service, which retained a strong sense of its own identity, and of civil servants in London – indeed 'rule from Whitehall' describes Ulster's position better than 'rule from Westminster'.

Education policy was different because Ulster had never abolished its grammar schools, and the Conservatives exerted no pressure for it to do so. There was no poll tax in Northern Ireland. Trade union legislation was applied in the province more slowly than on the mainland. The delay was justified on the grounds that industrial relations posed less severe problems in Ulster than they did on the mainland. In view of the role that the Ulster Workers' Council had played in opposing government policy in 1974, with a strike that was much more blatantly political than anything attempted by the NUM, this was a bizarre argument – though the simple fact that there were no coal mines in Ulster may have played a role in government thinking. The truth was that trade unions in Northern Ireland were so intertwined with sectarian divisions that even Norman Tebbit preferred not to open this particular *panier de crabes.*

What of Thatcherism's relation with the wider world, and particularly with that substantial part of it that had once been ruled by Britain? In 1978 a group of

Tory MPs had said: 'The Nation has been damaged ... by the denigration of its "colonialist" history. Let's stop apologizing for our history.'[20] There was, in fact, little evidence that Thatcher had ever started 'apologizing for our history'. She carried little imperial baggage. For her, the Empire was an admirable chapter in the British story but a chapter that was now finished. She repeatedly insisted that she was proud of the Empire and she sometimes did so in extraordinary contexts (inhabitants of the Congo must have been disconcerted to hear the European civilizing mission lauded in a speech that she gave in Belgium). However, Thatcher never expressed regret about the loss of Empire either and seems to have had remarkably little sense that Britain might in any way be overshadowed by its imperial past. One of her admirers wrote:

> For the fifty years before Thatcherism, the Conservative Party struggled with Britain's imperial heritage, never quite shaking off a belief in or at least a nostalgia for empire. Thatcherism, in its post-imperial modernity, has suffered no such hang-ups. It has concentrated instead on the revival of Britain as an independent island power.[21]

Thatcherites sometimes regarded the attachment to particular pieces of land as mere sentimentality. Nicholas Ridley put matters bluntly when, discussing the Falklands with Argentine diplomats in 1981, he said that the only former British possession that he cared about was Bordeaux – 'because of the wine'.[22]

Some saw the Falklands War as associated with a bid to restore an imperial quality to Britain's role in the world. The truth is that the Falklands War did not mark any turning point in Britain's world role. It was justified on the very unimperialist principle of 'self-determination'. Military success may have seeped into British self-perceptions but the Falklands themselves hardly did so at all: there was no sense that the islands constituted some exciting new frontier. Most of all, the Falklands War did not change British strategy towards any of its other dependencies. There was, in particular, no attempt to change the timetable for handing over Hong Kong, a more economically and strategically important residue of Empire, to China.

The area of the world in which the legacies of the British Empire still mattered most was southern Africa. Here two governments – in South Africa and Rhodesia – had broken away from the British Empire in order to resist the imposition of black majority rule. Britain had, eventually, imposed economic sanctions on both countries. A large group of Tory MPs, and a noisy group in the Conservative Party outside parliament, were, however, against sanctions. Thatcher's own views were open to more than one interpretation. She expressed doubts about sanctions. She said that they were hypocritical, because they were not applied to regimes that repressed their people on the basis of something other than race, and cruel, because they caused unemployment and suffering amongst the black population. In 1978, after the government of Rhodesia had made some concessions to the majority population, party whips ordered Conservative MPs to abstain in the vote on renewing sanctions, but 114 Tories voted against renewal. Many of these rebels – George Gardiner, Stephen Hastings, Julian Amery and Patrick Wall – regarded themselves as being personally loyal to Margaret Thatcher and sometimes believed that she took an indulgent view of their rebellion.[23] Stephen Hastings was knighted in 1983; Julian Amery was given to understand that he might be made foreign secretary. All this might mean that Thatcher was privately in favour of white minority rule, or at least that she regarded it as the least bad of the available options, but that she was obliged to support sanctions for reasons of political advantage. It might equally well mean that Thatcher simply found discreet gestures of consideration towards some right-wing MPs to be a good way to keep the support of a useful group in the party.

One clear fact is that Thatcher rarely gave a member of the pro-South Africa and Rhodesia lobby any office that might have given them influence over government policy. This was particularly striking in the case of Julian Amery. He was the son of a senior minister, Leo Amery, and the son-in-law of a former prime minister, Harold Macmillan. He had been a junior minister in the early 1960s, but he never held any office at all, let alone that of foreign secretary, under

Thatcher. Furthermore, though support for white minority rule often went with personal loyalty to Thatcher, it was not much associated with Thatcherites – that is to say those people who were most involved in implementing the broad range of government policies, particularly those that related to economics. Thatcher's first chancellor, Geoffrey Howe, was the strongest opponent of white rule in South Africa on the Conservative front bench. He had made an unauthorized visit to Soweto during the 1970s[24] and, when he became foreign secretary, he sent British soldiers to protect Botswana against South African raids.

In practical terms, the affairs of southern Africa impinged most sharply on the Thatcher government during its first year in office. Rhodesia's rulers had come to recognize that white rule could not survive. They hoped to manage a relatively gentle transition away from this regime with a constitution that protected some white privileges and with a government that would be formed by Bishop Abel Muzorewa, who was seen as the least threatening representative of black rule. The British government convoked a conference of interested parties at Lancaster Gate in London in 1979, and Lord Soames was sent out as the last governor of Rhodesia to preside over elections, which were won by Robert Mugabe's radical Patriotic Front. Thatcher claims, rather improbably, that she did not appreciate the significance of the Lancaster Gate settlement because she did not realize that

Mugabe's party was likely to win. More generally, historians have tended to assume that the real architect of Lancaster Gate was Lord Carrington, the foreign secretary, and that Margaret Thatcher, inexperienced in foreign affairs and still unsure of herself in cabinet, was manoeuvred into an agreement that went against her own instincts.

The coming of black majority rule in Rhodesia was significant for another reason. For much of the twentieth century some British people had seen the Empire/Commonwealth as a place in which 'British values' might thrive even if they were snuffed out in the British Isles themselves. After 1945 the sense that parts of the Commonwealth might provide a refuge from socialism and economic decline at home grew stronger. H.V. Morton, who had written evocatively about *'l'Angleterre profonde'* in the 1930s, made his home in South Africa. Noël Coward and Ian Fleming spent much of their time in the West Indies, and it was to Fleming's Jamaican house that Anthony Eden went when he was licking his wounds after Suez. Nevil Shute fantasized about Australia as a land of new opportunity for dynamic Europeans, in which the voting system would be changed to reflect the rights of education, property and service. Race also played an important part in these fantasies. As immigrants from Africa and Jamaica arrived in England, certain kinds of English people were attracted to places where blacks knew their place (as seemed to be the case in the West Indies until the 1970s) or where black people were shown their place (as in southern Africa or, until the 1960s, in Australia).

Some of Thatcher's ministers had been tempted by emigration.[25] In 1976 Thatcher talked of 'those who leave this country in increasing numbers for other lands'.[26] In the 1970s Thatcher told a friend that she and her husband would stay if socialism came to power again, but that they would ensure that their children were settled in Canada.[27] The idea of Britain overseas, however, seemed less and less reassuring. Thatcher had remarked as early as 1961 that 'Many of us do not feel quite the same allegiance to Archbishop Makarios or Doctor Nkrumah or to people like Jomo Kenyatta as we do towards Mr Menzies of Australia.'[28] By 1980 even Australia – more republican and less 'white' than it had been in the 1960s – was not an entirely comfortable place for an English conservative.

Rhodesia was the last place in which the notion of an overseas refuge could still seem plausible. Its white population had come mainly from England and had mostly done so quite recently. The capital city had the air of an English provincial town and bore the name of a Tory prime minister. The prime minister – Ian Smith – was a former Spitfire pilot who argued that Winston Churchill would have felt more at home in Rhodesia than in present-day England. Giving up Rhodesia meant giving up the notion that there was anywhere for English conservatives to run. It was, though Thatcher probably did not appreciate it, as symbolically important as the moment when the Romans burnt their boats on the coast of Kent. After this, a certain section of the English middle class had no choice but to stand and fight in their own country.

All this brings us back to Britain and, especially, to England. Thatcherism was an English phenomenon. It never commanded an electoral majority in any of the other constituent parts of the United Kingdom. Its most cherished policies worked better in England – especially southern England – than they did in Scotland, Wales and Ulster. The Thatcher government was pretty much indifferent to Britain's former imperial possessions overseas and never seems to have been infected with any nostalgia for the 'greater Britain' of Empire.

The policies of the Thatcher government provoked various forms of nationalist reaction in Wales, Scotland and Northern Ireland. Thatcherites were, however, remarkably unconcerned with the nationalistic implications of their own acts. The Falklands War, to choose an obvious example, was seen as having important implications for the United Kingdom by Unionists in Northern Ireland, which was why they supported it so vigorously, as well as by nationalists in Wales – Plaid Cymru was the only party represented in parliament to oppose the war (partly because there were so many Welsh-speakers in Patagonia). The government, however, seems not to have thought about such matters at all. Even the decision that the Scots and Welsh Guards should be sent to the South

Atlantic seems to have been taken on grounds of military expediency, without regard for any messages about Scottish or Welsh national feelings.

Thatcher often talked of patriotism and of Britain, but this was a curiously undefined concept in her mind. She seems, in private at least, to have allowed for the possibility that both Ulster and Scotland might split away from England. The American alliance was the centre of her thinking. She saw America both as the pivot of a Cold War coalition against Communism and as the leading country in an axis of English-speaking peoples. Even her apparently 'English' enthusiasms – Kipling, Churchill and the English language – were very transatlantic ones. The American and/or anti-Soviet alliance often cut across any particularly British loyalties. Thatcher barely protested in 1983 when the Americans, in the name of anti-Communism, invaded the island of Grenada, which was a member of the Commonwealth and which recognized Elizabeth II as head of state. The Tory writer T.E. Utley complained that Thatcher cared more about the anti-Soviet guerrillas of Afghanistan than about the Unionists in Ulster.[29]

Religion underlay a great deal of nationalism in Wales, Scotland and, especially, Ulster. It is revealing that the Thatcher government's periodic spats with the Church were concerned entirely with matters of social and economic policy. No mainstream Tory ever took much interest in what might have been *English* about the Church of England. Questions of liturgy, language and the nature of authority over the established Church were all discussed during the 1980s – especially when it seemed that the Church was seeking to circumvent parliamentary control over the prayer book.[30] But these were matters that concerned only a handful of eccentric parliamentarians and there was no particularly Tory approach to them.

Most strikingly, the Thatcher government said little about English nationalism. Some significant Conservatives – such as Stanley Baldwin and Enoch Powell – had talked a great deal about Englishness. Both Baldwin and Powell had delivered important speeches to the Royal Society of St George. Thatcher was to become a vice president of the society in 1999, but there is not much evidence that she took any interest in England's patron saint when she was in power – indeed, the only time she mentioned St George was on 1 April 1987, when she drew attention to the fact that he was also the patron saint of Georgia.[31]

Race played a peculiar role in Thatcherism. The perception that the Conservatives were 'tough' on immigration certainly played a role in their electoral success, especially in 1979. However, Thatcher's enemies were wrong to say that her party was simply 'racist' or unable to conceive of an English identity that was not white. In some ways the problem for Thatcherism was that Thatcherites could not agree on any conception of English identity at all. There were men, such as Howe and Nott, who stood on the Left

298

of their party, and indeed to the Left of James Callaghan, on race and immigration. However, even those Thatcherites who were most 'right-wing' on this issue, did not really live, or want to live, in a racially 'pure' society. The back-bench MP George Gardiner was opposed to immigration and supported the Apartheid regime in South Africa, but he was also close to leaders of the British Sikh community, whom he saw as incarnating the robust moral and martial qualities that Thatcherites admired. Thatcher was Philo-Semitic – she occasionally talked as though the Chief Rabbi was the head of the established Church – and some of her most important allies were Jews. This too meant that Conservatives approached issues of race with mixed feelings. In 1975 Keith Joseph had told the shadow cabinet: 'Mass immigration was imposed against the wishes and forebodings of the overwhelming majority of the people. The concept of the nation has been progressively diminished towards becoming a mere residence qualification.'[32] However, Joseph does not seem to have felt comfortable with a political appeal based on race, and he urged his colleagues not to make immigration an electoral issue. Both Joseph and Lawson, who had also talked about immigration in internal party documents,[33] were disconcerted when it emerged in 1983 that the Conservative Party had attracted a former member of the National Front as a parliamentary candidate.[34]

Nationalism in the United Kingdom was associated with the political death throes of Margaret Thatcher.

There was a Welsh element in the opposition to Thatcherism inside the Conservative Party. Sir Anthony Meyer, the first person to challenge Thatcher for the leadership of the party, sat for a Welsh constituency (though he was also an upper-class English Europhile of German-Jewish descent who had served in the Scots Guards), and Michael Heseltine believed that every single one of the three ministers at the Welsh Office voted against Thatcher in the leadership challenge that he made to her in the following year.[35]

Scotland also played a part in the general crisis that seemed to beset Thatcher during the last two years of her government. The poll tax was introduced in Scotland a year before it was introduced in England and Wales (see chapter 11). Though there was less violent disorder during protests against the tax than in England, resistance to paying was in fact more determined in Scotland.[36] Thatcher attempted to impose a more ideologically committed leader of the Conservative Party north of the border. She also used an address to the General Assembly of the Church of Scotland on 21 May 1988 as an opportunity to lecture the Scots on the virtues of her economic policy. Neither of these moves was terribly successful. In October 1990 Thatcher was obliged to accept that Michael Forsyth, the man whom she had imposed as chairman of the Scottish Conservative Party in the previous year, did not command enough support. She replaced him with the more 'traditional' Lord Russell Sanderson.[37] All the evidence showed that the attempt to Thatcherize Scotland failed. When Thatcher attended the Scottish Cup final between Celtic and Dundee at Hampden Park in 1988, the fans waved specially issued red cards to 'send her off'.

The irony of this was that Thatcher was beginning to talk, apropos of European integration, about the inherent instability of federal states at the very moment that some of the British nations seemed most hostile to her government. In the aftermath of Thatcher's Bruges speech, some of her supporters began to use the phrase 'nation state' as a rough translation of de Gaulle's *patrie'*. This was a dangerous phrase to use – since a defining quality of de Gaulle's 'Europe des Patries' was that it should exclude the British Isles. Furthermore, there is not much evidence that British Conservatives actually understood what might be particularly national about the kind of state that they desired. When Alan Clark was challenged on the subject by the economist Samuel Brittan, he could only say: 'If you don't *know* what the Nation State is, you're decadent.'[38]

Chapter 10

EUROPE

The Lady is going to make a speech at Bruges on the occasion of some Euro-anniversary or other. The Eurocreeps have written for her a really loathsome text, *wallowing* in rejection of our own national identity ... They even managed to delete a ritual obeisance to Churchill, his ideals, all that and substituted the name of *Schuman.* Really!

Alan Clark, September 1988[1]

The Bruges speech of September 1988 did not turn out as the 'Eurocreeps' had intended. Instead of making the 'positive' statement on Europe that the foreign secretary had hoped for when he first suggested that she make the speech, Thatcher delivered her most celebrated attack on the European Community. Towards the end of her time in office, and perhaps more importantly after it, some admirers of Margaret Thatcher talked as though opposition to European integration was the defining element of her philosophy. The Bruges speech was treated as a kind of political testament – the Bruges Group, established by an Oxford undergraduate in early 1989, became one of the most important guardians of the Thatcher shrine. Thatcher's downfall was rooted partly in argument over Europe, and she became increasingly bitter in her denunciations of pro-European Tories, even urging members of her own party to vote against a three-line whip on the Maastricht Treaty of 1993. Foreign secretaries who served under Thatcher had trouble in explaining the evolution of her views. Douglas Hurd thought that she moved 'slowly from the vague enthusiasm for the EEC which she had shown during the referendum campaign of 1975 to the almost total hostility to Europe which she has shown in recent years'.[2] Geoffrey Howe wrote:

> I was driven finally to conclude that for Margaret the Bruges speech represented, subconsciously at least, her escape from the collective responsibility of her days in the Heath Cabinet – when European policy had arrived, as it were, with the rations ... Margaret had waited almost fifteen years to display her own distaste for the European policies which she had accepted as a member of that same government.[3]

Her civil service advisers were equally confused. Charles Powell, her private secretary for foreign affairs from the end of 1983, said that Thatcher had come into power with little experience of foreign affairs but:

> She had certain strong instincts, and one of them was the importance of a very close attachment to the United States of America. The second was a very strong sense of anti-communism, that

communism was evil and had to be confronted. Also, one has to say, a strong support for British membership of the European Community. She had led the Conservative 'Yes' Campaign in the referendum in the early 1970s and therefore came with a basis of belief that Britain had a role in Europe and had to play that role.[4]

Percy Cradock was the prime minister's foreign policy adviser and had an office just yards away from Powell's in Number 10 Downing Street, but he recalled her attitude to Europe in very different terms: '[it] ranged from suspicion to undisguised hostility. She did not like the Europeans; she did not speak their languages; she had little time for their traditions ... Continental penchant for grand generalizations offended her lawyer's mind.'[5]

Thatcher's downfall owed much to the way in which her attitude to Europe irritated Howe and Nigel Lawson (see chapter 11). Europe split her party. In the autumn of 1980 George Gardiner, a Thatcher loyalist who had stressed Thatcher's 'Europeanism' in the admiring biography that he had written of her, was elected as chairman of the Parliamentary Committee on European Affairs, defeating Hugh Dykes. In his memoirs, Gardiner suggested that this marked the beginning of a civil war in the party between 'federalists' who wanted European union to be political and those, like himself, who merely hoped for a common market.[6] By 1998 Europe had taken both

Dykes and Gardiner out of the Conservative Party altogether – the former joined the pro-European Liberal Democrats; the latter joined the Referendum Party, which campaigned for a plebiscite on Britain's continued membership of the European Union. However, divisions such as these became apparent only slowly. In the early 1980s Dykes was still sufficiently sure of the Tory Party's pro-Europeanism to resist an invitation to join the Social Democratic Party.[7] Gardiner would still have described himself as pro-European. Alistair McAlpine, the Tory treasurer, would eventually join Gardiner in the Referendum Party but until the mid-1980s most people would still have assumed that his position was defined by his role in organizing the 'Yes' vote in the 1975 referendum on continued British membership of the European Community.

Thatcher never opposed Britain's membership of the European Community/Union. One of her earliest statements on the matter, in 1961, sounded remarkably like the kind of thing that pro-European Conservatives were to say thirty years later when they attacked the Bruges speech: 'Sovereignty and independence are not ends in themselves. It is no good being independent in isolation if it involves running down our economy and watching other nations outstrip us in both trade and influence.'[8] For most of her time as leader of the Conservative Party, Thatcher emphasized her *pro*-European feelings as something that divided her from Labour. She appointed and promoted pro-European ministers throughout her time in office. Hurd, for example, joined the cabinet in 1984, and Kenneth Clarke did so in 1987.

Europe reveals the difficulty of looking for some consistent spirit of 'real Thatcherism' that underlay the twists and turns of political expediency. The truth was that the position of both Thatcher and of other Thatcherites changed, but also that these changes were linked to the way in which the whole political spectrum, in terms of world alliances as well as British parties, changed.

Edward Heath was the politician who engineered Britain's entry into the Common Market. However, Thatcher's challenge to Heath was not seen to involve hostility to his European policy. On this issue, Thatcher had always supported Conservative policy, which since the early 1960s had been to secure British entry into the Common Market. After she had become leader of the party, Thatcher paid tribute to Heath who had 'brilliantly led the nation into Europe in 1973'.[9]

In 1975 Harold Wilson called a referendum to decide on whether Britain should remain in the Common Market, a move which owed much to his need to manage divisions in his own party. Thatcher opposed the very idea of a referendum as being outside British constitutional tradition. Both parties left their members free to campaign as they wished in the referendum. In practice, however, opposition to British membership came mainly from the Left of the Labour Party and from groups such as the Ulster Unionists. Thatcher stressed that Conservative MPs were overwhelmingly in favour of Britain remaining in the EEC, and that both the shadow cabinet and all the members of the last Conservative cabinet were united on this issue.

Some observers pointed out that Thatcher said relatively little about European integration during her campaign for the leadership of her party, and that she allowed Heath to make the running in the 'Yes' campaign in the 1975 referendum. No one, however, regarded these facts as particularly significant. Most assumed that Thatcher was just seeking to avoid alienating one or other wing of the Conservative Party – it was, perhaps, a sign of her success that people disagreed about which wing she belonged to.

Whatever Thatcher's personal feelings may have been, the Conservative Party was seen as pro-European, until at least halfway through her premiership. Simple electoral advantage played a part in this. The Labour Party was divided over Europe during the 1970s, and in 1980 the party conference passed a motion calling for British withdrawal – a motion that was eventually finessed into an expression of support for withdrawal within the lifetime of the next Parliament. The two men whose influence in the Labour Party rose most during the early 1980s (Tony Benn and Michael Foot) were almost caricatures of 'Britishness' – Benn had even complained about the new European passports that had begun to be issued in the 1970s. Labour Party strategists, who thought that their party's position on this issue would lose them votes, were slightly surprised that the Conservatives did not make more of the issue in the 1983 election.

The Conservative Party itself was touched by the process of European integration. The European parliament, previously made up of representatives delegated from national parliaments, was to be chosen by direct elections from the late 1970s onwards. Douglas Hurd recalled that Thatcher 'never challenged the principle of direct election, but she found it uncongenial'.[10] The prospect of direct elections meant that European parties had an interest in forming alliances across national frontiers. This presented the Conservatives with interesting problems. The most important non-Socialist parties in Europe – especially in Belgium, Holland, West Germany and Italy – were Christian Democrats. Christian Democracy implied an opposition to Marxism, a defence of private property and a belief in the family. However, Christian Democrat parties were not 'conservative' – they were mostly new parties and keen to play down any associations with embarrassing political ancestors from before the Second World War. They were also emphatically not 'liberal', which in continental terms meant that they were not supporters of an unrestricted free market. Christian Democrats also worked in political systems that contained more than two parties, and they sometimes governed in coalition with Socialists.

Douglas Hurd was put in charge of negotiations with European parties. The most important of his interlocutors was the German CDU. This was a successful party in a successful country and the very nature of West Germany, founded and defended by the Western allies, forced its leaders to think in international terms. The CDU was at the centre of an alliance of Christian Democrat groups (the European People's Party) that eventually contested elections to the European parliament in 1979, but it was also interested in a wider alliance of Centre-Right groups (which would include parties that were not Christian Democratic and countries that were not part of the EEC). Hurd himself became a moving force behind this latter group, which was eventually christened the European Democratic Union (EDU).[11] Debate about the value of 'Christian democracy' rumbled on amongst the more thoughtful Tories for many years:[12] Hurd was to describe himself as a 'Christian democrat' when he stood for the leadership of the Conservative Party in 1990. Conservatives seem to have regarded the EDU as a success. Thatcher met Helmut Kohl, the leader of the CDU, for the first time in 1976. Hurd's diary entry on this meeting indicated some of the reasons why there might in the long run be tension between Kohl and Thatcher. The former, Hurd wrote, had 'very much Ted's philosophy of human nature'.[13] However, at the time and for many years to come, Thatcher seems to have admired Kohl. Indeed, in the 1980s she was to describe Kohl, along with herself and Reagan, as the 'Trinity' of Cold War leaders.[14]

In an address to the EDU in April 1978, Thatcher managed to make the British Conservative Party sound remarkably like a continental Christian Democratic party – she even emphasized the role that trade unionists played in the party.[15] The centrist language that the Conservatives often spoke during the late 1970s owed a great deal to the need to maintain good relations with continental parties. Thatcher drew explicit links between the association of European political parties and the association of European states (and implied that she thought that both processes were good):

> It is nearly two years since I spoke at the Congress of the C.D.U. in Hanover. This was one of the first major European commitments which I undertook after becoming Leader of the Conservative Party, and it made a deep impression on me. I came home from Germany confirmed in my belief that the main inspiration behind the European ideal was political rather than economic – and convinced that the Parties of the Centre and Right in Europe had so much in common and so much at risk that they must learn to work together more effectively.[16]

Conservative enthusiasm for links with continental Europe went with enthusiasm for capitalism. The party's leaders were painfully aware that productivity was higher in France and Germany than in Britain and that, in some ways, capitalism was more secure in these countries. Enoch Powell said that the British bourgeoisie was 'bolting for Europe' because it had lost faith in its ability to defend capitalism with its own resources in its own country. Thatcher referred to the German president, Helmut Schmidt, as 'that rare person, a Socialist who believes in the market economy';[17] she even claimed in 1976 that some Communist parties of continental western Europe were less 'extreme' than the Labour Party.[18] Even more importantly, support for Europe went with opposition to Communism. Thatcher became leader of the Conservative Party at a time when the Soviet threat seemed to be increasing. Soviet protégés took power in Vietnam and Angola. Discussions amongst Conservative leaders involved much agonizing about the weakness of the West, and about the alleged links between foreign threat and internal subversion. Under these circumstances, the European Community was important partly because it underwrote an alliance of west European states that were grouped under the American aegis. Even during her anti-European old age, Thatcher continued to stress that Jean Monnet had been a vigorous supporter of the Atlantic alliance.[19] Thatcher was very conscious that West Germany was the front line of the Cold War in Europe. Her speech to the conference of the German CDU on 25 May 1976 was largely devoted to calling for both military and intellectual defence against Communism.[20] In her article of 1978 for a Hamburg newspaper, Thatcher talked of the alliance between Conservative and Christian Democrat parties in western

Europe as rooted in the need to contain 'Marxism'.[21] Sometimes, indeed, she described the whole EEC in these terms. After a meeting with Thatcher in 1979, Roy Jenkins noted that she was 'thinking always a little too much of the EEC and NATO as two bodies that ought to be amalgamated'.[22]

The Cold War got colder in the late 1970s and early 1980s. The Soviet Union invaded Afghanistan on Christmas Day 1979, and in 1981 the Communist government of Poland declared martial law in a bid to contain the Solidarity trade union. The Thatcher government's response to these events was to strengthen its links with the 'Western alliance', and 'Western allies' were, in large measure, European ones.

America was the richest and most powerful of the NATO countries, but Thatcher did not initially regard the United States with unqualified admiration. American society in the 1970s did not provide a model that many English Conservatives – often worried by crime, racial tension and social disintegration in their own country – were keen to imitate. As her party's education spokesman, Thatcher had suggested that American schools epitomized all the dangers of comprehensive education.[23] Thatcher disliked the policies of détente that had been pursued by Henry Kissinger in the early 1970s, and she did not have good relations with Jimmy Carter, the American president from 1976 until 1980. Relations were, of course, better once Ronald Reagan entered the White House, but they were not without tension. West

Europeans and Americans clashed when the Americans wanted to impose economic sanctions on the Soviet Union and in particular to prevent the construction of a pipeline to transport Soviet gas to western Europe. Over sanctions, Thatcher was strongly in the west European camp. Debates on American missile deployment also brought out a specifically European dimension to Thatcher's strategic thinking. She was against Reagan's Strategic Defence Initiative and against plans to reduce the number of long-range nuclear weapons, because she felt that such policies might leave Europe without American support. American short-range cruise missiles did lead the Thatcher government to take a pro-American stance (to an extent that was unpopular with the British electorate), but these policies also brought Thatcher closer to other west European governments. The missiles were, after all, being deployed very largely in Germany. Furthermore, it was the Socialist, but anti-Communist, François Mitterrand (president of a country that was in the EEC but not in NATO) who pronounced the most robust defence of cruise missiles – when he told his own compatriots in 1983 that 'The missiles are in the East and the pacifists are in the West.'

Why, then, did Thatcher's attitude to European integration change during the 1980s? Money had something to do with it. The Thatcher government made much of the fact that British contributions to the community budget were disproportionately large, especially in view of the fact that Britain was now poorer than France or Germany. During her first few years in office, Thatcher devoted much of her energy to negotiating a rebate on British contributions; her determination on this point disconcerted even some of her more abrasive ministers. It is indicative of the extent to which the EEC was seen in terms of anti-Communism that some of her own backbenchers, men usually seen as being on the Left of the party, implied that Thatcher was wrong to 'divide' the Western allies at a time when the Soviet peril was so high.[24]

More generally the very satisfaction that Thatcher came to feel about her own achievements in Britain made her less admiring of continental Europe. Before 1979 British Conservatives had pointed to Germany as a country where unions accepted capitalism more easily than their English counterparts. This seemed less attractive after, say, 1985, when British unions themselves had been so clearly humbled. Furthermore, Thatcher came to see the European Community itself as a means by which statism or corporatism might be imposed on member countries. The most striking passage in the Bruges speech was this: 'We have not successfully rolled back the frontiers of the state in Britain, only to see them reimposed at a European level, with a European super state exercising a new dominance from Brussels.'

Finally, changes in the Communist world affected Thatcher's attitude to Europe. In late 1984 her aides hunted around for a Soviet leader from the younger generation with whom the prime minister might talk. They vaguely thought that Viktor Grishin, the Moscow party secretary, or Grigory Romanov, from Leningrad, might fit the bill. As it turned out, the first person to respond to their invitations was Mikhail Gorbachev, recently appointed to the Politburo with special responsibility for agriculture. The meeting between Gorbachev and Thatcher was a success and Thatcher concluded it with the statement that she and Gorbachev could 'do business together'. Just a few months later, Gorbachev was general secretary of the Soviet Communist Party.

Reform in the Soviet Union had implications for Thatcher's attitude to the rest of Europe. West European unity had mattered to her largely because it promised to help contain the Soviet Union; if the Soviet Union ceased to be a threat, European unity mattered less. Changes in the Communist world also opened up the possibility of a new kind of Europe. Even before the advent of Gorbachev, Thatcher and her ministers had made discreet overtures to the Communist-ruled nations of central Europe. Hungary, the most liberal state in the Warsaw Pact, was the first target for the British government's attempts at seduction. Janos Kadar, the general secretary of the Hungarian Communist Party, was invited to Britain and Thatcher visited Hungary. Later Poland, which Thatcher visited in 1988, became the most important focus of Britain's attention. The shift was significant, perhaps more so than Thatcher's advisers realized at the time. In Hungary, 'reform' meant primarily a move towards free-market economics and was conducted under the aegis of the Communist government. In Poland, 'reform' meant the Solidarity trade union. It was less economic (the union defended the Gdansk shipyards at a time when heavy industry was being shut down in Britain), more nationalistic and less likely to be contained within a system dominated by the Soviet Union.

Whatever the broad reasons for Thatcher's change of emphasis over Europe, the change was not quick or clear-cut. Many of her closest associates seem to have been genuinely perplexed by her behaviour during the second half of the 1980s. In late 1985 Thatcher attended the Luxembourg conference which led to the signing of the Single European Act, by which European governments ceded some of their powers to the Commission. She claimed, in retrospect, that 'The Single European Act, contrary to my intentions and my understanding of formal undertakings given at the time, had provided new scope for the European Commission and the European Court to press forward in the direction of centralization.'[25] Howe, Thatcher's foreign secretary, and Charles Powell, her private secretary for foreign affairs, men who recalled matters from very different perspectives, both insisted that Thatcher had a clear sense of what she wanted out of the Luxembourg discussions, though Powell did believe that the Commission subsequently took advantage of agreements that they had secured, and that 'we should have been more alert to the Commission's duplicity in some of these matters'.[26]

Thatcher seems to have gone along with the Single European Act because it removed so many barriers to free trade in Europe. Much of the work to prepare for this had, in fact, been done by Arthur Cockfield, who had been one of Thatcher's ministers from 1979 until he was dispatched to Brussels as a European commissioner in 1984. Howe defined this as 'Thatcherism on a European scale', and argued that the concessions that Britain made to secure this agreement were calculated and moderate.[27]

Even on the national currency, Thatcher's position had not always been inflexible. Ever since the 1970s a number of European currencies had been linked to the Exchange Rate Mechanism, which prevented currencies from moving against each other by more than a certain margin. In 1978 Thatcher had mocked the Labour government for its refusal to take sterling into the ERM, and pledged that the Conservatives would do so, when the time was right. In practice, the matter was not much discussed during the early years of the thatcher government – though Lawson, as financial secretary to the treasury, raised the possibility of joining the ERM in June 1981,[28] and Thatcher apparently asked him, when the pound had seemed about to fall to parity with the dollar in January 1985, why sterling was not already in the ERM and thus 'protected from all this'.[29]

During the second Thatcher government, support for the ERM amongst Thatcher's ministers became more vocal. At a key meeting in November 1985, John Biffen was the only minister who spoke against the proposal, but Thatcher vetoed it outright. Attitudes to sterling were to haunt her for the next five years. Lawson believed that, even if Germany was no longer a microeconomic model for Britain to emulate, she could still be a macro-economic one, and that tying sterling to the Deutschmark might create 'international monetarism'. To this end, he ensured that the value of sterling shadowed that of the Deutschmark during the late 1980s. The policy was never announced in any official way and Thatcher claimed that she found out about it only when journalists from the *Financial Times* showed her a graph that illustrated the movements of the two currencies. Lawson's policy with regard to the Deutschmark broke down in the spring of 1988 under financial pressure from the markets and political pressure from the prime minister. However, Lawson and Howe finally faced Thatcher down on the eve of the Madrid summit in 1989. Apparently with threats of resignation, they forced her to concede that sterling should now move towards entering the Exchange Rate Mechanism.

Though monetary union became important to Thatcher, it was not an issue on which there was a clear-cut division between Thatcherites and their opponents in cabinet. Norman Tebbit, usually seen as Thatcherite and anti-European, had to everyone's surprise supported joining the ERM in November 1985. Howe and Lawson – both Thatcherite opponents of Thatcher on monetary issues – did not agree about the most desirable outcome. Howe was in favour of creating a single currency eventually; Lawson merely wanted to achieve greater stability in the exchange rate.

In any case, arguments over Europe became intertwined with other disputes – often of a rather petty nature. Cockburn was dismissed, partly because Thatcher saw his support for European tax harmonization as a sign that he had 'gone native' in Brussels. Jacques Delors, the president of the European Commission, became a particular target for Thatcher's ire. Delors was a Socialist and a trade unionist – though one whose links to the Catholic Church probably made him the closest thing that Fifth Republic France had to a Christian Democrat. Thatcher had a high opinion of Delors's ability, which may be why she was annoyed by his public statements and especially by two of his speeches in 1988. In one, he claimed that 80 per cent of legislation affecting member states would soon be enacted by the European parliament; in another, delivered to the British Trade Union Congress, he urged unions to undertake collective bargaining at European level.

All of this fed into Thatcher's Bruges speech of September 1988. Howe had originally urged her to make the speech because he hoped that it would give her the opportunity to lay out a slightly more pro-European position – though, as drafts of the speech were passed from the Foreign Office to Downing Street and back, it became clear that Howe was going to be disappointed. Alan Clark wrote: 'by their [the Foreign Office's] interference and provocation they have turned a relatively minor ceremonial chore into what could now well be a milestone in redefining our position towards the Community.'[30]

The Bruges speech took up many characteristic Thatcher themes. It insisted Europe was older than the European Community. It also drew attention to a Europe that extended beyond the members of the Community and, indeed, into the Communist world: 'We shall always look on Warsaw, Prague and Budapest as great European cities.' It insisted on the importance of national cultures. It urged that the Community should be based on a minimum of regulation – 'we in Britain would fight attempts to introduce collectivism and corporatism at the European level – although what people would wish to do in their own countries is a matter for them'. A large part of the speech was devoted to insistence on the continuing importance of NATO and nuclear weapons.

Like many of Thatcher's most notorious pronouncements, the speech was notable for its tone rather than for containing any concrete proposals for a change in policy. Nothing in it implied that the EEC should not exist or that Britain should not be a member of it. One diplomat noted that, with a slightly different spin and in a slightly different context, parts of the speech might have been interpreted as 'pro-European'. There was no marked change in British policy after Bruges and there seemed to be an uncomfortable tension between what everyone now took to be Thatcher's private beliefs and her government's actions. Geoffrey Howe likened his time as foreign secretary during this period to the experience of a vicar's wife whose husband has said that he does not believe in God.

If Thatcher was not pro-European, what was she? Her speech was applauded by Enoch Powell and John Biffen; Howe suggested that Thatcher had revealed some true 'Powellite' identity. However, Powell and Biffen had both voted against British accession to the EEC; they were both clear that defence of the 'Nation' should be put above the defence of free-market economics. Powell associated opposition to the EEC with fierce anti-Americanism. Biffen associated opposition to Franco-German domination with a call for a Europe that would be wider, looser and somehow less worthy – when the EEC first began to expand beyond its original core, he had implied that he rather welcomed the fact that the 'European club' was becoming less like the Athenaeum and more like the Playboy.[31] Thatcher did not really go along with either of these visions.

The Bruges speech contained a revealing line: 'Utopia never comes, because we know that we should not like it if it did.' In some ways, the greatest problem for Thatcher was precisely that Europe did seem to totter on the brink of a kind of Utopia in 1989 and

1990. Thatcher's whole vision of the world had been formed during the Cold War. Her own success owed much to the sense that she had been particularly resolute in standing up to the Soviet Union. The Cold War had also meant that Britain was able to use its military power to increase its leverage in Europe; during a sterling crisis in late 1986, Thatcher had threatened to withdraw the Rhine Army if the Bundesbank did not buy pounds.[32] The end of the Cold War, however, raised awkward questions about what the victors might really want. This was particularly noticeable with regard to the issue that absorbed much of Thatcher's attention in early 1990 – the reunification of Germany. Ostensibly, reunification had been the aim of the Western allies for many years. But, as late as October 1987, even those Foreign Office discussions that were specifically initiated to plan for reunification did so on the assumption that it would not happen for many years. An official remarked that Thatcher had always been in favour of German reunification 'as long as it was not a realistic prospect'.[33] With the fall of Communist rule in the German Democratic Republic, reunification suddenly seemed all too possible. America and, after some hesitation, France supported it. Thatcher was unhappy, though there was, as it happened, little that she could do to stop Germany from reunifying, or to prevent the unified state from being admitted to the EEC and NATO. She made much of German refusal to guarantee its frontiers with Poland. Nicholas Ridley had to resign from her cabinet after giving a tactless interview in which he said that handing the European Union over to a unified Germany under Kohl would be like handing it over 'to Hitler'.

In two respects, Thatcher's position was contradictory, or at least ambiguous. First, she had always insisted that European unity should not come at the expense of relations with the United States (it was a point that she had made emphatically at Bruges), and yet her own relations with America took a turn for the worse in 1988, as Ronald Reagan left the White House and was replaced by George Bush. She was particularly discomfited by the fact that Bush turned out to be a supporter of German reunification. Secondly, Thatcher was keen to help Gorbachev in the Soviet Union and argued that German reunification might weaken his position. British diplomats complained that their own country was 'more pro-Russian than the Russians'.[34] However, she was also worried about the prospect that western Europe might prove too weak in the face of some future incarnation of the Soviet Union, and consequently she was hostile to any suggestion that Germany might be disarmed or distanced from NATO. Personal relations played a role in Thatcher's attitude. Her growing dislike for Kohl was one aspect, but so too was her respect for Mitterrand and Gorbachev. One British diplomat maliciously recalled: 'Mrs Thatcher, as she noted interestingly in her memoirs, was hoping for a sort of alliance between her and Gorbachev and Mitterrand in order somehow or other to stop something or other.'[35]

Was there such a thing as Thatcherite, rather than Thatcher's, policy on Europe? Some of her admirers (Tebbit and Ridley) thought there was, and rooted this in an Anglo-Saxon concern for intellectual clarity and legal principle. There were some wonderfully confused references to racial characteristics – Lord Young thought that Helmut Kohl had a typically Latin outlook. Thatcher's enemies also came to believe that anti-Europeanism was hardwired into Thatcherism. Stuart Hall and Martin Jacques wrote:

> Since the whole project has been hinged, ideologically, around the narrowest, most racist, exclusive and backward-looking definition of English national identity, and focused on the ancient symbols of empire and nation, hearth and family, kin and culture, the idea that Thatcherism could lead the nation to embrace a European identity and future always lacked conviction.[36]

It was wrong to say that there had been a consistent Thatcherite line on Europe and silly to say that Thatcher's attitude to Europe was rooted in racism (there were, in any case, plenty of racists in the European parliament), but Hall and Jacques were on to something when they suggested that Europe exposed the 'contradictions' of Thatcherism. There had always been a certain conflict between the populist element of Thatcherism, often concerned with non-economic issues, and the governmentalist element, which had often meant the willingness to take unpopular economic measures. Thatcher had contained this conflict by implying that on certain issues she was a populist opponent of her own front bench. This approach worked with regard to short-term issues (such as interest rates in the early 1980s or the pace of trade union reform); it worked with issues that were seen as unimportant (such as whether or not to continue sanctions against South Africa); and it worked on issues that were not matters of party policy (such as the death penalty). The tactic could not, however, work on Europe. Thatcher could hardly disassociate herself from the Single European Act, which she had signed; she could hardly claim that the question of sterling's relation to other European currencies was a peripheral matter and, if she had stayed in power for long enough, she could not have avoided facing the simple question of whether or not she wanted Britain to stay in the European Union.

In the short term, Thatcher's European policy distanced her from the two men who had been most influential in her governments during the 1980s – Howe and Lawson – and brought her closer to people who played more minor roles in British politics – Alan Clark believed that he was helping her to compose 'Bruges II' in early 1990, though he also recognized that he might be helping her to 'dig her own grave'.[37] During her early years in power, Thatcher had devoted much of her energy to domestic policy and left much diplomacy to the Foreign Office. She had also focused in all her policies on what was concrete and attainable rather than on grand abstractions. During her last years in power, Thatcher changed. Her distrust of the Foreign Office, which dated back at least to the Falklands War, was now more openly expressed. She thought more about world affairs and less about domestic ones. Her last six months in office were framed by two grand international summits (in Houston and Paris). She also began to look to the long sweep of history. She cited Paul Kennedy's book on the Great Powers to an interviewer from the *Wall Street Journal*, 38 and she convoked a group of historians to Chequers to discuss the possible consequences of German unification in March 1990. The minutes of this meeting, quickly leaked to the press, listed 'abiding' German characteristics in alphabetical order: 'angst, aggressiveness, assertiveness, bullying, egotism, inferiority complex, sentimentality'.[39]

Thatcher opened the Chequers meeting with historians by saying that 'Europe had come to the end of the post-war period.' However, whilst others interpreted this end as meaning that they should move forward and concentrate on things that had happened since the fall of the Berlin Wall, Thatcher seemed to feel that the pre-1945 past was now pushing its way out of the history books and back into contemporary politics. Welcoming Vaclav Havel to Britain, as the president of an independent Czechoslovakia, she expressed her shame at the Munich agreement. More than any major politician, she wanted Britain to make some formal statement about the Nazi murder of the European Jews.

Thatcher's reinvention of herself as an actor in world history, rather than in British politics, came at an inopportune time. She liked to claim that she had 'prophesied' the fall of Communism and the end of the Cold War. The truth was, however, that the Cold War had helped Britain to conceal – perhaps mainly from itself – its long-term decline in power. Thatcher's own prestige had owed much to the perception that she was particularly resolute in standing up to the Soviet Union and particularly loyal to the United States. As Communism fell, these qualities mattered less. Britain now had to face the fact that it was, as it had been for decades, a middle-ranking European power.

Chapter 11

THE FALL

One is, after all, finite.

Margaret Thatcher, 24 October 1989[1]

Thatcherism's ending has to be explained too. Otherwise it might seem as if it was a gigantic experiment, which ultimately failed – like some vast science fiction concept which missed out one vital consideration and was never heard of again.

Nicholas Ridley, 1991[2]

I wish that cow would resign.

Intercepted telephone call from Richard Needham (minister at the Northern Ireland Office), 11 November 1990[3]

Margaret Thatcher never lost an election. Under her, the Conservative Party won parliamentary majorities in 1979, 1983 and 1987. On the last of these occasions, the Conservative Party obtained a majority of 101 seats – a smaller margin of victory than in the 1983 election but still bigger than the one the Conservative Party had enjoyed in 1979. Winning another large majority without the patriotic surge of 1983 and after the sharp dip in Tory fortunes that followed the Westland affair in 1986 (see below) was impressive. In retrospect the victory of 1987 carried intimations of trouble. Apparent Tory invincibility, and the more general sense of upper-middle-class prosperity, made even the government's supporters feel uneasy. Peregrine Worsthorne, editor of the *Sunday Telegraph,* complained of 'bourgeois triumphalism'. Furthermore, the Conservatives had been elected on an unusually detailed manifesto (very different from those of 1979 and 1983). The old hands in the party who remembered their manifesto of 1970 (or, for that matter, those who had bothered to read the Labour manifesto of 1983) thought that such specific commitments were unwise. Thatcher herself believed that the manifesto was the best ever produced by the Conservative Party – though the fact that the party had been so explicit about its intentions does not seem to have done it much good when the electorate began to turn against its policies.

Thatcher also won all the internal elections that she fought in her party. On the three occasions when she stood for the leadership of the Conservative Party (in 1975, 1989 and 1990) she obtained more votes than any other candidate – though on the last of these occasions her support fell short of the absolute majority that would have prevented a second round of the contest, and, as Thatcher eventually recognized, this left her too weak to continue as leader. The nature of her political demise encouraged some to hint darkly that she had been the victim of a conspiracy by ambitious rivals. Thatcher herself became convinced that her colleagues had behaved badly. This belief soured her relations with her successor, and overshadowed the Conservative Party for a decade. Actually, there is not much evidence of a conspiracy; the various actors in Thatcher's downfall do not seem to have worked together. It *is* true that many Conservatives wanted Thatcher to resign as leader, and that at least one of them believed that he would be the right person to replace her. However, few Conservatives wanted her to leave in the circumstances in which she did. Some came to regret that she had resigned – not because they thought that she could realistically have resurrected her leadership of the party, but rather because they came to believe that the party would have been better off if she had been allowed to go down to defeat in a general election.

Thatcher's biggest problem was not her enemies but her friends. She was increasingly isolated from ordinary life. She was, especially after the Brighton bomb of 1984, surrounded by bodyguards. It was probably twenty years since she had last had a conversation with anyone who did not know who she was. A group of advisers provided her with much of her information. The two most important members of her entourage were Bernard Ingham, her press secretary, and Charles Powell, who had become her private secretary for foreign affairs in 1983, though he sometimes preferred to be known as her foreign policy adviser. Ingham and Powell were different kinds of men. The former had spent his early years in Hebden Bridge, Yorkshire and worked his way up through jobs on local newspapers to a staff post on the *Guardian.* He had been a member of the Labour Party and, before working for Thatcher, his most significant post had been with Tony Benn.[4] Powell was a diplomat and married to a glamorous Italian socialite. What he and Ingham had in common was their peculiarly close relation to the prime minister. Both men were nominally civil servants but had, in practice, escaped from the usual routine of the civil service – one colleague from the Foreign Office said that Powell was as much a 'courtier' as a clerk.[5] Nigel Lawson wrote that Powell considered that his job was not to challenge Thatcher's prejudices but to 'refine the language in which they were expressed'.[6] Powell and Ingham resisted attempts to move them on (an increasingly desperate Foreign Office had tried to tempt Powell out of Downing Street with the offer of various embassies). Both men probably knew that their official career would pretty much end with Thatcher's departure, and both knew that the prestige and contacts they had acquired would serve them well in the outside world.

Advisers sometimes crossed swords with ministers. Powell seems to have encouraged Thatcher to redraft the Bruges speech in terms that were bound to annoy the foreign secretary (see chapter 10). Ingham had provoked a run on the pound in 1985, when he had told journalists that the government was not attached to any particular value of sterling, thus arousing the ire of Nigel Lawson.[7] Tim Bell, an advertising executive who remained close to Thatcher personally even when he left the agency Saatchi and Saatchi that held the Tory account, quarrelled with Norman Tebbit, the chairman of the Conservative Party, during the 1987 election campaign.

The adviser at the centre of Thatcher's most spectacular row with her senior ministers was the economist Alan Walters. Unlike Powell or Ingham, Walters was not a civil servant and not a fixture in Downing Street. He had advised Thatcher informally in opposition and worked in Downing Street for a time in the early 1980s before taking up an academic post in America. In 1989 he returned when Thatcher was in a state of undeclared war with her chancellor over the exchange rate. Walters was from a humble background and had made his reputation with work on a quite specialized area – the economics of transport. All this aroused much scorn from the Keynesians of Trinity and King's, and a little condescension from some of the grander monetarists. Lawson resented the fact that the prime minister was taking advice on the economy from someone other than himself. In October 1989 Walters indicated that he did not believe in the Exchange Rate Mechanism, which Lawson and Howe had just persuaded Thatcher to agree to join. Lawson demanded that Thatcher dismiss her adviser. When she refused, Lawson resigned – though Walters also resigned immediately afterwards.

What of the cabinet itself? By late 1990 no one talked of 'wets' and 'dries'. Thatcher's most bitter opponents in Cabinet – Pym, Prior, Gilmour and Soames – had gone, but so had her most fiercely loyal supporters – Tebbit and Ridley. There was a technocratic flavour to Thatcher's last government. In the acknowledgements to *Britain Can Work* – his anti-Thatcherite tract of 1983 – Gilmour had thanked three Tory MPs. By 1989 all three of them were in the government,[11] and one was in the cabinet. This did not mean that they had changed their views or that Thatcher had changed hers; it simply showed that senior Conservatives had in large measure given up discussing what their policies ought to be and now dedicated their energies to seeing how policies might be implemented and sold to the public.

Increasingly ministers were chosen because of their perceived competence rather than because of their ideological sympathy. For much of the later 1980s, Thatcher's favourite minister was David Young. Young had trained as a solicitor and then made a fortune in business. He was closer to being one of Thatcher's advisers than he was to being an ordinary minister – he had been parachuted into the House of Lords without having held a seat in the Commons. He entered the cabinet in 1984 and became secretary of state for trade and industry in 1987. Thatcher said of him: 'Others bring me problems; David brings me solutions.' In practice the 'solution' that Young preached most fervently was 'enterprise', which on close examination turned out to mean producing a lot of expensive advertisements to show how companies would flourish if they were given a certain indefinable 'whosh' that would be imparted by reading glossy brochures from the DTI, itself briefly renamed the Department of Enterprise. Young resigned to pursue his own business interests in July 1989. His place as Thatcher's favourite purveyor of 'solutions' was taken by Kenneth Baker. Baker had entered the cabinet in 1985 and become chairman of the Conservative Party in July 1989. 'Technology' had for a time been his own magic cure for the nation's ills, and, in the early 1980s, whilst the battles over monetarism raged in cabinet, Baker had invented a job for himself as minister for technology and spent much of his time getting photographed with clumsy-looking pre-Amstrad computers.

By the time Thatcher resigned, Douglas Hurd was the longest-serving member of her cabinet. The son and grandson of Tory MPs, Hurd had been educated at Eton and Trinity College Cambridge, joined the Foreign Office and then worked for Edward Heath before entering parliament in 1974. He was associated with those who wanted to modernize the Conservative Party (such as his friend Chris Patten) whilst also thinking of himself as rooted in the traditional values of Anglicanism (he was one of the few senior Tories who cared about the Church) and rural England. On a personal level he did not much like the new men who began to rise up the Conservative Party under Thatcher: 'stiff-collared accountants from Stratford on Avon'.[8] Hurd's position, however, might better be characterized as 'post-Thatcherite' than 'anti-Thatcherite'. He entered parliament shortly before Thatcher took over the party and he joined the cabinet only after Thatcher and her allies had won the economic debates of the early 1980s. He had sympathized with the 'wets' and advised Ian Gilmour to resign rather than wait to be sacked. Hurd himself, however, never seems to have contemplated resignation. He worked within the Thatcherite order, sometimes achieving concessions by stealth rather than confrontation. The fact that he never held a position in an economic ministry kept him out of the firing line, and he seems to have found it useful to cultivate the impression that he knew nothing of economics – though his business career since leaving politics suggests that he was not as innocent as he liked to pretend.

Thatcher's last appointments were all men who could at best be seen as efficient implementers of her policy rather than passionate believers in her vision. Tony Newton, who took over Social Security in July 1989, or Chris Patten, who became secretary of state for the environment in the same month, were known to be on the Left of the party. Thatcher's last appointment of all – William Waldegrave – was also seen as being on the Left, though he managed to maintain good relations with both Enoch Powell and Edward Heath. He was an old Etonian fellow of All Souls from an aristocratic family, who had once been engaged to Lord Rothschild's daughter. It looked as though the ghost of Ian Gilmour had come back to haunt the cabinet table – though Thatcher described Waldegrave as 'a sort of Norman St John-Stevas without jokes'.[9]

Thatcher's own view of her ministerial colleagues was an odd one. She could be a bully. Paddy Ashdown recorded her behaviour at the ceremony of remembrance in November 1988 in his diary: 'Maggie fussed around, bullied us into two lines ... then she proceeded to go down the lined-up Cabinet like a sergeant major, inspecting new recruits, straightening the Foreign Secretary's tie, flicking specks of dust off the Chancellor's coat etc.'[10]

Thatcher was not always able or willing to reward loyalty. She had made, and then disposed of, a succession of protégés. Cecil Parkinson had once been her favourite, but she had not been able to keep him in her government after it was revealed, in 1983, that he had broken a promise to marry his pregnant mistress. Parkinson came back to the cabinet in 1987, but he was now badly weakened. A man who might once have been chancellor or foreign secretary had to content himself with being secretary of state for energy and then transport. Furthermore, Parkinson's behaviour – his undignified return to his wife rather than his original affair – had made him look ridiculous, even in the eyes of his admirers. Parkinson knew that he had nothing going for him except Thatcher's affection. He did not try to stay in the cabinet after her resignation.

Tebbit too had been weakened by personal misfortune. He had been injured in the IRA attack at Brighton in 1984, which had left his wife crippled. After this, he had less energy for politics and, having returned to the front-rank as chairman of the party, he stepped down in 1987. Tebbit remained loyal to Thatcher – though some Tories had the uncomfortable sense that she, always dubious about any minister with an independent power base, was not completely loyal to him. Tebbit refused Thatcher's invitation to rejoin her cabinet, as education secretary, in early November 1990.

Other men rose and fell with disconcerting speed. Leon Brittan had owed his rise largely to Thatcher's favour. He had entered the cabinet, as chief secretary to the treasury in 1981, just seven years after being elected to parliament. Two years later, he was home secretary. He had seemed almost slavish in his willingness to do the bidding of his mistress – solemnly repeating her absurd view that people who refused to denounce terrorism in Ulster should be 'denied the oxygen of publicity' and calling for the restoration of the death penalty, when many believed that he was privately against it. However, Thatcher demoted Brittan as soon as he seemed to fail at the

Home Office, and then sacrificed him during the Westland crisis of early 1986. John Moore was the next minister to rise on the strength of Thatcher's patronage, and was talked of as a possible successor. He too entered the Commons in 1974, joined the cabinet as minister for transport in 1986 and became minister for health and social security in the following year. However, the health part of his portfolio was taken away from him after just over a year, and a year after that he was out of the cabinet for good.

Ministers were moved around like pawns on a chess board. John Major, Thatcher's last protégé and the one who had the dubious good fortune of holding the parcel when the music stopped, rose from almost nowhere to occupy two of the most important offices of state (foreign secretary and then chancellor of the exchequer) in the space of less than six months. Thatcher did not like being reminded of her own political mortality and, for this reason, being her anointed dauphin was always an uncomfortable position. She constantly implied that the only potential heirs were 'not ready yet'. In her memoirs, she claimed that she had become convinced that her successor must be drawn from a generation younger than her own, but her definition of 'young' in this context was arbitrary – the 'younger generation' included Hurd (born in 1930) but not Heseltine (born in 1933).[11]

Two politicians had partly alleviated the impact of Thatcher's isolation. William Whitelaw was useful to her because he possessed the qualities that she lacked. He was popular and well connected in the party and particularly close to those sections of it – aristocrats, Heathites and people with liberal views on law and order – who sometimes felt estranged from Thatcher. He was suspicious of ideology and good at listening to people. On the other hand, he was also a man with a strong sense of duty to the leader, as he had shown in 1974, and, at least after the Falklands War, he never seems to have considered supporting any move to dislodge Thatcher. He was the only major politician who could argue with Thatcher without making her doubt his loyalty, and he saw it as his job to head off dangerous initiatives and to maintain amicable working relations between ministers. Whitelaw, however, was ill and old. He went into the House of Lords in 1983, and withdrew from the cabinet in 1988.

Much was also made of Ian Gow. Gow, born in 1937, sometimes seemed to be a caricature of a particular kind of Tory MP. When he first stood for parliament in 1966, *The Times* wrote that he wore his 'public school manner as prominently as his rosette'.[12] He had, like Whitelaw and many of Thatcher's associates, been educated at Winchester. He had performed his national service in the cavalry, and then worked as a solicitor at Joynson-Hicks (a firm founded by a Conservative Home Secretary who had himself been something of a caricature). Gow was Thatcher's parliamentary private secretary from 1979 to 1983 and served as a link between her and the Conservative back benches – planting questions, massaging egos and keeping an eye on potential opposition. As a Powellite free marketeer, he was sympathetic to the government's aims and he was fiercely loyal to Thatcher personally. Gow, however, ceased to be Thatcher's parliamentary private secretary in 1983 and took office as a junior minister, first for housing and construction and then at the Treasury. He resigned from the government in 1985, in protest at the Anglo-Irish agreement. On 30 July 1990 he was killed by an IRA bomb that had been planted under his car.

Some thought that Gow's political antennae would have saved Thatcher from some of the faux pas that she made during her last two years in office, and, particularly, that he might have healed the rift between her and Geoffrey Howe – Gow was a friend of Howe and had managed his leadership bid in 1975. However, it is hard to see how Gow could have remained as Thatcher's parliamentary private secretary for ever, and his access to the prime minister had always depended on holding this post. Personal friendship might have healed the Thatcher/Howe rift but it is equally possible that Gow's own Eurosceptic opinions would have made things worse, or that his loyalty would simply have made Thatcher more impervious to criticism. It is not, in any case, clear what Gow would have wanted to do. In May 1990 Alan Clark and Gow talked in the smoking room of the House of Commons. After the conversation, Clark wrote in his diary: 'What could we do to succour the Lady? Do we even want to?'[13] In one sense at least, Gow's assassination certainly damaged Thatcher: it brought a by-election at Eastbourne in October 1990, which the Tories lost.

All of this tied in with wider problems that afflicted the Conservatives during their last few years in power. The first of these, discussed in a previous chapter, was Europe. Within a few years, the role of Europe in British electoral politics was turned on its head. It went from being an issue that gave the, mainly pro-European, Conservatives an advantage over a divided Labour Party to being an issue that divided the Conservatives themselves. Disputes over Europe underlay the resignations of Nigel Lawson in 1989 and Geoffrey Howe in 1990. These resignations were bad blows. Both men made carefully judged resignation speeches in the House of Commons that were designed to damage Thatcher. Howe's speech contained the line 'It is now time for others to consider their own response to the tragic conflict of loyalties with which I myself have wrestled perhaps for too long.' It was hard to interpret this as anything other than a call for Thatcher's removal from office.

The changing role of Europe in British politics was in part linked to the fact that the European Community of 1989 was different from that of 1979. However, it was not inevitable that these changes would have the particular impact that they did on the Conservative Party nor that they should prove so damaging to

Thatcher's position. After all, Thatcher had gone along with the Single European Act and the possibility of British entry into the European Exchange Rate Mechanism. What annoyed her pro-European colleagues was the tone of her remarks, especially those she made off-the-cuff, rather than the specific policies she advocated.

The second problem that afflicted the Tories was public service reform, particularly of the National Health Service. The cost of health care was increasing (because of ever more expensive treatments and an ageing population) and the difficulty of managing health care costs would have faced any government in the late 1980s. However, health was a difficult issue for a right-wing Conservative government, for the same reasons that defence had been a difficult issue for a left-wing Labour Party. The electorate was likely to suspect that any move to control costs reflected a lack of commitment to fund the service at all. The appointment of Kenneth Clarke as secretary of state for health in July 1988 did not make things any easier. Thatcher recognized that Clarke was not on her wing of the party but argued that he was 'an energetic and persuasive bruiser, very useful in a brawl or an election'.[14] She might have added that Clarke's breezy bad manners made him an awkward man to have on your side if you were trying to explain the need for complicated reform of a popular public service. In 1988 ambulance crews struck for higher pay. It was probably the first major strike to attract wide public support since 1972; Clarke's tone, and particularly his description of the strikers as 'glorified taxi drivers', grated.

The third problem for the government in the late 1980s was local government finance. Money for local government had been raised by charging home owners and businessmen 'rates' in proportion to the value of the property that they owned. Thatcher, and some of her supporters, had always disliked the rates, believing them to be unfair because only part of the population paid (especially unfair because ratepayers were likely to be drawn from 'our people'). Thatcher was deeply rooted in the politics of municipal resentment – her own father had represented a ratepayers' alliance in Grantham.

Resentment of the rates was nothing new in the Conservative Party. There was much talk of 'little old ladies' living on their own who paid the same rates as large families living next door to them – this talk was particularly common in Tory constituency associations, which tended to contain a lot of old ladies.[15] Various alternatives to the rates had been discussed, but nothing had come of them. Thatcher had talked of abolition during the general election of October 1974, but, when she got into power, she was in no hurry to act in this matter. When Michael Heseltine said in 1979 that the revaluation of rateable properties would generate discontent, Thatcher briskly responded that the way to avoid this was not to revalue.[16]

Pressure to do something about the rates came partly from Tories in Scotland, where legislation made it impossible to defer the revaluation of property beyond the mid-1980s. Reform of the rates also became part of a more general struggle between the government and Labour-controlled local councils. The government disliked the profligacy of councils, especially when that profligacy involved support for left-wing causes. The conflict had all sorts of fall-out. The metropolitan counties and the Greater London Council, the latter led by Ken Livingstone, were abolished in 1986. The government also began to 'cap' rates in a bid to contain local government spending and this brought it into conflict with some councils that simply refused to set rates.

Some wanted to abolish the rates and replace them with a flat-rate direct local tax that would be paid by all adults. New arrangements were bound to be expensive and bureaucratic. There was, in fact, something ominously Heathite about the whole discussion of local government finance. Indeed, the key advice was given by a group of civil servants, ministers and advisers – notably, William Waldegrave, Anthony Mayer and Victor Rothschild – who had first worked together in Heath's think tank. It was never entirely clear that the various advisers entirely believed in their own proposals. Some of them seem simply to have relished the challenge of grappling with a complex problem but not to have considered the political consequences of their proposal.[17]

Thatcher was initially sceptical about reform, but, in 1985, she finally agreed to the proposal for a new tax (soon to be known as the 'community charge' and to be christened by its enemies as the 'poll tax'). From then on, Thatcher embraced the new scheme with enthusiasm. Some of her younger and less obviously ideological ministers seem to have promoted it because they thought that doing so would demonstrate their loyalty to the prime minister. Opposition often came from the battle-hardened veterans of the first Thatcher government. Lawson hated the poll tax. It brought new people into the tax system when he was trying to take them out, it introduced new complexities when he was trying to simplify, and it seemed likely that the whole thing would end up costing central government money (first to pay for establishing the new scheme and then to provide subsidies that would alleviate its effects). Biffen, a man whose dislike of complicated novelties was even greater than Lawson's, found it hard to disguise his disdain as he 'defended' the proposal in the House of Commons.[18]

The poll tax illustrated the curious disintegration of the Thatcher government. Her early cabinets had been characterized by simplicity and clarity of thought. They focused on the essentials and they did not get into fights that could not be won. They avoided complicated legislation that would be difficult to enforce – Norman Tebbit had once remarked that the key aim of his trade union legislation was to *prevent* any trade unionist from having an excuse to get himself locked up. After 1985, and even more after 1987, ministers got buried in a complicated and messy legislative programme. A new law appeared to be the response to any problem. When a madman opened fire in Hungerford, the government introduced new restrictions on the possession of firearms – a measure calculated to annoy millions of rural Tories. When it emerged that a couple of old men who might once have been concentration camp guards were living in Scotland, the government introduced a war crimes bill – a retroactive measure that was bound to disturb Conservative lawyers. Thatcher's hyperactivity became a source of derision – one journalist claimed that he carried a card saying: 'In the event of an accident, I do not wish to be visited by the Prime Minister.'

Legislating for the poll tax was a long and wearing process. There was a bill for Scotland, introduced at the end of 1986, and one for England and Wales, introduced at the end of 1987. Many Tory MPs had doubts. Michael Heseltine, who had walked out of the cabinet on another issue minutes before it was due to endorse the poll tax in January 1986, was one of those who voted against its implementation in England. Whips twisted arms, called in favours and, in doing so, stoked up a mood of ill-will and confusion. Tory peers had to be dragged away from their estates to vote the measure through the House of Lords. In the end, the tax was introduced in Scotland in April 1989; it came to England and Wales a year later.

The poll tax had particularly awkward consequences for the Tories. Opponents of the tax rioted. Magistrates sent people to prison for refusal to pay – though the law surrounding such punishments was complicated and many sentences were overturned on appeal. The demonstrations and riots were not in themselves important. They involved a relatively small group of people and one that was not, in any case, likely to vote Tory, or to vote at all. Labour leaders feared that violent protests might in fact damage the Left. More importantly, the tax provoked discontent amongst middle-class people; Chris Patten described it as a 'heat-seeking missile aimed at voters in marginal constituencies'.[19] It annoyed the kind of self-righteous people who are liable to write letters to the authorities – often, one suspects, the same 'little old ladies' who had previously complained about the rates. Tory MPs found themselves buried under a deluge of correspondence, much of which required specific and detailed answers. The Tory chief whip had to deal with one of Thatcher's most loyal backbenchers, who was worried about the impact of the tax in Surrey, and had to explain to another irate MP why the tax in Spelthorne was more than twice as high as it was in neighbouring Slough.[20]

No amount of muttering in the tea room of the House of Commons would have had any effect on Thatcher's position if no one had been willing to stand against her. Technically, leaders of the Conservative Party were required to submit themselves for reelection every year; in practice, no other candidate had put themselves forward during Thatcher's first fourteen years in the post. In the autumn of 1989 this changed. Sir Anthony Meyer announced that he would challenge Margaret Thatcher. Meyer was a little-known MP from Wales who gave the impression of being a character escaped from *A Dance to the Music of Time,* an impression strengthened by his heroic lack of contrition when the press revealed that he had conducted a twenty-five-year affair with the jazz singer Simone Washington. His background and style evoked the world of patrician superiority that so exasperated some Thatcherites. He was formed by Eton (his father turned down a scholarship to prevent him from being corrupted by contact with clever boys), Oxford, the Guards (he was badly wounded in 1944) and the Foreign Office. Meyer came to play up to his upper-class image. He described his visit to Cecil Parkinson, when the latter was chairman of the Conservative Party and was trying to persuade Meyer to stand down as a parliamentary candidate, thus:

> I have to say that I felt as if I had strayed into the servants' hall of a not very well run stately home, rather than the nerve centre of a great political party at a critical stage in its battle for supremacy. I also reflected on how very differently Lord Thorneycroft, the previous Party Chairman, would have handled the interview with me. I am sure he would have had me round to lunch at Whites, oysters and champagne, a lot of talk

about how he was sure I would understand the needs of the Party at a time like this, a vague suggestion that there would be all sorts of ways in which I could render great service to the state in some other place, and would have come away from the lunch, quite possibly having agreed to stand down, or, if not, feeling that I was behaving like a cad.[21]

Meyer saw himself as being on the liberal end of the Conservative Party. He had, however, supported the economic policies of the government during the early 1980s, and he expressed misgivings about government economic policy (or at least about its social consequences) only after other issues had alienated him from the bulk of the Conservative Party. The turning point of his career was the Falklands War. He was one of the few MPs to speak out against the war. He despised the jingoism of the House of Commons – though he seems to have been more concerned about the fate of Lord Carrington than that of Welsh Guardsmen or Argentine conscripts.

After the Falklands, Meyer was increasingly recognized as an awkward MP by Tory whips, who would probably not have been sorry to see him lose his seat in parliament. European unity had always been the political cause closest to Meyer's heart and, as Thatcher's tone became increasingly anti-European, he became increasingly anti-Thatcher. Meyer's criticisms of the prime minister were couched in a code of transparently insincere loyalty that anyone in Westminster could have cracked. He invited her to pay homage to the memory of Jean Monnet, or to celebrate the measures that Peter Walker, the last supporter of government economic intervention left in the cabinet, was taking to revive the Welsh economy.[22]

In himself, Meyer posed no threat to Thatcher. He was not a serious candidate for high office, he had no following in the parliamentary party and he was unknown to the general public. During the Westland crisis, the Thatcher loyalist George Gardiner had sarcastically offered to sign the nomination papers if Meyer ran against the prime minister. In the very different context of the autumn of 1989, however, Meyer was more dangerous. His very obscurity meant that the choice between him and Thatcher was all the more stark. This was not an election that pitted two rival candidates or rival programmes against each other. The thirty-three MPs[23] who voted for Meyer were, in effect, saying 'anyone but Thatcher'.

The real, though undeclared, rival to Margaret Thatcher was Michael Heseltine. Heseltine, a flamboyant and famously ambitious man, had made a fortune in publishing and property before establishing a reputation as an effective minister and barnstorming performer at Conservative Party conferences. Thatcher had remarked privately in the early 1970s that Heseltine had 'everything that it takes to succeed in politics except brains'.[24] It was widely said that he had, as an undergraduate at Oxford, sketched a career plan on a restaurant menu. The plan involved becoming a millionaire in the 1960s and a cabinet minister in the 1970s before becoming prime minister in the 1990s.[25]

Heseltine, who had been secretary of state for defence since January 1983, resigned from the cabinet on 9 January 1986 over the fate of the Westland helicopter company. Westland was in financial trouble, and its management were keen to sell a stake to the American Sikorsky company. Heseltine suddenly took an interest in this comparatively small operation. He wanted Westland to join a consortium of European manufacturers and he tried to persuade a group of European 'National Armaments Directors' (i.e. officials responsible for buying weapons) that non-European manufacturers should be excluded from future European purchases. This produced a bitter argument between him and Thatcher, which also came to involve Leon Brittan, who, as secretary of state for trade and industry, was responsible for authorizing the takeover.

What was the dispute about? Heseltine favoured European integration. He also sometimes seemed to be interested in a policy of industrial intervention (the cabinet position that he most coveted, after that of prime minister, was trade and industry). However, this was not really a dispute that divided the cabinet on such lines – Norman Tebbit, one of the anti-European and anti-interventionist ministers, was initially sympathetic to Heseltine's proposal. Nor was it really, as Heseltine liked to claim, a dispute about the collective responsibility of the cabinet – collective responsibility imposes obligations on ministers but does not give them rights, and in any case almost all cabinet ministers seem to have concluded that Heseltine's 'European option' was just not realistic. The points on which Heseltine was subsequently able to embarrass Thatcher, and which almost brought her downfall, involved nice questions of constitutional procedure. A civil servant leaked a letter from the solicitor general to Heseltine, and thus breeched the convention that the advice of law officers to ministers should remain secret, and Leon Brittan denied having received a letter from the chairman of British Aerospace, thus opening him to the charge of having misled the House of Commons. Brittan was forced to resign and for a brief period Thatcher feared that she would have to do the same.

Westland was not significant because it raised important issues, but rather because it showed how the Thatcher government was increasingly vulnerable to the damage caused by comparatively trivial matters. Thatcher and her allies would have won the debate in cabinet easily if they had been more patient. They could probably have damaged Heseltine if they had allowed him to pursue his 'European option'. Instead Westland showed the prime minister's impatience, her tendency to use civil servants and advisers against ministers whom she regarded as disloyal (there was much dark muttering about the role of Bernard Ingham during the Westland affair) and her inability to help ministers, such as Brittan, who had been loyal.

Heseltine did not call for Thatcher's resignation after Westland (the only Tory MP to do so was Anthony Meyer), and he ostentatiously voted in the government lobbies during the vote of confidence that was moved by the opposition in the aftermath of the affair. For the next four years, Heseltine was to insist that he 'could not foresee the circumstances' under which he might challenge Margaret Thatcher for the leadership of the party.

Being a very rich man (he even took his ministerial driver with him when he resigned), Heseltine could afford to conduct a long private campaign to maintain his reputation in the Conservative Party. He addressed endless constituency associations (108 of them during the 1987 election campaign) and wrote a couple of worthy books. Michael Mates and Keith Hampson became unofficial parliamentary private secretaries and fixers for Heseltine in the House of Commons.

But Heseltine was in an awkward position. His links with those who had remained in the cabinet were weak. He was not a clubbable man and was actively disliked by some powerful ministers. Whitelaw, probably the man who most resented Heseltine's habit of wearing a Brigade tie on the strength of a few months' national service with the Welsh Guards, was an enemy. After his own resignation, Geoffrey Howe rebuffed an approach from Heseltine. Heseltine's resignation looked bad – probably even worse to those who believed Heseltine's own story that it was carried out in a moment of spontaneous exasperation than to those who assumed that it was a calculated challenge to the prime minister. Heseltine was also acutely aware that the Tory rank and file valued loyalty and would not forgive him for an open challenge to the leader. A Tory whip commented on his 'delicate balancing act between rebellion and oblivion'.[26] Heseltine summed up his dilemma with the phrase: 'He who wields the dagger never wears the crown.'

Michael Heseltine did not publicly support Meyer's candidacy and abstained in the vote on the leadership in 1989 – though one of his associates did talk to Meyer, apparently without Heseltine's authorization. Heseltine's enemies argued that he was seeking to damage Thatcher, in the hope that she would resign, whilst not being willing to take her on directly. An article in *The Times,* which Heseltine believed to have been inspired by Ingham, said that he should 'either put up or shut up'. Heseltine felt that such accusations were damaging him. Like Meyer before him, he also seems to have been annoyed by the belief that his enemies had agitated in his own constituency. Quite large parts of his account of the events leading to his decision to stand involve the machinations of obscure people in Henley-on-Thames rather than politicians in Westminster. Finally, on the day after Howe's resignation speech of 13 November, Heseltine announced: 'I am persuaded that I would now have a better prospect than Mrs Thatcher of leading the Conservatives to a fourth electoral victory and preventing the ultimate calamity of a Labour government.'

Thatcher responded badly to the challenge. Her campaign, which had been so well organized in 1975, was inept in 1990. George Younger was nominally the leader of Thatcher's campaign but was distracted by his business commitments. Norman Tebbit became recognized as the real leader – though he was hardly the man to draw together a broad coalition and though, like other senior Tories, he seems by this stage to have been more interested in stopping Heseltine than preserving Thatcher.[27] Peter Morrison was Thatcher's parliamentary private secretary. A wealthy man from an established political family (his father and brother had both supported Heath against Thatcher in 1975), he was not well equipped for the kind of street-fighting that his mistress needed in 1990. He seems to have pursued his canvassing of MPs with remarkably little vigour. He told Thatcher that 'if you have not won then an awful lot of Conservative MPs are lying' – a remark that will live on in the annals of political naïvety.[28]

Some blamed Thatcher for going to attend a meeting of leaders of industrial powers in Paris at a crucial moment when Heseltine was campaigning vigorously. This probably misunderstands Thatcher's nature. She had won the leadership when fighting as an outsider against an aloof and unpopular leader, but she was not the kind of person who could have won MPs over with displays of intimacy and bonhomie in 1990.

In any case, the notion that getting the extra few votes to give her an absolute majority in the first round of the leadership election would have saved Margaret Thatcher is far-fetched. She would have been wounded by the leadership election under any circumstances and would almost certainly have found it impossible to restore her fortunes afterwards. Indeed, Heseltine's campaign manager – Michael Mates – was later to reproach himself for having missed a trick by not having his candidate withdraw after the first round. If Heseltine had done this, he would have looked gracious, and he would have denied other candidates the chance to compete in the second round. However, he would not in reality have saved Margaret Thatcher. She would have limped on for a few months before being finished off when the next crisis made the Conservative Party nervous.

In truth, Margaret Thatcher's authority was ebbing away in 1990 for reasons that were only partially linked to the electoral arithmetic behind a formal leadership bid. A parliamentary party with a large majority is, almost by definition, nervous, because it contains many MPs who represent relatively marginal seats. In addition to this, the social changes of the 1980s created problems. The cost of bourgeois life had increased (school fees were an object of special concern to many Tory MPs), but the means that MPs had to pay for such a life diminished. Relatively few of them now had private incomes; the new professionalism and urgency of business life made it harder to combine a career in parliament with one in the City or at the Bar. Most Conservatives lived on their salary, their parliamentary allowances and (in many cases) on business activities that involved peddling political influence. Some of the new-style Tories would have found it hard to make a living outside Westminster. Such men were frightened at the thought that the next election must occur no later than 1992, and that public opinion polls were turning against them.

Lack of faith in Thatcher acquired a circular quality. Once Tory MPs began to feel that Thatcher would not last, then their thoughts increasingly turned to the question of who would be her successor. The prime minister's powers of patronage disappeared when no one believed that she would be able to exercise them in the long term.[29] This ebbing of support was illustrated by Alan Clark. Thatcher recalls a slightly farcical meeting with him after the first round of the leadership contest, in which he told her that she should fight on – not because she could win but because 'it was better to go out in a blaze of glorious defeat than to go gentle into that good night.' She does not seem to have taken Clark very seriously; she likened the meeting to the porter's scene in Macbeth, but she was glad 'to have someone unambiguously on my side even in defeat'.[30]

In reality, there was nothing 'unambiguous' about Clark's support for Thatcher. As early as April 1990 he had doubted whether she ought to stay on. The month before her fall, he had encouraged Douglas Hurd to put himself forward as Thatcher's replacement.[31] Clark was almost obsessively concerned with prime ministerial powers of patronage. When Carla Powell, a significant figure in Thatcher's personal court, asked for his help in reversing the dismissal of Bruce Anderson, a journalist on the *Daily Telegraph,* Clark said: 'we were all in limbo. No one, not even Mrs T herself could today cut any ice at all with anyone.'[32] Clark worried about the impact that a new prime minister would have on his career – on whether he would get into the cabinet, whether he would get on to the Privy Council, whether he would get a knighthood.

Clark got none of the things he desired – a more realistic man might have understood that he had actually been lucky to achieve office as a junior minister. In such circumstances, it is hardly surprising that cabinet ministers, who really did have something to lose, were reluctant to stand at the salute on the sinking battleship of HMS Thatcher. The only unqualified support for the prime minister came from those political kamikazes – Ridley and Powell – whose political careers were already destroyed.

Thatcher saw the leadership contest as a matter of 'loyalty', but loyalty could mean more than one thing. Some who respected Thatcher personally had reached the point when they genuinely believed that her own reputation would suffer if she stayed in office. Many put loyalty to the party, and particularly to its election prospects, above loyalty to its leader. Rank-and-file Tory members had much influence on the MPs who represented them, and opinions amongst this group were more complicated than the orchestrated displays of enthusiasm at the annual conference made them appear. Most members of the Conservative Party were old; they understood that the party had existed before Thatcher and hoped that it would exist after her. It is significant that members of the Conservative Party seem to have been especially loyal to John Major in the early 1990s, at the very moment when Thatcher was beginning to regard him as a 'traitor'.[33] Conservatives were reluctant to express their concerns in public – for reasons that may have been linked to feelings about good form as much as calculation of personal interest. George Walden conducted an interesting experiment. He asked his constituency officers in Buckinghamshire for a show of hands over whether Thatcher should stay. Most said that she should. He then approached those who had voted in favour of Thatcher and asked them their private opinions: three quarters said that she should go.[34]

After the first round of the leadership contest (in which Thatcher got 204 votes and Heseltine got 152), Thatcher consulted her cabinet colleagues. Almost all of them said, with various nuances, that they would support her if she maintained her candidature, but that they thought it unlikely that she could win. She was later to rage at the betrayal involved in the polite formula. Hurd, Waldegrave and Baker were amongst the very few ministers who left a favourable impression. It does not seem to have occurred to Thatcher that all three of these men had been intimates of Edward Heath, and consequently had some experience in handling a defeated leader who felt bitter at 'betrayal'.

The defeat for Thatcher was not a defeat for the policies that had been espoused by the early Thatcher governments. Even Anthony Meyer, who had been a critic of the Thatcher government since 1982, stressed that he was favourable to much of its economic and social legacy. Heseltine had served in the Thatcher governments for seven years and never implied that he regretted much that he had done in that position. The two people whose resignations did most to bring Thatcher down – Lawson and Howe – were both Thatcherites *de la première heure.* Will Hopper, a former member of the European parliament, who had supported the chancellor over the 1981 budget, urged Howe to make a leadership bid in 1990, precisely in order to make it clear that opposition to Thatcher was not a 'wet European thing', but that it went with a restoration of the austere virtues of the first Thatcher government.[35] No one suggested that overthrowing Thatcher should go with reversing her government's policy on trade unions, the sale of council houses, the promotion of the free market or privatization: John

Wakeham was distracted from his duties in the Thatcher leadership campaign team partly by his efforts to privatize the electricity companies.

Thatcher's opponents sometimes disliked the poll tax – though this was hardly, except in Thatcher's own mind, a matter of great principle. Europe was a more substantial issue (the only matter of policy that was mentioned at all in Heseltine's declaration of his intention to stand for the leadership of the party). However, this too was hardly a matter on which policy differences brought Thatcher down. Her opponents were themselves divided on matters such as the desirability of a single currency. Only opposition to Thatcher united them, and this opposition was aroused more by her tone than by any concrete proposal that she made.

In a curious way, Thatcher's fall might be interpreted as a sign that Thatcherism had succeeded. She was a natural leader at a time of conflict. Her image was burnished at the height of the Cold War. She had challenged the leader of her own party at a time when no one else dared to do so and fought for four years against a Labour government. She had persisted with unpopular policies in the early 1980s, led her country in a war and denounced the 'enemies within'. Her success had changed the very circumstances that had once made her supporters regard her as uniquely useful. By the time she resigned, Soviet troops were pulling out of Eastern Europe, the National Union of Mineworkers was broken and over a million council houses had been sold. The problem for this unconsensual politician was that she had created a new consensus.

CONCLUSION

Is it serious or is it just the usual wank?

William Shelton, junior education minister, to Ferdinand
Mount, head of Number 10 Policy Unit[1]

William Shelton was, by any definition, a Thatcherite. He was a monetarist who had despaired during the last years of the Heath government. He was one of just two MPs whose support Margaret Thatcher knew she could rely on when she first declared her candidacy for the leadership of the Conservative Party in 1975.[2] The fact that such a man could also see that many individual policies of the Thatcher government were silly, contradictory or unoriginal does not mean that he did not also recognize that there was some overall thrust behind the Thatcher government which made it, in his eyes, worthwhile. In short, Shelton recognized that the frequently drawn contrast between the Thatcher government as an ideologically driven revolution and the Thatcher government as just another piece of Tory 'statecraft' is misleading. There were always elements of both, and the fact that Thatcherism was often mythologized, by its most unworldly supporters as well as by its bitterest enemies, does not mean that it was a myth.

What did Thatcherites themselves mean by Thatcherism? Nigel Lawson gave a speech on

Thatcherism to Swiss bankers in 1981, which in his memoirs he recalled thus:

> Thatcherism is, I believe, a useful term, and certainly was at the time. No other modern Prime Minister has given his or her name to a particular constellation of policies and values. However, it needs to be used with care ... The right definition involves a mixture of free markets, financial discipline, firm control over public expenditure, tax cuts, nationalism, 'Victorian values' (of the Samuel Smiles self-help variety), privatization and a dash of populism.[3]

Lawson's definition of Thatcherism is revealing. He mentions privatization, which hardly featured in the 1979 manifesto and was not much practised until after the 1983 election, and 'Victorian values' – a phrase that was coined by a television interviewer and only really used by Thatcherites themselves for a few months in 1983. His 1992 definition, on the other hand, makes no mention of monetarism, though this would have been seen as a crucial aspect of Thatcherism until at least 1982 and Lawson's lecture of 1981 had in fact been mainly about control of the money supply. As for populism, no one would deny that it was an element of Thatcherism – though a paper that Lawson had helped draft in 1978 came close to suggesting that populism and the practice of free-market economics might prove mutually exclusive.[4] Neither in 1981 nor in 1992 did Lawson mention the issue that many came to define as central to Thatcherism, and that eventually produced the rift between Lawson himself and Thatcher: Europe.

One might argue that there were really several different Thatcherite projects and that they overlapped only to a limited extent. Before the 1979 election, Thatcherism meant, in large measure, certain attitudes to crime, race and disorder. It was known that powerful Conservatives were monetarists, but it was not clear how far the party leader had embraced this doctrine or how far it would be applied in government. After the 1979 election, the focus on a particular kind of economic policy became so intense that many commentators talked as though monetarism was a synonym for Thatcherism. After the 1983 election, monetarism was discussed less. Privatization played an increasing role in the government's image, as did the booming stock market. After 1988, and even more after 1990, Thatcherism was increasingly interpreted as meaning opposition to Britain's further integration into Europe – though, in fact, some prominent people associated with early Thatcherism supported such integration.

Does all this mean that, as some came to argue, there was no continuity or coherence in Thatcherism? There is a peculiar risk that a political phenomenon will be dismissed because of its success. If Margaret Thatcher had been forced to resign in 1981, then historians would find it easier to agree on what her government stood for. The very fact that the government remained in power for so long meant that it was bound to encounter new problems, to adjust to circumstances and to seem 'inconsistent'.

Underneath the tactical adjustments, however, it is possible to discern certain general themes in the Thatcher government. It sought to promote the free market, to reduce public spending (or at least to reduce its rate of increase) and to place the control of inflation above that of unemployment. Economics was at the core of Thatcherism – this explains why Thatcher always placed her allies in economic ministries while being less concerned with who occupied, for example, the Home Office; it also explains how a man like Geoffrey Howe, who disagreed with Thatcher on many areas of social and foreign policy, could still think of himself as a Thatcherite. It would, however, be wrong to assume that Thatcherism was just about economics or that economics could be entirely separated from other elements of the project. A concern for 'order' or 'discipline' was discernible in almost everything the Thatcher governments did and to some extent this concern transcended the division between economic and non-economic policies. Dealing with strikes and trade unions, to take an obvious example, can be seen as both an attempt to re-establish order (something that should be placed alongside Thatcherite concern with crime), and as an attempt to make the economy more productive. It is true that there was nothing particularly new or distinctive about many broad aims of Thatcherite economic policies. T.E. Utley argued in 1986: 'Her two major achievements – the control of inflation and the reduction of the trade unions to size – were simply the climax of a series of unsuccessful attempts by Labour and Tory governments alike to cope with what were increasingly seen as the two most important evils from which the country was suffering.'[5] There were, however, two distinct novelties. First, the techniques by which the Thatcher government tackled both inflation and labour relations – particularly its refusal to use formal pay controls – were different from those used by governments in the 1970s. Secondly, and crucially, there is a difference between governments that *try* to do things and governments that *do* things, especially when they do things over a long period of time, as in the case of the Thatcher government.

THATCHERITE MORALITY

During the 1970s both Thatcher's supporters and her opponents understood that the political battle was not likely to be won or lost entirely, or even mainly, through debates on economics.[6] Discussions of electoral strategy in the shadow cabinet made much of immigration, crime and patriotism. Thatcher's opponents sometimes argued that Thatcherism needed to be understood as part of a larger movement that took in Enoch Powell's attitudes to race and the views of Mary Whitehouse on sexual morality.[7]

The rejection of progressive 'Keynesian' conservatism was therefore also accompanied by ... marked hardening of the party's attitudes on questions of immigration, law and order and the family. From a feminist perspective the Thatcherite project was very successful in exploiting gender and race issues to win popular support for its wider programme.[8]

Sexual morality intersected with the discussion of other political issues in all sorts of peculiar ways during the 1980s. The feminists who campaigned against nuclear weapons at the Greenham Common airbase were pitched against Lady Olga Maitland's Families for Defence. Supporters of striking miners made much of the transformation of women's status that was alleged to have taken place in pit villages during the strike; whilst the Union of Democratic Miners (which represented men who had refused to strike) supported a Parents' Rights Group in its bid to sue Haringay Council for supporting homosexual causes.[9] William Rees-Mogg suggested in 1983 that there was a link between Keynes's disregard for the 'natural' rules of economics and the homo-erotic atmosphere of Forsterian Cambridge.[10]

There was never, however, as clear a link between politics and morality in Britain as there was in America during the 1980s. Religion was a more pervasive and explicit influence on politics in America. The American 'moral majority' was united by commitment to particular policies – in favour of the death penalty and against abortion. There was no such coherence in Britain. There was not always a link between particular positions on race, crime and sexual morality. Enoch Powell was the most prominent opponent of non-white immigration, but he was also one of the most articulate opponents of the death penalty. On sexual matters, Powell was 'liberal' over homosexuality and 'illiberal' over abortion. Victoria Gillick, who campaigned to prevent girls under sixteen from being given contraceptive advice without their parents' consent, had taken a Powellite line on immigration during the early 1970s. She seemed to change her position during the 1980s though, partly because some black and Muslim groups sympathized with her view of sexual morality.[11] Conservatives were particularly numerous amongst those who voted in favour of restoring the death penalty or restricting abortion, but these were never matters on which political parties imposed whips, and the running was primarily made by backbench MPs – often people, such as Jill Knight, Cyril Townsend, Bernard Braine or Geoffrey Dickens, who were not taken very seriously by their senior colleagues. Voting on all these issues cut across party lines.

Conservatives, and even Thatcherites, were never united around a single line. Thatcher refused to admit that she was a 'feminist', but many MPs in her party – ranging from Teresa Gorman on the libertarian Right to Emma Nicholson on the liberal Left – would have described themselves in that way. Christine Chapman – the journalist who once told Thatcher, 'We still believe in Thatcherism but I wonder if you still do'[12] – had no time for moral authoritarianism. Thatcher's two most important chancellors sought to reform the tax system in ways that would give equality to married women, and at least one of them thought of this in feminist terms.

The Conservative leadership's association with 'moral' issues was strongest during the period when Thatcher was leader of the opposition. Some prominent Tories seem to have seen such issues largely as a matter of electoral advantage, and the attempt to present Thatcherism in terms of some overall moral code resurfaced briefly before the 1983 election. Thatcherites as policy makers were very different from Thatcherites as electoral campaigners. On some issues – notably immigration – the Conservatives did not really differ much (in terms of policy rather than tone) from Labour, whilst on other issues they took no party line. Dealing with Gillick's campaign against the provision of contraceptive advice to girls under sixteen, the Conservative government managed to give the impression that it supported the general moral thrust of the campaign whilst appealing against legal judgments that went in Gillick's favour.[13]

Hostility to homosexuality was often seen as an important part of the Thatcher government's morality – especially when a clause seeking to prevent councils from 'promoting' homosexuality was inserted into the local government bill of 1988.[14] In fact, though, the fuss over this single clause, which was vague to the point of meaninglessness and which was never tested in court, helped to conceal the fact that the Thatcher government had in many ways been remarkably liberal. It had responded to the AIDS crisis with medical advice rather than moral homilies 15 and it had, in accordance with European law, legalized homosexuality in Northern Ireland.[16]

The gulf between words and action was particularly notable with reference to the two issues with which Thatcher had been strongly associated during her early career: comprehensive education and the death penalty. In practice, the Conservative government did almost nothing to reverse the move towards comprehensive schools that had occurred during the 1960s and 1970s. As for capital punishment, this undoubtedly played an important part in Thatcher's public image. In her memoirs she implies that the failure of more Conservative MPs to vote in favour of restoration in 1983 was an omen of disappointments and betrayals to come. However, the Conservative leadership was never united on this issue – many Thatcherite ministers were opposed to restoration – and, as Thatcher must have known, putting the matter to a free vote was tantamount to accepting that it would be defeated (a number of Tory MPs voted in favour of hanging only because they knew that the motion that they 'supported' had no chance of winning). Thatcher's own position seems to have been more complicated than she admitted, perhaps even to herself. Jim Prior, who was sitting next to her on the government benches when the result of the 1983 vote in the Commons was announced, believed that she was privately relieved and that she would not have welcomed the practical difficulties that would have sprung from being forced to put her own principles into action.[17]

For all this, race, crime and family were important to the image of Thatcherism and part of the electorate clearly saw the Thatcher government as having a consistent and coherent position on such matters, even if it did not do so. Here, as was often the case, attacks on Thatcherism helped to define it in the public mind. There was a strange tacit complicity between parts of the Left and parts of the Right on certain kinds of disputes that revolved around 'values'. It suited the Left to be shocked by Thatcherites and it suited the Thatcherites to shock. Both sides could avoid asking awkward questions about their own positions. The Left could avoid asking how the election of Britain's first woman prime minister could be construed as an assertion of 'patriarchy' or whether Yorkshire miners were the natural allies of feminists. The Right could avoid stating precisely which bits of the 'permissive society' it would seek to destroy. Both sides reduced their dispute into a vague and ahistorical juxtaposition of two periods. 'Progressive' values were associated with 'the radical movements and political polarizations of the 1960s, for which "1968" must stand as a convenient, though inadequate, notation'.[18]

Just as the 'Sixties' came to be the expression of everything that Thatcherites were supposed to dislike, so the Victorian age was used to sum up everything that they were supposed to like. The history of the phrase 'Victorian values' is itself revealing. It was coined not by Thatcher but by the television interviewer Brian Walden. Walden had been a Labour MP and was sometimes seen as Thatcher's most hostile journalistic interlocutor[19] (he once asked her whether she was 'off her trolley').[20] But he had seriously contemplated defecting to the Conservative Party during the late 1970s and seems to have been close to Thatcher in private during the 1980s.[21] 'Victorian values' illustrated the curious way in which references to Thatcherism's morality could be double edged – descriptions perceived as attacks by the Left could be seen as benign by Thatcherism's own supporters. Thatcherites adopted the phrase 'Victorian values' with enthusiasm but this enthusiasm was fairly brief, mainly confined to the period immediately before the 1983 election. The Left's interest in the phrase was more durable (books on the subject were still pouring off the presses when Thatcher resigned) and almost certainly played into her hands by helping to give her government a certain moral brand – Michael Foot's introduction to Labour's catastrophically unsuccessful 1983 manifesto pledged to 'end the long Victorian night'.[12]

Some discerned a 'contradiction' between Thatcherism's economic policies and its attitudes to other matters. They believed that there was something incongruous about the fact that a government that seemed so committed to freedom in economic affairs was authoritarian and moralistic in other spheres. They saw a conflict between an expensive defence policy and the desire to cut public spending or protect capitalism. Thatcherites themselves sometimes recognized that their policy was double-sided and that, for example, the Falklands War involved a conflict between desire to reassert British greatness and desire to cut public spending.

More commonly, however, Thatcherites argued that their attitudes to economics, foreign policy and morality fitted together. There were three elements to this. First, Thatcherites were not in fact defenders of an utterly unrestricted free market. All of them recognized the need for social services that were provided by the state. All of them also recognized that the state needed to regulate economic activity in certain respects – indeed their criticism of British politics in the 1970s revolved around the fact that the state had become too 'big' (in that it interfered in too many things) but also that it had become too 'weak' (in that it was unable to enforce its will in those things that really mattered).

Secondly, Thatcherite policies, including economic policies, were not just about economics. Keith Joseph wrote in 1975:

It is characteristic of the past two decades that almost exclusive obsession with economics by governments, and competitive claims to usher in utopia, have coincided with economic failure. A healthy economy is possible only in a healthy body politic – with self reliance, thrift, respect for laws and confidence in a system of rewards and sanctions.[22]

Thatcher's opponents often presented the battle against her as a battle between the market and morality. Thatcherites, however, thought that the market was moral. The free market encouraged individual virtue. It produced people who were robust, independent and willing to take responsibility for the consequences of their own actions. Shirley Robin Letwin, who both commented on and influenced Thatcherism, wrote that 'The Thatcherite conception of the individual is the most important and at the same time the least understood element of Thatcherism.'[23] For Letwin, this aspect of Thatcherism revolved around promoting the 'vigorous virtues'. She argued, for example, that privatization might have raised more money, and done more to promote industrial efficiency, if it had involved the sale of state assets to existing companies rather than attempts to spread share-ownership as widely as possible. She added:

[T]he privatization programme has indeed been 'ideologically driven', in the sense that it had aims other than that of merely increasing economic rationality. The privatization programme has been specifically designed not merely to resuscitate economic vitality, but also to promote the vigorous virtues in individuals, to strengthen the family, and to bring the paradigm shift to bear on industrial policy.[24]

Thirdly, economic success was seen as a prerequisite for national greatness. The sense of crisis that afflicted the British establishment in the 1970s, and which helped to give birth to Thatcherism, was always a crisis about *relative* decline rather than about the extent to which people enjoyed the fruits of prosperity within their own frontiers – indeed some 'declinists' seemed to think that the British people needed to live *less* comfortable lives. The Thatcher government was always interested in British prestige and influence. Ministers were reluctant to cut defence spending and, when Britain was at war in 1982, the government disregarded financial considerations entirely. Margaret Thatcher admired Switzerland, but she never thought that a nation exercising no influence beyond its frontiers could be a model for Britain.

THE ECONOMY

As she left Downing Street for the last time, Margaret Thatcher said 'we are very happy that we leave the United Kingdom in a very, very much better state than when we came here eleven and a half years ago'. How far, in economic terms, was this true?

Generally speaking, judgements on the Thatcher government's economic record have been marked by grudging and reluctant concessions on the part of Thatcher's critics. Andrew Gamble wrote: 'There was an improvement in the 1980s, but no miracle.'[25] At first glance, this is not very extravagant praise, but the mere suggestion that Thatcherism should be discussed in terms of 'improvement' shows how far debate has shifted since the 1980s – a time when Gamble's commentaries were published in an official organ of the British Communist Party[26] and when one of Britain's best-known economists talked of imminent 'apocalypse'.[27]

British productivity improved during the 1980s. Those who are less favourable to the government's record point out that the improvement was smaller than that enjoyed by some other countries during the 1980s and than that which Britain itself had enjoyed during the 1960s.[28] These are unfair comparisons. Britain always faced the problems of apparent relative decline that came from having been the first industrial nation. In terms of international comparison, two points are worth noting. First, by the mid-1980s, some foreign observers had come to regard some aspects of the British economy as a model to be imitated, which would certainly not have been the case in the mid-1970s. Secondly, those who were least favourable about British economic growth tended to move the goal posts – they compared Britain with France in 1978, Japan in 1987 and increasingly with a variety of entities – the Rhone–Alps corridor, for example – that had been dreamt up in research seminars.

Britain was not the most 'successful' economy in the world at any point during the 1980s (or, for that matter, at any point since 1851). There were, however, important, and unexpected, successes in the 1980s. At the time many worried about the nature of these successes. The diplomat Nicholas Henderson wrote in 1987, consciously making himself a spokesman for establishment opinion, that the recession of the early 1980s had done irredeemable damage to much of British manufacturing industry. He thought it unlikely that an economy based on services would be able to fill the gap that was left by this.[29]

Sir Nicholas was right about the collapse of manufacturing industry. This is also an area in which it is fair to look at the Thatcher government's record, because Thatcherites did assume that 'reversing decline' meant improving the state of British manufacturing – indeed Henderson's own lament on this subject in 1979 influenced Thatcher and some of her associates. Members of the Thatcher government did not want or expect the recession of the early 1980s to be as severe as it was. The emphasis on 'services' in Thatcherite economic discourse emerged largely as a rhetorical expedient to justify the unintended consequences of government economic policy.

Having said this, the consequences of Thatcherite economic policy did not turn out to be as bad as many, including some of Thatcher's supporters, feared they might be. An economy based on services did produce prosperity for parts of Britain – especially because of the, largely unplanned, way in which reforms in the City of London intersected with the growth of international finance. Nicholas Henderson himself did rather well out of this new economy – in retirement he became a consultant for Hambros merchant bank and a director of Sotheby's auction house. As for the losers of the early 1980s – those who worked in manufacturing industry – it is not, in retrospect, clear what might have been done to help them. Manufacturing industry declined in most of the more prosperous Western countries during the 1980s and 1990s. Britain had particular long-term problems of low investment, poor industrial relations and weak technical training that would have meant that industry performed badly even in the best of circumstances. The most brutally simple verdict on the Thatcher government's relations with industry in the early 1980s was that it merely turned off the life-support system for a patient that was already dead.

A defender of the Thatcher government's economics might also point out that these need to be seen as a whole. The shock of its policies – particularly during the recession of the early 1980s or the miners' strike of 1984 to 1985 – was meant to be therapeutic. Thatcherites probably did not then understand the full scope of the policies they were going to implement, but they did know that things were going to have to change dramatically and that the country needed to be prepared for a new kind of economy. They might argue with some justice that the 'successful' policy of privatization would not have been possible without the humiliation of the trade unions, seen most clearly with the miners' strike, and that the defeat of the miners would not have been possible if the high unemployment of the early 1980s had not left much of the rest of the working class too subdued to help the miners.

There was also a sense in which the whole debate about economics and society changed during the 1980s. Enoch Powell once said: 'The life of nations no less than that of men is lived largely in the imagination.'[13] The remark was sometimes quoted disapprovingly as an example of Britain's flight from the hard realities of the economic world. Curiously, commentators from parts of the Left, which had once made much of material conditions, became more sympathetic to interpretations that stressed subjective experience during the late 1970s and 1980s, and this influenced their views of Thatcherism. In 1989 Charles Leadbeater (whose own curious status on the frontiers of financial journalism, business consultancy and policy advice reflected the social transformations wrought by Thatcherism) pointed out that 'progress' had once been measured largely at national level and largely in quantifiable terms relating to material goods and accepted by both Right and Left. In the previous decade, all this had changed:

> A simple balance sheet of progress and regress is not enough because the accounting conventions to draw up the balance sheet are changing. They are changing with the shift to new times and post-Fordism. But Thatcherism is ensuring that they are shifted to the Right as they are brought up to date.[30]

Thatcher's own advisers, especially from the world of advertising, were increasingly influenced by the knowledge that there was not a precise relationship between people's economic situation and their own perception of their social class and/or political interests. It is significant that the most important resource for British sociologists in the 1960s and 1970s was *British Social Trends.* In 1984 this annual publication was supplemented by another – entitled *British Social Attitudes.*

WHIG OR TORY?

It was often alleged that Thatcher had broken with a true Tory tradition that saw social obligations as more important than market relations. The charge was levelled from both the Left and the Right. Ian Gilmour talked of a 'traditional' Toryism that was defined by interest in fairness and, in particular, in reducing unemployment. On the other side of the spectrum, journalists – such as T.E. Utley and Peregrine Worsthorne – talked of a Conservatism that was defined in terms of hierarchy and deference: both men were close to the historian Maurice Cowling who had written in 1978 that the free market interested Conservatives only in so far as it was a means 'to maintain existing inequalities or restore lost ones'. A few of Thatcher's supporters occasionally showed interest in the notion that she was not really a Tory. John Nott wrote in 1982: 'I am a nineteenth-century Liberal. So is the Prime Minister. That is what this government is all about.'[31] There clearly were people around Thatcher who felt some affinity with Liberalism (or at least with the Liberal Party of an earlier age). Geoffrey Howe had voted Liberal in 1945 and Nott had technically been elected to parliament as one of the last representatives of the National Liberals, who did not finally and formally merge into the Conservative Party until 1974.

It would, however, be wrong to make too much of this. It is not possible to draw a clear line between Liberalism and Toryism – after all, Gladstone was once a Tory and Winston Churchill was a Liberal for a time. Late twentieth-century Conservatism drew from a variety of traditions (an important group of Thatcher's advisers had once been active on the Left), but it confronted problems that would have been inconceivable in the nineteenth century. There was an element of point-scoring in the use of historical analogies – and it is significant that both Thatcherites and 'wets' were prone to label their enemies in the party as 'Whigs'.

In any event, the case that Thatcher was 'not really a Tory' was never made very convincingly. Nott himself changed his mind on Thatcher's Liberalism. He came to argue that she was never really sympathetic to the logic of free trade and that 'it is a complete misreading of her beliefs to depict her as a nineteenth-century Liberal'.[32] Characteristically, Nott did not mention the fact he himself had put this particular myth into circulation. Besides, there were other Thatcherites who emphatically saw themselves as not being Liberal. In particular, Nigel Lawson – one of the most vigorous defenders of free-market economics in the government – insisted that his political ancestor was Disraeli not Gladstone, though he also pointed out that Disraeli and Gladstone had actually shared important economic assumptions.[33] Finally, it is worth pointing out that Thatcherites made most of 'Liberalism' at a time when they seemed threatened by an alliance of the Liberal and Social Democrat parties – it seems likely that a large part of their enthusiasm was rooted in the well-established Tory tradition of electoral calculation.

The self-appointed spokesmen of 'true Toryism' did not put a very consistent case. In many respects, Gilmour was to the Left of his friend Roy Jenkins and recognized in retrospect that his references to Burke served mainly as 'covering fire'[34] for suggestions that owed much to Keynes. As for Worsthorne and

Utley, they represented a dissident faction within Thatcherism, rather than a Tory opposition to it. When the chips were down, as they often were in the late 1970s and early 1980s, both men described themselves as 'Thatcherites'.[35] Besides, there was a degree of affectation in those Tories who pretended that they cared about fox hunting and the prayer book more than they cared about crushing the unions and controlling inflation. In February 1979, Utley talked of 'the scrannel piping of some of the agitated economists who surround Mrs Thatcher',[36] but this did not prevent him from writing speeches for the leader of the opposition.

Denunciations of Thatcher for departing from 'Toryism' often implied that the market in which she placed such faith was a thing of 'Gradgrindesque' impersonality – hence the glee with which her detractors fastened on her remarks about there being 'no such thing as Society'. These denunciations missed the point. For some Conservatives, the market itself could be an organic and natural thing. Strains of such thinking can be found in Keith Joseph and Nigel Lawson – both men who combined a defence of the free market with an insistence that they were 'Tories'.[37] Thatcher expressed such ideas to the conference of the Scottish Conservative Party in 1990:

> We realise, with Edmund Burke, that 'to be attached to the subdivision, to love the little platoon we belong to in society, is the first principle (the germ as it were) of public affection.

It is the first link in the series by which we proceed towards a love to our country and to mankind'. What the class warriors of the Left refuse to grasp, however, is that markets are living, bustling, spontaneously generated communities. And it's not surprising that the first great champion of markets, Adam Smith, was the friend of Edmund Burke.[38]

THATCHER'S PERSONAL ROLE

How much did Margaret Thatcher personally confer coherence on the Conservative Party during the time she led it? Her closest associates were sometimes rather dismissive of her. Alfred Sherman wrote: 'In the eight years that we worked closely together I have never heard her express an original idea or even ask an insightful question. She left no memorable sayings, apart from one quoted against her out of context.'[39]

Thatcher drew heavily on the opinions of advisers. Her speeches were mainly composed by other people. Some of the key phrases of the Thatcherite revolution were in the first instance coined by its enemies – what single phrase did more to define Thatcher than 'Iron Lady', first used in the pages of the Red Army newspaper? It is certainly true that Thatcher's exposition of Thatcherism was less systematic than that of some of her advisers and ministers. She did not value intellectual coherence as an end in itself, and she made few general statements of principle. Her very importance sprang from these facts. For all her apparent dogmatism, she was, at least at crucial moments in her career, a pragmatist who avoided fights that could not be won and who recognized the importance of tactical flexibility.

Those who worked with Thatcher also recognized that – though she often seemed to lack a theory of politics – she did have certain beliefs or instincts that pervaded much of what she did. She rarely coined phrases, but when presented with choices she often had a strong sense of which words might capture her views. As has been suggested, she preferred 'community' to 'society' and 'popular capitalism' to 'people's capitalism'. She disliked 'privatization', 'supply side' and 'detente' – though no one ever came up with satisfactory alternatives to these words. One aide summed up Thatcher's speech-writing manner thus:

> A speech-writing discussion with Margaret Thatcher was like a session on the psychiatrist's couch, though I was unsure who was the patient and who the psychiatrist. One would usually sit with others, in her study at No.10, pen poised over notepad, hanging on her every word. Phrases, themes, single words would be scribbled down as one tried to identify – from the stream of consciousness, often inchoate, that poured from her brow furrowed and with that penetrating gaze turned inward – some thread from which to form sentences and paragraphs. One could sense the

specks of gold in the ore, but it was agonizingly difficult to capture them as she darted quickly from subject to subject and from theme to theme.[40]

Margaret Thatcher's image was always an important part of the reason for her government's success – not because she was popular, but because she had a particular appeal for a part of the electorate that would not otherwise have voted Conservative. Here Thatcher's apparent lack of systematic and clear thinking often turned out to be an advantage, in that she conveyed the impression that she disliked many aspects of elite liberal thinking, but she did so without being explicit about how she would do things differently and without making many binding promises.

AGAINST CONSENSUS?

Thatcher hated the word 'consensus'.[41] Many of her enemies assumed that this hatred focused on a particular kind of consensus – that which had grown up around Keynesian economics and the welfare state in post-war Britain. Some of her colleagues also came, at least after 1990, to relish the image of themselves as enemies of the political orthodoxies that had allegedly pervaded both parties during the 1950s and 1960s. There are three reasons, however, why we should hesitate before labelling Thatcher as the destroyer of the post-war consensus. First, the Thatcher government's attack on government spending, especially welfare spending, was less dramatic than its enemies alleged. Government spending in many areas rose during the 1980s. Secondly, the Thatcher government never really denounced the whole post-war period. Thatcher herself was polite about the ministers of the Labour governments who held office immediately after the war. None of Thatcher's ministers ever suggested that it might, for example, be desirable to dismantle the National Health Service. For all their occasional talk about Victorian values or periodic attempts to rehabilitate the 1930s, it was, in fact, pretty clear that the golden age for Thatcherites was the 1950s.[42] This was the very period during which the Conservatives had embraced the post-war consensus. Thatcher recalled the 1950s thus:

> I am always astonished when people refer to that period as a time of repression, dullness or conformity – the Age of Anxiety etc. The 1950s were, in a thousand different ways, the reawakening of normal happy life after the trials of wartime and the petty indignities of post-war austerity.[43]

There was a sense in which Thatcherites attacked the 'progressive consensus'; that is to say, the way in which establishment opinion evolved during the 1960s and early 1970s. In an important shadow cabinet discussion of 1975, Angus Maude dated the moment at which the 'consensus' had moved to the Left very precisely: 1962.[44] Thatcher thought 'things started to go wrong in the late Sixties'.[45] Thatcherites did not challenge the existence of the welfare state but they did complain about the growing proportion of the national wealth that it consumed. They resented specific aspects of 'progressive' opinion – notably that relating to comprehensive schools. However, even if the 'progressive' rather than the 'postwar' consensus is considered, attacks on it had more effect in terms of Thatcherite rhetoric than policy – the Thatcherites did not in fact reverse many of the policies that had been enacted in the late 1960s.

Secondly, the post-war consensus was not just about Keynesianism and the welfare state. It also encompassed a view of Britain's role in the world. The two parties agreed that loss of the Empire should not mean the loss of Britain's great power status. They both sought to maintain this through membership of NATO, through a particularly intimate alliance with the United States and through Britain's possession of an independent nuclear bomb. Both parties also accepted, though neither was very successful at doing anything about it, that they needed to reverse Britain's economic decline relative to other countries, particularly in western Europe, that became visible during the 1960s. By the mid-1970s most major politicians agreed that British membership of the European Economic Community was a crucial part of reversing this decline.

In the contexts of great power status and attitudes to economic decline, the Thatcher government did not merely accept the post-war consensus; it was a strong defender of it. Thatcher's relatively conventional views on this matter in the 1960s and 1970s are thrown into focus by comparison with someone who really did challenge the consensus: Enoch Powell. Later the most revealing comparison was with the political Left: in 1983 it was Thatcher's Conservative Party that defended the pre-1979 consensus – revolving around the American alliance, nuclear weapons and the EEC. It was Michael Foot's Labour Party that attacked it.

There was, however, one sense in which Thatcher did attack consensus. This did not involve the specific policies of the postwar period; rather it was a question of style. Thatcher's attacks on consensus did not on the whole involve reference to post-war Britain at all. Sometimes she just attacked the very notion of consensus: 'a soft wishy washy word'.[46] Often her insistence on the superiority of 'conviction' to 'consensus' swept across the centuries to take in Greek philosophers, old testament prophets and reformation theologians.[47] She represented a view of politics that saw vigorously expressed disagreement as inherently desirable.

In early 1979 Norman Tebbit explained what he saw as being special about Margaret Thatcher in revealing terms:

> She's not a Conservative like, say, Stanley Baldwin or some of those leaders who were essentially compromisers and stayers in office and trimmers

to keep the ship of state just going that way. She sees that we need a much more radical change of direction than that, and that's what made her attractive to people like myself.[48]

The reference to Baldwin is significant. He could hardly be accused or representing the post-war consensus – some suggested that such a consensus had been built in conscious opposition to everything that Baldwin stood for.[49] What Thatcherites disliked about Baldwin was his manner rather than his policies. He was a tough-minded politician in terms of what he *did* (it was, after all, as a result of Baldwin's economic policies that Norman Tebbit's father had been obliged to 'get on his bike and look for work'), but he was emollient and conciliatory in terms of what he *said.* Baldwin had an odd afterlife during the 1980s. Though he had been the most electorally successful Tory prime minister of the twentieth century, Thatcher could barely bring herself to say his name – indeed, she referred to Jack Baldwin, the professor of organic chemistry at Oxford, almost as often as she referred to Stanley Baldwin the politician.[50] Baldwin also became a significant figure for those Conservative politicians who wanted to distance themselves from Thatcher's style without condemning her policies. Julian Critchley, delighted to find something that would annoy both Michael Foot and Margaret Thatcher, campaigned during the early 1980s to erect a statue of Baldwin in the House of Commons.[51] William Whitelaw gave the Baldwin Memorial Lecture in 1980,[52] Edward

392

Heath insisted that Baldwin represented the true Conservative Party,[53] and Thatcher's successor, John Major, announced that Stanley Baldwin was his political hero.

Thatcher's combative style accounted for much of her early success but it also explained the increasing distance between her and her ministers: many of them worried that their leader saw conflict as an aim in itself. After a shadow cabinet discussion of trade union reform, Hailsham wrote in his diary: 'Margaret wants to fight. But about what?'[54] Radical Thatcherites allowed for the possibility that they would have some hard fights to impose their vision on Britain, but, like Howe, they saw no gain to be had from unnecessary disagreement and, like Lawson, they anticipated a moment when a consensus might be built, or resurrected, around their own ideas.[55] John Biffen illustrates the changes in the Conservative Party most strikingly. Biffen was willing to take unpopular positions when he thought it necessary – Thatcher regarded his open support for Powell as an act of political suicide in the early 1970s. However, Biffen's apparently extreme stance was designed for a specific and limited purpose. He told John Hoskyns that 'wild men on the Right' would help move the centre of the Conservative Party.[56] By the mid-1980s Biffen believed that redefinition of the party's centre had gone far enough and began to talk about 'balanced tickets' and consolidation. Men such as Biffen were increasingly worried by what they saw as Thatcher's 'Maoist' enthusiasm for new battles even after the old ones had been won.

A THATCHERITE PEOPLE?

Thatcher won three general elections with comfortable majorities, but opinion polls showed that Thatcher personally was not always popular with the electorate. They also showed that two thirds of British people in the late 1980s regarded the phrase 'Thatcher's Britain' as evoking something unpleasant.[57] Polls consistently showed that British people were suspicious of free-market values and sympathetic to notions of communal solidarity – particularly as expressed in the welfare state.

All this evidence needs to be used with care. Opinion poll results depended on the questions people were asked. Voters often seemed to distinguish between what was 'good' and what was 'good for me'. Polls about 'values' often implied the existence of a scale with 'collectivism' or 'government action' at one end and 'individualism' at the other, but such a scale did not really capture the complexity of the choices in British politics during the 1980s.[58] Respondents tended to dislike unrestrained free-market economics and anything that they perceived as a threat to the welfare state. On the other hand, they were positive about, say, trade union reform. Indeed, in this area, the Thatcher government was marked by caution rather than radicalism. Norman Tebbit said that he aimed in his trade union legislation to 'stay one step behind public opinion'. An important part of the electorate was also quite closely aligned with Thatcherism, or at least with what was perceived as being Thatcher's personal position, on issues such as race and crime. One might in any case argue that people's statements about economic 'values' reflected a sense of the worthy opinions they were expected to express but that the votes they cast in general elections were a more realistic reflection of the ways in which they calculated their own interest. Thatcher's ministers seem to have been cynically aware that the electorate was 'unThatcherite' in every respect except its repeated willingness to re-elect governments led by Margaret Thatcher.[59]

Another interpretation would stress the peculiarity of the British electoral system. Margaret Thatcher's Conservative Party obtained more votes than any other party in every election that it contested, but it never got a majority of British people's votes. In fact, the Conservative share of the vote declined between 1979 and 1983 – though the Conservative representation in parliament increased between these two dates. Part of the reason lay in the foundation of the Social Democratic Party (SDP) in 1981. Initially, it seemed likely that the SDP would eat into the Conservative electorate. However, Conservative fortunes revived, particularly after the Falklands War, and this transformed the electoral position of the three main parties. The Conservatives, gaining more votes than any other party, won a disproportionate share of seats in the 1983 election. The SDP and their Liberal allies, gaining fewer votes than the other parties, won a disproportionately small number of seats in parliament.

Some commentators argued that this reflected the fact that Thatcherism had not succeeded in electoral terms, but rather that its opponents had failed. They pointed to the division of the 'anti-Thatcher vote'. They also, at least in 1983, often talked about the 'unelectability' of the Labour Party: committed, particularly on defence, to policies that were unpopular with the electorate and led by a man, Michael Foot, who was seen as an improbable prime minister.[60] Often debate about the electoral success of Thatcherism was tied in with debates about the post-war consensus. Those who urged the unification of the anti-Thatcher vote assumed that postwar consensus was a kind of default option to which a large part of the electorate would revert as soon as squabbles on the Left were resolved. This analysis understates the extent to which Thatcher was actually a defender of the post-war settlement, especially in the 1983 election, and to which the Labour Party was its enemy. It also underestimates the extent to which individual voters regarded their votes as having a significance that went beyond the simple instrumental question of whether or not they managed to eject a government they disliked. It overestimates the extent to which there was some natural centre ground on which the Labour Party and the SDP, or at least their voters, might have been able to come together. In fact, it is wrong to see a clear division between a broad mass of leftist and centrist positions and an extreme right-wing Thatcherite position. Many issues cut across the party divisions in ways that aligned parts of the political centre with Thatcherism. Nuclear weapons was not an issue that divided a broad Left from the Conservative Party – on the contrary this was an issue that placed the Conservatives, along with the SDP and part of the Labour Right, on one side, with the Labour Left and part of the Liberal Party on the other. On industrial relations, the Labour Party – especially its 'moderate', centrist wing – was closely attached to the trade unions. The SDP leadership, on the other hand, had broken away from the Labour Party partly in protest at the institutionalization of trade union power. SDP MPs were divided on the trade union laws that the Thatcher government introduced in 1982 – five of them voted against and seventeen voted in favour. Most rank-and-file members of the SDP were hostile to trade unions.

On economic management, there was, again, no clear-cut division. Those who talked of a broad anti-Thatcher coalition sometimes wanted to revive a 'Keynesian' consensus. The truth was, though, that the Labour Party official policy (at least during the early 1980s) was not very Keynesian. Its emphasis was on direct state control rather than broad macro-economic management. As for the SDP, its members seem to have wanted to see higher levels of state spending (perhaps because some of them worked for the public sector) but the position of its leaders vis-à-vis economic Thatcherism was not one of unqualified hostility.

Most of all, emphasis on Thatcherism's electoral failure assumes that Thatcherism ought to have been different from any other political movement and that it ought to have converted a majority of the population to its point of view. There is no evidence that Conservative electoral strategists thought in these terms – they were happy with a working parliamentary majority and not overly exercised by the question of how it was obtained.

The 'success' of Thatcherism did not necessarily mean electoral success. Thatcher certainly wanted to win elections and stay in Downing Street. Some of her supporters, however, were very aware of the difference between being 'in office' and being 'in power' and were sure that they preferred the latter to the former. As a young radical in the Centre for Policy Studies during the early 1980s, John Redwood recalled that a great deal of his work was predicated on the assumption that the Conservatives were in fact likely to lose the next election, and for this reason 'In our policy discussions we would always include the question of whether the change we were proposing could be made irreversible.'[61] The area in which Redwood and his colleagues were most successful in establishing 'irreversibility' was, eventually, privatization. Privatization stood in an odd relation to electoral success. The Conservatives needed to be reasonably secure in office before they could get significant numbers to buy shares in privatized industries and, at least as long as Labour threatened to renationalize, privatization may have contributed to Conservative success. But privatized companies were never popular; rather, like nationalized companies in the 1960s and 1970s, they were simply accepted as part of the economic landscape. The Conservatives had not so much won the argument as persuaded the British people that there was no argument to be had.

How far, though, did the Thatcher government mobilize some wider change in values? Thatcher was pessimistic. Referring to the period after the 1983 election, she wrote:

> there was still too much socialism in Britain. The fortunes of socialism do not depend on those of the Labour Party: in fact, in the long run it would be truer to say that Labour's fortunes depend on those of socialism. And socialism was still built into the institutions and mentality of Britain. We had sold thousands of council homes; but 29% of the housing stock remained in the public sector. We had increased parents' rights in the education system; but the ethos in the classrooms and teachers' training colleges remained stubbornly Left wing. We had grappled with the problem of bringing more efficiency into local government; but the Left's redoubts in the great cities still went virtually unchallenged. We had cut back trade

union power; but still almost 50 per cent of the workforce in employment was unionized.[62]

Perhaps looking for ways in which the British public might have embraced Thatcherism with enthusiasm is deceptive. Marxists who were interested in how Thatcherism might achieve ideological hegemony in Britain often talked about the way in which it might change perceptions of 'common sense'. This is a significant phrase because it was one that Thatcherites, especially Margaret Thatcher herself, frequently used.[63] Common sense did not necessarily imply a belief that Thatcherite policies were good, but rather that they were inevitable or 'natural'. The success of Thatcherism in these terms was to be measured not just in the way that its supporters expressed their enthusiasm, but also in the ways that its opponents (or victims) expressed their acquiescence. Unemployed people who recognized that unemployment was 'no one's fault' were, in one sense, Thatcherite, even if they did not belong to that section of the unemployed (24 per cent in 1983) who voted Conservative.[64]

Some argued that submission was not the same as acceptance. They stressed the ways in which 'dull compulsion of economic relations' forced people to do things without implying that they had undergone any sort of ideological or cultural conversion. However, even 'the dull compulsion of economic relations' is a cultural construct. The fact, for example, that increasing numbers of workers sought to protect their jobs by accepting increasing levels of workplace flexibility rather than by going on strike is a sign that they had to some extent accepted the government's definition of 'economic realism'. Indeed the ways in which Thatcherism redefined 'economic realism' can be seen amongst those Tories who did not think of themselves as Thatcherites. In 1978 a secret report warned Thatcher of the 'harsh reality' that 'Strong unions and advanced technology operated by their members ... mean that no government these days can "win".'[65] Fourteen years later, Ian Gilmour, who had been a member of the committee that drew up the secret report, argued that the decline in working-class power was the 'harsh reality' and that 'the succession of British acts of parliament registered rather than caused the decline of the trade unions'.[66]

The complexity of what it might mean to 'accept' or 'submit' to Thatcherism is illustrated by the single group of people whose opinions were most intensively studied during the 1980s: miners during the strike of 1984–5. At first glance, the division amongst miners might seem a simple one between those who struck and those who crossed picket lines. The former were the warrior class of the British Left in the mid-1980s; the latter were 'scabs' despised by the Left for their selfishness. The first problem with this division is it does not work for all miners. Only a minority of them worked throughout the strike and only a minority held out until the National Union of Mineworkers called for a return to work in March 1985. Between these two extremes lay a large group of men who struck (and who were sometimes militant supporters of the strike) but who returned to work before March 1985. Strikers themselves sometimes distinguished, after the event, between 'super scabs', who had worked from the beginning, and 'hunger scabs', who had returned to the pits halfway through the strike. This is a division that seems to overlap with that between people who accepted Thatcherism and those who merely submitted to the 'dull compulsion of economic relations'.

It should be stressed, however, that even the 'super scabs' of the Nottingham coalfield were not enthusiastic supporters of the Thatcher government. As far as can be told, few of them voted Conservative. Furthermore, in one respect the stated aims of those who broke the strike were rather similar to those of men who struck: both wanted to preserve their own jobs in a nationalized industry. Working miners remained members of a trade union. It is true that some broke away to join the Union of Democratic Miners, but even then a large proportion of the members of the UDM would have liked to reunite with the NUM. Whatever their enemies may have said, working miners thought of their interests in very collective terms – indeed most working miners, just like most strikers, seem to have been driven by a desire to fit in with their neighbours and workmates. There were also ways in which the more general values of the 1980s cut across the division between strikers and strike-breakers in the coalfields. Both sides were very affected by that most Thatcherite institution: home ownership. Men who worked often did so because they needed to pay mortgages; equally strikers often believed that owning their houses had given them a particular attachment to their pit villages and sometimes argued that the closure of pits would bring a fall in house prices.[67]

LEGACY

What was left of Thatcherism after Margaret Thatcher had gone? Thatcher was by this stage an emphatic believer in a Thatcherism that would go on after her political demise. Her desire to secure the election of John Major as her successor was partly linked to the desire to secure the survival of Thatcherism – though it also had a good deal to do with personal bitterness, and her feelings about the succession were not shared by all Thatcherites. To many people's surprise, the Conservative Party did win the 1992 general election, but it was not a successful party for most of the fifteen years after Thatcher's resignation. Between 1997 and 2005, it ran through four different leaders and lost three general elections. Some commentators had always worried, or hoped, that Thatcher would induce intolerable divisions in her own party. As early as 1983, one of her admirers wrote: 'History's verdict on Mrs Thatcher could yet be that she saved the nation, and dished her party. It might be a verdict that all three deserved.'[68] In 2005 John Sergeant expressed a common argument when he wrote that 'Maggie's fatal legacy' had been to destroy the Conservative Party. Sergeant attributed this destruction to divisions over Europe and to the bitterness caused by the circumstances of Thatcher's departure.[69]

The notion that the Conservative Party has been 'destroyed' looks less convincing in 2009 than it did in 2005. Besides, viewing Thatcher as the 'destroyer of the Conservative Party' risks, as is often the case with interpretations of Thatcherism, painting an excessively benign picture of what came before 1979. For one thing, such a view assumes that there was a secure patrician 'old' party that was displaced by Thatcherism during the 1970s. Actually, the party had already changed frequently, which was partly why it was so electorally successful. Besides, Thatcher did not simply sweep away an old Tory style of patrician paternalism and social liberalism. Even 'traditional' Conservatives had often concluded that 'old' solutions, particularly with regard to labour relations, were not working during the 1970s. Furthermore, Thatcherism did not just mean free-market economics. The ultimate Tory grandee – Alec Douglas-Home – was closer to Margaret Thatcher on issues of race or foreign policy than he was to Edward Heath. Major General Sir Brian Wyldbore-Smith DSO was very much an oldstyle Tory. He was a Master of Hounds for the Belvoir Hunt who regretted the passing of national service, disliked professional politicians and thought immigration and urbanization would destroy English values. He was, however, also a moderately important Thatcherite – director of the Conservative Board of Finance from 1970 until 1992 and a trustee of the Thatcher Foundation.[70]

There is in any case no reason why political parties should survive and, judged in an international context, it is odd that British politics should still be so influenced by a party that was founded in the early nineteenth century and that exists, in theory at least, to defend the monarchy, the Union and the established Church. Between 1974 (the moment when Heath called for a government of national unity) and 1982 (the moment when electoral support for the Social Democrat Party began to decline), there was a period when many thought that the British party system might be restructured in ways that would mean the end of the Conservative Party. Thatcher was one of the very few Tory politicians who believed that the battle against socialism could be carried out exclusively through her own party and, in this sense, she was the saviour of her party rather than its destroyer.

Alongside the view of Thatcher as the destroyer of her party has often gone the view that Thatcherism was the intellectual ancestor of New Labour. In March 1986 the journalist Woodrow Wyatt met John Smith – Labour's shadow chancellor who was to become leader of the party six years later. Apparently, Smith agreed with Wyatt that the Labour Party owed a 'big debt' to Thatcher for having 'tamed the unions' and made reform of the Labour Party possible. Wyatt subsequently told Thatcher about this meeting and suggested that she had 'shifted the centre about two hundred miles to the Right', to which Thatcher replied: 'Yes but not far enough.'[71] The changes in the Labour Party that happened after 1990, of course, dwarfed those that had happened during the 1980s. In 1984 Andrew Gamble wrote:

> The real question to ask about Thatcherism ... is how far it is creating [a] ... broader consensus for its policies and objectives ... the Labour Party must be brought to accept it or the Labour Party must never govern again. In the first case this would mean the Labour Party abandoning Clause IV; accepting the priority given to the control of inflation; renouncing protectionism ... to shield any sector of the British economy from the need to be competitive; and accepting a much smaller state sector, with lower taxation, selective rather than universal welfare provision, as well as permanent weakening of trade union organizations ... No one really expects Labour to head down this road.[72]

By 1997 Labour had in fact adopted many of the policies that Gamble regarded as being inconceivable in 1984. Indeed, there was an odd personal flirtation between Margaret Thatcher and Labour prime ministers: Tony Blair attended her eightieth birthday party and Gordon Brown invited the woman whom he had once derided as an 'Anglo Poujadist' to tea at Number 10 Downing Street.

Does this mean that the Labour Party had become Thatcherite? Clearly Labour accepted that elements of what the Thatcher government had done were now irreversible. There was no attempt to renationalize companies that had been privatized. The trade union laws of the 1980s were not repealed. However, there was such a wide shift in all political attitudes between the mid-1970s and the mid-1990s that it is sometimes hard to construct a meaningful spectrum on which politicians can be compared. There is no doubt that John Smith was a more right-wing Labour leader than Michael Foot, but saying whether Tony Blair was more right-wing than James Callaghan is a trickier proposition – partly because the Labour Party turned through such a collection of sharp political hairpin bends in the 1980s and partly because some of the issues that confronted politicians in the late 1990s were just different from those that had confronted politicians in the late 1970s.

It should also be stressed that changes in the Labour Party should not just be seen as a reaction to Thatcherism. They were also in part responses to international changes that affected left-wing parties throughout western Europe regardless of what kind of opponents they faced. Capitalism seeped into the most unexpected corners of political life. A monument to Antonio Gramsci (whose writings exercised such an influence over English Marxist understanding of

Thatcherism) is now located in the entrance hall to the business school of the accountancy firm Ernst and Young, which bought the building that had formerly housed the headquarters of the Italian Communist Party.

Changes in the Labour Party lead us to the broader sorts of change in the whole pattern of politics. What would the Thatcherite position on the break-up of Yugoslavia be? Thatcher was vigorously pro-Bosnian, but some of her advisers took exactly the opposite point of view. What might a Thatcherite position on climate change be – especially in an era when support for coal-fired power stations is seen as a 'right-wing' policy? What about international events since September 2001? Thatcher always laid a heavy emphasis on international law (including the legal restraint that might prevent states from pursuing terrorists outside their own frontiers). Thatcherites are divided on whether British involvement in the invasion of Iraq in 2003 was a good thing and, indeed, disagree with each other on what Lady Thatcher's own position on this matter might be.[73] In 1983 Conservatives denounced Labour proposals to nationalize banks; now (early 2009) both Labour and Conservative politicians seem to recognize that the acquisition of a controlling interest in British banks by the state is a necessary and, they devoutly hope, temporary evil.

The truth is that Thatcherism was not composed of political constants that can be traced back to the nineteenth century or transported forward into the twenty-first. It was rooted in particular problems posed by the expansion of Soviet power after the Vietnam War, the development of 'progressive opinion' after 1968 and the British elite's obsession with notions of economic decline during the 1970s. Thatcherism also exploited certain opportunities opened up by North Sea Oil, the growth of international finance, the election of Ronald Reagan as president of the United States and the spread of reform in Communist Europe. Thatcherism belonged to a particular time, and it is probably significant that Thatcher seems to have become most interested in the idea of Thatcherism as a timeless phenomenon at precisely the moment when she was herself losing touch with political reality.

SOME THOUGHTS ON SOURCES

The way to study Conservatives is to meet Conservatives; and here Leftist writers are at a loss. They resemble early Victorian anthropologists, whose willingness to pronounce on the nature of man bore no relation to their readiness to commune with natives by sleeping in straw huts. Naturally self-imprisoned in their intellectual ghetto, Leftists concentrate on the printed text, which, in Tory terms, means the ephemeral, the tangential and the epiphenomenal.

John Vincent[1]

Professor Vincent is unfair to 'Leftists' – to judge from the interview pages of Marxism Today in the late 1980s, of which more below, one might think that Beatrix Campbell and her colleagues spent practically all their time talking to Tories. Furthermore, some Thatcherites took ideas seriously: the 'printed text' was less 'ephemeral' to, say, Nigel Lawson than it would have been to Alec Douglas-Home.

The peculiar circumstances of the 1980s also did something to subvert another distinction that is dear to historians: that between primary and secondary sources. Many books and articles about Thatcherism deserve to be treated as primary sources – either because they draw directly on the experience of the authors or because they were themselves intended to be political statements. Equally, many of Thatcher's allies were aware of their own historical importance. Their memoirs are rarely just based on memory. Ministers and advisers knew quite a lot about the academic debate that swirled around the events in which they had taken part – sometimes ministerial memoirs were in fact ghostwritten, edited or otherwise influenced by professional historians. Mark Garnett, to take the most obvious example, is a historian who has produced his own accounts, and also a kind of academic midwife who has helped Tory politicians deliver their accounts. He wrote biographies of Keith Joseph and William Whitelaw – the latter book being an official biography that seems, with the complicity of its subject, to have revealed things that had been skated over in Whitelaw's own memoirs.[2] However, Garnett also edited Alfred Sherman's bilious attack on the Thatcher government from the Right and encouraged Sir Ian Gilmour to produce his display of urbane sulkiness from the Left of the Conservative Party.[3] In writing their autobiographies, ministers drew on accounts by other people of the governments in which they had served.[4] They also looked to historians to place their own actions in some longer-term context. The work of Andrew Roberts was so important in moulding the retrospective view that Thatcherites had of what they had done[14] that intelligent observers often assume that Roberts came to prominence in the 1980s[5] – actually, he must have been at school in 1980 and did not publish his first book until 1991.

Because journalistic accounts were so important to the image of the Thatcher government, including the image that its members often had of themselves, it is worth pausing to think about the backgrounds of the British political journalists – Peter Hennessy, Peter Jenkins, Simon Jenkins, Peter Riddell and Hugo Young – who wrote most about Thatcher. All belonged to that fraction of the British establishment that encompasses academia, parts of Fleet Street (especially pre-Murdoch *The Times* and the *Economist)* and the administrative civil service. The title of Hugo Young's biography of Margaret Thatcher – *One of Us* – is an implicit joke because Young, and most of his readers, did not really think that Thatcher was 'their kind of person'. Looking back, however, I wonder whether the joke was not on 'us' rather than her. Thatcher, after all, was explicit about what she stood for. People who wrote about her often did so through the prism of unspoken assumptions that sprang from their own background. Young writes that Thatcher 'possessed no trace of the effortless superiority of the Balliol men, Macmillan and Heath, who went before her'.[6] Readers of these lines might not be surprised to hear that Young himself was a Balliol man.

The grander journalists drew from their extensive connections with the great and the good. Sometimes it seems to me that they end up being sucked into the spider's web of their well-placed sources. For example, Simon Jenkins insists that Britain would have been unable to fight the Falklands War if it had taken place after the defence cuts envisaged by John Nott had been implemented.[7] No doubt this is what senior figures in the Admiralty told their journalistic contacts, but it is almost impossible to predict the outcome of a hypothetical war fought with hypothetical resources. Anyone who reads Jenkins's confident pronouncements on this subject might do well to recall that he is the man who said that the battle for Baghdad in 2003 would be as savage as that for Stalingrad in 1943.[8]

In a similar vein, consider one of the most striking passages in Hugo Young's biography of Margaret Thatcher. Young describes Thatcher's propensity to interfere in every aspect of policy and illustrates this with an account of how she threatened to take personal control of the hunt for the Yorkshire ripper (a serial killer of women) in 1980: 'so vexed was the prime minister that she summoned the Home Secretary and announced her intention of going to Leeds that weekend to take personal charge of the investigation'.[9] This story seems to refer to a meeting between Thatcher and the home secretary (in the presence of various civil servants) on 25 October 1980.[10] An account of it is now in the public domain. It reveals that Thatcher said that violence against women was a serious matter, suggested that the local police had not been very effective and asked whether it might be useful to hand over the enquiry to Scotland Yard. The official transcript of the meeting gives no hint of a threat to take personal charge of the case. All of Thatcher's comments sound sensible and her intervention may have had an effect because the team investigating the case was changed shortly after it and the murderer was caught. It is easy to imagine how this story might have passed from a succession of civil servants to a succession of journalists (probably over a succession of lunches at the Garrick) and become progressively more colourful in the telling – 'Have you heard what happened to Willie? Now the bloody woman thinks she's Sherlock Holmes.'

There were of course some influential journalists who were, at least to start with, self-consciously outside the establishment. Particularly important in the 1980s was the journal *Marxism Today.* Founded in 1957, it was the official organ of the Communist Party of Great Britain (CPGB). Nigel Lawson described it as 'recherché' and 'briefly influential' – the mere fact that a senior Conservative minister could be bothered to be rude about it is probably a sign of its importance. The journal had an odd symbiotic relation with Thatcherism. Martin Jacques became editor in 1977 and began to rethink the politics of the Left. The fact that the British Communist Party entertained no real fantasies about ever holding power gave some of its intellectuals an Olympian open-mindedness. During the 1980s *Marxism Today's* circulation grew from 4,000 to 15,000 (its readership was larger than the membership of the CPGB), and it became a glossy magazine that stood uncomfortably on the doorstep of consumerism – it carried advertisements for Nicaraguan rum and Zimbabwean wines. Leading Tories (Biffen, Heath, Heseltine) were interviewed in its pages and, on at least one occasion, Thatcher quoted from it.[11] It ran important articles by Hall, Jessop, Gamble and others, some of which formed the basis of later books.

Marxism Today was, however, neither a party-line Communist journal nor the exponent of a systematic theoretical viewpoint. Marxists often denounced work that appeared in *Marxism Today,* and, indeed, it seemed as though the most bitter arguments about Thatcherism took place between different kinds of Marxist. Roger Scruton – surveying matters from the other side of the spectrum, or perhaps just the other side of Birkbeck senior common room – parodied an Open University sociology course that pitted Dave Spart, who believed that 'the capitalist class as a class controls the means of production', against Chris Toad, who believed that 'the bourgeoisie as a class controls the power structures from which workers as a class are excluded'.[12]

For some contributors to *Marxism Today,* the urgency of their day-to-day analysis of Thatcherism seems to have gone with a declining interest in Marxist theory. It would certainly be hard to tell from his articles in the journal whether or not Andrew Gamble considered himself to be a Marxist.[13] Arthur Seldon, one of *Marxism Today's* many Thatcherite admirers, argued that the second word in its title was more important that the first.[14] Between 1975 and 1990 a certain kind of left-wing affiliation sometimes seemed more like a fashion statement than a political or intellectual manifesto – this was a period when a group of art school students named their pop band Scritti Politti, in homage to the work of Antonio Gramsci. The jibe by Peter Jenkins that Thatcherism was 'more a style than an ideology' might equally well have been directed at many British Marxists and, indeed, the article in which the very unMarxist Jenkins made this point was published in *Marxism Today*.[15]

As time went on, the analysis of some left-wing writers began to bear an odd resemblance to that of some writers who were looking at matters from a more obviously establishment perspective.[16] This was particularly notable with regard to the sentimentalization of the period between 1945 and 1979. At first, writers from the Left tended to be highly critical of post-war social democracy, and often saw Thatcherism as associated with changes that had begun a long time before Thatcher's arrival on the stage of British politics. However, the Falklands War and the Conservative victory in the 1983 election seem to have brought a change. Anthony Barnett's *Iron Britannia* (published in 1982 and written at the beginning of the Falklands campaign) was probably the last left-wing analysis to emphasize the things that Thatcherism and post-war social democracy had in common rather than the things that separated them. After this, left-wingers were increasingly prone to see themselves as part of a broad anti-Thatcher alliance, and to celebrate the pre-1979 period. Eric Hobsbawm was the most important contributor to this new mood. He was a regular writer for *Marxism Today* and a card-carrying member of the Communist Party, but he saw political salvation in a political alliance of the Labour and Social Democratic parties, and he seems to have had more respect for Healey than for Benn, Foot or Kinnock. His notion of a 'golden age' throughout the Western world from 1945 to 1975, a notion that influenced many historians of Europe, seems in effect to have meant 'anything before Thatcher'.

Questions about sources are particularly pressing now because the thirtieth anniversary of Thatcher's election, when this book is to be published, is also the time when the cabinet papers relating to the Thatcher government will begin to be opened to historians. Is it folly to write without having full access to the sources that will soon be available? My own feeling is that the archives to be opened over the next decade will be useful to historians in all sorts of ways. I dare say that some of my own assumptions will be proved wrong, that some questions will be answered, and some new questions (quite a large number I suspect) will be raised.

I am, however, sceptical about the idea that there is some pot of gold at the end of the archival rainbow.[17] Consider, for example, the Westland crisis, which almost brought Thatcher down in 1986. Many participants in this believe that there is a document somewhere that will vindicate them, or reveal what really happened. Leon Brittan told a friend that the truth of the matter would come out 'after thirty years' (i.e. when the cabinet papers were opened). Michael Heseltine became obsessed with finding out what 'really happened'. He nagged the Italian industrialist Gianni Agnelli, who had been involved in a takeover bid for Westland, to tell him – Agnelli wisely said that he could not remember.[18] Heseltine even printed his own email address in his memoirs in case a reader could shed light on the matter.[19] One journalist believed that Colette Bowe, a civil servant at the centre of the case, had her own account locked away in a safe.[20]

All this reveals the slight absurdity of an interest in 'secret' documents. What document is likely to reveal something that none of the principal participants in the affair knew or understood themselves? Over half of the ministers who sat in cabinet on the day that Heseltine walked out have now published their memoirs. But these accounts do not agree about the most simple details of the affair – whether Heseltine intended to resign when he first arrived for the meeting and whether Thatcher was already prepared for him to do so. Nicholas Ridley opens his account by saying: 'I have a clear memory of the first Cabinet in 1986 after the Christmas recess, on 16 January.'[21] The meeting actually took place on 9

January. Geoffrey Howe describes his own contribution to cabinet discussion and then adds, with a characteristic mixture of asperity and self-deprecation, that no one else seems to recall his intervention.[22] In any case, Westland hardly revolved around hidden documents; the whole scandal was rooted in the fact that so many documents had been improperly leaked to the press. There were no fewer than three official enquiries into Westland, which means that the events surrounding a small Somerset firm in late 1985 and early 1986 have been investigated in more depth than almost any other episode in recent British history. It is very hard to imagine that cabinet papers will tell us anything that we do not already know. Perhaps the fury of the main protagonists in the affair sprang from the fact that they themselves were uncertain of what had really happened.

The Westland affair does draw our attention to sources that are available, even before the opening of cabinet papers. Firstly Thatcher's ministers were notoriously indiscreet. Furthermore, a group of journalists built up particularly good personal relations with important figures in the Conservative Party during the fifteen years when Margaret Thatcher led it. By the time he came to write his account of Thatcher's fall, Alan Watkins reckoned that he was on first-name terms with over a hundred Tory MPs and that it was quicker to list those people who had refused to talk to him than to acknowledge those who had done so.[23] Sometimes leaks were used, especially by the prime minister's own entourage, as a means of conducting political battles. Sometimes indiscretion seems to have been built into the psychology of the government in ways that divided even men who agreed with each other about policy. Cecil Parkinson, not the most discreet of men, believed that John Wakeham, leader of the House of Commons, had briefed journalists about cabinet business even as he walked back from Downing Street.[24]

All this makes it easier to study Thatcherism but leaks have to be used with care. Indeed my general sense is that the release of archives will not produce startling 'revelations' but rather tend to put information that has already been revealed into a context that will make it appear a bit less startling. One of the important leaks from Thatcher's shadow cabinet concerned the Ridley report, which apparently anticipated a confrontation between a future Tory government and the National Union of Mineworkers. The report was published in the *Economist* in 1978 under the headline 'CIVIL WAR OR APPOMATTOX'. Six years later, when the government did take on the miners, many left-wingers assumed that it was acting on the Ridley plan and well-thumbed photocopies of the *Economist* article circulated on picket lines. However, the shadow cabinet papers, which are now available, remind us that Ridley's view on the miners formed just one small part of a long report on other matters, and that Ridley was a relatively junior figure. His report probably illustrated the way in which senior

Conservatives were thinking but it did not necessarily *influence* that thinking much. Ministers in 1984 were not following the Ridley plan – it is not clear, in fact, that anyone in Central Office even knew where Ridley's report had been filed.[25]

The second source for the study of the Thatcher government lies in the memoirs published by those who participated in politics during the period. Almost twenty of the people who held office in Thatcher's cabinets have now published some kind of autobiography – as have many other Tory politicians and other well-connected figures in British public life. Once again, the very acrimony that the Thatcher government generated means that these memoirs can be revealing. The bland tones of self-satisfaction and mutual congratulation that characterize an earlier generation of Tory autobiography are usually absent. Enoch Powell famously likened reading Harold Macmillan's memoirs to 'chewing on cardboard'. Anyone who reads the memoirs of, say, Alistair McAlpine or John Nott will sometimes feel as though they are choking on broken glass.

A willingness to say frank things does not, of course, mean that authors are being frank about everything, especially their own motives. In his diaries, Alan Clark, a junior minister in the late 1980s, describes amongst other things his intermittent desire to stand on the window ledge outside his seventh-floor office in the Department of Trade and Industry and urinate on the passers-by in Victoria Street beneath him.[26] On the other hand, the entry in this diary for 29 October 1990 does not mention the fact that on that day Clark went to urge a senior minister to put himself forward as Thatcher's replacement as leader of the Conservative Party.[27]

The very differences between the accounts provided by various participants in the Thatcher government can themselves be revealing. Kenneth Baker suggests that Nicholas Ridley considered the Falklands War to be 'mad', something that the reader would not learn from Ridley's own memoirs.[28] On the other hand, a reader of Baker's memoirs would not discover that Baker had, according to his friend Max Hastings, said in the late 1970s that a future Conservative government should avoid conflict with the miners.[29] Geoffrey Howe draws attention to the support that Tebbit apparently gave in 1985 to British entry into the Exchange Rate Mechanism,[30] a support that Tebbit does not mention in his own memoirs.[31] Several of Thatcher's advisers allege that it was Thatcher, acting on the advice of Alan Walters, who forced Geoffrey Howe into his radical budget of 1981. In his own memoirs, Howe comments on the commentaries thus: 'Most of the participants have been keen to take credit ... So there has been no lack of over-simplification ... Most of the subsequently alleged battle-lines were by no means apparent (to me at least) at the time.'[32] Howe, himself, however, is not always above 'oversimplification'. He cites the speeches that he delivered in August and September

1978 as examples of the way in which Conservative policy on trade unions was developing.[33] He makes no mention of the draft speech on trade unions that he sent to Thatcher in January 1978 and on which she wrote: 'Geoffrey this is not your subject. The press will crucify you for this.'[34]

The ways in which an autobiography can reveal and conceal are illustrated by the works of Douglas Hurd – works that are interesting precisely because Hurd writes in a more serene and less obviously partisan tone than many of his colleagues. Hurd has written three books about his own political involvement. First, he kept a diary throughout his career. This diary has never been published – though Hurd quotes it in other works and also read out long chunks of it to his biographer.[35] Hurd writes interestingly about the diary, suggesting that entries made at the end of an exhausting or annoying day may be less 'true' than recollections recorded at a greater distance.

Secondly, he published an *End to Promises* in 1979, an account of the government of Edward Heath, whom Hurd had served as an adviser. Hurd sought to defend aspects of Heath's record, but his book was also addressed to the people who had taken power in the Conservative Party after Heath's fall. Hurd recognized that the age that had produced Heath and Macmillan might now seem as remote as the age of Baldwin had seemed to those who had risen to prominence after the Second World War.[36] Hurd was frank about the government's faults, and the diary entry that he quotes from February 1972 – 'The Government now wandering vainly over the battlefield looking for someone to surrender to – and being massacred all the time'[37] is probably the single sentence that is most often cited in accounts of Heath's failure.

Thirdly, Hurd published his memoirs in 2004. Most of his cabinet colleagues had already published their memoirs and, though he is rarely explicit about it, this gives Hurd the last word on some matters. Quotations from the diary were less inhibited in 2004 than in 1979. He quotes his entry for 23 November 1975: 'Listen to a talk by a typical Thatcherite – dark suited, articulate, 55, accountant, full of sourness.'[38] It is revealing that Hurd seems privately to have regarded 'Thatcherite' as a term of abuse – all the more interesting when we remember that he served in Thatcher's cabinets for longer than Nott or Parkinson, and that he was still serving in one of them after both Howe and Lawson had resigned.

In his memoirs Hurd discusses his personal life to a greater extent than most of his colleagues and sometimes he does so in ways that raise interesting questions – one notes, for instance, how many prominent Conservatives got divorced, or lived through some other personal crisis, in the mid-1970s, and one wonders how this might have been related as cause and/or effect to their wider sense of crisis about British politics during the period. Finally, Hurd's memoirs are often most interesting for what they leave out. For example, though his political career involved foreign affairs, security and Ulster, he says nothing at all about an episode that was associated with all three of these – the shooting by British soldiers of three members of the IRA on Gibraltar in 1987.

I should end by emphasizing that any study of Thatcherism published now or at any point in the near future will have a provisional quality. In addition to the opening of papers under the thirty-year rule, documents that are currently exempt from Freedom of Information legislation, such as letters from working miners during the miners' strike of 1984–5, will one day be available to historians.[15] Many of Thatcher's ministers have not published their memoirs, and some of them will presumably do so. Charles Moore, who, as editor of the *Spectator* from 1984 to 1990, was a participant in Conservative politics during the 1980s, is writing the official biography of Margaret Thatcher.

I have sought to stress throughout this book that the Thatcher government should be seen as an episode in history rather than an aspect of present-day politics. All the same, views of the 1980s will clearly be influenced by things that have happened more recently. I am writing these words in October 2008. In the last few weeks Britain has seen a financial crash, a burst of state intervention in the economy and an apparent revival in the fortunes of the Labour Party. I must admit to worrying that aspects of my book may seem quaintly out of date by the time I see the proofs.

NOTES

Place of publication is London, unless otherwise specified. Date of publication refers to the edition cited in this book.

Abbreviations used:

TFW – Margaret Thatcher Foundation website
NA – National Archives

INTRODUCTION

[1]   Ian Deary, Simon Wessely and Michael Farrell, 'Dementia and Mrs Thatcher', *British Medical Journal,* 291, 21–28 December 1985.

[2]   *The Times,* 8 December 2005.

[3]   Andrew Gamble, *The Free Economy and the Strong State* (1994, first published 1988); Stuart Hall and Martin Jacques (eds.), *The Politics of Thatcherism* (1983); Bob Jessop et al., *Thatcherism. A Tale of Two Nations* (Cambridge, 1988); Peter Jenkins, *Mrs Thatcher's Revolution. The End of the Socialist Era (1987); Dennis Kavanagh, Thatcherism and British Politics. The End of Consensus?* (Oxford, 1990, first published 1986); Peter Riddell, *The Thatcher Decade. How Britain Changed during the 1980s (Oxford, 1989); Robert Skidelsky (ed.), Thatcherism*

(1988); Hugo Young, One of Us. A Biography of Margaret Thatcher (1990).

[4]   Stuart Hall, 'The Great Moving Right Show', *Marxism Today,* January 1979.

[5]   Raphael Samuel, Barbara Bloomfield and Guy Boanas (eds.), *The Enemy Within. Pit Villages and the Miners' Strike of 1984–5* (1986), p.20.

[6]   TFW, Thatcher interview with David Frost for TV-AM, 7 June 1985 (105826).

[7]   John Campbell, *Margaret Thatcher,* Vol.1, *The Grocer's Daughter* (2000) and Vol.2, *The Iron Lady* (2003).

[8]   Andrew Gamble, 'The Reading of a Decade', *Marxism Today,* May 1989: 'The term was first used by Stuart Hall in *Marxism Today* ... [whose] seminal article "The Great Moving Right Show" appeared in January 1979.'

[9]   Nigel Lawson used Thatcherism, as he believed, for the first time in 1981, but then wrote: 'I later discovered that it had been used by the recherché and now defunct journal *Marxism Today* before we had even taken office in 1979', Nigel Lawson, *The View from No.11. Memoirs of a Tory Radical* (1993), p.64.

[10]   T.E. Utley, *Spectator,* 9 August 1986, reprinted in Philip Marsden-Smedley (ed.), *Britain in the*

Eighties. The Spectator's View of the Thatcher Decade (1989), pp.146–50.

[11]   Bob Jessop, Kevin Bonnett, Simon Bromley and Tom Ling, 'Authoritarian Populism, Two Nations and Thatcherism', *New Left Review,* 1, 147, September–October 1984.

[12]   TFW, Thatcher speech to Conservative Central Council, 15 March 1975 (102655): 'Do we become extremist Right-Wingers? Because that is what our opponents will say, that's what they've been saying. To stand up for liberty is now called Thatcherism. (Laughter.)' Thatcherism was also quite widely used in the press during the late 1970s. See for example, *The Times,* Business Diary, 2 September 1977.

[13]   John Hoskyns, *Just in Time. Inside the Thatcher Revolution (2000), p.118.* The phrase was coined by Norman Strauss.

[14]   Peter Clarke, *A Question of Leadership. From Gladstone to Thatcher (1991); E.H.H. Green, Thatcher (2006).*

[15]   David Cannadine, 'How I Inspired Thatcher'. A Point of View from BBC website, 9 December 2005. Cannadine wrote an article on that very unThatcherite hero Harry Flashman in *New Society* and later heard that his friend Matthew Parris had drawn the article to Thatcher's attention.

[16]   Campbell, *The Grocer's Daughter,* p.60.

[17]   'Playing with the Casino's Money', John Mortimer interview with Tebbit, *Spectator,* 24 May 1986, reprinted in Marsden-Smedley (ed.), *Britain in the Eighties.* pp.139–46.

[18]   E.H.H. Green, *Ideologies of Conservatism* (Oxford, 2001), p.221.

[19]   The only Thatcher minister to refer to Law in his memoirs is John Nott, but these memoirs were published some time after Nott's resignation and Nott quite often draws the general historical background of his memoirs from the works of historians rather than personal memory. John Nott, *Here Today, Gone Tomorrow, Recollections of an Errant Politician* (2003), p.134.

[20]   Simon Jenkins, *Thatcher and Sons. A Revolution in Three Acts (2006).*

CHAPTER 1. THATCHER BEFORE THATCHERISM

[1]   Alfred Sherman, *Paradoxes of Power. Reflections on the Thatcher Interlude,* edited by Mark Garnett (Exeter, 2005), p.20.

[2]   TFW, Margaret Thatcher, enclosing account of her early career to Donald Kaberry MP, 16 March 1956 (109939).

[3]   Margaret Thatcher, *The Path to Power* (1996), p.xiii.

[4]   TFW, Memorandum of conversation between Margaret Thatcher and official of US embassy at Connaught Hotel, 22 May 1973, enclosed with letter from Annenberg to State Department, 25 June 1973 (110554).

[5]   George Gardiner, *Margaret Thatcher. From Childhood to Leadership (1975)*.

[6]   On the circumstances of his biography's composition and his own life, see George Gardiner, *A Bastard's Tale* (1999).

[7]   Paul Halloran and Mark Hollingsworth, *Thatcher's Fortunes. The Life and Times of Mark Thatcher (2005)*.

[8]   Leo Abse, *Margaret Daughter of Beatrice. A Politician's Psycho Biography of Margaret Thatcher* (1989).

[9]   John Campbell, *Margaret Thatcher,* Vol.1, *The Grocer's Daughter* (2000), p.33.

[10]   Ibid., pp.8–15.

[11]   For an account by one of her less privileged fellow pupils, who seems not to have fond memories of Margaret Roberts, see Joan Bridgman, 'At School with Margaret Thatcher', *Contemporary Review,* 9 January 2004.

430

[12]   Julian Critchley, *A Bag of Boiled Sweets* (1995), p.49.

[13]   TFW, Thatcher speech to Conservative Party conference, 13 October 1989 (107789): 'I went to Oxford, but I've never let it hold me back.'

[14]   *The Fourth Protocol* was published in 1984. It concerns an attempt by elements in the Soviet Union to bring Thatcher's downfall and engineer the election of a left-wing Labour government in 1987. Forsyth dabbled in Conservative politics. See Frederick Forsyth, *Britain and Europe. The End of Democracy? Tenth Ian Gow Memorial Lecture* (2001).

[15]   Percy Cradock, *In Pursuit of British Interests. Reflections on Foreign Policy under Margaret Thatcher and John Major* (1997), p.20.

[16]   On Thatcher's meeting with Bloom, see George Walden, *Lucky George. Memoirs of an Anti-Politician* (1999), p.273.

[17]   Anthony Powell, *Journals, 1982–1986* (1995), p.40, entry for 26 October 1982.

[18]   TFW, Thatcher speech on the opening of Buckingham University, 6 February 1976 (102954).

[19]   TFW, Speech by Harry Giles, 24 February 1950 (100873).

[20]   Angus Calder, *The Myth of the Blitz* (1991).

[21]   TFW, Thatcher speech to rally in Cardiff, 16 April 1979 (104011): 'Is this the nation that stood alone in 1940 against the collapse of European Civilization?'

[22]   TFW, Thatcher speeches: 21 May 1985 (106055), 1 November 1989 (107812) and 29 August 1990 (108179).

[23]   TFW, Thatcher speech to Conservative Party conference, 13 October 1989 (107789): 'Let us never forget Poland's role in our own finest hour.'

[24]   George Urban, *Diplomacy and Disillusion at the Court of Margaret Thatcher. An Insider's View* (1996), p.34: 'I provided some Churchillian words and metaphors for Margaret Thatcher, not because I believed her to be quite of Churchillian stature – though my respect for her was immense – but rather because I thought that she was the most persuasive and eye-catching representative of the new Western determination to stop the Soviet Union.'

[25]   TFW, Nigel Lawson, 'The New Conservatism', speech to Bow Group, 4 August 1980 (109505): 'This, for a whole generation, was Britain's finest hour: it was also a time when the State was seen to arrogate to itself, in a cause whose rightness was not open to question, all the apparatus of central planning and direction of labour. In fact what is sensible

in war, when there is a unique unity of national purpose and when a simple test can be applied to all economic activities (namely whether or not they further the success of the war effort), is wholly inappropriate in time of peace, when what is needed is a system that brings harmoniously together a diversity of individual purposes of which the State need not even be aware. Nevertheless, the apparent beneficence, rationality and justice of central planning cast a spell that long outlived the wartime world to which it belonged.'

[26] Peter Tatchell, the unsuccessful Labour candidate in the Bermondsey by-election of 1983, expressed his admiration for Wintringham in his pamphlet, *Democratic Defence. A Non-Nuclear Alternative (1985)*.

[27] TFW, Thatcher speech to Scottish Conservative Party conference, 10 May 1985 (106046): 'One of the world's ugliest tyrannies had to be defeated so that we could live in peace and human dignity. It was a war of the common man – our own, Russian, French and American. We all fought, rich and poor, men at the front, women in the factories, fought together in a common cause which transcended all our differences ... Many were at constant risk – in London streets; at Anzio, at Coventry, at Murmansk.'

[28] Richard Hillary, *The Last Enemy* (1942).

[29] Barbara Cartland, *Ronald Cartland* (1942).

[30] John Peyton, *Without Benefit of Laundry* (1997), p.1.

[31] Peter Rawlinson, *A Price Too High. An Autobiography* (1989), p.17.

[32] TFW, Waldron Smithers to J.P.L. Thomas, 5 February 1949. This document is quoted in the editorial comments attached to the memo from Cook to Thomas, 1 February 1949 (109917).

[33] Roy Jenkins, *A Life at the Centre* (1994), p.554.

[34] James Prior, *A Balance of Power* (1986), p.17.

[35] Carol Thatcher, *Below the Parapet. The Biography of Denis Thatcher (1996).*

[36] Woodrow Wyatt, *The Journals of Woodrow Wyatt,* Vol.1, *1985–1988,* edited by Sarah Curtis (2000), entry for 19 January 1986, p.62.

[37] Petronella Wyatt, *Father, Dear Father. Life with Woodrow Wyatt* (1999), p.158.

[38] Thatcher's candidacy seems to have been supported by Central Office but resisted by constituency associations. John Ramsden, *The Winds of Change. Macmillan to Heath, 1957–1975* (1996), p.117.

[39] TFW, Harris to Kaberry, 15 July 1958 (109944).

[40] Dennis Walters, *Not Always with the Pack* (1989), p.104.

[41] Rawlinson, *A Price Too High,* p.246.

[42] TFW, Thatcher to Kaberry, 18 August 1958 (109946).

[43] TFW, 'What My Daughter Must Learn in the Next Nine Years', Thatcher article for *Daily Express,* 4 March 1960 (100948).

[44] Campbell, *The Grocer's Daughter,* p.95.

[45] TFW, Thatcher interview for the *Hornsey Journal,* 21 April 1978 (103662). Thatcher denied being a feminist – though the interviewer tried to insist that the mere fact of being leader of the Conservative Party made her a feminist, if not a militant one.

[46] The quickest way to find all her statements on feminism is to do a keyword search on the Thatcher Foundation website with the word 'strident'. See, for example, TFW, Thatcher press conference in Glasgow, 26 April 1979 (104045).

[47] TFW, Thatcher interview for Thames TV, 13 December 1982 (105071).

[48] TFW, Thatcher general election address, 3 February 1950 (100858).

[49] Denis Healey, *The Time of My Life* (1990), p.487.

[50] Most literature on the subject in recent years has, in fact, been devoted to showing that consensus was a 'myth'. See Dennis Kavanagh, *Thatcherism and British Politics. The End of Consensus?* (Oxford, 1988); Ben Pimlott, 'The Myth of Consensus' in Lesley Smith (ed.), *The Making of Britain. Echoes of Greatness* (1988); Harriet Jones and Michael Kandiah (eds.), *The Myth of Consensus* (1996); Scott Kelly, *The Myth of Mr Butskell. The Politics of British Economic Policy, 1950–1955 (Aldershot, 2002).*

[51] Norman Tebbit, *Unfinished Business* (1991), pp.17–19.

[52] Nicholas Ridley, *My Style of Government. The Thatcher Years* (1991), p.3.

[53] Thatcher, *The Path to Power,* p.116.

[54] Campbell, *The Grocer's Daughter,* p.151.

[55] TFW, Interview for Scottish Television, 21 February 1975 (102632). Thatcher said, 'He [Macmillan] was a marvellous politician and it was fascinating to work with him and watch him. He was working towards the things which I believe in.'

[56] Gardiner, *Margaret Thatcher,* pp.67 and 68: 'Even now, Macmillan is the Tory leader for

whom Margaret seems to have the greatest admiration.'

[57]   TFW, Thatcher interview for the Finnish newspaper *Suomen Kuvalehti,* 7 November 1984 (105512). Interviewed by Alastair Burnet for *TV Eye,* 24 January 1985 (105949), Thatcher drew attention again to the fact that Macmillan had been in power at a time when public spending consumed about 33.3 per cent of national income – though now, at a time when Macmillan's attacks on her were becoming more open, her own tone was more petulant. On 22 February 1983, Hugo Young, interviewing Thatcher for the *Sunday Times* (105088), asked: 'Were the Macmillan years an aberration?' Thatcher replied: 'I don't think I have changed the direction of Conservatism ... don't forget that in the Macmillan years the proportion of public expenditure was lower than it is now.'

[58]   TFW, Thatcher interviewed by Brian Walden, *Weekend World,* 1 February 1981 (104472).

[59]   TFW, Thatcher interviewed by Hugo Young, *Sunday Times,* 22 February 1983 (105088): 'The Employment 1944 White Paper is excellent but it's on my side.' Later in the same interview, she said: 'I really am the true Keynesian, when you take him as a whole.' Favourable references to Keynes from Thatcher

were relatively rare – though they were quite common in the speeches of her mentor Sir Keith Joseph.

[60] TFW, Thatcher speech to the Institute of Socio-Economic Studies in New York, 'Let Our Children Grow Tall', 15 September 1975 (102769).

[61] Richard Cockett, *Thinking the Unthinkable. Think Tanks and the Economic Counter-Revolution, 1931–1983 (1995).*

[62] John Nott, *Here Today, Gone Tomorrow. Recollections of an Errant Politician* (2003), p.137.

[63] Geoffrey Howe, *Conflict of Loyalty* (1994), pp.30–31.

[64] TFW, Thatcher speech to Conservative Political Centre, 'What's Wrong with Politics?, 11 October 1968 (101632).

[65] *The Times,* 5 November 1969.

[66] Oliver Franks, *Britain and the Tide of World Affairs. The BBC Reith Lectures, 1954* (1955).

[67] Thatcher, *The Path to Power,* p.91.

[68] TFW, *Sun,* 10 April 1970 (101809).

[69] John Pardoe cited in Campbell, *The Grocer's Daughter,* p.155.

[70] TFW, Thatcher speech in Friern Barnet, 3 April 1959 (101016).

[71] *Financial Times,* 23 October 1969.

[72] Thatcher interview for *The Times,* 5 November 1969.

[73] TFW, Thatcher speech at Haberdasher's Aske School, 17 September 1971 (102138).

[74] On Heath's life, see his autobiography – *The Course of My Life* (1998) – and John Campbell, *Edward Heath. A Biography (1993).* On the Heath government, see Martin Holmes, *The Failure of the Heath Government* (1997) and Stuart Ball and Anthony Seldon (eds.), *The Heath Government, 1970–1974. A Reappraisal (1996).* For the sense of crisis in the early 1970s, it is worth reading Victor Rothschild, *Meditations on a Broomstick* (1977).

[75] John Ramsden, *The Making of Conservative Party Policy. The Conservative Research Department since 1929 (1980).*

[76] TFW, transcript of meeting at Selsdon Park Hotel, morning session, 31 January 1970 (109512).

[77] TFW, 'Advance hints on Walden's thinking', with covering letter signed Bruce Anderson, 14 September 1977 (archive/2008/gl.pdf).

[78] Howe, *Conflict of Loyalty,* p.76.

[79] Jeremy Smith, 'Relations between the Conservative Party and the Ulster Unionist Party during the Twentieth Century', *English Historical Review,* CXXI, 490 (2006), pp.70–103. See also Jeremy Smith, 'Walking a Real Tight-Rope of Difficulties: Sir Edward Heath and the Search for Stability in Northern Ireland, June 1970–March 1971', *Twentieth Century British History,* 18, 2 (2007), pp.219–53.

[80] TFW, 'Events leading to the resignation of Mr Heath's administration, 4 March 1974' (thorpe .pdf): Telegram from Mr Harry West, 2 March; Mr Pym's advice on Mr West's Telegram; reply to Mr West's Telegram; note of the meeting with Thorpe on 2 March. See also John Ramsden, *The Winds of Change. Macmillan to Heath, 1957–1975* (1996), p.387.

[81] NA, PREM 15/985, Strike Report 5/6 February (day 28/9) 1972.

[82] NA, PREM 15/986, Note to or from Prime Minister signed E, 23 February 1972.

[83] Douglas Hurd, *An End to Promises* (1979), p.81.

[84] For an account of Heath's fall, see TFW, 'Events leading to the resignation of Mr Heath's Administration on 4 March 1974' by Robert Armstrong, 16 March 1974 (110605). This

document is different from the one listed above with the same title.

[85] Nott, *Here Today, Gone Tomorrow,* p.146.

[86] Arthur Scargill, interviewed in *Marxism Today,* April 1981.

[87] Gerald Nabarro, *Exploits of a Politician* (1973), p.101.

CHAPTER 2. THATCHERISM BEFORE THATCHER? ENOCH POWELL

[1] Cited in Douglas Schoen, *Enoch Powell and the Powellites* (1977), p.261.

[2] Simon Heffer, *Like the Roman. The Life of Enoch Powell* (1998), p.958.

[3] TFW, House of Commons, Prime Minister's Question Time, 4 June 1981 (104660).

[4] *The Times* diary, 10 September 1974.

[5] *Observer,* quoted in Richard Shepherd, *Enoch Powell* (1996), p.217.

[6] Schoen, *Powell and the Powellites,* p.11: 'The deepest instinct of the Englishman – how the word 'instinct' keeps forcing itself in again and again – is for continuity.' The Tory MP Stephen Hastings wrote of Powell's 'massive castles of logic steadily constructed rampart upon

unassailable rampart, yet sometimes founded on some simple, instinctive, romantic conviction'. Stephen Hastings, *The Drums of Memory* (1994), p.240.

[7]   'No answers blowing in the wind' first published in the *Spectator,* 9 October 1976, reprinted in Rex Collings (ed.), *Reflections of a Statesman. The Writings and Speeches of Enoch Powell* (1991), pp.341–5.

[8]   'A battalion in which fifty per cent deserve the VC is a battalion that destroys itself ... Still, you have to have somebody within the ranks who says, "I'll charge that machine gun!"' Powell quoted in John Ranelagh, *Thatcher's People* (1991), p.184.

[9]   Shepherd, *Enoch Powell,* p.231.

[10]   Quoted in ibid., p.246.

[11]   Douglas Hurd, *An End to Promises* (1979), p.23.

[12]   Geoffrey Howe quotes Powell's speech approving of the abolition of exchange controls in *Conflict of Loyalty* (1994), p.143. Note too one of the rare occasions when Thatcher herself said: 'I entirely accept the right honourable gentleman's rebuke', House of Commons, Prime Minister's Question Time, 13 May 1980 (104363). Powell had rebuked her for suggesting that the civil service made policy.

442

[13] Douglas Hurd, *Memoirs* (2003), p.308.

[14] Collings (ed.), *Reflections of a Statesman,* p.137. Powell replied that he was not sure that what Thatcher meant by Powellism was the same as what he himself meant by the term.

[15] Cecil Parkinson, *Right at the Centre* (1992), p.124.

[16] John Nott, *Here Today, Gone Tomorrow. Recollections of an Errant Politician* (2003), pp.135–8.

[17] Powell used the phrase in a speech in Birmingham on 13 June 1970.

[18] Powell has excited an extraordinary amount of attention from biographers; Simon Heffer has written the definitive work. T.E. Utley, *Enoch Powell. The Man and His Thinking* (1968) is also very important – Utley was sceptical about some aspects of the Powell myth, perhaps because he himself had done a good deal to invent it.

[19] TFW, Thatcher speech to Finchley League of Jewish Women, 18 November 1968, reported in the *Finchley Press,* 22 November 1968 (101636).

[20] TFW, Memorandum of conversation between Margaret Thatcher and official of US embassy at Connaught Hotel, 22 May 1973, enclosed

with letter from Annenberg to State Department, 25 June 1973 (110554).

[21] John Ramsden, *The Winds of Change. Macmillan to Heath, 1957–1975* (1996), p.279.

[22] Thatcher's remarks about Powell in her own constituency were always made in terms of studied inscrutability. Asked about Powell's views on immigration in November 1968, she said: 'I think that you should always be willing to take your views to the final test; and I hope that Enoch will put his views before the parliamentary forum.' TFW, Thatcher speech to Finchley League of Jewish Women, 18 November 1968 (101636).

[23] Shepherd, *Enoch Powell,* p.292.

[24] TFW, Thatcher speech to Young Conservative conference, 12 February 1978 (103487).

[25] Christopher Bland, reviewing T.E. Utley's biography of Powell in a liberal Tory journal, argued that Powell's views on race were the least interesting and attractive part of his political platform, *Crossbow,* January–March 1969.

[26] Howe, *Conflict of Loyalty,* pp.476 and 480.

[27] Quoted in Heffer, *Like the Roman,* p.748.

[28] Cited by Ronald Butt in 'The Importance of Being Enoch', *Crossbow,* April–June 1966.

444

[29] Cited in Shepherd, *Enoch Powell,* p.388.

[30] Ibid., p.427.

[31] Heffer, *Like the Roman,* p.97.

[32] Collings (ed.), *Reflections of a Statesman,* p.577.

[33] Schoen, *Powell and the Powellites,* p.11. Powell made these remarks in 1964.

[34] John Wood (ed.), *Enoch Powell. Freedom and Reality* (1969), p.241.

[35] Shepherd, *Enoch Powell,* p.248.

[36] Ridley was speaking on *Panorama;* quoted in Collings (ed.) *Reflections of a Statesman,* p.12.

[37] Quoted in Shepherd, *Enoch Powell,* p.267.

[38] TFW, Thatcher interviewed by David Frost for TV-AM, 30 December 1988 (107022).

[39] Simon Heffer, *Like the Roman,* p.934.

CHAPTER 3. BECOMING LEADER

[1] Quoted in Patrick Cosgrove, *Margaret Thatcher. A Tory and Her Party* (1978), p.11.

[2] TFW, Annenberg to State Department, 25 June 1973 (110554).

[3] David Butler and Dennis Kavanagh, *The British General Election of October 1974* (1975), pp.237

and 264. According to Hailsham, Thatcher, Macmillan (fils) and Joseph had been the only members of the shadow cabinet to oppose an approach to the Liberals in March 1974, TFW, Hailsham diary, entry for 1 March 1974 (111117).

[4]   TFW, Joseph speech, 'Inflation is Caused by Governments', Preston, 5 September 1974 (110607).

[5]   Morrison Halcrow, *Keith Joseph. A Single Mind* (1989), p.9.

[6]   Cited in John Ranelagh, *Thatcher's People* (1991), p.137.

[7]   Bruce Anderson, *The Times,* 31 August 2006.

[8]   Alfred Sherman, *Paradoxes of Power. Reflections on the Thatcher Interlude,* edited by Mark Garnett (Exeter, 2005), p.97.

[9]   Ferdinand Mount cited in Halcrow, *Keith Joseph,* p.90.

[10]   Sherman, *Paradoxes of Power,* p.55.

[11]   Denis Healey, *The Time of My Life* (1990), p.488.

[12]   TFW, Hailsham diary, 9 March 1977 (111176). Hailsham seems to have been reporting remarks made by Jo Grimond and Lord Plowden.

[13] Ibid., entry for 29 March 1977 (111182), after meeting Carrington.

[14] Ibid., entry for 6 October 1977 (111187), after meeting Carrington and Whitelaw.

[15] The precise purpose of the speech is unclear. Joseph's biographer believes that it was designed to form part of a bid for the leadership of the Conservative Party, Halcrow, *Keith Joseph,* p.81.

[16] Sherman, *Paradoxes of Power,* p.56.

[17] Halcrow, *Keith Joseph,* pp.86–7.

[18] Margaret Thatcher, *The Path to Power* (1996), p.266.

[19] Cited in Halcrow, *Keith Joseph,* p.76.

[20] Edward du Cann, *Two Lives. The Political and Business Careers of Edward du Cann (Upton upon Severn, 1995).*

[21] Nigel Fisher, *The Tory Leaders. Their Struggle for Power* (1977), p.146. For Fisher's activities earlier in the year, see TFW, 'Events leading to the resignation of Mr Heath's administration, 4 March 1974' (thorpe.pdf): 'Message from Mr Nigel Fisher', 3 March 1974. Fisher, a friend of Jeremy Thorpe's, said that he believed the Liberals would find supporting the government easier if it had a different leader.

[22]   Baker says that Kitson was the manager. Kenneth Baker, *The Turbulent Years. My Life in Politics* (1993), p.44. John Ramsden says that Baker and Kitson jointly managed the campaign. John Ramsden, *The Winds of Change. Macmillan to Heath, 1957–1975* (1996), p.447.

[23]   For an analysis of the votes in the 1975 leadership election (conducted with access to private documents and anonymous interviews), see Philip Cowley and Matthew Bailey, 'Peasants' Uprising or Religious War? Re-Examining the 1975 Conservative Leadership Contest', *British Journal of Political Science,* 30, 4 (2000), pp.599–629.

CHAPTER 4. OPPOSITION, 1975–9

[1]   TFW, Hailsham diary, 29 March 1977 (111182).

[2]   TFW, Kissinger briefing for Ford, 8 January 1975 (110510).

[3]   Edmund Dell, *A Hard Pounding. Politics and Economics Crisis, 1974–1976 (Oxford, 1991), p.vii.*

[4]   TFW, Angus Maude and others, 'Themes', 16 February 1978 (109853).

[5] TFW, Thatcher speech to Institute of Socio-Economic Studies, 'Let Our Children Grow Tall', 15 September 1975 (102769).

[6] See Peter Jay, 'How is Your Gloom Resistance?', *The Times,* 8 July 1974 and 'Pursuit of Group Self-Interest Seen as Main Threat to Liberal Democracy', *The Times,* 4 September 1974.

[7] Auberon Waugh, 'Of Human Bondage', *New Statesman,* 13 September 1976. Reprinted in Auberon Waugh, *In the Lion's Den* (1978), pp.71–4.

[8] TFW, shadow cabinet, 11 April 1975 (109958). Tim Raison said: 'We should support Mr Healey if he produces a sensible budget.'

[9] *Sun,* 15 October 1972.

[10] Alistair McAlpine, *Once a Jolly Bagman* (1998), p.211.

[11] James Prior, *A Balance of Power* (1986), p.112.

[12] Kenneth Morgan, *Callaghan. A Life (Oxford, 1997).*

[13] This remark was apparently quoted by Tim Bell to Larry Lamb; see Mark Hollingsworth, *The Ultimate Spin Doctor. The Life and Fast Times of Tim Bell* (1997), p.71.

[14] TFW, Steering Committee, 13 May 1975 (109965).

[15] John Nott, *Here Today, Gone Tomorrow. Recollections of an Errant Politician* (2003), p.174 and McAlpine, *Once a Jolly Bagman*, p.205.

[16] *The Times,* 30 May 1978, 'Loyalty and Leadership'.

[17] In her memoirs, Thatcher suggests that Patten's main use was to turn the CRD into a 'secretariat for the Shadow Cabinet'; a secretariat was particularly necessary because the shadow ministers were so often divided amongst themselves. Margaret Thatcher, *The Path to Power* (1995), p.293. In fact, Thatcher eventually took away Patten's functions as secretary to the shadow cabinet though she stressed that this was in no way a demotion. See Thatcher letter to *The Times,* 31 May 1978.

[18] John Hoskyns, *Just in Time. Inside the Thatcher Revolution (2000), p.16.*

[19] Ibid., p.28.

[20] Thatcher, *The Path to Power,* p.399.

[21] Stephen Hastings, the right-wing Tory MP who was also involved in some of these committees, described Crozier's account as 'rather colourful'. Stephen Hastings, *The Drums of Memory* (1994), p.236.

[22] Brian Crozier, *Free Agent. The Unseen War, 1941–1991* (1993), pp.128–48.

[23] TFW, Patten, 'Implementing our Strategy', 21 December 1977 (109847).

[24] TFW, Joseph, 'Notes Towards the Definition of Policy', 4 April 1975 (110098).

[25] TFW, Shadow cabinet, 11 April 1975 (109958).

[26] TFW, Hailsham's note on shadow cabinet meeting, 11 April 1975 (111134).

[27] TFW, Shadow cabinet, 11 April 1975 (109958). Raison argued: 'that the fulcrum of the political see-saw lay not between the Labour and Conservative Parties but half way across the Labour Party'.

[28] Ibid.

[29] David Stirling expressed his support for a written constitution. TFW, Hailsham diary, entry for 8 November 1974 (111124).

[30] TFW, Joseph to Thatcher, 22 July 1975 (111219), on meeting with Val Duncan, of RTZ, Marcus Sieff and Hector Laing. Joseph alluded to 'a brief reference to the old subject of electoral reform' – though he suggested that Duncan was more realistic about the limited benefits of such reform than some of the industrialists whom he represented.

[31]   TFW, Maudling, 'Incomes Policy', 24 May 1976 (110140). Adam Ridley sent the paper to Thatcher with a note saying that he had tried, and failed, to persuade Maudling to amend his paper to allow that 'monetary policy and the level of demand did have some influence on the rate of inflation'.

[32]   TFW, Joseph lecture, 'Monetarism is not Enough', 5 April 1976 (110796).

[33]   TFW, Howe, 'The Economic Prospect and the Party's Political Position', 16 December 1975 (110128).

[34]   TFW, Kissinger briefing for Ford, 16 September 1975 (110527).

[35]   TFW, Thatcher interviewed by Peter Jay on *Weekend World*, 9 May 1976 (102836). Thatcher said: 'There are times when for temporary purposes you have to have an incomes policy.' Pressed on whether the Labour government's current pay policy was necessary, Thatcher replied: 'I certainly thought that the initial impact was temporarily needed.'

[36]   TFW, Maudling, 'Incomes Policy', 24 May 1976 (110140).

[37]   TFW, Lawson to Thatcher, 'Thoughts on "Implementing Our Strategy"', 15 January 1978 (110321).

[38]   Geoffrey Howe, *Conflict of Loyalty* (1994), p.100.

[39]   Ibid., p.63.

[40]   TFW, Howe, 'The Economic Education of the Public. Proposals for Concerted Action and Fighting Inflation', 16 May 1977 (109761).

[41]   TFW, Thatcher annotation on letter from Howe, 26 May 1977 (109784).

[42]   TFW, Thatcher annotation on Howe proposed speech on trade unions, 11 January 1978 (109796).

[43]   Thatcher, *The Path to Power,* p.423. For the discussion of the Stepping Stones report, see TFW, Meeting of leader's steering committee, 30 January 1978 (109832).

[44]   Norman Fowler, *Ministers Decide. A Personal Memoir of the Thatcher Years* (1991), p.93.

[45]   Nott, *Here Today, Gone Tomorrow,* p.172.

[46]   'Tory Leader Denies Split in Party Over Closed Shop', *The Times,* 14 September 1988.

[47]   Thatcher, *The Path to Power,* p.451.

[48]   Konrad Zweig wrote a pamphlet, prefaced by Howe, on the social market economy for the Centre for Policy Studies. He also published *The Origins of the German Social Market*

Economy. Leading Ideas and Their Intellectual Roots with the Adam Smith Institute in 1980.

[49] TFW, Howe, 'The Economic Education of the Public. Proposals for Concerted Action and Fighting Inflation', 16 May 1977 (109761).

[50] TFW, Maudling, 'Incomes Policy', 24 May 1976 (110140).

[51] Peter Hennessy, 'Mrs Thatcher Warned in Secret Report of Defeat in Confrontation with Unions', *The Times,* 18 April 1978. For a more detailed, and less defeatist, account of this committee, see TFW, Authority of Government Policy Group, Final Report, 22 June 1977 (111394).

[52] TFW, 'Themes' by Angus Maude and others, 16 February 1978 (109853).

[53] TFW, Hailsham diary, entry for 20 January 1976 (111153).

[54] It is worth noting Callaghan's own remarks on the eve of the 1979 election: 'You know there are times, perhaps once every thirty years, when there is a sea-change in politics. It does not matter what you say or what you do. There is a shift in what the public wants and what it approves of. I suspect there is now such a sea-change – and it is for Mrs Thatcher.' See Bernard Donoughue, *Prime Minister. The Conduct of Policy under Harold Wilson and James Callaghan* (1987), p.191. The remarks

are widely quoted in memoirs of the period – see, for example, David Owen, *Time to Declare* (1991), p.413.

[55] David Butler and Dennis Kavanagh, *The British General Election of 1979* (1980), p.337.

[56] TFW, Joseph, 'Our Tone of Voice and our Tasks', 7 December 1976 (110178).

[57] TFW, *Weekend World,* 18 September 1977 (103191).

[58] Howe, *Conflict of Loyalty,* p.104.

[59] The Tories proposed a register of Commonwealth citizens whose family links might give them the right to settle in Britain. Their home affairs spokesman privately regarded the proposal as unworkable and, after the election, it was dropped. Howe, *Conflict of Loyalty,* p.104.

[60] Hoskyns, *Just in Time,* p.94.

CHAPTER 5. PRIMITIVE POLITICS, 1979–83

[1] Nigel Lawson, *The View from No 11. Memoirs of a Tory Radical* (1993), p.46.

[2] Robert Armstrong and Clive Priestley in 'The Civil Service Reforms of the 1980. The Demise of the Civil Service Department and the Resignation of

Sir Ian Bancroft as Head of the Civil Service, November 1981', seminar held 17 November 2006, Centre for Contemporary British History, 2007, p.67.

[3]   John Newsinger, *Dangerous Men. SAS and Popular Culture (1997).*

[4]   TFW, Hailsham diary, entry for 8 November 1974 (111124).

[5]   John Harvey-Jones, *Getting it Together. Memoirs of a Troubleshooter* (1991), p.361.

[6]   Nicholas Henderson, *Mandarin* (1994), p.406, entry for 4 July 1981. Henderson added, however: 'I am not sure that it's Maggie's fault or that it will not come right in the end.'

[7]   TFW, Richard Allen, memo for the president, 31 July 1981 (110522).

[8]   Quoted in Henderson, *Mandarin,* p.363, entry for 3 October 1980.

[9]   Denis Healey, *The Time of My Life* (1990), p.433.

[10] Geoffrey Howe, *Conflict of Loyalty* (1994), p.144. Howe did not believe that his party should have committed itself to sustain such increases in defence spending.

[11] Edmund Dell, *A Hard Pounding. Politics and Economics Crisis, 1974–1976* (Oxford, 1991), p.70.

[12] Howe, *Conflict of Loyalty,* p.204. Lawson, *The View from No.11,* p.93.

[13] Tim Renton went home as the measure taxing banks was put to parliament, hoping that the opposition would not force a vote and expose his absence. As it was, there was a vote and the whips gave Renton a choice between inventing some duplicitous excuse for his absence or resigning. He resigned. He was quickly offered office again, but was reluctant to forgo his lucrative City employment (perhaps becoming known as a defender of banks had not done his extra-parliamentary career any harm). Tim Renton, *Chief Whip* (2005), p.12.

[14] Milton Friedman comment on Patrick Minford, 'Inflation, Unemployment and the Pound' in Subroto Roy and John Clarke (eds.), *Margaret Thatcher's Revolution. How it Happened and What it Meant* (2005), pp.50–66, p.66: 'I am a great admirer of Margaret Thatcher, but I have no great expertise on recent British experience.'

[15] American ambassador in London to secretary of state, 15 September 1983 (109408): 'Thatcher and Howe are skeptical of Administration arguments that inflationary

expectations – rather than deficits – are the major influence on interest rates.'

[16] On Tory resentment at the programmes by Galbraith, and the suggestion that the BBC restore 'proper balance' by broadcasting Friedman or Hayek, see TFW, Howe to Joseph, 22 March 1976, 'Economics and the BBC' (110039).

[17] Biffen, interviewed by Beatrix Campbell in *Marxism Today,* 6 December 1989.

[18] John Hoskyns, *Just in Time. Inside the Thatcher Revolution (2000), p.135.*

[19] Ibid., p.127.

[20] Quoted in David Richards, *The Civil Service under the Conservatives, 1979–1997* (1997), p.191.

[21] Peter Hall, *Governing the Economy. The Politics of State Intervention in Britain and France* (1986), p.97.

[22] Enoch Powell, 'The Conservative Party', in Dennis Kavanagh and Anthony Seldon (eds.), *The Thatcher Effect. A Decade of Change* (1989), pp.80–88, p.81.

[23] Lawson, *The View from No.11,* p.45.

[24] Howe, *Conflict of Loyalty,* p.109.

[25] Ibid., p.162.

458

[26] TFW, Lawson, 'The New Conservatism', speech to the Bow Group, 4 August 1980 (109505).

[27] The financial secretary to the treasury ended the practice, begun by the Labour government in 1975, whereby the government imposed limits on the amount that building societies were allowed to lend in each quarter. However, he discreetly refrained from breaking up the cartel that existed amongst building societies, because it suited him that some interest rates at least should not fluctuate. Lawson, *The View from No.11,* pp.86–7.

[28] Lawson, The *View from No.11,* pp.78–80.

[29] TFW, 'Fentiman Road Economic Seminar', 18 May 1975 (109968): 'It [a floating exchange rate] poses the threat of higher interest rates, with the consequent difficulty of "dealing with" the mortgage situation ... Probably the most important political and practical constraint on monetary policy, particularly in the context of a floating rate, is the housing mortgage market. A stabilization scheme that would have the effect of insulating this is an essential concept to have on hand ... The question arises whether this two-tier interest rate structure needs to be extended in other directions.'

[30] Gordon Pepper, *Inside Thatcher's Monetarist Revolution* (1998); Gordon Pepper and Michael Oliver, *Monetarism under Thatcher. Lessons for*

the Future (2001); Patrick Minford, *The Supply Side Revolution in Britain* (1991).

[31] Ferdinand Mount claims that 'Alan Walters was the driving force behind the 1981 budget', Ferdinand Mount, *Cold Cream. My Early Life and Other Mistakes* (2008), p.283.

[32] Ian Gilmour, *Dancing with Dogma. Britain under Thatcherism* (1992), p.26.

[33] Patrick Minford, 'Inflation, Unemployment and the Pound', in Roy and Clarke (eds), *Margaret Thatcher's Revolution,* pp.50–66.

[34] Philip Booth (ed.), *Were 364 Economists All Wrong?* (2006). This pamphlet can be downloaded from the website of the Institute of Economic Affairs.

[35] *Guardian,* 16 March 1982, cited in Howe, *Conflict of Loyalty,* p.209.

[36] Mount, *Cold Cream,* p.283.

[37] *The Times,* 9 March 1984, letter from Hahn and Solow.

[38] Peter Bazalgette in *Philips and Drew Market Review,* cited in David Kynaston, *The City of London, IV, A Club No More, 1945–2000* (2001), p.587.

[39] TFW, Nigel Lawson, 'Thoughts on the Coming Battle', 15 October 1973 (110312).

[40]   James Prior, *A Balance of Power* (1986), p.129.

[41]   Margaret Thatcher, *The Downing Street Years* (1995), p.151.

[42]   George Gardiner, *A Bastard's Tale* (1999), p.141. The rebels wanted to remove legal immunity from unions involved in all secondary action (not just strikes), to require unions to hold ballots before strikes and to require ballots on all existing closed shops.

[43]   Peter Dorey, 'One Step at a Time: the Conservative Government's Approach to the Reform of Industrial Relations since 1979', *Political Quarterly,* 64, 1 (1993), pp.24–36. And Simon Auerbach, 'Mrs Thatcher's Labour Laws: Slouching Towards Utopia?' in ibid., pp.37–48.

[44]   Peter Ingram, David Metcalf and Jonathan Wadsworth, 'Strike Incidence in British Manufacturing in the 1980s', *Industrial and Labor Relations Review,* 46, 4 (July 1993), pp.704–17.

[45]   Roy Jenkins, *European Diary, 1977–81* (1998), p.479, entry for 14 July 1979.

[46]   Hoskyns, *Just in Time,* p.147.

[47]   Michael Edwardes, *Back from the Brink* (1983), p.89.

[48]   TFW, Thatcher interview for *Weekend World,* 18 September 1977 (103191): 'I've never seen

anyone take Clive Jenkins to the cleaners as Hugh Scanlon does.'

[49]   Donald MacDougall, *Don and Mandarin. Memoirs of an Economist* (1987), p.231.

[50]   Brian Wyldbore-Smith, *March Past* (2001), p.135.

[51]   On the decline in donations to the Tory party, see the report by the Labour Research Department of 1977 – mentioned in *The Times* Business Diary, 2 September 1977. On 29 March, Hailsham reported Carrington's view that 'they [the big industrialists] much resented the hectoring way she lectured them'. TFW, Hailsham diary, 29 March 1977 (111182).

[52]   Hoskyns, *Just in Time,* p.345.

[53]   Lawson, *The View from No.11,* p.58. MacDougall denies that the CBI leaders 'caved in' during their subsequent meeting with Thatcher.

[54]   Ivor Crewe and Anthony King, *SDP. The Birth, Life and Death of the Social Democratic Party* (Oxford, 1995), p.113.

[55]   David Butler and Dennis Kavanagh (eds.), *The British General Election of October 1974* (1975), p.237.

[56]   TFW, Meeting of shadow ministers and economists, 8 July 1975 (109986).

[57]   TFW, Joseph speech at Preston, 'Inflation is Caused by Governments', 5 September 1974 (110607): 'But you will ask, how do I square this with the monthly unemployment statistics which receive banner headlines and strike gloom into politicians' hearts – 500,000 – 600,000 – 800,000 – fears of one million unemployed?'

[58]   MacDougall, *Don and Mandarin,* p.211. MacDougall himself prepared a report in November 1979 which suggested that, by 1983, inflation would stand at 5 per cent, output would barely regain its 1979 level and unemployment would reach 2 million. He thought that the Tories would find it hard to win an election with such statistics – as it turned out, they won with inflation and output at roughly the levels MacDougall had guessed, and unemployment at 3 million.

[59]   Kenneth Morgan, *Michael Foot. A Life (2007).*

[60]   Eric Heffer, *Never a Yes Man. The Life and Politics of an Adopted Liverpudlian* (1991), p.176. Heffer identifies the key figures behind Foot's candidacy as being himself, Clive Jenkins, Ian Mikardo, Moss Evans, Bill Keyes, Alec Smith and Arthur Scargill.

[61]   TFW, CBTV programme, 13 December 1982 (105071): Child: 'What's the three things you admire in Michael Foot?' PM: 'Oh my goodness

me. Can I give you just one? He's a very effective journalist.'

[62] David Butler and Dennis Kavanagh (eds.), *The British General Election of 1983* (1984), pp.60–63.

[63] Cecil Parkinson, *Right at the Centre* (1992), p.229. McAlpine himself gives a slightly different figure. Alistair McAlpine, *Once a Jolly Bagman* (1998), p.254.

[64] David Owen, *Time to Declare* (1991), p.495.

[65] William Rodgers, *Fourth Amongst Equals* (2000), p.201.

[66] John Golding, *Hammer of the Left. Defeating Tony Benn, Eric Heffer and Militant in the Battle for the Labour Party,* edited by Paul Farrelly (2003).

[67] Ken Spencer, Andy Taylor, Barbara Smith, John Mawson, Norman Flynn and Richard Batley, *Crisis in the Industrial Heartland. A Study of the West Midlands* (Oxford, 1986), p.42.

[68] David Lazar, *Markets and Ideology in the City of London* (1990), p.42.

[69] Gallup Poll, 21–26 May 1987, cited in David Butler and Dennis Kavanagh (eds.), *The British General Election of 1987* (1988), p.248.

[70] *British Social Attitudes Survey* (1984), pp.48–9.

[71]   Paul Bagguley, *From Protest to Acquiescence? Political Movements of the Unemployed* (1991), p.202.

[72]   In December 1982, only 38 per cent of unemployed people blamed the government for their plight. Martin Holmes, *Thatcherism. Scope and Limits, 1983–1987* (1989), p.92. Paul Bagguley did stress that the attitudes of the unemployed varied according to how questions were phrased and how much contact they had with wider political movements. Bagguley, *From Protest to Acquiescence?*

CHAPTER 6. UNEXPECTED VICTORY: THE FALKLANDS

[1]   TFW, James Rentschler, 'Falklands Diary', 1 April–25 June 1982, entry for 1 April.

[2]   Julian Critchley, *A Bag of Boiled Sweets* (1995), p.181.

[3]   Lawrence Freedman, *The Official History of the Falklands Campaign,* Vol.1, *The Origins of the Falklands War* (2005), pp.114–27.

[4]   Sir Michael Armitage, in 'The Falklands War', seminar held 5 June 2002, http:/www.icbh.ac.uk/witness/Falklands/, p.22.

[5]   Cecil Parkinson, *Right at the Centre* (1992), p.165.

[6]   TFW, Telegram from American embassy, Buenos Aires, for Assistant Secretary of State Enders, 3 March 1982 (109418): 'He [Galtieri] reportedly wants to find a formula that will permit him to continue in a dual capacity [i.e. as head of the army and head of state]. This is likely to emerge as the key political question in the months ahead.'

[7]   The precise reasons for the Argentine decision to invade the Falklands at the moment when they did are still a matter of debate. Lawrence Freedman and Virginia Gamba-Stonehouse suggest that the British reaction to the Argentine landing in South Georgia forced the Argentinians to act before the British could send forces to the Falklands. Lawrence Freedman and Virginia Gamba-Stonehouse, *Signals of War* (1990), pp.65–83.

[8]   Douglas Hurd, *Memoirs* (2003), pp.88 and 280.

[9]   Henry Leach, in 'The Falklands War', seminar held 5 June 2002, http://www.icbh.ac.uk/witnes s/Falklands/, p.29.

[10]   Sir Michael Quinlan denied that the money for Trident had come from the navy budget, 'The Nott Review', seminar held 20 June 2001, htt p://www.icbh.ac.uk/witness/nott/, p.36.

[11]   John Nott, *Here Today, Gone Tomorrow. Recollections of an Errant Politician* (2003), p.240.

[12]   Keith Speed, *Sea Change. The Battle for the Falklands and the Future of Britain's Navy (1982), p.109.*

[13]   Kim Sabido (ITN correspondent), cited in Robert Harris, *Gotcha. The Media, the Government and the Falklands Crisis* (1983), p.26.

[14]   Ewen Southby-Tailyour. *Reasons in Writing. A Commando's View of the Falklands War* (2003). It illustrates the relative unimportance of the islands to British planners that Southby-Tailyour had been posted to the Falklands, in 1978, as an unofficial punishment after an argument with a superior.

[15]   Rentschler, 'Falklands Diary', p.3.

[16]   Jacques Attali, *Verbatim. I. Première Partie, 1981–1983* (1993), pp.298–9.

[17]   Nott, *Here Today, Gone Tomorrow,* p.305.

[18]   See, for example, Anthony Barnett, *Iron Britannia,* special issue of the *New Left Review* (1982): 'If the "profusion" of unexploded Argentine bombs had gone off, the story might have had another ending.'

[19]   Sandy Woodward with Patrick Robinson, *One Hundred Days. The Memoirs of the Falklands Battle Group Commander* (1997), p.99.

[20]   Roger Jackling referred to a letter from John Nott's office to the prime minister which said: 'from four to six escorts and an aircraft carrier – they were likely losses.' 'The Falklands War', seminar held 5 June 2002. http://www.icbh.ac.uk/witness/Falklands/, p.45. Leach said that he was never told of this and that he never asked directly about possible losses but that he would have expected them to amount to 'six destroyers/frigates, I would have been perfectly prepared to tolerate at least double that number'. He added that the landing might have been cancelled if both aircraft carriers had gone before it, but that they would have pressed on if the carriers had been destroyed after it. Leach to ibid., p.46. Woodward said, in ibid., that he had understood that the loss of one carrier would mean that the landing would have been called off.

[21]   Roger Curtis, in 'The Falklands War', seminar held 5 June 2002, http://www.icbh.ac.uk/witness/Falklands/, p.45, said that he had taken the figure 'from the top of his head' to impress the seriousness of the affair on the war cabinet. Roughly 3000 men took part in the first landings at San Carlos Bay. So perhaps

Leach's 'worst-case scenario' simply anticipated that all of these would be lost.

[22] Cecil Parkinson, in 'The Falklands War', seminar held 5 June 2002, http://www.icbh.ac.uk/witness/Falklands/, p.44.

[23] Quintin Hailsham, *A Sparrow's Flight. Memoirs* (1991), p.408: 'The one thing I had always been taught in the army was that an opposed landing from the sea was a peculiarly hazardous undertaking, required air superiority, and should be undertaken only with a secure and fairly short line of communications.'

[24] Julian Thompson, *No Picnic. 3 Commando Brigade in the South Atlantic, 1982* (1992), p.31.

[25] Nott, *Here Today, Gone Tomorrow*, p.247.

[26] Guy Bransby, *Her Majesty's Interrogator* (1996), p.48. It should be added that the Falklands War involved an unspoken alliance with Pinochet's regime in Chile. Bransby's wife was the daughter of a Chilean officer.

[27] Kevin Foster, *Fighting Fictions. War, Narrative and National Identity* (1998), p.28.

[28] Alan Clark, *Diaries, 1972–1982. Into Politics* (2001), p.366, entry for 29 October 1982.

[29] Ibid., p.370, letter to Michael Jopling, 4 November 1982.

[30]   Hugh McManners, *Falklands Commando* (1987), p.24.

[31]   Ted Rowlands, cited in Freedman, *The Falklands War,* p.75.

[32]   Jock Bruce-Gardyne, *Ministers and Mandarins. Inside the Whitehall Village (1986), p.166.*

[33]   Kenneth Baker, *The Turbulent Years. My Life in Politics* (1993), p.69: 'I also remember Nick Ridley telling me ... that ... "She is mad and will have to go."' Ridley himself mentions no such conversation in his memoirs.

[34]   Geoffrey Howe, *Conflict of Loyalty* (1994), p.453. In *Cold Cream. My Early Life and Other Mistakes* (2008), Ferdinand Mount, an opponent of the Falklands War who was appointed as an adviser to Thatcher immediately after it, gives a more colourful account of Walters's proposals and suggests that they were, in fact, put to Thatcher at the time.

[35]   Ian Lang, *Blue Remembered Years* (2002), p.58.

[36]   Geoff Eley, 'Finding the People's War: Film, British Collective Memory, and World War II', *American Historical Review*, 106, 3 (2001): 'Thatcherite reinscription of Churchillian "greatness" in the little-Englander animus against "Europe" licensed by the Falklands-Malvinas War.' Eley also writes: 'By

1983, Thatcherism was evoking the other Churchill of late imperial militarism and racialized cultural superiority, exchanging ideals of social justice for patriotism pure and simple.'

[37] Cecil Parkinson, in 'The Falklands War', seminar held 5 June 2002, http://www.icbh.ac.uk.witness/Falklands/, p.70.

[38] David Butler and Dennis Kavanagh (eds.), *The British General Election of 1983* (1984), p.256. Only 28 per cent of their sample of Conservative candidates referred directly to the Falklands.

[39] Harris, *Gotcha,* p.89.

[40] Eric Hobsbawm, 'Falklands Fallout', in Stuart Hall and Martin Jacques (eds), *The Politics of Thatcherism* (1983), pp.257–70.

CHAPTER 7. VICTORY FORETOLD: THE MINERS

[1] Andrew Richards, *Miners on Strike. Class, Solidarity and Division in Britain* (1996), p.125.

[2] Brian Towers, 'Running the Gauntlet: British Trade Unions under Thatcher, 1979–1987', *Industrial and Labor Relations Review,* 42, 2 (1989), pp.163–88.

[3] Norman Tebbit, *Upwardly Mobile* (1989), p.302.

[4]   TFW, Thatcher interview for *Weekend World,* 18 September 1977 (103191). Walden anticipated a first successful strike over pay and then a second strike over pit closures that would challenge the authority of the government.

[5]   TFW, Report of the Nationalized Industries Policy Group, 30 June 1977 (110795).

[6]   See, for example, Penny Green, *The Enemy Without. Policing and Class Consciousness in the Miners' Strike* (1990), p.29. Alex Callinicos and Mike Simons, *The Great Strike. The Miners' Strike of 1984–5 and its Lessons* (1985), p.36: 'Thatcher's six years in office have followed with eerie precision the pattern laid out in the Ridley Report'. John Saville, 'An Open Conspiracy: Conservative Politics and the Miners' Strike, 1984–5', *Socialist Register* (July–August 1985), pp.295–329: 'The Ridley plan began to be inserted into the statute book within a year of the Thatcher government taking office.'

[7]   Martin Adeney and John Lloyd, *The Miners' Strike, 1984–5. Loss Without Limit* (1986), p.73. Tim Eggar was apparently unable to find a copy of the report when drafting the 1983 manifesto. The report had anticipated confrontation between six and eighteen months after a Conservative election victory. Anyone reading it in 1982 might well have concluded that the report had already been implemented in the government's handling

of strikes in steel and the civil service or, for that matter, in the government's 'surrender' to the miners in February 1981. According to *The Times,* the annex to the report was not circulated to members of the shadow cabinet, Michael Hatfield, 'Tory Views on Unions Embarrass Leaders', *The Times,* 27 May 1978.

[8] TFW, Report of the Nationalized Industries Policy Group, 30 June 1977 (110795).

[9] John Hoskyns, *Just in Time. Inside the Thatcher Revolution (2000), p.73.* On 13 November 1978, an opposition working group had asked: 'What is a Tory government's response to an "unbeatable strike" (miners' or power-workers')?' Prior apparently told Hoskyns in 1977 that he believed a government would have no option but to surrender to the miners. Ibid., p.39.

[10] Ian MacGregor with Rodney Tyler, *The Enemies Within. The Story of the Miners' Strike, 1984–5* (1986), p.145.

[11] Hoskyns, *Just in Time,* p.143.

[12] Alan Clark, *Diaries. Into Politics, 1972–1982 (2001), entry for 25 January 1974, p.40.*

[13] Joe Gormley, *Battered Cherub* (1982), p.186.

[14] Roy Ottey, *Strike. An Insider's Story (1985), p.41.* Ottey resigned from the NUM executive

in October 1984 in protest at Scargill's refusal to hold a strike ballot.

[15]   Eric Heffer, *Never a Yes Man. The Life and Politics of an Adopted Liverpudlian* (1991), p.180. After reading an article in the *Financial Times,* Scargill rebuked Heffer for having refused to support Tony Benn in the election for deputy leader of the Labour Party.

[16]   'The New Unionism', *New Left Review,* July–August 1975, pp.3–33. Scargill interviewed by 'RB' and 'HW'.

[17]   Peter Walker, *Staying Power. An Autobiography* (1991), p.167.

[18]   'The New Unionism', *New Left Review.*

[19]   Sir John Herbecq, 'The Civil Service Reforms of the 1980s: the 1981 Civil Service Strike', seminar held 17 November 2006, Centre for Contemporary British History, http://icbh.a.uk/downloads/civilservicereforms, p.40: 'It was absolutely clear [after the civil service strike of 1981] that there would be a succession of strikes by the more familiar suspects, those who really would cause the government trouble. In July 1979, Christopher Foster ... and I were having private meetings with one or two other outsiders and Michael Portillo (who was special adviser to David Howell at the Department of Energy) about a miners' strike. It actually took

until the scare of the spring of 1981 to get the government to grapple with preparing for a miners' strike, which conservatively we reckoned would take two years.'

[20]   Gormley, *Battered Cherub,* p.173.

[21]   Nigel Lawson, *The View from No.11. Memoirs of a Tory Radical* (1993), pp.145–51.

[22]   Margaret Thatcher, *The Downing Street Years* (1995), p.341.

[23]   Lawson, *The View from No.11,* p.154.

[24]   Thatcher expressed her dislike of both Ezra and Villiers, of British Steel, in private conversations as early as July 1979, see Roy Jenkins, *European Diary, 1977–1981* (1989), p.480, entry for 14 July 1979.

[25]   Roy Mason, *Paying the Price* (1999), pp.73–6 and 236; Lawson, *The View from No.11,* p.156. Mason knew that his name had been discussed as chairman of the NCB and believed that Thatcher had vetoed his appointment.

[26]   Giles Shaw, *In the Long Run* (2001), p.128.

[27]   MacGregor, *The Enemies Within,* pp.168, 171 and 209.

[28]   Bob Haslam, *An Industrial Cocktail* (2003), p.113.

[29] MacGregor, *The Enemies Within,* p.146. Mick McGahey of the NUM met Jimmy Cowan of the NCB at Christmas. In spite of their differences, the two men were friends and McGahey advised Cowan to get out of the industry because there would soon be a strike.

[30] Ibid., p.166.

[31] Andrew Taylor, *The NUM and British Politics,* Vol.2, *1969–1995* (Aldershot, 1995), p.229. There were nine regional ballots of which only one, in Northumberland, favoured the strike – though the result in Derbyshire was very close.

[32] Adeney and Lloyd, *The Miners' Strike,* p.262.

[33] In May 1984 Eric Hammond, the right-wing leader of the electricians' union, wrote a private letter to an NUM official offering to shut the power stations if only the NUM executive won a ballot of its members on the strike. Eric Hammond, *Maverick. The Life of a Union Rebel* (1992), p.47. The letter was apparently sent to Peter Heathfield of the NUM on 24 May 1984. Hammond must have known by this stage that there was no chance that the NUM executive would hold a ballot.

[34] MacGregor insists that he himself decided to abandon the NCB's legal action and that he also discouraged other heads of nationalized

industries from suing. MacGregor, *The Enemies Within,* p.218.

[35]   Walker, *Staying Power,* p.173.

[36]   Haslam, *An Industrial Cocktail,* p.105.

[37]   Adeney and Lloyd, *The Miners' Strike,* p.93.

[38]   Bill Sirs, *Hard Labour* (1985), pp.122–4.

[39]   Mike Ironside and Roger Seifert, *Facing up to Thatcherism. The History of NALGO, 1979–1993* (Oxford, 2000), pp.171–2.

[40]   Adeney and Lloyd, *The Miners' Strike,* p.152.

[41]   Walker, *Staying Power,* p.175. Walker claims that he dissuaded the cabinet from sacking MacGregor on the grounds that this would appear to give Scargill a victory. Walker seems to have approached Robert Haslam, then at British Steel, in 1985 and suggested that he be appointed to the NCB in a move to force MacGregor out. Haslam did become deputy chairman of the NCB and did eventually replace MacGregor as chairman. Haslam, *Industrial Cocktail,* p.113.

[42]   TFW, Peter Walker to Ian MacGregor, 12 February 1985 (strikend.pdf); the letter is taken from MacGregor's files – the originals of which can be found at Kew, National Archives Coal 31/438.

[43] National Archives, Coal 26/500. Tables on number of strikers. The NCB believed that 43 per cent of miners were not on strike on 1 February 1985 and that 52 per cent of them were not on strike on 1 March.

[44] Woodrow Wyatt also seems to have helped the National Working Miner's Committee, though the precise nature of the help was often rather symbolic. After the strike, most leaders of working miners seem to have felt rather marginalized. Wyatt helped one of them, Tony Morris, to obtain a sufficiently good redundancy deal from the NCB to buy himself a bar in Marbella. Woodrow Wyatt, *The Journals of Woodrow Wyatt,* Vol.1, *1985–1988,* edited by Sarah Curtis (1998), pp.224 and 336, entries for 14 November 1986 and 30 April 1987.

[45] Peter Gibbon and David Steyne (eds.), *Thurcroft. A Village and the Miners' Strike. An Oral History* (1986), p.152.

[46] Tony Parker, *Redhill. A Mining Community* (1986), p.41. Interview with Harry Hartley: 'most of them were only 9 out of 10 mentally ... They didn't know what day it was ... What was worse they didn't know what would happen to them.'

[47] Roger Seifert and John Urwin, *Struggle Without End. The 1984/85 Miners' Strike in North Staffordshire* (Newcastle, Staffs, 1987), p.6.

478

[48]   *The Times,* 5 March 1985.

[49]   Herbecq, 'The Civil Service Reforms of the 1980s', p.40.

[50]   Hammond, *Maverick,* p.56. Basnett and Laird both criticized the NUM after the strike was over.

[51]   Tony Benn, *The Benn Diaries, 1940–1990,* edited by Ruth Winstone (1996), p.564, entries for 5 May and 15 May 1984.

[52]   Gibbon and Steyne (eds.), *Thurcroft,* p.148.

[53]   Quoted in David Waddington, Maggie Wykes and Chas Critcher, *Split at the Seams. Community, Continuity and Change after the 1984–5 Coal Dispute* (Milton Keynes, 1991), p.97.

[54]   Raphael Samuel, Barbara Bloomfield and Guy Boanas (eds.) *The Enemy Within. Pit Villages and the Miners' Strike* (1986), interview with Iris Preston, pp.240–50.

[55]   Tebbit, *Upwardly Mobile,* p.302.

[56]   Introduction to Seifert and Urwin, *Struggle Without End.*

[57]   Samuel et al., *The Enemy Within,* interview with Steve Ciebow, pp.199–202.

[58]   Peregrine Worsthorne, Preface, in Subroto Roy and John Clarke, *Margaret Thatcher's*

Revolution. How it Happened and What it Meant (2005), pp.vii–xvi.

[59]   Cited in Wyatt, *The Journals,* entry for 29 September 1986, p.198.

[60]   Samuel et al., *The Enemy Within,* p.xi, Meyer does not mention this speech in his own autobiography.

CHAPTER 8. SERIOUS MONEY, 1983–8

[1]   Margaret Thatcher, Tribute to Nicholas Ridley, *Sunday Times,* 7 March 1993.

[2]   Ross McKibbin, *London Review of Books,* 23 November 1989. 'Although Mrs Thatcher and Mr Lawson are closely associated in the public mind their aspirations are very different. Mrs Thatcher, for her part, is not really interested in the economy at all. She has little idea how it works, no notion of its complicated and delicate relationships and only the most elementary conception of how it might work better ... Mr Lawson is not in her sense a Thatcherite, not one of us. A form of economic neo liberalism is central to his politics – not, as with her, secondary. He differs also from Mrs Thatcher in other important respects: he is a bon viveur, is not, I would think, an admirer of Mrs Whitehouse and has openly declared his dislike of the inquisitorial and moralizing state which seems

to mean so much to the prime minister. Mr Lawson has been called "the brains of Thatcherism" in the press: but that he and Mrs Thatcher adhere to apparently similar economics is partly accidental and partly just a matter of convenience.'

[3]   Margaret Thatcher, *The Downing Street Years* (1995), p.308: 'if it comes to drawing up a list of Conservative – even Thatcherite – revolutionaries I would never deny Nigel a leading place on it'.

[4]   Nigel Lawson, *The View from No.11. Memoirs of a Tory Radical* (1993), p.64.

[5]   Graham Greenwell, letter to *The Times,* 25 June 1971. The letter, which also contained reference to 'the Guards', banging of drums in 'primitive countries' and doctrinaire dons, 'possibly of the female sex', aroused embarrassed dissent from younger brokers, including Greenwell's own son.

[6]   Peter Carrington, *Reflect on Things Past. The Memoirs of Lord Carrington* (1988), p.20.

[7]   John Campbell, *Margaret Thatcher,* Vol.1, *The Grocer's Daughter* (2000), p.30.

[8]   John Nott, *Here Today, Gone Tomorrow. Recollections of an Errant Politician* (2003), p.95.

[9]   Cecil Parkinson, *Right at the Centre* (1992), p.87: 'Insider trading could not have been made

illegal in the Fifties, it was almost a way of life. The best stockbrokers were the best connected. Through their connections they found out what was going on, and passed on to their clients as "tips" the information gained quite often over that famous institution, the two-hour city lunch.'

[10]   *Economist,* 'The City Revolution. Big Bang and After' (1986), p.3.

[11]   Karl Van Horn, Head of Asset Management at Amex, quoted in ibid., p.16.

[12]   Dominic Hobson, *The Pride of Lucifer. The Unauthorized Biography of Morgan Grenfell (1991), pp.211 and 200.*

[13]   David Kynaston, *Cazenove & Co. A History* (1991), pp.301–32.

[14]   Woodrow Wyatt, *The Journals of Woodrow Wyatt.* Vol.1, *1985–1988,* edited by Sarah Curtis (1998), p.27, entry for 8 December 1985.

[15]   *Spectator,* 15 March 1986, reprinted in Philip Marsden-Smedley (ed.), *Britain in the Eighties. The Spectator's View of the Thatcher Decade* (1989).

[16]   Elaine Aston, *Caryl Churchill* (2001), p.74.

[17]   Parkinson, *Right at the Centre,* p.67.

[18]   Bob Jessop, Kevin Bonnett, Simon Bromley and Tom Ling, 'Authoritarian Populism, Two Nations and Thatcherism', *New Left Review,* 1, 147 (September–October 1984).

[19]   Nicholas Henderson, *Mandarin.* (1994), p.269, entry for 24 May 1979. For a sceptical response to Henderson, see R.W. Johnson, 'Dear Peter...' in *The Politics of Recession* (1985), pp.13–17, first published in *New Society,* 21 June 1979.

[20]   TFW, Thatcher off-the-record press briefing after meeting French president, 5 June 1979 (104089): 'I must say that I found it a very, very interesting despatch. If I might say so, some of the things which [Lord Carrington] Peter and I have been saying with my *[sic]* less panache and much less style were said in that.'

[21]   TFW, Thatcher to House of Commons, 22 November 1990 (108256): 'I remind the House that, under socialism, this country had come to such a pass that one of our most able and distinguished ambassadors felt compelled to write ... a famous dispatch, a copy of which found its way into *The Economist.'*

[22]   For an idea of the impact made by this book, see James Raven, 'British History and the Enterprise Culture', *Past and Present,* 123 (1989), pp.178–204.

[23] John Ranelagh, *Thatcher's People* (1991), p.186. Henderson did cite Wiener in his book *Channels and Tunnels* (1987), in which he revisited the debate that he had aroused in 1979.

[24] On Barnett's influence, see Lawson, *The View from No.11,* p.607.

[25] Shirley Robin Letwin, *The Anatomy of Thatcherism* (1992), p.251.

[26] Curiously, Wiener suggested, in retrospect, that his book was written as a hostile response to Heath: 'He had absorbed this whole anti-urban and anti-enterprise culture.' Interview with Martin Wiener in Richard English and Michael Kenny (eds.), *Rethinking British Decline* (2000), pp.25–36, p.34. I think that Wiener is rewriting his own history here. In 1981, he had seen Heath as a proponent of modernization – though not necessarily a successful one. See Martin Wiener, *English Culture and the Decline of the Industrial Spirit, 1850–1980* (Cambridge, 1981), p.164.

[27] Henderson, *Mandarin,* p.250, entry for 25 February 1979.

[28] John Hoskyns, *Just in Time. Inside the Thatcher Revolution (2000), p.110.*

[29] Jacques Attali, *Un homme d'influence, Sir Siegmund Warburg, 1902–1982.* (1985).

[30]   John Redwood, *Singing the Blues. The Once and Future Conservatives* (2004), p.35. Redwood claimed that, at least in the 1970s, his opinions were considered unorthodox by his fellow bankers.

[31]   For the extent to which Henderson's views were shared by other senior diplomats, see Percy Cradock, *In Pursuit of British Interests. Reflections on Foreign Policy under Margaret Thatcher and John Major* (1997), p.28.

[32]   Tessa Blackstone and William Plowden, *Inside the Think Tank* (1988), p.162.

[33]   Thatcher expressed reservations about business studies. TFW, Thatcher speech to First Engineering Assembly, 3 September 1985 (106120).

[34]   Nicholas Crickhowell, *Westminster, Wales and Water* (Cardiff, 1999), p.69.

[35]   TFW, Thatcher speech in Friern Barnet, 3 April 1959 (101016).

[36]   Nicholas Ridley, *My Style of Government. The Thatcher Years* (1991), p.4.

[37]   TFW, 'Notes Towards the Definition of Policy', 4 April 1975 (110098).

[38]   TFW, Nationalized Industries Policy Group, 12 January 1977 (110844).

[39]   Ibid.

[40]   Norman Fowler, *Ministers Decide. A Personal Memoir of the Thatcher Years* (1991), p.97. See also Joseph to Heseltine, 10 September 1976 (111237), reporting a conversation with industrialist Arnold Hall 'who believes that we would be wrong to commit ourselves to total denationalisation of the aircraft industry – since that would only renew uncertainties'.

[41]   Fowler, *Ministers Decide,* p.99.

[42]   Donald MacDougall, *Don and Mandarin. Memoirs of an Economist* (1987), p.231.

[43]   TFW, Joseph to Thatcher, 19 July 1976 (111232). Joseph had met the banker Minos Zombanakis who believed that Healey was looking for an excuse for *'nationalization à la française'.* See also, Thatcher speech to Institute of Directors, 6 June 1975 (102702); Thatcher article for CBI review, 3 November 1975 (102794).

[44]   Michael Ivens wrote the introduction to Ian Gow, *A Practical Approach to Denationalization* (1977). Ivens seemed more radical than Gow and lamented that 'many Conservatives seem to have accepted that the extending frontiers of nationalization cannot be flung back'.

[45]   Leo Pliatzky, *The Treasury under Mrs Thatcher* (1989), p.106.

[46] Bob Haslam, *An Industrial Cocktail* (2003), p.112.

[47] Karin Newman, *The Selling of British Telecom* (1986), p.77.

[48] Lazard consistently refused to underwrite privatizations. See Nott, *Here Today, Gone Tomorrow,* p.336.

[49] TFW, Letter from a variety of American bankers (apparently led by Goldman Sachs) to Sir Peter Middleton (permanent secretary to the treasury), 28 October 1987, about the losses that they had endured from underwriting BP shares. This letter is attached to the letter from Howard Baker to Goldman Sachs, 8 December 1987 (110640).

[50] Nott, *Here Today, Gone Tomorrow,* p.171; Parkinson, *Right at the Centre,* p.137.

[51] On Thatcher's attempt to quash the case involving British Airways and the by now defunct, Laker Airways, see TFW, Memorandum for the president from William P. Clark, attached to letter from Reagan to Thatcher, 6 April 1983 (109328).

[52] David Lazar, *Markets and Ideology in the City of London* (1990), p.33.

[53] Leslie Hannah, 'Mrs Thatcher, Capital Basher', in Dennis Kavanagh and Anthony Seldon (eds.),

The Thatcher Effect. A Decade of Change (Oxford, 1989), pp.38–48. Stephen Martin and David Parker, *The Impact of Privatizations. Ownership and Corporate Performance in the UK (1997).*

[54] Newman, *The Selling of British Telecom,* p.77.

[55] Enoch Powell, 'The Conservative Party', in Kavanagh and Seldon (eds.), *The Thatcher Effect,* pp.80–88.

[56] Anne Power and Rebecca Tunstall, *Swimming Against the Tide. Polarization or Progress on 20 Unpopular Council Estates, 1980–1995* (1996), p.15.

[57] Patrick Minford, Paul Ashton and Michael Peel, 'The Effects of Housing Distortions on Unemployment', *Oxford Economics Papers,* 40, 2 (1988), pp.322–45.

[58] Alan Murie, 'Housing and the Environment', in Kavanagh and Seldon (eds.), *The Thatcher Effect,* pp.213–25.

[59] Alistair McAlpine, *Once a Jolly Bagman* (1998), p.255.

[60] Power and Tunstall, *Swimming Against the Tide,* p.32.

[61] Anne Power, *Property before People* (1987), p.114.

[62]   TFW, Thatcher article for *Daily Telegraph,* 'The Owner-Occupier's Party', 1 July 1974 (102377).

[63]   Murie, 'Housing and the Environment', in Kavanagh and Seldon (eds.), *The Thatcher Effect,* pp.213–25.

[64]   Margaret Reid, 'Mrs Thatcher and the City', in ibid., pp.48–63.

[65]   Pliatzky, *The Treasury under Mrs Thatcher,* p.148.

CHAPTER 9. DIVIDED KINGDOM?

[1]   TFW, Joseph, 'Notes Towards the Definition of Policy', 4 April 1975 (110098).

[2]   TFW, 10 October 1986 (106498).

[3]   Dylan Griffith, *Thatcherism and Territorial Politics. A Welsh Case Study* (1996), p.63.

[4]   Ibid., p.25.

[5]   TFW, Thatcher speech to Scottish Conservative Party conference, 13 May 1988 (107240).

[6]   Griffith, *Thatcherism and Territorial Politics,* p.77.

[7]   Cited in Marc Mulholland, *Northern Ireland at the Crossroads. Ulster Unionism in the O'Neill Years, 1960–1969* (2000), p.ix.

[8]   Ivor Stanbrook, *A Year in Politics* (1988). No pagination, but see entry for 16 January 1986,

for an attempt to found a 'nation-wide' organization of unionists. On 30 January Stanbrook complained that Thatcher herself had started to talk of union 'as long as the majority in Northern Ireland want it'.

[9] Ferdinand Mount, 'Hypernats and Country Lovers', *The Spectator,* 18 February 1989, reprinted in Philip Marsden-Smedley (ed.), *Britain in the Eighties. The Spectator's View of the Thatcher Decade (1989), pp.158–68.*

[10] Ferdinand Mount, *Cold Cream. My Early Life and Other Mistakes* (2008), p.334.

[11] On Thatcher's surprise at hearing of Powell's position see TFW, Mrs Thatcher's call on the prime minister, 10 September, report dated 11 September 1975 (110717).

[12] TFW, Thatcher speech to the American Bar Association meeting, 15 July 1985 (106096). Thatcher's phrase about denying terrorists the 'oxygen of publicity', which was subsequently used as a justification for the ban on broadcasting the voices of some Northern Irish politicians, was first used in a speech to American lawyers with no suggestion that this remark was particularly linked to Ulster.

[13] Douglas Hurd, *Memoirs* (2003), p.302.

[14] Margaret Thatcher, *The Downing Street Years* (1995), pp.420–1.

[15]   TFW, Report of Howe's visit to Ulster, 3 and 4 July 1977 (109789).

[16]   Ian Aitkin cited in Frank Gaffikin and Mike Morrissey, *Northern Ireland. The Thatcher Years* (1990), p.35.

[17]   Ibid., p.76.

[18]   Ibid., p.28

[19]   Ibid., p.47.

[20]   TFW, Angus Maude and others, 'Themes', 16 February 1978 (109853).

[21]   Shirley Robin Letwin, *The Anatomy of Thatcherism* (1992), p.37.

[22]   Lawrence Freedman, *The Official History of the Falklands Campaign,* Vol.1, *The Origins of the Falklands War* (2005), p.107.

[23]   George Gardiner, *A Bastard's Tale* (1999), p.127.

[24]   Geoffrey Howe, *Conflict of Loyalty* (1994), p.476.

[25]   Cecil Parkinson, *Right at the Centre* (1992), p.83. Angus Maude had, in fact, lived in Australia for a time during the 1960s.

[26]   TFW, Thatcher speech to Conservative Party conference, 8 October 1976 (103105)

[27]   John Campbell, *Margaret Thatcher,* Vol.1, *The Grocer's Daughter* (2000), p.362.

[28]   TFW, Thatcher speech to Finchley Conservatives, 14 August 1961 (101105).

[29]   T.E. Utley, 'A Monstrous Invention', *Spectator,* 20 October 1987.

[30]   See David Martin, 'The Stripping of the Words: Conflict over the Eucharist in the Episcopal Church', *Modern Theology,* 15, 2 (1999), pp.247–61. See also Bernard Palmer, *High and Mitred. A Study of Prime Ministers as Bishop-Makers (1992).* Charles Moore, A.N. Wilson and Gavin Stamp. *The Church in Crisis* (1986).

[31]   TFW, Thatcher speech at official dinner in Georgia, 1 April 1987 (106784).

[32]   TFW, Joseph, 'Notes Towards the Definition of Policy', 4 April 1975 (110098).

[33]   TFW, Lawson, 'Thoughts on "Implementing our Strategy"', 15 January 1978 (110321): 'we must not shirk the immigration issue'.

[34]   David Butler and Dennis Kavanagh, *The British General Election of 1983* (1984), p.99.

[35]   Michael Heseltine, *Life in the Jungle* (2000), p.365.

[36]   Rodney Barker, 'Legitimacy in the United Kingdom: Scotland and the Poll Tax', *British Journal of Political Science,* 22, 4 (1992), pp.521–33.

[37]   Ian Holliday, 'Scottish Limits to Thatcherism', *Political Quarterly,* 63, 4 (2005), pp.448–59. Holliday argues that Forsyth continued to exercise some influence, via Downing Street, even after he ceased to be chairman of the party.

[38]   Alan Clark, *Diaries* (1993), p.301, entry for 8 June 1990.

CHAPTER 10. EUROPE

[1]   Alan Clark, *Diaries* (1993), p.225, entry for 13 September 1988.

[2]   Douglas Hurd, *Memoirs* (2003), p.244.

[3]   Geoffrey Howe, *Conflict of Loyalty* (1994), p.538.

[4]   TFW, Charles Powell interviewed by Chris Collins, 12 September 2007 (111049).

[5]   Percy Cradock, *In Pursuit of British Interests. Reflections on Foreign Policy under Margaret Thatcher and John Major* (1997), p.125.

[6]   George Gardiner, *A Bastard's Tale* (1999), p.136.

[7]   Ivor Crewe and Anthony King, *SDP. The Birth, Life and Death of the Social Democratic Party* (Oxford, 1995), p.114.

[8]   TFW, Thatcher speech to Finchley Conservatives, 14 August 1961 (101105).

[9]   TFW, Thatcher speech to Conservative Party conference, 10 October 1975 (102777).

[10]   Hurd, *Memoirs,* p.243.

[11]   TFW, Hurd and Baroness Elles, 'The European Democratic Union', circulated paper for shadow cabinet, 12 April 1978 (110134) and Hurd, 'Alliance of Centre/Right Parties in Europe', 22 March 1976 (110314).

[12]   See David Willets, 'Conservatism and Christian Democracy', speech to Viennese Institute for Human Sciences, 9 December 2003.

[13]   Hurd, *Memoirs,* p.246.

[14]   Ian Lang, *Blue Remembered Years* (2002), p.57.

[15]   TFW, Thatcher speech to founding conference of EDU in Salzburg, 24 April 1978 (103663).

[16]   TFW, Thatcher article for *Hamburger Adenblatt,* 13 May 1978 (103683).

[17]   TFW, Thatcher speech to Engineering Employers' Federation, 21 February 1978 (103622): 'A few years ago when Helmut Schmidt – that rare

person, a Socialist who believes in the market economy – visited this country, he was compared by *The Times* to "the headmaster of a famous public school, come to give out prizes at a struggling comprehensive".'

[18] TFW, Thatcher speech to Conservative Party conference, 8 October 1976 (103105).

[19] TFW, Thatcher speech to Aspen Institute, 4 August 1995 (108346).

[20] TFW, Thatcher speech to CDU, 25 May 1976 (103034).

[21] TFW, Thatcher article for *Hamburger Adenblatt,* 13 May 1978 (103683).

[22] Roy Jenkins, *European Diary, 1977–1981* (1989), p.450, entry for 21 May 1979.

[23] TFW, Thatcher speech to National Association of Head Teachers conference, 25 May 1970 (101752): 'America has spent a good deal more on education than on defence; she has had virtually a total comprehensive education system ... But she still has colossal problems.' See also Thatcher speech to Westminster Catholic Parents Association, 1 May 1970 (101742): 'In the USA they have had all children going to the same school for a long time, yet it doesn't seem to me that they have created either the kind of society that would suit us, nor have they got rid of their social

problem, nor have they got supreme educational standards.'

[24] *The Times,* 1 May 1980, letter from Sir Anthony Meyer: 'Is it acceptable that the attention of Europe and America should be concentrated during the next few weeks on side issues when the Soviet threat is so huge and so imminent?' See also the letter in the same issue from Hugh Dykes.

[25] Margaret Thatcher, *The Path to Power* (1995), p.473.

[26] TFW, Charles Powell interviewed by Chris Collins, 12 September 2007 (111049).

[27] Howe, *Conflict of Loyalty,* p.456.

[28] Philip Stephens, *Politics and the Pound. The Tories, the Economy and Europe* (1997), p.16.

[29] Ibid., p.29.

[30] Clark, *Diaries,* p.227, entry for 16 September.

[31] John Biffen, 'The Europe of Tomorrow', in ibid., *Political Office or Political Power. Six Speeches on National and International Affairs,* foreword by Margaret Thatcher (1977), pp.19–25.

[32] Stephens, *Politics and the Pound,* p.65.

[33] Colin Munro, 'Anglo-German Relations and German Reunification', seminar held 18 October 2000, Institute of Contemporary British History,

http://www.icbh.ac.uk/icbh/witness/germanreun//, p.37.

[34]   Hurd, *Memoirs,* p.383.

[35]   Sir Roderic Braithwaite, 'Anglo-German Relations and German Reunification', seminar held 18 October 2000, Institute of Contemporary British History, http://www.icbh.ac.uk/icbh/witness/germanreun//, p.28.

[36]   Stuart Hall and Martin Jacques, 'March without a Vision', *Marxism Today,* December 1990.

[37]   Clark, *Diaries,* p.281, entry for 20 February 1990.

[38]   TFW, Interview with Robert Keatley, *Wall Street Journal,* 24 January 1990 (107876).

[39]   TFW, Charles Powell's minutes of meeting held at Chequers on 24 March 1990 (111047).

CHAPTER 11. THE FALL

[1]   TFW, Thatcher interview for TV-AM, 24 November 1989 (107829).

[2]   Nicholas Ridley, *My Style of Government. The Thatcher Years* (1991), p.2.

[3]   Richard Needham, *Battling for Peace. Northern Ireland's Longest Serving British Minister (Belfast, 1998), pp.209–22.*

[4]   Robert Harris, *Good and Faithful Servant. The Unauthorized Biography of Bernard Ingham (1990).*

[5]   Percy Cradock, *In Pursuit of British Interests. Reflections on Foreign Policy under Margaret Thatcher and John Major* (1997), p.15.

[6]   Nigel Lawson, *The View from No.11. Memoirs of a Tory Radical* (1993), p.680.

[7]   Ibid., p.485.

[8]   Douglas Hurd, *Memoirs* (2003), p.234, quoting diary entry for 23 November 1975.

[9]   Margaret Thatcher, *The Downing Street Years* (1995), p.835.

[10]   Paddy Ashdown, *The Ashdown Diaries,* Vol.1, *1988–1997* (2002), p.18, entry for 11 November 1988.

[11]   Thatcher, *The Downing Street Years,* p.755.

[12]   *The Times,* 19 March 1966.

[13]   Alan Clark, *Diaries* (1993), p.296, entry for 1 May 1990.

[14]   Margaret Thatcher, *The Downing Street Years,* p.835.

[15]   David Butler, Andrew Adonis and Tony Travers, *Failure in British Government. The Politics of the Poll Tax* (Oxford, 1993), p.52.

[16] Ibid., p.61.

[17] Ibid., p.48.

[18] Ibid., p.103.

[19] Quoted in John Sergeant, *Maggie. Her Fatal Legacy* (2005), p.91.

[20] Tim Renton, *Chief Whip* (2005), p.37.

[21] Anthony Meyer, *Stand Up and Be Counted* (1990), p.101.

[22] TFW, Prime Minister's Question Time, 10 November 1988 (107378) and 16 June 1988 (107263).

[23] Robin Oakley, 'Victory with Just a Dent', *The Times,* 6 December 1989. For an assessment of the political situation after Meyer's challenge see TFW, Post-Mortem Notes, prepared by George Younger and a number of Thatcher's supporters in parliament, 6 December 1989 (111437). The notes concluded that the result was less good than the figures made it appear, Tristan Garel-Jones said: 'We are talking about the beginning of the end of the Thatcher era.' Everyone seemed to agree that Thatcher's advisers were a serious problem: 'Charles must go ... Bernard is the one they all really hate.'

[24] TFW, Memorandum of conversation between Margaret Thatcher and official of US embassy at Connaught Hotel, 22 May 1973, enclosed

with letter from Annenberg to State Department, 25 June 1973 (110554).

[25] Julian Critchley, *Heseltine. The Unauthorised Biography (1987).*

[26] Renton, *Chief Whip,* p.13.

[27] Kenneth Baker, *The Turbulent Years. My Life in Politics* (1993), p.387.

[28] Perhaps Morrison was not really so naïve. Bernard Ingham reports that Morrison had built a 'lie factor' of 15 per cent into his calculations; Bernard Ingham, *Kill the Messenger* (1991), p.393.

[29] On 15 November 1990 John Major told Edwina Currie: 'Don't be too close to her, or you could go down with her too.' Edwina Currie, *Diaries, 1987–1992* (2002), p.209.

[30] Thatcher, *The Downing Street Years,* p.853.

[31] Hurd, *Memoirs,* p.398.

[32] Clark, *Diaries,* p.357, entry for 20 November 1990.

[33] Paul Whiteley, Patrick Seyd and Jeremy Richardson, *True Blues. The Politics of Conservative Party Membership* (1994), p.61. Asked to rank Tory leaders, at a time when Major was particularly unpopular with the electorate as a whole, party members gave

him an average rating of 80; this compared to 78 for Thatcher, 70 for Hurd, 64 for Heseltine and 41 for Heath.

[34] George Walden, *Lucky George. Memoirs of an Anti-Politician* (1999), p.302.

[35] Geoffrey Howe, *Conflict of Loyalty* (1994), p.610.

CONCLUSIONS

[1] Ferdinand Mount, *Cold Cream. My Early Life and Other Mistakes* (2008), p.313.

[2] Nigel Fisher, *The Tory Leaders. Their Struggle for Power* (1977), p.163.

[3] Nigel Lawson, *The View from No.11. Memoirs of a Tory Radical* (1993), p.64.

[4] TFW, Angus Maude and others, 'Themes', 16 February 1978 (109853).

[5] 'A Monstrous Invention', *Spectator,* 9 August 1986. Note that eighteen months after having proclaimed the non-existence of Thatcherism Utley was writing: 'I deplore the end of Thatcherism'; see 'Why I Shrink from 1988', *The Times,* 28 December 1987.

[6] Stuart Hall, 'The Great Moving Right Show', *Marxism Today,* January 1979: 'Neither

Keynesianism nor Monetarism win votes in the electoral market place.'

[7]   Whitehouse was a particular target of mockery for left-wing intellectuals. In *Policing the Crisis* (1978), Hall wrote that Whitehouse's Festival of Light gave the Right 'considerable popular depth of penetration in the aroused middle classes'. See Martin Durham, *Moral Crusades, Family and Morality in the Thatcher Years* (New York, 1991), p.162.

[8]   Andrew Gamble, *The Free Economy and the Strong State* (1994, first published 1988), p.198.

[9]   Anna Marie Smith, *New Right Discourse on Race and Sexuality: Britain, 1968–1990* (Cambridge, 1994), p.194.

[10]   William Rees-Mogg, 'Confessions of a Justified Monetarist', *The Times,* 10 November 1983.

[11]   Durham, *Moral Crusades,* p.39.

[12]   TFW, Chapman interviewing Thatcher for Channel 4's *Diverse Reports,* 16 July 1985 (106097).

[13]   Beatrix Campbell, 'A Taste of Edwina Currie', *Marxism Today,* 20 March 1987. Campbell suggested that Thatcher supported Gillick and Whitehouse – though she seemed to recognize that Currie was not part of this moral consensus. In her book, *Iron Ladies. Why Do*

Women Vote Tory? (1987), Campbell suggested that Kenneth Clarke, the secretary of state for health, opposed Gillick whilst Thatcher supported her.

[14] Adam Lent and Merle Storr, introduction, no pagination, 'Section 28 and the Revival of Lesbian, Gay and Queer Politics in Britain', seminar held 24 November 1999, icbh.ac.uk/downloads/section28.pdf., p.11.

[15] Norman Fowler, *Ministers Decide. A Personal Memoir of the Thatcher Years* (1991), p.252.

[16] Note that Matthew Parris used the legalization of homosexuality in Northern Ireland in 1982 as the occasion to try to announce his own homosexuality to the House of Commons. It is indicative of the atmosphere of the times that it suited both sides to ignore his declaration. Matthew Parris, *Chance Witness. An Outsider's Life in Politics (2002), p.261.*

[17] James Prior, *A Balance of Power* (1986), p.225: 'On the one hand, her strong personal prejudice meant that she wanted to win, but on the other, her reason told her that she would be very happy to lose.' See also Douglas Hurd, *Memoirs* (2003), p.341: 'She was reasonably content with a situation in which she could record her own views, ... without any chance of their prevailing.'

[18]   Hall, 'The Great Moving Right Show', *Marxism Today,* January 1979.

[19]   Gertrude Himmelfarb – a rare example of an academic historian who was sympathetic to both Margaret Thatcher and to Victorian values – thought that Walden had used the phrase 'Victorian values' 'rather derisively'. Gertrude Himmelfarb, *The Demoralization of Society. From Victorian Virtues to Modern Values (1995), p.3.*

[20]   TFW, 28 October 1989, 'The Walden Interview' (107808).

[21]   TFW, Hailsham diary, entry for 1 October 1976 (11159). Ronald Millar, *A View from the Wings. West End, West Coast, Westminster* (1993), p.293.

[22]   TFW, 'Notes Towards the Definition of Policy', 4 April 1975 (110098).

[23]   Shirley Robin Letwin, *The Anatomy of Thatcherism* (1992), p.32.

[24]   Ibid., p.101.

[25]   Andrew Gamble, 'Theories and Explanations of National Decline', in Richard English and Michael Kenny (eds.), *Rethinking British Decline* (2000), pp.1–22, p.19.

[26]   In fairness, one should say that *Marxism Today* had by the end of Thatcher's premiership begun

to express a remarkably nuanced view of government economic achievements; see John Wells, 'Miracles and Myths', *Marxism Today,* May 1989.

[27] Margaret Jones, *Thatcher's Kingdom. A View of Britain in the Eighties* (1984), p.15. Wynne Godley apparently objected to an article that Jones had written on the grounds that it was not pessimistic enough. He predicted 'apocalypse'.

[28] Christopher Johnson, *The Economy under Mrs Thatcher, 1979–1990* (1991).

[29] Nicholas Henderson, *Channels and Tunnels. Reflections on Britain and Abroad* (1987), pp.109–140. Henderson lists about fifty people whose opinions he had canvassed about the British economy.

[30] Charles Leadbeater, 'Back to the Future', *Marxism Today,* May 1989.

[31] Cited in E.H.H. Green, *Thatcher* (2006), p.31.

[32] John Nott, *Here Today, Gone Tomorrow. Recollections of an Errant Politician* (2003), p.183.

[33] TFW, Lawson, 'The New Conservatism', speech to the Bow Group, 4 August 1980 (109505): 'Those Conservatives who none the less feel ill at ease with the new Conservatism are inclined

to suggest that it smacks far too much of classical liberalism. The charge is a strange one. Nineteenth-century politics was about wholly different issues. There was, behind the rhetoric, a fundamental consensus on economic policy. Disraeli may have used the Corn Laws and protection to secure the leadership of the Conservative Party, but in practice he was operating in precisely the same world of non-intervention in industry, adherence to the gold standard (and thus to stable money) and free trade as was Gladstone. They had their differences outside the field of economic policy, but what matters to us today is what they had in common – which is scarcely surprising given that Gladstone himself was a Conservative Cabinet Minister before becoming the embodiment of Liberalism. Of all forms of heresy-hunting, this variety seems particularly futile.'

[34] Ian Gilmour, *Dancing with Dogma. Britain under Thatcherism* (1992), p.25.

[35] Peregrine Worsthorne, Preface in Subroto Roy and John Clarke (eds.), *Margaret Thatcher's Revolution. How it Happened and What it Meant* (2005), pp.vii–xvi, p.vii: 'This excellent book has reminded me why, from the beginning of "the Thatcherite era" to the bitter end, I was an ardent fan, devoted both to the person and the creed.' Characteristically, Worsthorne follows

this with several pages denouncing much of what Thatcher did.

[36]   *Daily Telegraph,* 11 February 1979.

[37]   TFW, 'Notes Towards the Definition of Policy', 4 April 1975 (110098): 'Our vision is embodied in social market policies, which recognise economic life as something organic but largely autonomous.'

[38]   Thatcher speech to Scottish Conservative Party conference, 12 May 1990 (108087).

[39]   Alfred Sherman, *Paradoxes of Power. Reflections on the Thatcher Interlude,* edited by Mark Garnett (Exeter, 2005), p.26.

[40]   Ian Lang, *Blue Remembered Years* (2002), p.82.

[41]   TFW, Thatcher article, 'Consensus or Choice' *Daily Telegraph,* 19 February 1969 (101650): 'In politics, certain words suddenly become fashionable. Sometimes they are just words. Sometimes they reveal a whole attitude of mind and influence the development of thought. Then they can be dangerous and set us on a false trail. Consensus is one of these.'

[42]   TFW, 'The Right Approach', Conservative Policy Statement, 4 October 76 (109439): 'In the 1950s, for example, there was a substantial and soundly based increase in prosperity.' There

were more guarded references to the 1950s in Keith Joseph, TFW 'Monetarism is not Enough', 5 April 1976 (110796), in which he talked of 'the mid 1950s, the silver age of Churchill's post-war administration' and in Geoffrey Howe's budget speech of 26 March 1980 (109498): 'Even in the 1950s and early 1960s our economy was lagging behind those of our competitors. But it was a period of low inflation and rising growth rates. Seen in retrospect, that period was something of a golden age.'

[43] Margaret Thatcher, *The Path to Power* (1995), p.77.

[44] TFW, Hailsham diary, 11 April 1975 (111134).

[45] TFW, Thatcher interviewed by Hugo Young for the *Sunday Times,* 22 February 1983 (105088).

[46] *The Times,* 3 May 1983.

[47] TFW, Speech to Conservative rally in Cardiff, 16 April 1979 (104011) and Sir Robert Menzies Lecture, Monash University, 6 October 1981 (104712).

[48] TFW, Norman Tebbit, interviewed on *Weekend World,* 7 January 1979 (103807). Note also Nicholas Ridley's sarcastic suggestion of 1978 that the Labour Party might sponsor a statue of Baldwin because Callaghan was his natural successor. 'Why a Tory Wants a Statue of Baldwin', *The Times,* 21 February 1978.

508

[49] Philip Williamson, 'Baldwin's Reputation. Politics and History, 1937–1967, *Historical Journal,* 47, 1 (2004), pp.127–68.

[50] For example, Thatcher referred to Stanley Baldwin in the speech that she made on the opening of Buckingham University – when she cited his view of 'intellectuals', TFW, 6 February 1976 (102954). She cited him again in a speech to the Cambridge Union, 12 March 1976 (102981). She referred to Jack Baldwin twice – in a speech at the Oxford Centre for Molecular Sciences on 4 August 1989 (107748) and in a speech to the Parliamentary and Scientific Committee on 6 December 1989 (107839).

[51] *The Times,* 27 February 1982, Julian Critchley, 'Why Baldwin Deserves His Place in the House'.

[52] Mark Garnett and Ian Aitken, *Splendid. Splendid! The Authorized Biography of Willie Whitelaw* (2002), p.263.

[53] No Prime Minister', interview between Hugo Young and Edward Heath, *Marxism Today,* 16 November 1988.

[54] TFW, Hailsham diary, entry for 2 February 1976 (111154).

[55] TFW, Lawson, 'The New Conservatism', Lecture to the Bow Group, 4 August 1980 (109505):

'The old consensus is in the process of being re-established.'

[56] John Hoskyns, *Just in Time. Inside the Thatcher Revolution (2000), p.39.*

[57] Ivor Crewe, 'Values: the Crusade that Failed', in Dennis Kavanagh and Anthony Seldon (eds.), *The Thatcher Effect. A Decade of Change* (Oxford, 1989), pp.239–50.

[58] Noel Malcolm, 'Margaret Thatcher, Housewife Superstar', *Spectator,* 25 February 1989, reprinted in Philip Marsden-Smedley (ed.), *Britain in the Eighties. The Spectator's View of the Thatcher Decade* (1989), pp.168–73: 'such a scale cannot measure the effects of a populism which favours both individualism in private life and a crude but powerful cult of government action'.

[59] Lawson, *The View From No.11,* p.696.

[60] Paul Hirst, *After Thatcher* (1989), p.11: '"Thatcherism" is a myth that tries to justify Conservative victory by ascribing it to fundamental social and attitudinal changes, rather than to the defeat of any credible political force.'

[61] John Redwood, *Singing the Blues. The Once and Future Conservatives* (2004), p.63.

[62] Margaret Thatcher, *The Downing Street Years* (1995), p.306.

[63] TFW, Thatcher speech at Conservative rally (European Election), 11 June 1984 (105703): 'It's interesting to see how catching these policies of sound finance have become – whether they're called honest money, or monetarism or just plain commonsense, or Thatcherism'. Press conference for American correspondents in London, 10 January 1986 (106300): 'many of them [European countries] have come closer to Thatcherism than they had ever intended. That is not because it is Thatcherism; it is because it is common sense!'

[64] Bob Jessop, Kevin Bonnet, Simon Bromley and Tom Ling, *Thatcherism. A Tale of Two Nations* (Cambridge, 1988), p.74.

[65] Peter Hennessy, 'Mrs Thatcher Warned in Secret Report of Defeat in Confrontation with Unions', *The Times,* 18 April 1978.

[66] Ian Gilmour, *Dancing with Dogma. Britain under Thatcherism* (1992), p.82.

[67] Peter Gibbon and David Steyne (eds.), *Thurcroft. A Village and the Miners' Strike. An Oral History* (1986), p.46.

[68] Jock Bruce Gardyne, *Mrs Thatcher's First Administration. The Prophets Confounded* (1984), p.82.

[69] John Sergeant, *Maggie. Her Fatal Legacy (2005).*

[70] Brian Wyldbore-Smith, *March Past* (2001).

[71] Woodrow Wyatt, *The Journals of Woodrow Wyatt. 1, 1985–1988, edited by Sarah Curtis (1998), entries for 17 and 20 March 1986.*

[72] Andrew Gamble, 'The Lady's Not For Turning: Thatcherism Mark III', *Marxism Today,* June 1984.

[73] See Douglas Hurd's review of Ferdinand Mount's *Cold Cream* in the *Spectator,* 9 April 2008.

SOME THOUGHTS ON SOURCES

[1] Quoted in Campbell Storey, 'The Poverty of Tory Historiography' in The School of Historical Studies Postgraduate Forum, e-Journal, Edition Three, 2004.

[2] Mark Garnett and Andrew Denham. *Keith Joseph. A Life* (2001); Mark Garnett and Ian Aitken, *Splendid, Splendid! The Authorized Biography of Willie Whitelaw* (2002); William Whitelaw, *The Whitelaw Memoirs* (1989).

[3] Ian Gilmour, *Dancing with Dogma. Britain under Thatcherism* (1992), preface and acknowledgements: 'Mark Garnett, who suggested I write this book, has given very freely of his own ideas and has been a tireless critic of mine.'

[4] See, for example, Norman Fowler, *Ministers Decide. A Personal Memoir of the Thatcher Years (1991), p.148, which draws on Hugo Young's biography.*

[5] Alan Bennett, 'The History Boy', *London Review of Books,* 3 June 2004.

[6] Hugo Young, *One of Us. A Biography of Margaret Thatcher* (1990), p.137.

[7] Simon Jenkins, *Thatcher and Sons. A Revolution in Three Acts* (2006), p.74: 'The war was won because the Argentinians invaded before her "weak" defence policy had been implemented.'

[8] 'Baghdad Will Be Near Impossible to Conquer', *The Times,* 28 March 2003.

[9] Young, *One of Us,* p.237.

[10] TFW, Account of this meeting in letter from Clive Whitmore to John Halliday of the Home Office, 25 November 1980 (110839). Other documents relating to the Ripper case can be found on the Home Office website.

[11] TFW, Thatcher speech to Conservative rally in Edinburgh, 2 June 1987 (106861).

[12] 'Chatshows with a Touch of Class,' *The Times,* 31 July 1984.

[13] This was particularly striking when events, such as the Westland crisis, invited an analysis

based on some theory about how capitalism worked, see Andrew Gamble, 'Tarzan Takes the High Ground', *Marxism Today,* February 1986. Gamble seems to have slipped discreetly away from Marxist language in his academic work. An intriguing note in the second edition of his book on Thatcherism informs us that the term 'economic strategy' has been substituted for 'accumulation strategy'. Andrew Gamble, *The Free Economy and the Strong State* (1994 edition), endnote p.257.

[14]   Steve Lohr, 'A Magazine Reflects a Shift in the British Left', *New York Times,* 25 April 1988.

[15]   Peter Jenkins, 'Thatcher's Statism', *Marxism Today,* July 1985.

[16]   Note how often *Marxism Today* published articles by non-Marxist authors such as Hugo Young or, as has already been mentioned, Peter Jenkins.

[17]   As an adviser to Margaret Thatcher, Ferdinand Mount sat in on a number of cabinet meetings. He suggests that minutes were often drafted in a manner that was designed to smooth over differences and that in any case the cabinet secretary could not always keep up with the pace of conversation. Ferdinand Mount, *Cold Cream. My Early Life and Other Mistakes (2008), pp.310 and 311.*

514

[18] Michael Heseltine, *Life in the Jungle* (2000), p.302.

[19] Ibid., p.326. MRDH@haynet.com.

[20] Alan Watkins, 'The Force is with Cook and He Will Prevail', *Independent,* 5 July 1998.

[21] Nicholas Ridley, *My Style of Government. The Thatcher Years* (1991), p.48.

[22] Geoffrey Howe, *Conflict of Loyalty* (1994), p.467.

[23] Alan Watkins, *A Conservative Coup* (1991), p.3. Watkins said that only three Tories had refused to speak to him and that these were Cranley Onslow, chair of the 1922 Committee, Sir Peter Morrison, Thatcher's parliamentary private secretary, and Tim Renton, the chief whip. Renton did subsequently publish his own account.

[24] Alan Clark, *Diaries* (1993), p.56, entry for 14 December 1983.

[25] Martin Adeney and John Lloyd, *The Miners' Strike, 1984–5. Loss Without Limit* (1986), p.73. According to these authors, Tim Eggar was unable to find a copy of the report when drafting the 1983 manifesto.

[26] Clark, *Diaries,* p.15, entry for 23 June 1983.

[27]   Douglas Hurd, *Memoirs* (2003), p.398. Hurd attributes Clark's silence on this point to a desire to make himself seem loyal to Thatcher. Actually Clark is pretty open about the fact that he thought Thatcher would have to go. My guess is that he did not want to reveal that he had supported Hurd for the leadership of the party at a time when John Major was prime minister.

[28]   Kenneth Baker, *The Turbulent Years. My Life in Politics* (1993), p.69.

[29]   Max Hastings, *Going to the Wars* (2001), p.271.

[30]   Howe, *Conflict of Loyalty,* p.449.

[31]   Norman Tebbit, *Upwardly Mobile* (1990) and *Unfinished Business* (1991).

[32]   Howe, *Conflict of Loyalty,* p.200.

[33]   Ibid., p.106.

[34]   Undated but referring to a speech that Thatcher had given on 9 January 1978.

[35]   Mark Stuart, *Douglas Hurd. Public Servant (1998).*

[36]   Douglas Hurd, *An End to Promises* (1979), p.91.

[37]   Ibid., p.103.

[38]   Hurd, *Memoirs,* p.234.

BIBLIOGRAPHY

Listed below are all books and journal articles referred to in this book. Articles in newspapers or individual documents taken from the Thatcher Foundation website are not listed. Readers seeking these should consult the Notes.

BOOKS

Abse, Leo, *Margaret, Daughter of Beatrice. A Politician's Psycho Biography of Margaret Thatcher* (1989)

Adeney, Martin and Lloyd, John, *The Miners' Strike, 1984–5. Loss Without Limit* (1986)

Ashdown, Paddy, *The Ashdown Diaries,* Vol.1, *1988–1997* (2002)

Aston, Elaine, *Caryl Churchill* (2001)

Attali, Jacques, *Verbatim. I. Première Partie, 1981–1983* (1993)

—, *Un homme d'influence, Sir Siegmund Warburg, 1902–1982.* (1985)

Bagguley, Paul, *From Protest to Acquiescence? Political Movements of the Unemployed* (1991)

Baker, Kenneth, *The Turbulent Years. My Life in Politics* (1993)

Ball, Stuart, and Seldon, Anthony (eds.), *The Heath Government, 1970–1974. A Reappraisal* (1996)

Barnett, Anthony, *Iron Britannia* (1982)

Benn, Tony, *The Benn Diaries, 1940–1990,* edited by Ruth Winstone (1996)

Biffen, John, *Political Office or Political Power. Six Speeches on National and International Affairs* (1977)

Blackstone, Tessa, and Plowden, William, *Inside the Think Tank* (1988)

Booth, Philip (ed.), *Were 364 Economists All Wrong?* (2006)

Bransby, Guy, *Her Majesty's Interrogator* (1996)

Bruce-Gardyne, Jock, *Ministers and Mandarins. Inside the Whitehall Village* (1986)

—, *Mrs Thatcher's First Administration. The Prophets Confounded* (1984)

Butler, David, and Kavanagh, Dennis (eds.), *The British General Election of October 1974* (1975)

—, *The British General Election of 1979* (1980)

—, *The British General Election of 1983* (1984)

—, *The British General Election of 1987* (1988)

Butler, David, Adonis, Andrew, and Travers, Tony, *Failure in British Government. The Politics of the Poll Tax* (Oxford, 1993)

Calder, Angus, *The Myth of the Blitz* (1991)

Callinicos, Alex, and Simons, Mike, *The Great Strike. The Miners' Strike of 1984–5 and its Lessons* (1985)

Campbell, Beatrix, *Iron Ladies. Why Do Women Vote Tory?* (1987)

Campbell, John, *Margaret Thatcher.*, Vol.1, *The Grocer's Daughter* (2000)

—, *Margaret Thatcher,* Vol.2, *The Iron Lady* (2003)

—, *Edward Heath. A Biography* (1993)

Carrington, Peter, *Reflect on Things Past. The Memoirs of Lord Carrington* (1988)

Cartland, Barbara, *Ronald Cartland* (1942)

Clark, Alan, *Diaries, 1972–1982. Into Politics* (2001)

—, *Diaries* (1993)

Clarke, Peter, *A Question of Leadership. From Gladstone to Thatcher* (1991)

Cockett, Richard, *Thinking the Unthinkable. Think Tanks and the Economic Counter-Revolution, 1931–1983* (1995)

Collings, Rex (ed.), *Reflections of a Statesman. The Writings and Speeches of Enoch Powell* (1991)

Cosgrove, Patrick, *Margaret Thatcher. A Tory and Her Party* (1978)

Cradock, Percy, *In Pursuit of British Interests. Reflections on Foreign Policy under Margaret Thatcher and John Major* (1997)

Crewe, Ivor, and King, Anthony, *SDP. The Birth, Life and Death of the Social Democratic Party* (Oxford, 1995)

Crickhowell, Nicholas, *Westminster, Wales and Water* (Cardiff, 1999)

Critchley, Julian, *A Bag of Boiled Sweets* (1995)

—, *Heseltine. The Unauthorised Biography* (1987)

Crozier, Brian, *Free Agent. The Unseen War, 1941–1991* (1993)

Currie, Edwina, *Diaries, 1987–1992* (2002)

Dell, Edmund, *A Hard Pounding. Politics and Economies Crisis, 1974–1976* (Oxford, 1991)

Donoughue, Bernard, *Prime Minister. The Conduct of Policy under Harold Wilson and James Callaghan* (1987)

du Cann, Edward, *Two Lives. The Political and Business Careers of Edward du Cann* (Upton upon Severn, 1995)

Durham, Martin, *Moral Crusades. Family and Morality in the Thatcher Years* (New York, 1991)

Edwardes, Michael, *Back from the Brink* (1983).

English, Richard, and Kenny, Michael (eds.), *Rethinking British Decline* (2000)

Fisher, Nigel, *The Tory Leaders. Their Struggle for Power* (1977)

Forsyth, Frederick, *Britain and Europe. The End of Democracy? Tenth Ian Gow* Memorial Lecture (2001)

—, *The Fourth Protocol* (1984)

Foster, Kevin, *Fighting Fictions. War, Narrative and National Identity* (1998)

Fowler, Norman, *Ministers Decide. A Personal Memoir of the Thatcher Years* (1991)

Franks, Oliver, *Britain and the Tide of World Affairs. The BBC Reith Lectures, 1954* (1955)

Freedman, Lawrence, *The Official History of the Falklands Campaign,* Vol.1, *The Origins of the Falklands War* (2005)

Freedman, Lawrence, and Gamba-Stonehouse, Virginia, *Signals of War* (1990)

Gaffikin, Frank, and Morrissey, Mike, *Northern Ireland. The Thatcher Years* (1990)

Gamble, Andrew, *The Free Economy and the Strong State* (1994, first published 1988)

Gardiner, George, *A Bastard's Tale* (1999)

—, *Margaret Thatcher. From Childhood to Leadership* (1975)

Garnett, Mark, and Aitken, Ian, *Splendid, Splendid! The Authorized Biography of Willie Whitelaw* (2002)

Garnett, Mark, and Denham, Andrew, *Keith Joseph. A Life* (2001)

Gibbon, Peter, and Steyne, David (eds.), *Thurcroft. A Village and the Miners' Strike. An Oral History* (1986)

Gilmour, Ian, *Dancing with Dogma. Britain under Thatcherism* (1992)

—, *Britain Can Work* (1983)

Golding, John, *Hammer of the Left. Defeating Tony Benn, Eric Heffer and Militant in the Battle for the Labour Party,* edited by Paul Farrelly (2003)

Gormley, Joe, *Battered Cherub* (1982)

Gow, Ian, *A Practical Approach to Denationalization* (1977)

Green, E.H.H., *Thatcher* (2006)

—, *Ideologies of Conservatism* (Oxford, 2001)

Green, Penny, *The Enemy Without. Policing and Class Consciousness in the Miners' Strike* (1990)

Griffith, Dylan, *Thatcherism and Territorial Politics. A Welsh Case Study* (1996)

Hailsham, Quintin, *A Sparrow's Flight. Memoirs* (1991)

Halcrow, Morrison, *Keith Joseph. A Single Mind* (1989)

Hall, Peter, *Governing the Economy. The Politics of State Intervention in Britain and France* (1986)

Hall, Stuart (ed.), *Policing the Crisis* (1978)

Hall, Stuart, and Jacques, Martin (eds), *The Politics of Thatcherism* (1983)

Halloran, Paul, and Hollingsworth, Mark, *Thatcher's Fortunes. The Life and Times of Mark Thatcher* (2005)

Hammond, Eric, *Maverick. The Life of a Union Rebel* (1992)

Harris, Robert, *Good and Faithful Servant. The Unauthorized Biography of Bernard Ingham* (1990)

—, *Gotcha. The Media, the Government and the Falklands Crisis* (1983)

Harvey-Jones, John, *Getting it Together. Memoirs of a Troubleshooter* (1991)

Haslam, Bob, *An Industrial Cocktail* (2003)

Hastings, Max, *Going to the Wars* (2001)

Hastings, Stephen, *The Drums of Memory* (1994)

Healey, Denis, *The Time of My Life* (1990)

Heath, Edward, *The Course of My Life* (1998)

Heffer, Eric, *Never a Yes Man. The Life and Politics of an Adopted Liverpudlian* (1991)

Heffer, Simon, *Like the Roman. The Life of Enoch Powell* (1998)

Henderson, Nicholas, *Mandarin* (1994)

—, *Channels and Tunnels. Reflections on Britain and Abroad* (1987)

Heseltine, Michael, *Life in the Jungle* (2000)

Hillary, Richard, *The Last Enemy* (1942)

Himmelfarb, Gertrude, *The Demoralization of Society. From Victorian Virtues to Modern Values* (1995)

Hirst, Paul, *After Thatcher* (1989)

Hobson, Dominic, *The Pride of Lucifer. The Unauthorized Biography of Morgan Grenfell* (1991)

Hollingsworth, Mark, *The Ultimate Spin Doctor. The Life and Fast Times of Tim Bell* (1997)

Holmes, Martin, *The Failure of the Heath Government* (1997)

—, *Thatcherism. Scope and Limits, 1983–1987* (1989)

Hoskyns, John, *Just in Time. Inside the Thatcher Revolution* (2000)

Howe, Geoffrey, *Conflict of Loyalty* (1994)

Hurd, Douglas, *Memoirs* (2003)

—, *An End to Promises* (1979)

526

Ingham, Bernard, *Kill the Messenger* (1991)

Ironside, Mike, and Seifert, Roger, *Facing Up to Thatcherism. The History of NALGO, 1979–1993* (Oxford, 2000)

Jenkins, Peter, *Mrs Thatcher's Revolution. The End of the Socialist Era* (1987)

Jenkins, Roy, *A Life at the Centre* (1994)

—, *European Diary, 1977–1981* (1989)

Jenkins, Simon, *Thatcher and Sons. A Revolution in Three Acts* (2006)

Jessop, Bob, Bonnet, Kevin, Bromley, Simon, and Ling, Tom, *Thatcherism. A Tale of Two Nations* (Cambridge, 1988)

Johnson, Christopher, *The Economy under Mrs Thatcher, 1979–1990* (1991)

Johnson, R.W., *The Politics of Recession* (1985)

Jones, Harriet, and Kandiah, Michael (eds.), *The Myth of Consensus* (1996)

Jones, Margaret, *Thatcher's Kingdom. A View of Britain in the Eighties* (1984)

Kavanagh, Dennis, *Thatcherism and British Politics. The End of Consensus?* (Oxford, 1990, first published 1986)

Kavanagh, Dennis, and Seldon, Anthony (eds.), *The Thatcher Effect. A Decade of Change* (Oxford, 1989)

Kynaston, David, *The City of London. IV. A Club No More, 1945–2000* (2001)

—, *Cazenove & Co. A History* (1991)

Kelly, Scott, *The Myth of Mr Butskell. The Politics of British Economic Policy, 1950–1955* (Aldershot, 2002)

Lang, Ian, *Blue Remembered Years* (2002)

Lawson, Nigel, *The View from No.11. Memoirs of a Tory Radical* (1993)

Lazard, David, *Markets and Ideology in the City of London* (1990)

Letwin, Shirley Robin, *The Anatomy of Thatcherism* (1992)

MacDougall, Donald, *Don and Mandarin. Memoirs of an Economist* (1987)

MacGregor, Ian, with Rodney Tyler, *The Enemies Within. The Story of the Miners' Strike, 1984–5* (1986)

Marsden-Smedley, Philip (ed.), *Britain in the Eighties. The Spectator's View of the Thatcher Decade* (1989)

Martin, Stephen, and Parker, David, *The Impact of Privatizations. Ownership and Corporate Performance in the UK* (1997)

Mason, Roy, *Paying the Price* (1999)

McAlpine, Alistair, *Once a Jolly Bagman* (1998)

McManners, Hugh, *Falklands Commando* (1987)

Meyer, Anthony, *Stand Up and Be Counted* (1990)

Millar, Ronald, *A View from the Wings. West End, West Coast, Westminster* (1993)

Minford, Patrick, *The Supply Side Revolution in Britain* (1991)

Moore, Charles, Wilson, A.N., and Stamp, Gavin, *The Church in Crisis* (1986)

Morgan, Kenneth, *Michael Foot. A Life* (2007)

—, *Callaghan. A Life* (Oxford, 1997)

Mount, Ferdinand, *Cold Cream. My Early Life and Other Mistakes* (2008)

Mulholland, Marc, *Northern Ireland at the Crossroads. Ulster Unionism in the O'Neill Years, 1960–1969* (2000)

Nabarro, Gerald, *Exploits of a Politician* (1973)

Needham, Richard, *Battling for Peace. Northern Ireland's Longest Serving British Minister* (Belfast, 1998)

Newman, Karin, *The Selling of British Telecom* (1986)

Newsinger, John, *Dangerous Men. SAS and Popular Culture* (1997)

Nott, John, *Here Today, Gone Tomorrow. Recollections of an Errant Politician* (2003)

Ottey, Roy, *Strike. An Insider's Story* (1985)

Owen, David, *Time to Declare* (1991)

Palmer, Bernard, *High and Mitred. A Study of Prime Ministers as Bishop-Makers* (1992)

Parker, Tony, *Redhill. A Mining Community* (1986)

Parkinson, Cecil, *Right at the Centre* (1992)

Parris, Matthew, *Chance Witness. An Outsider's Life in Politics* (2002)

Pepper, Gordon, *Inside Thatcher's Monetarist Revolution* (1998)

Pepper, Gordon, and Oliver, Michael, *Monetarism under Thatcher. Lessons for the Future* (2001)

Peyton, John, *Without Benefit of Laundry* (1997)

Pliatzky, Leo, *The Treasury under Mrs Thatcher* (1989)

Powell, Anthony, *Journals, 1982–1986* (1995)

Power, Anne, *Property before People* (1987)

Power, Anne, and Tunstall, Rebecca, *Swimming Against the Tide. Polarization or Progress on 20 Unpopular Council Estates, 1980–1995* (1996)

Prior, James, *A Balance of Power* (1986)

Ramsden, John, *The Winds of Change. Macmillan to Heath, 1957–1975* (1996)

—, *The Making of Conservative Party Policy. The History of the Conservative Research Department since 1929* (1980)

Ranelagh, John, *Thatcher's People* (1991)

Rawlinson, Peter, *A Price Too High. An Autobiography* (1989)

Redwood, John, *Singing the Blues. The Once and Future Conservatives* (2004)

Renton, Tim, *Chief Whip* (2005)

Richards, Andrew, *Miners on Strike. Class, Solidarity and Division in Britain* (1996)

Richards, David, *The Civil Service under the Conservatives, 1979–1997* (1997)

Riddell, Peter, *The Thatcher Decade. How Britain Changed during the 1980s* (Oxford, 1989)

Ridley, Nicholas, *My Style of Government. The Thatcher Years* (1991)

Rogers, William, *Fourth Amongst Equals* (2000)

Rothschild, Victor, *Meditations on a Broomstick* (1977)

Roy, Subroto, and Clarke, John (eds.), *Margaret Thatcher's Revolution. How it Happened and What it Meant* (2005)

Samuel, Raphael, Bloomfield, Barbara, and Boanas, Guy (eds.), *The Enemy Within. Pit Villages and the Miners' Strike of 1984–5* (1986)

Schoen, Douglas, *Enoch Powell and the Powellites* (1977)

Seifert, Roger, and Urwin, John, *Struggle Without End. The 1984/85 Miners' Strike in North Staffordshire* (Newcastle, Staffs, 1987)

Sergeant, John, *Maggie. Her Fatal Legacy* (2005)

Shaw, Giles, *In the Long Run* (2001)

Shepherd, Richard, *Enoch Powell* (1996)

Sherman, Alfred, *Paradoxes of Power. Reflections on the Thatcher Interlude,* edited by Mark Garnett (Exeter, 2005)

Sirs, Bill, *Hard Labour* (1985) Skidelsky, Robert (ed.), *Thatcherism* (1988)

Smith, Anna Marie, *New Right Discourse on Race and Sexuality: Britain, 1968–1990* (Cambridge, 1994)

Southby-Tailyour, Ewen, *Reasons in Writing. A Commando's View of the Falklands War* (2003)

Speed, Keith, *Sea Change. The Battle for the Falklands and the Future of Britain's Navy* (1982)

Spencer, Ken, Taylor, Andy, Smith, Barbara, Mawson, John, Flynn, Norman, and Batley, Richard, *Crisis in the Industrial Heartland. A Study of the West Midlands* (Oxford, 1986)

Stanbrook, Ivor, *A Year in Politics* (1988)

Stephens, Philip, *Politics and the Pound. The Tories, the Economy and Europe* (1997)

Stuart, Mark, *Douglas Hurd. Public Servant* (1998)

Tatchell, Peter, *Democratic Defence. A Non-Nuclear Alternative* (1985)

Taylor, Andrew, *The NUM and British Politics,* Vol.2, *1969–1995* (Aldershot, 1995)

Tebbit, Norman, *Unfinished Business* (1991)

—, *Upwardly Mobile* (1989)

Thatcher, Carol, *Below the Parapet. The Biography of Denis Thatcher* (1996)

Thatcher, Margaret, *The Path to Power* (1995)

—, *The Downing Street Years* (1995)

Thompson, Julian, *No Picnic. 3 Commando Brigade in the South Atlantic, 1982* (1992)

Urban, George, *Diplomacy and Disillusion at the Court of Margaret Thatcher. An Insider's View* (1996)

Utley, T.E., *A Tory Seer. The Selected Journalism of T.E. Utley* (1989)

—, *Enoch Powell. The Man and His Thinking* (1968)

Waddington, David, Wykes, Maggie, and Critcher, Chas, *Split at the Seams. Community, Continuity and Change after the 1984–5 Coal Dispute* (Milton Keynes, 1991)

Walden, George, *Lucky George. Memoirs of an Anti-Politician* (1999)

Walker, Peter, *Staying Power. An Autobiography* (1991)

Walters, Dennis, *Not Always with the Pack* (1989)

Watkins, Alan, *A Conservative Coup* (1991)

Waugh, Auberon, *In the Lion's Den* (1978)

Whitelaw, William, *The Whitelaw Memoirs* (1989)

Whiteley, Paul, Seyd, Patrick, and Richardson, Jeremy, *True Blues. The Politics of Conservative Party Membership* (1994)

Wiener, Martin, *English Culture and the Decline of the Industrial Spirit, 1850–1980* (Cambridge, 1981)

Wood, John (ed.), *Enoch Powell. Freedom and Reality* (1969)

Woodward, Sandy with Robinson, Patrick, *One Hundred Days. The Memoirs of the Falklands Battle Group Commander* (1997)

Wyatt, Petronella, *Father, Dear Father. Life with Woodrow Wyatt* (1999)

Wyatt, Woodrow, *The Journals of Woodrow Wyatt, Vol.1, 1985–1988,* edited by Sarah Curtis (2000)

Wyldbore-Smith, Brian, *March Past* (2001)

Young, David, *The Enterprise Years. A Businessman in the Cabinet* (1990)

Young, Hugo, *One of Us. A Biography of Margaret Thatcher* (1990)

Zweig, Konrad, *The Origins of the German Social Market Economy. Leading Ideas and Their Intellectual Roots* (1980)

ARTICLES

Auerbach, Simon, 'Mrs Thatcher's Labour Laws: Slouching Towards Utopia?', *Political Quarterly,* 64, 1 (1993), pp.37–48

Barker, Rodney, 'Legitimacy in the United Kingdom: Scotland and the Poll Tax', *British Journal of Political Science,* 22, 4 (1992), pp.521–33

Biffen, John, interviewed by Beatrix Campbell in *Marxism Today,* December 1989

Bland, Christopher, review of T.E. Utley's biography of Enoch Powell, *Crossbow,* January–March 1969

Bridgman, Joan, 'At School with Margaret Thatcher', *Contemporary Review,* 9 January 2004

Butt, Ronald, 'The Importance of Being Enoch', *Crossbow,* April–June 1966

Cowley, Philip, and Bailey, Matthew, 'Peasants' Uprising or Religious War? Re-Examining the 1975 Conservative Leadership Contest', *British Journal of Political Science,* 30, 4 (2000), pp.599–629

Crewe, Ivor, 'Values the Crusade that Failed', in Dennis Kavanagh and Anthony Seldon (ed.), *The Thatcher Effect. A Decade of Change* (Oxford, 1989), pp.239–50

Currie, Edwina, interviewed by Beatrix Campbell, *Marxism Today,* March 1987

Deary, Ian, Wessely, Simon, and Farrell, Michael, 'Dementia and Mrs Thatcher', *British Medical Journal,* 291, 21–28 December 1985

Dorey, Peter, 'One Step at a Time: The Conservative Government's Approach to the Reform of Industrial Relations since 1979', *Political Quarterly,* 64, 1 (1993), pp.24–36

Eley, Geoff, 'Finding the People's War: Film, British Collective Memory, and World War II', *American Historical Review,* 106, 3 (2001), pp.818–38

Gamble, Andrew, 'The Reading of a Decade', *Marxism Today,* May 1989

—, 'Tarzan Takes the High Ground', *Marxism Today,* February 1986

—, 'The Lady's Not for Turning: Thatcherism Mark III', *Marxism Today,* June 1984

Hall, Stuart, and Jacques, Martin, 'March without a Vision', *Marxism Today,* December 1990

Hall, Stuart, 'The Great Moving Right Show', *Marxism Today,* January 1979

Hannah, Leslie, 'Mrs Thatcher, Capital Basher', in Dennis Kavanagh and Anthony Seldon (eds.), *The Thatcher Effect. A Decade of Change* (Oxford, 1989), pp.38–48

Heath, Edward, interviewed by Hugo Young, *Marxism Today,* November 1988

Hobsbawm, Eric, 'Falklands Fallout', in Hall, Stuart, and Jacques, Martin (eds.), *The Politics of Thatcherism* (1983), pp.257–70

538

Holliday, Ian, 'Scottish Limits to Thatcherism', *Political Quarterly,* 63, 4 (2005), pp.448–59

Ingram, Peter, Metcalfe, David, and Wadsworth, Jonathan, 'Strike Incidence in British Manufacturing in the 1980s', *Industrial and Labor Relations Review,* 46, 4 (1993), pp.704–717

Jenkins, Peter, 'Thatcher's Statism', *Marxism Today,* July 1985

Jessop, Bob, Bonnet, Kevin, Bromley, Simon, and Ling, Tom, 'Authoritarian Populism, Two Nations and Thatcherism', *New Left Review,* (September–October, 1984)

Leadbeater, Charles, 'Back to the Future', *Marxism Today,* May 1989

Martin, David, 'The Stripping of the Words: Conflict over the Eucharist in the Episcopal Church', *Modern Theology,* 15, 2 (1999), pp.247–61

Minford, Patrick, Ashton, Paul, and Peel, Michael, 'The Effects of Housing Distortions on Unemployment', *Oxford Economics Papers,* 40, 2 (1988), pp.322–45

Murie, Alan, 'Housing and the Environment', in Dennis Kavanagh and Anthony Seldon (eds.), *The Thatcher Effect. A Decade of Change* (Oxford, 1989), pp.213–25

Pimlott, Ben, 'The Myth of Consensus', in Lesley Smith (ed.), *The Making of Britain. Echoes of Greatness* (1988)

Powell, Enoch, 'The Conservative Party', in Dennis Kavanagh and Anthony Seldon (eds.), *The Thatcher Effect. A Decade of Change* (Oxford, 1989), pp.80–88

Raven, James, 'British History and the Enterprise Culture', *Past and Present,* 123 (1989), pp.178–204

Saville, John, 'An Open Conspiracy: Conservative Politics and the Miners' Strike, 1984–5', *Socialist Register,* July–August 1985, pp.295–329

Scargill, Arthur, interview, *Marxism Today,* April 1981

—, interview, *New Left Review,* July–August 1975

Smith, Jeremy, 'Walking a Real Tight-Rope of Difficulties: Sir Edward Heath and the Search for Stability in Northern Ireland, June 1970–March 1971', *Twentieth Century British History,* 18, 2 (2007), pp.219–53

—, 'Relations between the Conservative Party and the Ulster Unionist Party during the Twentieth Century', *English Historical Review,* CXXI, 490 (2006), pp.70–103

Towers, Brian, 'Running the Gauntlet: British Trade Unions under Thatcher, 1979–1987', *Industrial and Labor Relations Review,* 42, 2 (1989), pp.163–88

Wells, John, 'Miracles and Myths', *Marxism Today,* May 1989

Willets, David, 'Conservatism and Christian Democracy', speech to Viennese Institute for Human Sciences, 9 December 2003

Williamson, Philip, 'Baldwin's Reputation: Politics and History, 1937–1967', *Historical Journal,* 47, 1 (2004), 127–68.

WEBSITES

Margaret Thatcher Foundation
www.margaretthatcher.org

The Margaret Thatcher Foundation has provided a unique historical resource by putting almost all of Margaret Thatcher's public statements online. This is a very important reserve of material – much larger than anything that exists for figures even as major as Churchill and de Gaulle. It is possible to carry out keyword searches of all Thatcher's statements which can yield interesting results. In view of the frequency with which her enemies invoked the links between the Conservative Party and Mary Whitehouse's Festival of Light, for example, it is significant that Thatcher used the words 'Festival of Light' only twice – both times she was referring to the Hindu festival of Diwali.

In addition to this, a number of speeches and writing by other people can be found on the Thatcher Foundation website. Particularly important are long speeches or lectures by Keith Joseph and Nigel Lawson.

Finally, the Thatcher Foundation website gives access to a number of archival sources, which is constantly expanding as new material is released. The most significant of these are documents from the National Archives relating to the Heath government; documents from the Conservative Party archives relating to Thatcher's early career; documents from the Conservative Party archives relating to the discussions of the shadow cabinet between 1975 and 1979; documents (released under the Freedom of Information Act) from the National Coal Board relating to the miners' strike of 1984–5; and documents from a variety of archives in the United States relating to aspects of British politics (not just Anglo-American relations).

Samuel Brittan
www.samuelbrittan.co.uk

The financial journalist Samuel Brittan has his own website. Its autobiographical component in particular will be interesting for anyone who wishes to understand the social and cultural context in which economic discussion took place.

Centre for Policy Studies
www.cps.org.uk

The website of the Centre for Policy Studies contains the full text of important pamphlets by people such as John Biffen.

Institute of Economic Affairs
www.iea.org.uk

The website of the Institute of Economic Affairs contains much interesting material – notably the text of the pamphlet (edited by Philip Booth) *Were 364 Economists All Wrong?* (2006), about the 1981 budget.

Marxism Today
www.amielandmelburn.org.uk/collections/mt/index_fra me.htm

The complete run of *Marxism Today* from 1978 to 1991 can be consulted online.

The Institute of Contemporary British History
www.icbh.ac.uk

The Institute of Contemporary British History has organized a succession of witness seminars that touch on the Thatcher years. These can all be consulted on the ICBH's website. Particularly important are those on German reunification; the Civil Service Reforms of the 1980s; the Nott Defence Review; the Falklands War; and the opposition to Clause 28.

NATIONAL ARCHIVES KEW, LONDON

PREM 15/985
PREM 15/986
Coal 26/500

ENDNOTES

[1]   Just after Sutton Coldfield.

[2]   It is said that Thatcher herself was told of Hollinghurst's novel but misheard the title as 'The Line of Duty', which suggests a different kind of book.

[3]   Hailsham, Joseph and Soames. Maude was a prisoner of war.

[4]   Carrington, Pym, Soames and Whitelaw.

[5]   The others were Sir John Farr and Nicholas Ridley.

[6]   Whitelaw was born in 1918; Joseph in 1918; Maudling in 1917; Pym in 1922; Peyton in 1919; Neave in 1916; Thorneycroft in 1909; Maude in 1912; Atkins in 1922; Havers in 1923; Hailsham in 1907; Carrington in 1919.

[7]   Strictly speaking it did not raise taxes but failed to increase allowances in line with inflation.

[8]   There were about 17,000 British passport holders in Argentina and around 100,000 people of British extraction.

[9]   With his unfailing instinct for getting the wrong end of every stick, Ian MacGregor, head of the

National Coal Board during the strike, attributed this remark to Stanley Baldwin,

[10]   The Conservative Party did authorize the formation of four associations in Northern Ireland in 1989.

[11]   Richard Needham, Chris Patten and John Patten.

[12]   Foot was quoting the Welsh poet Idris Davies.

[13]   The remark was originally made in a speech at Trinity College Dublin in 1946.

[14]   Roberts's work is cited by John Hoskyns and John Nott.

[15]   I made requests under the Freedom of Information Act to see the following collections of documents in the National Archives: Coal 31/362, Coal 31/441 and Coal 26/510. My requests were turned down.

Printed in Great Britain
by Amazon

67194815R00341